RISKS OF FAITH

ALSO BY JAMES H. CONE

Speaking the Truth: Ecumenism, Liberation,
   and Black Theology

God of the Oppressed

Black Theology and Black Power

Martin & Malcolm & America:
   A Dream or a Nightmare

The Spirituals and the Blues:
   An Interpretation

A Black Theology of Liberation

My Soul Looks Back

For My People: Black Theology
   and the Black Church

Risks of Faith

James H. Cone **THE EMERGENCE OF**

A BLACK THEOLOGY

OF LIBERATION, 1968–1998

BOSTON   *Beacon Press*

Beacon Press
25 Beacon Street
Boston, Massachusetts 02108-2892
www.beacon.org

Beacon Press books
are published under the auspices of the
Unitarian Universalist Association of Congregations.

05   8 7

This book is printed on recycled acid-free paper that meets
the uncoated paper ANSI/NISO specifications for permanence
as revised in 1992.

Text design by Wesley B. Tanner/Passim Editions
Composition by Wilsted & Taylor Publishing Services

Library of Congress Cataloging-in-Publication Data

Cone, James H.
    Risks of faith : the emergence of a Black theology of liberation,
  1968–1998 / James H. Cone.
        p.   cm.
    Includes bibliographical references and index.
    ISBN 0-8070-0950-4 (cloth)
    ISBN 0-8070-0951-2 (pbk.)
    1. Black theology.   2. Black power.   I. Title.
  BT82.7.C675   1999
  230'.089'96073—dc21   99-28327

FOR GAYRAUD S. WILMORE

My friend and colleague in the black theology movement,
who was never afraid to take risks for black people

And for communities of color throughout the world,
for whom risks of faith are a daily reality

Contents

Introduction
Looking Back, Going Forward

This book provides an opportunity for me to reflect on the origin and development of my theological perspective. When I think about my vocation, I go back to my childhood years in Bearden, Arkansas—a rural community of approximately 1,200 people. I do not remember Bearden for nostalgic reasons. In fact, I seldom return there in person, because of persistent racial tensions in my relations to the whites and lingering ambivalence in my feelings toward the blacks. I am not and do not wish to be Bearden's favorite son. My brother, Cecil, also a theologian and a preacher, has been bestowed that honor by the African-American community, a distinction he gladly accepts and a role he fulfills quite well.

I remember Bearden because it is the place where I first discovered myself—as *black* and *Christian*. There, the meaning of black was defined primarily by the menacing presence of whites, which no African-American could escape. I grew up during the age of Jim Crow (1940s and early '50s). I attended segregated schools, drank water from "colored" fountains, saw movies from balconies, and when absolutely necessary greeted white adults at the back doors of their homes. I also observed the contempt and brutality that white law meted out to the blacks who transgressed their racial mores or who dared to question their authority. Bearden white people, like most Southerners of that time, could be mean and vicious, and I, along with other blacks, avoided them whenever possible as if they were poisonous snakes.

The Christian part of my identity was shaped primarily at Macedonia A.M.E. Church. Every Sunday and sometimes on weeknights I encountered Jesus through rousing sermons, fervent prayers, spirited gospel songs, and the passionate testimonies of the people. Jesus was the dominant reality at Macedonia and in black life in Bearden. The people walked with him and told him about their troubles as if he were a trusted friend who understood their trials and tribulations in this unfriendly world. They called Jesus "the lily of the valley and the bright and morning star," the "Rose of Sharon and the Lord of life," a "very present help in time of trouble." The people often shouted and danced, clapped their hands and stamped their feet as they bore witness to the power of Jesus' Spirit in their midst—"building them up where they are torn down and propping them up on every leaning side."

Like the people of Macedonia, Jesus became a significant presence in my life, too. I do not remember the exact date or time I "turned to Jesus," as the conversion experience was called. At home, church, and school, at play and at work, Jesus was always there, as the anchor of life, giving it meaning and purpose and bestowing hope and faith in the ultimate justice of things. Jesus was that reality who empowered black people to know that they were not the worthless human beings that white people said they were.

There were no atheists in "Cotton Belt," as the "colored" section of Bearden was called—no proclaimers of Nietzsche's "God is dead" philosophy and none of the "cultured despisers" of religion that Friedrich Schleiermacher wrote to in 1799. The closest to Nietzsche's atheists and Schleiermacher's "cultured despisers" were the bluespeople who drank corn whiskey and boogied slowly and sensually to the deep guttural sound of the raunchy music at the jook joints every Friday and Saturday night. The sounds of Bessie Smith, Muddy Waters, and Howlin' Wolf took center-stage as they belted out the lowdown dirty blues in songs like "I Used to Be Your Sweet Mama," "Hoochie Coochie Man," and "Somebody in My Home."

Unlike the churchpeople, the bluespeople found the Sunday religion of Jesus inadequate for coping with their personal problems and the social contradictions they experienced during the week. As churchpeople soothed their souls with the song "Lord, I Want to Be a Christian in My Heart," the people at the honky-tonk transcended their agony by facing it with stoic defiance or, as James Baldwin called it, "ironic tenacity"[1]: "I got the blues, but I'm too damned mean to cry."

Sometimes sharp tensions emerged between the celebrants of Saturday night and those of Sunday morning. But each group respected the other, because both knew that they were seeking, each in its own way, to cope with the same troubles of life. Some people moved between the two groups during different periods of their lives, as my father did. But it was not possible to be a member in good standing in both groups at the same time, because the church demanded that an individual make a choice between the blues and the spirituals, between the "devil's music" and the "sweet melodies of Jesus." Baptist and Methodist churches, the only black denominations in Bearden, regularly accepted backsliders back into the fold, provided they repented of their wrongdoing and declared their intentions to lead good and righteous lives in service to the Lord. My father had a few lapses in faith, because he found it hard to cope with life's adversities without taking a nip of gin and hanging out with the bluespeople in order to add a little spice to life not found at the church. But my mother monitored him closely, and Macedonia readily received him back into the community of the faithful as often as he publicly repented.

What puzzled me most during my childhood about the religion of Jesus were not the tensions between Saturday night and Sunday morning in black life but rather the conspicuous presence of the color bar in white churches. In Bearden, like the rest of America, Sunday was the most segregated day of the week. Black and white Christians had virtually no social or religious dealings with each other, even though both were Baptists and Methodists—reading the same Bible, worshiping the same God, and reciting the same confessions of faith in their congregations.

Although whites posted "Welcome" signs outside their churches, ostensibly beckoning all visitors to join them in worship, blacks knew that the invitation did not include them. "What kind of Christianity is it that preaches love and practices segregation?" my brother Cecil and I, budding young theologians, often asked each other. "How could whites exclude black people from their churches and still claim Jesus as their Savior and the Bible as their holy book?" We talked about testing the theological integrity of white faith by seeking to integrate one of their churches, but felt that the risks of bodily harm were too great.

Despite the ever present reality of white supremacy, I do not ever remember experiencing a feeling of inferiority because of what whites said about me or about other black people. One reason was the stellar example my father and mother set for me. They were part of that cloud of black witnesses that James Baldwin wrote about who "in the teeth of the most terrible odds, achieved an unassailable and monumental dignity."[2] They taught me what Baldwin told his nephew: "You can only be destroyed by believing that you really are what the white world calls a *nigger.*"[3]

My parents were strong and self-confident—exhibiting a determined opposition to white supremacy and creative leadership and great courage when they and the black community faced adversity. Charlie and Lucy, as the people in Bearden called them, were immensely intelligent, even though they had little opportunity for formal education, having completed only the sixth and ninth grades, respectively. (With the support and encouragement of my father, my mother went back and completed high school where her sons had graduated earlier and also went on to finish her college degree four years later. She then returned to teach in Bearden. I was struck by her determination.) Their education, they often told their sons, came from the "school of hard knocks"—the experience of surviving with dignity in a society that did not recognize black humanity.

The faith of Macedonia, which my parents imbibed deeply, was a powerful antidote against the belief that blacks were less than whites. According to this faith, God created all people equal—as brothers and sisters in the church and the society. No person or group is better than any other. As evidence for that claim, preachers and teachers often cited the text from the prophet Malachi: "Have we not all one father? Hath not one God created us?" (2:10 Authorized [King James] Version). They also quoted Paul, *selectively*—carefully avoiding the ambiguous and problematic texts, especially in *Philemon* where Paul returned the slave Onesimus to his master and in *Ephesians* where servants were told to "be obedient to them who are your masters . . . as unto Christ" (Eph. 6:5 AV).

Preachers and Sunday School teachers at Macedonia were quite skilled in picking biblical texts that affirmed their humanity. They especially liked Luke's account of Paul's sermon on Mars' Hill where he said God "made of one blood all nations of men [and women] to dwell on the face of the earth" (Acts 17:26 AV). They also quoted Paul's letter to the Galatians: "There is neither Jew nor Greek . . . neither slave nor free . . . neither male nor female." We are "all one in Christ Jesus" (3:28 AV)—blacks and whites, as well as other human colors and orientations. When one truly believes that gospel and internalizes it in one's way of life, as I and many black Christians in Bearden did, it is possible to know that "you are somebody" even though the world treats you like nobody.

From the time I was conscious of being black and Christian, I recognized that I was a problem for America's white politicians and invisible to most of its practitioners of religion. I did not quite understand what made me a problem or invisible since skin color appeared to be a minor difference between human beings. Yet politicians found it difficult to pass laws to protect black humanity. Even those passed were rarely enforced. White ministers seemed not to notice the daily white assault on black humanity. They preached sermons about loving God and thy neighbor as if the violence that whites committed against blacks did not invalidate their Christian identity.

While struggling to understand how whites reconciled racism with their Christian identity, I also encountered an uncritical faith in many black churches. Blacks not only seemed to tolerate anti-intellectualism as whites tolerated racism; but, like most whites in relation to racism, often promoted it. It was as if the less one knew and the louder one shouted Jesus' name, the closer one was to God.

I found it hard to believe that the God of Jesus condoned ignorance as if it were a virtue. It contradicted what my parents and teachers taught me about the value of education and a disciplined mind. It also contradicted what I read in history books about black slaves who risked life and limb in order to learn to read and write so they could understand more clearly the meaning of the freedom to which God had called them. I was, therefore, deeply troubled by the anti-intellectualism that permeated many aspects of the ministry in the Black Church.

How could ministers preach the gospel in a world they did not understand? How can they understand the gospel without disciplined reflections and critical debate? "A religion that won't stand the application of reason and common sense," wrote W. E. B. Du Bois, "is not fit for an intelligent dog."[4]

The search for a reasoned faith in a complex and ever changing world was the chief motivation that led me to study at Garrett Theological Seminary (now Garrett-Evangelical). It seemed that the more I learned about the gospel through a critical study of the Bible, history, theology, and the practice of ministry the more I needed and wanted to know about it. I wanted to explore its meanings for different social, political, and cultural contexts, past and present.

Theology quickly became my favorite subject in seminary because it opened the door to explore faith's meaning for the current time and situation in which I was living. I loved the give-and-take of theological debate and eagerly waited for the opportunity during and after classes to engage my professors and fellow students on the burning theological issues of the day. That was why I remained at Garrett and Northwestern University for the Ph.D. in systematic theology. While writing a dissertation on Karl

Barth's anthropology, I thought I had enough knowledge of the Christian faith to communicate it to persons anywhere in the world. Who would not feel adequately endowed after plowing through twelve volumes of Barth's *Church Dogmatics?*

In a way, my education was pulling me away from my people. The educational quest focused on mastering the theological systems of the well-known European theologians of the past and present. We students spent most of our time obediently reading books, listening to lectures, and writing papers about their views of God, Jesus, the Holy Spirit, and the church.

The Civil Rights movement of the 1960s awakened me from my theological slumber. As I became actively involved in the black freedom movement that was exploding in the streets all over America, I soon discovered how limited my seminary education was. The curriculum at Garrett and Northwestern did not deal with the questions black people were asking as they searched for the theological meaning of their fight for justice in a white racist society. And as individuals and isolated students within a demanding educational system, neither I nor the token number of black students had the intellectual resources to articulate them. I found myself grossly ill-prepared, because I knew deep down that I could not repeat to a struggling black community the doctrines of the faith as they had been reinterpreted by Barth, Bultmann, Niebuhr, and Tillich for European colonizers and white racists in the United States. I knew that before I could say anything worthwhile about God and the black situation of oppression in America I had to discover a theological identity that was accountable to the life, history, and culture of African-American people.

Recognizing the community to whom I was accountable, I wanted to know more than just what Europeans and the white Americans who emulated them thought about sacred reality. I was searching for a way to create a Christian theology out of the black experience of slavery, segregation, and the struggle for a just society. When I asked my professors about what theology had to do with the black struggle for racial justice, they seemed surprised and uncomfortable with the question, not knowing what to say, and anxious to move on with the subject matter as they understood it. I was often told that theology and the struggle for racial justice were separate subjects, with the latter belonging properly in the disciplines of sociology and political science. Although I felt a disquieting unease with that response, I did not say much about it to my professors as they skirted around talking about what the gospel had to say to black people in a white society that had defined them as nonpersons.

While reading Martin Luther King, Jr., and Malcolm X, the blackness in my theological consciousness exploded like a volcano after many dormant years. No longer able to accept black invisibility in theology and getting angrier and angrier at the white brutality meted out against Martin King and other civil rights activists, my southern, Arkansas racial identity began to rise in my theological consciousness.

"You are a racist!" I yelled angrily at my doctoral advisor who was lecturing to a theology class of about forty students. "You've been talking for weeks now about the wrongdoings of Catholics against Protestants in sixteenth and seventeenth century Europe," I continued, raising my voice even higher, "but you've said absolutely nothing about the monstrous acts of violence by *white* Protestants against Negroes in the American South *today!*"

Devastated that I—who was a frequent presence in his office and home —would call him a racist, my advisor, a grave and staid English gentleman, had no capacity for understanding black rage. He paced back and forth for nearly a minute before he stopped suddenly and stared directly at me with an aggrieved and perplexed look on his face. Then he shouted, "That's simply not true! Class dismissed."

He stormed out of the classroom to his office. I followed him. "Jim," he turned in protest, "*you* know I'm not a racist!" "I know," I said with an apologetic tone but still laced with anger. "I'm sorry I blurted out my frustrations at you. But I am angry about racism in America and the rest of the world. I find it very difficult to study theology and never talk about it in class." "I'm concerned about racism, too," he retorted with emphasis. We then talked guardedly about racism in Britain and the U.S.

The more I thought about the incident, then and later, the more I realized that my angry outburst was not about the personal prejudices of my advisor or any other professor at Garrett. It was about how the discipline of theology had been defined so as to exclude any engagement with the African-American struggle against racism. I did not have the words to say to my advisor what I deeply felt. I just knew intuitively that something was seriously wrong with studying theology during the peak of the Civil Rights era and never once reading a book about racial justice in America or talking about it in class. It was as if the black struggle for justice had nothing to do with the study of theology—a disturbing assumption, which I gradually became convinced was both anti-Christian and racist. But since I could not engage in a disinterested discussion about race as if I were analyzing Karl Barth's christology, I kept my views about racism in theology to myself and only discussed them with the small group of African-American students who had similar views.

After I completed the Ph.D. in systematic theology in the fall of 1964, I returned to Arkansas to teach at Philander Smith College in Little Rock. No longer cloistered in a white academic environment and thus free of the need of my professors' approval, I turned my attention to the rage I had repressed during six years of graduate education. Martin Luther King, Jr., and the Civil Rights movement helped me to take another look at the theological meaning of racism and the black struggle for justice. My seminary education was nearly worthless in this regard, except as a negative stimulant. My mostly neo-orthodox professors talked incessantly about the "mighty acts of God" in biblical history. But they objected to any effort to link God's righteousness with the political struggles of the poor today, especially among the black poor fighting for justice in the United States. God's righteousness, they repeatedly said, can never be identified with any human project. The secular and death-of-God theologians were not much better. They proclaimed God's death with glee and published God's obituary in *Time* magazine. But they ignored the theological significance of Martin King's proclamation of God's righteous presence in the black freedom struggle.

It is one thing to think of Martin King as a civil rights activist who transformed America's race relations and quite another to regard the struggle for racial justice as having theological significance. King was a public theologian. He turned the nations' television networks into his pulpit and classroom, and he forced white Christians to confront their own beliefs. He challenged all Americans in the church, the academy, and every segment of the culture to face head-on the great moral crisis of racism in the U.S. and the world. It was impossible to ignore King and the claims he made about religion and justice. While he never regarded himself as an academic theologian, he transformed our understanding of the Christian faith by making the practice of justice an essential ingredient of its identity.

It could be argued that Martin King's contribution to the identity of Christianity in America and the world was as far-reaching as Augustine's in the fifth century and Luther's in the sixteenth.[5] Before King, no Christian theologian showed so conclusively in his actions and words the great contradiction between racial segregation and the gospel of Jesus. In fact, racial segregation was so widely accepted in the churches and societies throughout the world that few white theologians in America and Europe regarded the practice as unjust. Those who did see the injustice did not regard the issue important enough to even write or talk about it. But after King no theologian or preacher dares to defend racial segregation. He destroyed its moral legitimacy. Even conservative white preachers like Pat Robertson and Jerry Falwell make a point to condemn racial segregation and do not want to be identified with racism. That change is due almost single-handedly to the theological power of King's actions and words.

Martin King was extremely modest about his political achievements and rather naive about the intellectual impact he made on the theological world. Theologians and seminarians also have been slow to recognize the significance of his theological contribution. But I am convinced that Martin Luther King, Jr., was the most important and influential Christian theologian in America's history. Some would argue that the honor belongs to Jonathan Edwards or Reinhold Niebuhr or even perhaps Walter Rauschenbusch. Where we come down on this issue largely depends upon how we understand the discipline of theology. Those who think that the honor belongs to Edwards or Niebuhr or Rauschenbusch regard intellect as more important than character in the doing of theology and thus do not think that the disparity between morality and intelligence affect theological insight. To place Edwards, Niebuhr, and Rauschenbusch over King means that one cannot possibly regard the achievement of racial justice as a significant theological issue, because none of them made justice for black people a central element of their theological program. Edwards, Rauschenbusch, and Niebuhr were *white* theologians who sought to speak only to their racial community. They did not use their intellectual power to support people of color in their fight for justice. Blacks and the Third World poor were virtually invisible to them.

Martin King is America's most important Christian theologian because of what he said and did about race from a theological point of view. He was a liberation theologian before the phrase was coined by African-American and Latin American religious thinkers in the late sixties and early seventies. King's mature reflections on the gospel of Jesus emerged primarily from his struggle for racial justice in America. His political practice preceded his theological reflections. He was an activist-theologian who showed that one could not be a Christian in any authentic sense without fighting for justice among people.

One can observe the priority of practice, as a hermeneutical principle, in his sermons, essays, and books. *Stride Toward Freedom* (1958), *Why We Can't Wait* (1964), and *Where Do We Go from Here?* (1967) were reflections on the political and religious meaning, respectively, of the Montgomery bus boycott (1955–56), the Birmingham movement (1963), and the rise of Black Power (1966). In these texts King defined the black freedom movement as seeking to redeem the soul of America and to liberate its political and religious institutions from the cancer of racism. I contend that as a theologian to America he surpassed the others, because he addressed our most persistent and urgent sickness.

But two other features of King's work elevate him above Edwards, Rauschenbusch, and Niebuhr. The first is his international stature and influence. I do not mean his Nobel Prize, but his contribution beyond the particularity of the Black American struggle. He influenced liberation movements in China, Ireland, Germany, India, South Africa, Korea, and the Philippines, and throughout Latin America and the Caribbean. Hardly any liberation movements among the poor are untouched by the power of his thought.

Secondly, King was North America's most courageous theologian. He did not seek the protection of a university appointment and a quiet office. One of his most famous theological statements was written in jail. Other ideas were formed in brief breathing spaces after days of exposure to physical danger in the streets of Birmingham, Selma, and Chicago and the dangerous roads of Mississippi. King did theology in solidarity with the least of these and in the face of death. "If physical death," he said, "is the price I must pay to free my white brothers and sisters from the permanent death of the spirit, then nothing could be more redemptive." Real theology is risky, as King's courageous life demonstrated.

From King black liberation theology received its Christian identity, which he understood as the practice of justice and love in human relations and the hope that God has not left the least of these alone in their suffering. However, that identity was only one factor that contributed to the creation of black liberation theology. The other was Malcolm X, who identified the struggle as a *black* struggle. As long as black freedom and the Christian way in race relations were identified exclusively with integration and nonviolence, black theology was not possible. Integration and nonviolence re-

quired blacks to turn the other cheek to white brutality, join the mainstream of American society, and do theology without anger and without
reference to the history and culture of African-Americans. It meant seeing
Christianity exclusively through the eyes of its white interpreters. Malcolm prevented that from happening.

Martin King helped to define my *Christian* identity but was silent about
the meaning of blackness in a world of white supremacy. His public thinking about the faith was designed to persuade white Christians to take seriously the humanity of Negroes. He challenged whites to be true to what
they said in their political and religious documents of freedom and democracy. What King did not initially realize was how deeply flawed white
Christian thinking is regarding race and the psychological damage done
to the self-image of blacks.

To understand white racism and black rage in America, I turned to Malcolm X and Black Power. While King accepted white logic, Malcolm rejected it. "When [people] get angry," Malcolm said, "they aren't interested
in logic, they aren't interested in odds, they aren't interested in consequences. When they get angry, they realize that the condition that they're
in—that their suffering is unjust, immoral, illegal, and that anything they
do to correct it or eliminate it, they're justified. When you develop that
type of anger and speak in that voice, then we'll get some kind of respect
and recognition, and some changes from these people who have been
promising us falsely already for far too long."[6]

Malcolm saw more clearly than King the depth and complexity of racism in America, especially in the North. The North was more clever than
the South and thus knew how to camouflage its exploitation of black people. White northern liberals represented themselves as the friends of the
Negro and deceived King and many other blacks into believing that they
really wanted to achieve racial justice in America. But Malcolm knew better and he exposed their hypocrisy. He called white liberals "foxes" in contrast to southern "wolves." Malcolm saw no difference between the two,
except that one smiles and the other growls when they eat you. Northern
white liberals hated Malcolm for his uncompromising, brutal honesty. But
blacks, especially the young people, loved him for it. He said publicly what
most blacks felt but were afraid to say except privately among themselves.

I first heard Malcolm speak while I was a student at Garrett but I did not
really listen to him. I was committed to Martin King and even hoped that
he would accept the invitation offered him to become a professor of theol-

ogy at Garrett. I regarded Malcolm as a racist and would have nothing to do with him. Malcolm X did not enter my theological consciousness until I left seminary and was challenged by the rise of the black consciousness movement in the middle of the 1960s. Black Power, a child of Malcolm, forced me to take a critical look at Martin King and to discover his limits.

It is one thing to recognize that the gospel of Jesus demands justice in race relations and quite another to recognize that it demands that African-Americans accept their blackness and reject its white distortions. When I turned to Malcolm, I discovered my blackness and realized that I could never be who I was called to be until I embraced my African heritage—completely and enthusiastically. He taught me that a colorless Christianity is a joke—only found in the imaginary world of white theology. It is not found in the real world of white seminaries and churches. Nor is it found in black churches. That black people hate themselves is no accident of history. As I listened to Malcolm and meditated on his analysis of racism in America and the world, I became convinced by his rhetorical virtuosity. Speaking to blacks, his primary audience, he said:

> Who taught you to hate the color of your skin? Who taught you to hate the texture of your hair? Who taught you to hate the shape of your nose? Who taught you to hate yourself from the top of your head to the sole of your feet? Who taught you to hate your own kind? Who taught you to hate the race you belong to so much that you don't want to be around each other? You should ask yourself, "Who taught you to hate being what God gave you?"[7]

Malcolm challenged me to take a critical look at Christianity, Martin King, and the Civil Rights movement. The challenge was so deep that I found myself affirming what many persons regarded as theological opposites: Martin and Malcolm, civil rights and Black Power, Christianity and blackness.

Just as Martin King may be regarded as America's most influential theologian and preacher, Malcolm X may be regarded as America's most trenchant race critic. As Martin's theological achievement may be compared to Augustine's and Luther's, Malcolm's race critique is as far-reaching as Marx's class critique and the current feminist critique of gender. Malcolm was the great master of suspicion in the area of race. No one before or after him analyzed the role of Christianity in promoting racism and its mental and material consequences upon the lives of blacks as Malcolm did. He has no peer.

Malcolm X taught black ministers and scholars that the identity of African-Americans as a people was inextricably linked with blackness. This was his great contribution to black theology. Malcolm gave black theology its *black* identity, putting blackness at the center of who we were created to be. Like Martin, Malcolm did not write a scholarly treatise on the theme of blackness and self. He revolutionized black self-understanding with the power of his speech.

The distinctiveness of black theology is the bringing together of Martin and Malcolm—their ideas about Christianity and justice and blackness and self. Neither Martin nor Malcolm sought to do that. The cultural identity of Christianity was not important to Martin because he understood it in the "universal" categories he was taught in graduate school. His main concern was to link the identity of Christianity with social justice, oriented in love and defined by hope.

The Christian identity of the black self was not important to Malcolm X. For him, Christianity was the white man's religion and thus had to be rejected. Black people, Malcolm contended, needed a black religion, one that would bestow self-respect upon them for being black. Malcolm was not interested in remaking Christianity into a black religion.

I disagreed with both Martin and Malcolm and insisted on the importance of bringing blackness and Christianity together. While Martin and Malcolm were prevented from coming together during their lifetime, I was determined to put them together in black liberation theology. Using their cultural and political insights, I discovered a way of articulating what I wanted to say about theology and race that not only rejected the need for my professors' approval, but challenged them to exorcise the racism in their theologies. Malcolm taught me how to make theology black and never again to despise my African origin. Martin showed me how to make and keep theology Christian and never allow it to be used to support injustice. I was transformed from a *Negro* theologian to a *black* theologian, from an understanding of theology as an analysis of God-ideas in books to an understanding of it as a disciplined reflection about God arising out of a commitment to the practice of justice for the poor.

The turn to blackness was an even deeper conversion-experience than the turn to Jesus. It was spiritual, transforming radically my way of seeing the world and theology. Before I was born again into thinking black, I thought of theology as something remote from my history and culture, something that was primarily defined by Europeans which I, at best, could only imitate. Blackness gave me new theological spectacles, which enabled me to move beyond the limits of white theology, and empowered my mind to think thoughts that were wild and heretical when evaluated by white academic values. Blackness opened my eyes to see African-American history and culture as one of the most insightful sources for knowing about God since the Bible was declared a canon. Blackness whetted my appetite for learning how to do theology with a black signature on it and thereby make it accountable to poor black people and not to the privileged white theological establishment. The revolution that Malcolm X created in my theological consciousness meant that I could no longer make peace with the intellectual mediocrity in which I had been trained. The more I trusted my experience the more new thoughts about God and theology whirled around in my head—so fast I could hardly contain my excitement.

Using the black experience as the starting point of theology raised the theodicy question in a profound and challenging way that was never mentioned in graduate school. It was James Baldwin's *The Fire Next Time* which poignantly defined the problem for me: "If [God's] love was so great, and if He loved all His children, why were we, the blacks, cast down so far?"[8] This was an existential, heart-wrenching question, which challenged the academic way in which the problem of evil was dealt with in graduate school. It forced me to search deep into a wellspring of blackness, not for a theoretical answer that would satisfy the dominant intellectual culture of Europe and the United States, but rather for a new way of doing theology that would empower the suffering black poor to fight for a more liberated existence.

"Christianity and Black Power" was the first essay I wrote following my black conversion. I vividly remember when I sat down at my desk in Adrian College (Adrian, Michigan) in the wake of the Newark and Detroit riots in July 1967. I could hardly contain my rage against the white church and its theology for their inability to see that the God of Jesus was at work in places they least expected—Black Power! That essay was the beginning of my theological journey. I was well aware of the risk I was taking in making such a radical break with my theological education. But with black people dying in the streets of America, I just could not keep silent. I had to speak a liberating word for my people. Once I took the first step, I kept on stepping—writing *Black Theology and Black Power* (1969) in a month's time in the summer of 1968.

In writing *Black Theology and Black Power*, I suddenly understood what Karl Barth must have felt when he first rejected the liberal theology of his professors in Germany. It was a liberating experience to be free of my liberal and neo-orthodox professors, to be liberated from defining theology with abstract theological jargon that was unrelated to the life-and-death issues of black people. Although separated by nearly fifty years and dealing with completely different theological situations and issues, I felt a spiritual kinship with Barth, especially in his writing of *The Epistle to the Romans* (1921) and in his public debate with Adolf Harnack, his former teacher.

As I think back to that time in the late 1960s, when white American theologians were writing and talking about the "death-of-God theology" as black people were fighting and dying in the streets, the energy swells once again. I was angry and could not keep it to myself. Like Malcolm X, I felt I was the angriest black theologian in America.[9] I had to speak out, as forcefully as I knew how, against the racism I witnessed in theology, the churches, and the broader society. And that was why I began to write.

Once I started writing I could not stop. The message I was seeking to communicate was "something like a burning fire shut up in my bones" (Jer. 20:9). I had to write or be consumed by my anger. As soon as I finished *Black Theology*, I dove immediately into writing *A Black Theology of Liberation* (1970). In the first book I addressed my race critique primarily to the white liberals in the church and society because they were the loudest in denouncing Black Power. White theology and the seminaries were a secondary concern. But as soon as I knew that I was leaving Adrian College to teach at Union Theological Seminary in New York, the most liberal and influential seminary in America, I decided that I had to address head-on white theology, the intellectual arm of the white church. Two of the world's most famous theologians had taught at Union—Reinhold Neibuhr and Paul Tillich. Although I respected their great intellectual contribution to theology and had learned much from their brilliant theological insights, I was not intimidated by their legacy. I was audacious enough to think that my understanding of the gospel was a simple truth, available to anyone who opened his/her heart and mind to the God revealed in the Scriptures and present in the world today. One does not need to be an intellectual giant to know that the God of the Bible is known as the liberator of the oppressed from physical and spiritual bondage. I did not regard this point as a brilliant insight. It was an obvious biblical truth and only white theologians' racism blinded them to it. In *A Black Theology of Liberation* I merely sought to remind them of it.

I did not limit my critique to white churches and their theologians. In *Black Theology and Black Power* I also leveled a sharp critique against the post–Civil War Black Church for its otherworldliness and indifference toward the political and cultural implication of Black Power. Black ministers were none too happy about that. To my surprise, even some black religion scholars questioned whether my focus on liberation was indigenous to the black religious experience or something I derived exclusively from the secular advocates of Black Power. "Black Spirituals: A Theological Interpretation" was my reply, followed by a book-length treatment on *The Spirituals and the Blues* (1972).

"Black Theology on Revolution, Violence, and Reconciliation" was written in the heat of theological debate and in the context of my involvement in the Black Power movement in the early 1970s. It was my standard address to white seminaries and churches that condemned Black Power as revolutionary and violent, saying it was unchristian. As the theologian of the Black Power movement, I felt that I had to give a theological reply to their misguided judgment.

"Black Theology and the Black Church: Where Do We Go from Here?" continues my affirmation and critique of the Black Church and also marks the beginning of a new development in my theological journey. Here I seek to connect the African-American struggle for justice with the struggles of the Third World poor in Africa, Asia, and Latin America. This is also the beginning of my recognition of the importance of Marxism as a tool of social analysis, largely through the influence of my dialogue with Latin American liberation theology in the Theology in the Americas (TIA) and the Ecumenical Association of Third World Theologians (EATWOT). Although our debates were heated (since I would not replace race with class as my starting point), I learned much from our dialogue.

The "Martin and Malcolm" section focuses on the two ministers most responsible for the rise of black liberation theology. Although I refer to them from the beginning of my reflections on black theology, they are not the subject of a sustained analysis. A disciplined investigation began in the 1980s with Martin King's theology where I was seeking to show that his thinking was primarily defined by the Black Church community and not white theology. I then proceeded to place him in conversation with Malcolm X, his most challenging critic. These essays were written before and after the publication of *Martin & Malcolm & America: A Dream or a Nightmare* (1991) and cover topics not developed there. All were presented as addresses at events celebrating Martin King's birthday and his significance for America and the church. Following the early focus on Martin's theology, I now almost never talk or write about Martin without giving similar attention to Malcolm. People are always asking me who of the two is the more important for my theological perspective. Some think Martin and others, Malcolm. I say both are equally important, because each contributes something essential to my theological identity.

The "Going Forward" section addresses the importance of solidarity across differences as we move into the next millennium. Nothing is more important than unity among black people and solidarity with all who are struggling to make a world that is safe and healthy for life in all its forms.

No issue is more urgent than the fight against patriarchy in the Black Church community. Unfortunately, I have not always been supportive of women in the ministry, at least not as forcefully as common sense and the gospel demanded. While I did not publicly oppose gender-consciousness in theology, I just kept silent about it and continued my writing and teaching about black liberation theology as if gender-inclusive language and black women's experience made no distinctive contribution to my understanding of liberation and its impact on theology. It was a sexist assumption, just as detrimental to humanity as racism. I was like white theologians who were silent about black theology. I broke my silence in the middle of the 1970s when black women students at Garrett-Evangelical Theological Seminary (October 1976) asked me to address a black women's conference on the theme "New Roles in the Ministry: A Theological Appraisal." It was my first halting effort. Since then, I have endeavored to always use inclusive language and engage gender issues in my teaching, writing, and way of life. Womanist theologians continue to challenge my thinking, reminding me that I still have a long way to go. I did not seek to remove the obviously male-centered language in my early essays, because I think it is important for me to acknowledge the limits of my perspective during the course of thirty years of writing.

In "Black Theology and the Black College Student" I address young blacks who were in danger of separating themselves from the religious roots of their elders. That danger is still present today. There is no future for the African-American community divided against itself. We need one another, the young and the elders, men and women, for together we stand and divided we fall.

I do not see any future for humankind unless people around the world come to their senses and learn how to treat one another as human beings. This is especially true for white people in relation to people of color. Unlike many black nationalists, past and present, I do not believe that whites by nature are more sinful than other people. They just have more power—intellectual, political, social, economic, military, and otherwise—to do evil. "Humans exhibit the greatest cruelty when they have uncurbed power to do so," especially "when mob or group actions override individual judgment and sensitivity."[10] As Reinhold Niebuhr was persistent in reminding us, powerful groups have very little capacity to restrain themselves from evil acts against the powerless.[11] No group has been more evil than whites, especially in relation to black people over such a long period of time. I emphasized this point nearly thirty years ago. What is still amazing to me is that white theologians and ethicists, the intellectual and spiritual conscience of America and the world, continue to write about everything under the sun *except* the cancer of racism. "White Theology Revisited" is another urgent call to white theologians to recognize that their theologies will never have integrity as long as they fail to incorporate a persistent and radical race critique in their discourse.

This same unity principle must be applied to the whole of humanity and indeed to life itself. Unless we learn how to live in harmony with one another and with the universe we will self-destruct. This is the central point of "Whose Earth Is It, Anyway?" presented at an ecology conference at Union Seminary.

Risks of Faith represents thirty years of searching for the truth of the gospel. I do not claim to have found the whole truth. I am still searching, for I know, as Paul knew, "we see in a mirror, dimly" and thus "know only in part," not fully (1 Cor. 13:12 New Revised Standard Version). The partial truths we see can be enlarged if we have the humility to open ourselves to the verity of other peoples' experiences. Let us hope that we will recognize our common humanity so that together we can create a world that is truly the "beloved community" of life.

Black Theology and Black Power

[Black Power] means that blacks accept the risk of defining themselves. Like our forefathers who rebelled against slavery, we know that life is not worth living unless we are fighting against its limits.

—*The Christian Century*, Sept. 16, 1970

I cannot de-emphasize the *literal* significance of blackness. My people were enslaved, lynched, and ghettoized in the name of God and country because of their color. No amount of theologizing can remove the reality of that experience from my consciousness. And because blacks were de-humanized by white-skinned people who created a cultural style based on black oppression, the *literal* importance of whiteness has historical referents.

—*The Christian Century*, Sept. 15, 1971

Christianity and Black Power

My purpose is to examine the concept of Black Power and its relationship to Christianity and the Church. Some religionists would consider Black Power the work of the Antichrist. Others would suggest that such a concept should be tolerated as an expression of Christian love to the misguided black brother. It is my thesis, however, that Black Power, even in its most radical expression, is not an antithesis of Christianity, nor is it a heretical idea to be tolerated with painful forbearance. It is rather Christ's central message to twentieth-century America. And unless the empirical denominational Church makes a determined effort to recapture the Man Jesus through a total identification with the suffering poor as expressed in Black Power, that Church will become exactly what Christ is not.

That most churches see an irreconcilable conflict between Christianity and Black Power is evidenced not only by the structure of their community (the 11:00 A.M. hour on Sunday is still the most segregated hour of any weekday), but by their typical response to riots: "I deplore the violence but sympathize with the reasons for the violence." What churchmen, laymen, and ministers alike apparently fail to recognize is their contribution to the ghetto-condition through permissive silence—except for a few resolutions which they usually pass once a year or immediately following a riot—and through their cotenancy with a dehumanizing social structure whose existence depends on the enslavement of black people. If the Church is to remain faithful to its Lord, it must make a decisive break with the structure of this society by launching a vehement attack on the evils of racism in all forms. It must become *prophetic*, demanding a radical change in the interlocking structures of this society.

Of course the Church must realize, in view of the Christian doctrine of man, that this is a dangerous task. But obedience to Christ is always costly. The time has come for the Church to challenge the power structure with the power of the *gospel*, knowing that nothing less than *immediate* and *total* emancipation of all people is consistent with the message and style of Jesus Christ. The Church cannot afford to deplore the means that oppressed people use to break the chains of slavery because such language not only clouds the issue but also gives comfort and assistance to the oppressor. Therefore, the primary purpose of this essay is to show that embracing Black Power is not only possible but necessary, if the Church wants to remain faithful to the traditions of Christianity as disclosed in the person of Jesus Christ.

Definition of Black Power

What does Black Power mean? It means nothing other than full emancipation of black people from white oppression by whatever means black people deem necessary. The methods may include selective buying, boycotting, marching, or even rebellion. Black Power, therefore, means black freedom, black self-determination, wherein black people no longer view themselves as animals devoid of human dignity but as men, human beings with the ability to carve out their own destiny. In short, as Stokely Carmichael would say, Black Power means T.C.B., Take Care of Business—black folk taking care of black folks' business not on the terms of the oppressor, but on those of the oppressed.

Black Power is analogous to Albert Camus's understanding of the rebel. The rebel is the man who says no and yes; he says no to conditions considered intolerable, and yes to that "something within him which 'is worth while . . .' and which must be taken into consideration."[1] He says no to "the humiliating orders of his master," and by so doing testifies to that something that is placed above everything else, including life itself. To say no means that death is preferable to life, if the latter is devoid of freedom. In the words of the black spiritual, "Before I be a slave I'll be buried in my grave." This is what Black Power means.

Unfortunately, many well-intentioned persons have insisted that there must be another approach, one that will not cause so much hostility, not to mention rebellion. Therefore, appeal is made to the patience of black people to keep their "cool" and not to get carried away by their feelings. These men argue that if any progress is to be made, it will be through a careful, *rational* approach to the subject. These people are deeply offended when black people refuse to listen and place such liberals in the same category as the most adamant segregationists. They simply do not see that such reasoned appeals merely support the perpetuation of the ravaging of the black community. Black Power, in this respect, is by nature *"irrational,"* that is, not denying the role of rational reflection, but insisting that human existence cannot be mechanized or put into neat boxes according to reason. Human reason, though valuable, is not absolute, because moral decisions—those decisions that deal with human dignity—cannot be made by using the *abstract* methods of science. Human emotions must be reckoned with. Consequently, black people must say no to all do-gooders who insist that they need more time. If such persons really knew oppression— knew it existentially in their guts—they would not be confused or disturbed at black rebellion, but would join black people in their fight for freedom and dignity. It is interesting that most people do understand why Jews can hate Germans. Why can they not also understand why black people, who have been deliberately and systematically murdered by the structure of this society, hate white people? The general failure of Americans to make this connection suggests that the primary difficulty is their inability to see black men as men.

This leads us to another reason why the concept of Black Power is rejected. Some persons would have us believe that advocating Black Power creates too much resentment or hate among black people and this makes significant personal relationship between black and white impossible. It should be obvious that the hate that black people feel toward white people is not due to the creation of the phrase *Black Power*. Rather it is a result of the deliberate and systematic ordering of society on the basis of racism, making black alienation not only possible but inevitable. For 350 years black people have been enslaved by the tentacles of white power, tentacles that worm their way into the guts of their being and "invade the gray cells of their cortex." For 350 years they have cried, waited, voted, marched, picketed, and boycotted, but whites still refuse to recognize their humanity. In light of this, attributing black resentment to the creation of Black Power is ridiculous, if not obscene.

Furthermore, while it is true that black people do hate whites, it is misleading to suggest that hatred is essential to the definition of Black Power. Quoting Carmichael's denial of the "black supremacy" charge: "There is no analogy—by any stretch of definition or imagination—between the advocates of Black Power and white racists. . . . The goal of the racists is to keep black people on the bottom, arbitrarily and dictatorially, as they have done in this country for over three hundred years. The goal of black self-determination and black self-identity—Black Power—is full participation in the decision-making processes affecting the lives of black people."[2] In hate one desires something that is not his; but the black man's intention is to claim what is his—freedom. Therefore, it is not the purpose of the black man to repudiate his enslaver's dignity, but only his right as an enslaver. The rebellion in the cities should not be interpreted as the work of a few blacks who want something for nothing but as an assertion of the dignity of black people. The black man is assuming that there is a common value which is recognizable by all as existing in all people, and he is testifying to that *something* in his rebellion. He is expressing his solidarity with the human race.

In reality, then, *accommodation* and *protest* seem to be the only options open to the black man. For three hundred years he accommodated, thereby giving credence to his own enslavement. Black Power means that he will no longer accommodate; that he will no longer tolerate white excuses for enslavement; that he will no longer be guided by the oppressor's understanding of justice, liberty, freedom, or the methods to be used in attaining it. He recognizes the difference between theoretical equality and great factual inequalities. He will not sit by and wait for the white man's love to be extended to his black brother. He will protest, violently, if need be, on behalf of absolute and immediate emancipation. Black Power means that black people will cease trying rationally to articulate the political advantages and moral rightness of human freedom, because the dignity of man is a self-evident religious, philosophical, and political *truth*, without which human community is impossible. When one group breaks the accepted human covenant (i.e., a mutual respect for human freedom), it begins to plant the seeds of rebellion.

Many concerned persons have pointed out the futility of black rebellion by drawing a vast contrast between the present conditions of the black man in the ghetto and other revolutionaries of the past. They say that revolution depends on cohesion, discipline, stability, and the sense of a stake in society. The ghetto, by contrast, is relatively incohesive, unorganized, unstable and numerically too small to be effective. Therefore, rebellion for the black man can only mean extermination.

The analysis is essentially correct. But to point out the futility of rebellion is to miss the *point* of black rebellion. Black people know that they compose less than 12 percent of the total population and are proportion-

ately weak with respect to economic, political, or military power. The rebellion in the cities is not a conscious organized attempt of black people to
take over; it is an attempt to say *yes* to their own dignity even in death.
Therefore, the question is not whether black people are prepared to die—
the riots testify to that—but whether whites are prepared to kill them. Unfortunately, it seems that that answer has been given through the riots as
well. Yet this willingness of black people to die is not novel but is rather a
part of the heritage of Christianity.

Christianity and Black Power

The black intellectual community is becoming increasingly suspicious of
Christianity because the oppressor has used it as a means of directing the
oppressed away from any concern for present inequalities by emphasizing
a heavenly reality beyond time and space. Naturally, as the slave begins
to question his existence as a slave, he also questions the religion of the
enslaver.

It is, therefore, appropriate to ask, "Is Black Power compatible with the
Christian faith, or are we dealing with two radically divergent perspectives?" To answer these questions we need to ask and answer a prior question: "What is Christianity?"

Christianity begins and ends with the Man Jesus—his life, death, and
resurrection. He is the essence of Christianity. Schleiermacher was not far
wrong when he said that "Christianity is essentially distinguished from
other faiths by the fact that everything in it is related to the redemption
accomplished by Jesus of Nazareth."[3] In contrast to many religions, Christianity revolves around a Person, without whom its existence ceases to
be. Christ and Christianity belong together; they cannot be separated.
Granted, there have been historical disagreements regarding the nature of
that connection. The relationship has been conceived as inward or as external and mechanical. But it is impossible to separate Christ from Christianity without robbing it of its uniqueness.

The central importance of Jesus Christ for Christianity is plainest of all
when we consider the New Testament picture of Jesus. According to the
New Testament, Jesus is the man for others who views his existence as inextricably tied to other men to the degree that his own Person is inexplica-
ble apart from others. *Others*, of course, refers to all men, especially the oppressed, the unwanted of society, the sinners. He is God Himself coming

into the very depths of human existence for the sole purpose of destroying all human tentacles of slavery, thereby freeing man from ungodly principalities and powers that hinder his relationship with God. Jesus himself defines the nature of his ministry in these terms:

> The Spirit of the Lord is upon me,
> because he has anointed me to preach the good news to the poor,
> He has sent me to proclaim release to the captives and recovering of
> sight to the blind,
> To set at liberty those who are oppressed,
> To proclaim the acceptable year of the Lord.
>
> *(Luke 4:18, 19)*

His work is essentially one of liberation. Becoming a slave himself, he opens realities of human existence formerly closed to man. Through an encounter with him, man now knows the full meaning of God's action in history and man's place within it.

The Gospel of Mark describes the nature of Jesus' ministry in this manner: "The time is fulfilled, the Kingdom of God is at hand; repent and believe the Gospel" (1:14, 15). On the face of it this message appears not to be too radical to our twentieth-century ears, but this impression stems from our failure existentially to bridge the gap between modern man and biblical man. In reality the message of the Kingdom strikes at the very center of man's desire to define his own existence in the light of his own interest at the price of his brother's enslavement. It means the irruption of a new age, an age that has to do with God's action in history on behalf of man's salvation. It is an age of liberation, in which "the blind receive their sight, the lame walk, the lepers are cleansed, the deaf hear, the dead are raised up, the poor have the good news preached to them" (Luke 7:22). This is not pious talk, and one does not need a seminary degree to interpret the passage. It is a message about the ghetto, Vietnam, and all other injustices done in the name of democracy and religion to further the social, political, and economic interests of the oppressor. In Christ, God enters human affairs and takes sides with the oppressed. Their suffering becomes his; their despair, divine despair. Through Christ the poor are offered freedom now to rebel against that which makes them other than human.

It is ironical that America with its history of injustice to the poor (especially regarding the black man and the Indian) prides itself as a Christian nation (is there really such an animal?). It is even more ironical that officials within the body of the Church have passively or actively participated in injustices. With Jesus, however, the poor were at the heart of his mission: "The last shall be first and the first last" (Matt. 20:16). That is why he was always kind to traitors, adulterers, and sinners and why the Samaritan came out on top in the parable. Speaking of Pharisees (the religiously elite of his day), he said: "Truly I say to you, the tax collectors (traitors) and harlots go into the Kingdom—but not you" (Matt. 21:31). Jesus had little tolerance for the middle- or upper-class religious snob whose attitude attempted to usurp the sovereignty of God and destroy the dignity of the poor. The Kingdom is for the poor and not the rich because the former has nothing to expect from the world while the latter's entire existence is grounded in his commitment to worldly things. The poor man may expect everything from God while the rich man may expect nothing because of his refusal to free himself from his own pride. It is not that poverty is a precondition for entrance into the Kingdom. But those who recognize their utter dependence on God and wait on him despite the miserable absurdity of life are usually poor, according to our Lord. And the Kingdom which the poor may enter is not merely an eschatological longing for escape to a transcendent reality, nor is it an inward serenity that eases unbearable suffering. Rather it is God encountering man in the very depths of his being-in-the-world and releasing him from all human evils, like racism, which hold him captive. The repentant man knows that even though God's ultimate Kingdom is in the future, it breaks through even now like a ray of light upon the darkness of the oppressed.

When we make it contemporaneous with our life situation, Jesus' message is clear enough. The message of Black Power is the message of Christ himself. To be sure, that statement is both politically and religiously dangerous. It is so politically because Black Power threatens the very structure of the American way of life. It is theologically dangerous because it may appear to overlook Barth's early emphasis on "the infinite qualitative distinction between God and man." In this regard, we must say that Christ never promised political security, but the opposite; and Karl Barth was mainly concerned with the easy identification of the work of God with the work of the State. But if Luther's statement "we are Christ to the neighbor" is to be taken seriously, and if we can believe the New Testament witness that proclaims Jesus as resurrected and thus active even now in the midst of human misery, then he must be alive in men who are where the action is. If the gospel is a gospel of liberation for the oppressed, then Jesus is where the oppressed are. Jesus is not safely confined in the first century. He is our contemporary, proclaiming release to the captives and rebelling against all who silently accept the structure. If perchance he is not in the ghetto, if he is not where men are living at the brink of existence, but is rather in the easy life of the suburb, then he lied and Christianity is a mistake. Christianity, therefore, is not alien to Black Power; it *is* Black Power!

There are perhaps many secular interpretations that could account for the present black rebellion as there were secular views of the Exodus or of the life and death of Jesus. But for the Christian, there is only one interpretation: Black rebellion is God himself actively involved in the present-day affairs of men for the purpose of liberating a people. Through his work, black people now know that there is something more important than life itself. They can afford to be indifferent toward death, because life devoid of freedom is not worth living.

The Church and Black Power

What is the Church and its relationship to Christ and Black Power? According to the New Testament, the Church is the *laos theou*, the "people of God." It is a community of people who have encountered God's action in history and thus desire to participate in Christ's continued work of liberation. As Bonhoeffer puts it, the Church is "Christ existing as community" or Christ's "presence in history." This means that the Church's work and message is nothing other than a continuation of the message and work of Christ. It is, as Barth puts it, "God's provisional demonstration of his intention for all humanity."

If the real Church is the *laos theou* whose primary task is that of being Christ to the world by proclaiming the message of the gospel *(kerygma)*, by rendering services of liberation *(diakonia)*, and by being itself a manifestation of the nature of the new society *(koinonia)*, then the empirical Church has failed on all counts. It certainly has not rendered service of reconciliation to the poor, evidently because it represents the values of a sick society that oppresses the poor. Some present-day theologians, like Hamilton and Altizer, taking their cue from Nietzsche and the present irrelevancy of the Church to modern man, have announced the death of God. It seems, however, that their chief mistake lies in their apparent identification of God's reality with the signed-up Christians. If we were to identify the work of God with the denominational Church, then, like Altizer, we must "will the death of God with a passion of faith." Or as Camus would say, taking his cue from Bakunin, "If God *did* exist, we should have to abolish Him!"

The Church has not only failed to render service to the poor, but also failed miserably at being a visible manifestation of God's intention for humanity and at proclaiming the message of the gospel to the world. It seems that the Church is not God's redemptive agent but rather an agent of the old society. It not only fails to create an atmosphere for radical obedience to Christ, but also precludes the possibility of becoming a loyal, devoted servant of God. How else can we explain that some church fellowships are more concerned with nonsmoking principles or temperances than with children who die of rat bites or men who are shot while looting a TV set. Men are dying of hunger, children are maimed from rat bites, women are dying of despair, and churches pass resolutions. While we may have difficulty in locating the source of evil, we know what must be done against evil in order to relieve the suffering of the poor. We know why men riot. Perhaps we cannot prevent riots, but we can fight against conditions that cause them. The Church is placed in question because of its contribution to a structure that produces riots.

Some churchmen may reply: "We do condemn the deplorable conditions which produce urban riots. We do condemn racism and all the evils arising from it." But to the extent that this is true, the Church, with the exception of a few isolated individuals, voices its condemnation in the style of resolutions that are usually equivocal and almost totally unproductive. If the condemnation was voiced, it was not understood! The Church should speak in a style that avoids abstractions. Its language should be backed up with relevant involvement in the affairs of people who suffer. It must be a grouping whose community life and personal involvement are coherent with its language about the gospel.

The Church does not appear to be a community willing to pay up personally. It is not a community that views every command of Jesus as a call to the cross—death. Rather, it is an institution whose existence depends on the evils that produce the riots in the cities. With this in mind, we must say that when a minister blesses by silence the conditions that produce riots and condemns the rioters, he gives up his credentials as a Christian minister and becomes inhuman. He is an animal, just like those who, backed by an ideology of racism, order the structure of this society on the basis of white supremacy. We need men who refuse to be animals and are resolved to pay the price, so that all men can be something more than animals.

Whether Black Power advocates are that grouping, we will have to wait and see. But the Church has shown many times that it loves life and is not prepared to die for others. It has not really gone where the action is with a willingness to die for the neighbor, but remains aloof from the sufferings of men. It is a ministry to middle-class America! How else can one explain its snail-like pace toward an inclusive membership? Even though Paul says that Christ "has broken down the dividing walls of hostility" (Eph. 2:14), the Church's community life reflects racism through and through. It is still possible to be a racist, a black-hater, and at the same time a member of the Church. It is my contention that the Church cannot be the Church of Christ and sponsor or even tolerate racism. The fact that the Church does indeed tolerate or sponsor racism is evidenced by its *whiteness*.

This leads me to conclude that Christ is operating outside the denominational Church. The real Church of Christ is that grouping that identifies with the suffering of the poor by becoming one with them. While we should be careful in drawing the line, the line must nevertheless be drawn. The Church includes not only the Black Power community but all men who view their humanity as inextricably related to every man. It is that grouping with a demonstrated willingness to die for the prevention of the torture of others, saying with Bonhoeffer, "when Christ calls a man, he bids him come and die."

Black Spirituals:
A Theological Interpretation

Contrary to popular opinion, the spirituals are not evidence that black people reconciled themselves with human slavery. On the contrary, they are black freedom songs that emphasize black liberation as consistent with divine revelation. For this reason, it is most appropriate for black people to sing them in this "new" age of Black Power. And if some people still regard the spirituals as inconsistent with Black Power and black theology, that is because they have been misguided and the songs misinterpreted. There is little evidence that black slaves accepted their servitude because they believed God willed their slavery. The opposite is the case. The spirituals speak of God's liberation of black people, his will to set right the oppression of black slaves despite the overwhelming power of white masters. . . .

And if "de God dat lived in Moses' time is jus de same today," then that God will vindicate the suffering of the righteous black and punish the unrighteous whites for their wrongdoings.

A large amount of scholarship has been devoted to the music and poetry of the black spiritual, but little has been written about its theology. Apparently most scholars assume that the value of the black spiritual lies in its artistic expression and not its theological content, which could be taken to mean that blacks can "sing and dance good" but cannot think. For example, almost everyone agrees with W. E. B. Du Bois's contention that "the Negro is primarily an artist"[1] and that his gift of music to America is unsurpassed. But what about the black person as a philosopher and theologian? Is it not possible that the thought of the spiritual is as profound as its music is creative, since without thought art is impossible? In this essay my purpose is to investigate the theological implications of the black spirituals, with special reference to the meaning of God, Jesus Christ, suffering, and eschatology.

I

No theological interpretation of the black spirituals is valid that ignores the cultural environment that created them, and understanding a culture means, in part, perceiving its history. Black history in America is a history of black servitude, a record of pain and sorrows, slave ships and auction blocks. It is the story of black life in chains and of what that meant for the souls and bodies of black people. This is the history that created the spirituals, and it must be recognized if we are to render a valid theological interpretation of these black songs.

The logical place to begin is 1619 when twenty black Africans were sold as indentured servants at Jamestown, Virginia. Actually, there was nothing historically unusual about that event, since indentured servitude was already in existence, and many whites were victims. But in 1661 the significance of 1619 was clearly defined when Virginia legalized black slavery, declaring that people of African descent would be slaves for life. Maryland legalized black slavery two years later, and soon after all colonies followed suit. America became the land of the free for white people only, and for blacks she became a land of bondage.

Physical slavery was cruel. It meant working fifteen to twenty hours per day and being beaten unmercifully if one displayed the slightest fatigue. The auction block became a symbol of "brokenness" because no family ties were recognized. Husbands were separated from wives and children from parents. There were few laws protecting the slaves, since most whites believed that Africans were only partly human (three-fifths was the fraction fixed by the Fathers in 1787). Later, to put down any lingering doubts, the highest court of the land decreed that black people had no rights that white people were bound to respect. Slaves were property, as were animals and objects; their owners could dispose of them as they saw fit—provided they did not endanger the welfare of the society as a whole.

It has been said that not all masters were cruel, and perhaps there is some truth in the observation—particularly if it is made from a perspective that does not know the reality of the slave-experience. But from the black perspective, the phrase "good" master is an absurdity, a logical contradiction. To speak of "good" masters is like speaking of "good" racists and "good" murderers. Who in their right minds could make such nonsensical distinctions, except those who deal in historical abstractions? Certainly not the victims! Indeed, it may be argued that the so-called good masters were in fact the worst, if we consider the dehumanizing effect of mental servitude. At least those who were blatant in their physical abuse did not camouflage their savagery with Christian doctrine, and it may have been easier for black slaves to make the necessary value-distinctions so that they could regulate their lives according to black definitions. But "good" Christian masters could cover up their brutality by rationalizing it with Christian theology, making it difficult for slaves to recognize the demonic. Undoubtedly, white Christianity contributed to the phenomenon of "house niggers" (not all domestic servants were in this category), those blacks who internalized the masters' values, revealing information about insurrections planned by their brothers. The "good" masters convinced them that slavery was their lot ordained by God, and it was his will for blacks to be obedient to white people. After all, Ham was cursed, and St. Paul did admonish slaves to be obedient to their masters.

Initially, white masters did not permit their slaves to be Christianized. Christian baptism implied manumission, according to some; and there were too many biblical references to freedom. But white missionaries and preachers convinced slavemasters that Christianity made blacks "better" slaves—obedient and docile. As one slaveholder put it: "The deeper the piety of the slave, the more valuable he is in every respect."[2] White Christianity assisted in the internalization of white values in the minds of slaves, reconciling them to the condition of servitude. The Christianity taught to black slaves was a distorted interpretation of the gospel, geared to the ideological enforcement of white racism. Black resistance to slavery was interpreted as sin; revolt against the master was said to be revolt against God, and that could only mean eternal damnation. To be sure, Christianity offered freedom, but for slaves it was interpreted to mean freedom from sin, the lust and passion that made them disregard the interests of their masters. Such was the history that created the spirituals.

II

But the history that created the spirituals contains much more than what white people *did* to black people. Black history is also the record of black people's historical strivings, an account of their perceptions of their existence in an oppressive society. What whites did to blacks is secondary. The primary reality is what blacks did to whites in order to restrict the white assault on their humanity.

When white people enslaved Africans, their intention was to dehistoricize black existence, to foreclose the possibility of a future defined by the African heritage. White people demeaned the sacred tales of the black fathers, ridiculing their myths and defiling the sacred rites. Their intention was to define man according to European definitions so that their brutality against Africans could be characterized as civilizing the savages. But white Europeans did not succeed, and black history is the record of their failure. Black people did not stand by passively while white oppressors demoralized their being. Many rebelled—physically and mentally. Black history in America is the history of that rebellion.

Black rebellion in America did not begin with the Civil Rights movement and Martin Luther King, nor with Black Power and Stokely Carmichael or the Black Panther Party. Black resistance has roots stretching back to the auction blocks and the slave codes. It began when the first black person decided that death would be preferable to slavery. If white government officials could just realize this, then they might be able to understand the Black Panthers and other black revolutionaries. White people should know about Harriet Tubman and her liberation of more than three hundred black slaves. They should know about Henry Garnett and his urgent call for rebellion among the slaves. Black slaves were not passive, and black history is the record of their physical resistance against the condition of human bondage.

To understand the history of black resistance, it is also necessary to know the black spirituals. They are historical songs that speak about the rupture of black lives; they tell us about a people in the land of bondage and what they did to hold themselves together and to fight back. We are told that the people of Israel could not sing the Lord's song in a strange land. But, for blacks, their *Being* depended upon a song. Through song, they built new structures for existence in an alien land. The spirituals enabled blacks to retain a measure of African identity while living in the midst of American slavery, providing both the substance and the rhythm to cope with human servitude.

Much has been said about the compensatory and otherworldly ideas in the black spirituals. While I do not question the presence of that theme, there is, nevertheless, another train of thought running through these songs. And unless this emphasis is considered, it is possible that the spirituals cannot be understood. I am referring to the emphasis on freedom in this world, and the kinds of risks blacks were willing to take in order to attain it.

> *Oh Freedom! Oh Freedom!*
> *Oh Freedom, I love thee!*
> *And before I'll be a slave,*
> *I'll be buried in my grave,*
> *And go home to my Lord and be free.*

The theme of freedom and activities it implied explains why slaveholders did not allow black slaves to worship and sing their songs unless authorized white people were present to proctor the meeting. And after the Nat Turner revolt, black preachers were declared illegal in most southern states. Black religious gatherings were often occasions for organizing resistance against the institution of slavery.

Black history is the stuff out of which the black spirituals were created. But the "stuff" of black history includes more than the bare historical facts of slavery. Black history is an experience, a soulful event. And to understand it is to know the Being of a people who had to "feel their way along the course of American slavery,"[3] enduring the stresses and strains of human servitude but not without a song. *Black history is a spiritual!*

III

The divine liberation of the oppressed from slavery is the central theological concept in the black spirituals. These songs show that black slaves did not believe that human servitude was reconcilable with their African past and their knowledge of the Christian gospel. They did not believe that God created Africans to be the slaves of Europeans. Accordingly they sang of a God who was involved in history—*their* history—making right what whites have made wrong. Just as God delivered Moses and the Children of Israel from Egyptian bondage, drowning Pharaoh and his army in the Red

Sea, so also he will deliver black people from American slavery. It is this certainty that informs the thought of the black spirituals, enabling black slaves to sing:

> Oh Mary, don't you weep, don't you moan,
> Oh Mary, don't you weep, don't you moan,
> Pharaoh's army got drownded,
> Oh Mary, don't you weep.

The basic idea of the spirituals is that slavery contradicts God; it is a denial of His will. To be enslaved is to be declared *nobody*, and that form of existence contradicts God's creation of men to be his children. Because black people believed that they were God's children, they affirmed their *somebodiness*, refusing to reconcile their servitude with divine revelation. They rejected white distortions of the gospel, which emphasized the obedience of slaves to their masters. They contended that God willed their freedom and not their slavery. That is why the spirituals focus on biblical passages that stress God's involvement in the liberation of oppressed people. Black people sang about Joshua and the battle of Jericho, Moses leading the Israelites from bondage, Daniel in the lions' den, and the Hebrew children in the fiery furnace. Here the emphasis is on God's liberation of the weak from the oppression of the strong, the lowly and downtrodden from the proud and mighty. And blacks reasoned that if God could lock the lion's jaw for Daniel and could cool the fire for the Hebrew children, then he certainly could deliver black people from slavery.

> My Lord delivered Daniel
> Why can't He deliver me?

Contrary to popular opinion, the spirituals are not evidence that black people reconciled themselves with human slavery. On the contrary, they are black freedom songs which emphasize black liberation as consistent with divine revelation. For this reason it is most appropriate for black people to sing them in this "new" age of Black Power. And if some people still regard the spirituals as inconsistent with Black Power and black theology, that is because they have been misguided and the songs misinterpreted. There is little evidence that black slaves accepted their servitude because they believed God willed their slavery. The opposite is the case. The spirituals speak of God's liberation of black people, His will to set right the oppression of black slaves despite the overwhelming power of white masters. For blacks believed that there is an omnipotent, omnipresent, and omniscient power at work in the world, and that he is on the side of the oppressed and downtrodden. As evidence they pointed to the blind man who received his sight, the lame who walked, and Lazarus who was received into God's Kingdom while the rich man was rejected. And if "de God dat lived in Moses' time is jes' de same today," then that God will vindicate the suffering of the righteous blacks and punish the unrighteous whites for their wrongdoings.

IV

Some will argue, with Marx, that the very insistence upon *divine* activity is always evidence that people are helpless and passive. "Religion is the sign of the oppressed creature, the heart of the heartless world . . . the spirit of a spiritless situation. It is the *opium* of the people."[4] There were doubtless some black slaves who *literally* waited on God, expecting him to effect their liberation in response to their faithful passivity; but there is another side of the black experience to be weighed. When it is considered that Nat Turner, Denmark Vesey, and Harriet Tubman may have been creators of some of the spirituals, that "Sinner, please don't let this harvest pass" probably referred to a slave resistance meeting,[5] that after 1831 over two thousand slaves escaped yearly,[6] and that black churches interpreted civil disobedience as consistent with religion, then it is most likely that many slaves recognized the need for their own participation in God's liberation. Indeed, many believed that the only hands that God had were their hands, and without the risk of escape or insurrection, slavery would never end. This may be the meaning of the song, "Singin' wid a sword in ma han'." The sword may be the symbol of the need of black slaves to strike a blow for freedom even though the odds were against them. Certainly the strict enforcement of the slave codes and the merciless beating of many slaves who sang spirituals tend to point in that direction.[7] What is certain is that Christianity did not dull the drive for liberation among all black slaves, and there is much evidence that slaves appropriated the gospel to their various styles of resistance.

Seeking to detract from the theological significance of the spirituals, some critics may point out that black slaves were literalists in their interpretation of the Scripture, and this probably accounts for their acceptance of the white masters' interpretation of the Bible. Of course, it is true that slaves were not biblical critics and were unaware of erudite white reflections on the origins of biblical writings. Like most of their contemporaries, they accepted the inerrancy of Scripture. But the critical point is that their very literalism supported a black gospel of earthly freedom. They were literal when they sang about Daniel in the lions' den, David and Goliath, and Samson and the Philistines. On the other hand, they dispensed with biblical literalism when white people began to use the curse of Ham and Paul as evidence that blacks ought to accept their slavery. As one ex-slave preacher put it:

> When I starts preaching I couldn't read or write and had to preach what Master told me, and he say tell them niggers iffen they obeys the master they goes to Heaven; but I knowed there's something better for them, but daren't tell them 'cept on the sly. That I done lots. I tells 'em iffen they keeps praying, the Lord will set 'em free.[8]

Black slaves were not naive as is often supposed. They knew that slavery contradicted humanity and divinity, and that was why they cited biblical references that focused on the liberation of the oppressed. They believed that God would deliver them. As he once locked the lion's jaw for Daniel, he would paralyze the power of white masters.

> Who lock, who lock de lion,
> Who lock, de lion's jaw?
> God, lock, God lock de lion's jaw.

The point is clear. God is the liberator, the deliverer of the weak from the injustice of the strong.

It is significant that theology proper blends imperceptibly into christology in the spirituals. No theological distinction is made between the Son and the Father. Jesus is understood as the King, the deliverer of men from unjust suffering. He is the comforter in time of trouble, the lily of the valley, and the bright morning star.

> He's King of Kings, and Lord of Lords,
> Jesus Christ, the first and last
> No man works like him.

The death and resurrection of Jesus are particular focal points of the spirituals. The death of Jesus meant that the savior died on the cross for black slaves. His death was a symbol of their suffering, their trials and tribulation in an unfriendly world. When Jesus was nailed to the cross and the Romans pierced him in the side, he was not alone; blacks suffered and died with him. That was why they sang:

> *Were you there when they crucified my Lord?*
> *Were you there when they crucified my Lord?*
> *Oh! sometimes it causes me to tremble, tremble, tremble;*
> *Were you there when they crucified my Lord?*

Black slaves were there! Through the experience of being slaves, they encountered the theological significance of Jesus' death. With the crucifixion, Jesus makes an unqualified identification with the poor and helpless and takes their pain upon himself. They were there at the crucifixion because his death was for them.

And if Jesus was not alone in his suffering, they also were not alone in their slavery. Jesus is with them! Herein lies the meaning of the resurrection. It means that Jesus is not dead but is alive.

> *He rose, he rose from the dead,*
> *An' de Lord shall bear my spirit hom'.*

The resurrection is the divine guarantee that their lives are in the hands of him who conquered death, enabling men to do what is necessary to remain obedient to the Father, the creator and sustainer of life.

V

Though black slaves believed that the God of Jesus Christ was involved in the historical liberation of oppressed people from bondage, the continued existence of American slavery seemed to contradict that belief. If God was omnipotent and in control of human history, how could His goodness be reconciled with human servitude? If God had the power to deliver black people from the evil of slavery as he delivered Moses from Pharaoh's army, Daniel from the lions' den, and the Hebrew children from the fiery furnace, why then were black slaves still subject to the rule of white masters? Why are we still living in wretched conditions when God could end this evil thing with one righteous stroke?

These are hard questions, and they are still relevant today. In the history of theology and philosophy, these questions are the core of the "problem of evil"; college and seminary professors have spent many hours debating them. But black slaves did not have the opportunity to investigate the problem of suffering in the luxury of a seminar room with all the comforts of modern living. They encountered suffering in the cotton fields of Georgia, Arkansas, and Mississippi. Under the whip and pistol, they had to deal with the absurdities of human existence. Every time they opened their eyes and visualized the contradictions of their environment, they realized they were "rolling through an unfriendly world." How could a good and powerful God be reconciled with white masters and overseers? What explanation could the Holy One of Israel give for allowing the existence of an ungodly slave institution?

In order to understand the black slave's reaction to his enslavement, it is necessary to point out that his reflections on the problem of suffering were not "rational" in the classical Greek sense, with an emphasis on abstract and universal distinctions between good and evil, justice and injustice. The black slave had little time for reading books or sitting in the cool of the day, thinking about neat philosophical answers to the problem of evil. It was not only illegal to teach slaves to read, but most were forced to work from daybreak to nightfall, leaving no spare time for the art of theological and philosophical discourse. The black slave's investigation of the absurdities of human existence was concrete, and it was done within the context of the community of faith. No attempt was made to transcend the faith of the community by assuming a universal stance common to "all" men. In this sense, his reflection on human suffering was not unlike the biblical view of Yahweh's activity in human history. It was grounded in the historical realities of communal experience.

The classic examples in biblical history are found in the prophet Habakkuk and the sage Job. Both raised questions about the justice of God, but they were clearly questions for the faithful—not for philosophers. They took on significance only if one were a member of the community of faith. Habakkuk was concerned about the violence and the destruction of the land as witnessed in the army of the Chaldeans, while Job questioned the deuteronomic success formula. But in each case, the ultimate sovereignty of God was not denied. What was requested was a divine explanation so that the faithful could understand the ways of the Almighty. There was no philosophical resolution of the problem of evil. Suffering was a reality of life, and the believer must be able to take it upon himself without losing faith.

VI

In the spirituals, the slave's experience of suffering and despair defines for him the major issue in his view of the world. He does not really question the justice and goodness of God. He takes for granted God's righteousness and vindication of the poor and weak. Indeed, it is the point of departure for his faith. The slave has another concern, centered on the *faithfulness* of the community of believers in a world full of trouble. He wonders not whether God is just and right but whether the sadness and pain of the world will cause him to lose heart and thus fall prey to the ways of evil. He is concerned about the *togetherness* of the community of sufferers. Will the wretched of the earth be able to experience the harsh realities of despair and loneliness and take this pain upon themselves and not lose faith in the gospel of God? There was no attempt to evade the reality of suffering. Black slaves faced the reality of the world "ladened wid trouble, an' burden'd wid grief," but they believed that they could go to Jesus in secret and get relief. They appealed to Jesus not so much to remove the trouble (though that was included), but to keep them from "sinkin' down."

Significantly, the note of despair is usually intertwined with confidence and joy that "trouble don't last always." To be sure, the slave sings, "Sometimes I feel like a motherless child, a long way from home"; but because he is confident that Jesus is with him and has not left him completely alone, he can still add (in the same song!), "Glory Hallelujah!" The black slaves did not deny the experience of agony and loneliness in a world filled with trouble.

> *Nobody knows the trouble I've seen,*
> *Nobody knows my sorrow.*
> *Nobody knows the trouble I've seen,*
> *Glory, Hallelujah!*

The "Glory, Hallelujah!" is not a denial of trouble; it is an affirmation of faith. It says that despite the pain of being alone in an unfriendly world the black slave is confident that God has not really left him, and *trouble* is not the last word on human existence.

> *Soon-a-will be done with the trouble of the world;*
> *Soon-a-will be done with the trouble of the world;*
> *Going home to live with God.*

It appears that the slave is not concerned with the problem of evil per se, as if he intuitively knows that nothing will be solved through a debate of that problem. He deals with the world as it *is*, not as it might have been if God had acted "justly." He focuses on present realities of despair and loneliness that disrupt the community of faith. The faithful seems to have lost faith, and he experiences the agony of being alone in a world of hardship and pain. That is why he sings:

> *I couldn't hear nobody pray.*
> *Oh I couldn't hear nobody pray.*
> *Oh way down yonder by myself,*
> *And I couldn't hear nobody pray.*

VII

Related to the problem of suffering was the future, the "not-yet" of black existence. How was it possible for black slaves to take seriously their pain and suffering in an unfriendly world and still believe that God was liberating them from earthly bondage? How could they *really* believe that God was just when they knew only injustice and oppression? The answer to these questions lies in the concept of heaven, which is the dominant idea in black religious experience as expressed in the black spirituals.

The concept of heaven in black religion has not been interpreted rightly. Most observers have defined the black religious experience exclusively in terms of slaves longing for heaven, as if that desire were unrelated to their earthly liberation. It has been said that the concept of heaven served as an opiate for black slaves, making for docility and submission. But to interpret black eschatology solely in terms of its outmoded cosmology fails to take seriously the culture and thought of a people seeking expression amidst the dehumanization of slavery. It is like discarding the Bible and its message as irrelevant because the biblical writers had a three-storied conception of the universe. While not all biblical and systematic theologians agree with Rudolf Bultmann's method of demythologization in his efforts to solve the problem of biblical mythology, most agree that he is correct in his insistence that the gospel message is not dependent on its pre-scientific world-picture. Is it not possible that the same analogy is true in regard to the heaven theme in the spirituals?

Let me admit, then, that the black slaves' picture of the world is not to be defended as a viable scientific analysis of reality; that their image of the Promised Land, where "the streets are pearl and the gates are gold," is not the best way of communicating to contemporary Black Power advocates with their stress on political liberation by any means necessary; that a "new" black theological language is needed if black religion is going to be involved in articulating the historical strivings of black people in America and the Third World; and that the language of heaven is a white concept given to black slaves in order to make them obedient and submissive. The question nevertheless remains: How was it possible for black people to endure the mental and physical stresses of slavery and still keep their humanity intact? I think the answer is found in black eschatology; and maybe what is needed is not a dismissal of the idea of heaven but a reinterpretation of this concept so that oppressed blacks today can develop styles of resistance not unlike those of their grandparents.

VIII

The place to begin is Miles Fisher's contention that the spirituals are primarily "historical documents." They tell us about the black movement for historical liberation, the attempt of black people to define their present history in the light of their promised future, not according to their past miseries. Fisher notes that heaven for early black slaves referred not only to a transcendent reality beyond time and space; it designated the earthly places that blacks regarded as lands of freedom. Heaven referred to Africa, Canada, and the states north of the Mason-Dixon line.[9] Frederick Douglass wrote about the double meaning of these songs:

> We were at times remarkably buoyant, singing hymns, and making joyous exclamations, almost as triumphant in their tone as if we had reached a land of freedom and safety. A keen observer might have detected in our repeated singing of
>
> > O Canaan, sweet Canaan,
> > I am bound for the land of Canaan,
>
> something more than a hope of reaching heaven. We meant to reach the North, and the North was our Canaan.[10]

But while it is true that heaven had its historical referents, not all black slaves could hope to make it to Africa, Canada, or even to the northern section of the United States. The failure of the American Colonization Society's experiments crushed the hopes of many black slaves who were expecting to return to their African homeland. And blacks also began to realize that the North was not as significantly different from the South as they had envisioned, particularly in view of the Fugitive Slave Act of 1850 and the Dred Scott Decision in 1857. Black slaves began to realize that their historical freedom could not be assured as long as white racists controlled the governmental process of America. And so they found it necessary to develop a style of freedom that included but did not depend upon historical possibilities. What could freedom mean for black slaves who could never expect to participate in the determination of society's laws governing their lives? Must they continue to define freedom in terms of the possibility of escape and insurrection as if their humanity depended on their willingness to commit suicide? It was in response to this situation that the black concept of heaven developed.

For black slaves, who were condemned to carve out their existence in human captivity, heaven meant that the eternal God has made a decision about their humanity that could not be destroyed by white slavemasters. Whites could drive them, beat them, and even kill them; but they believed that God nevertheless had chosen black slaves as his own and that this election bestowed upon them a freedom to *be*, which could not be measured by what oppressors could do to the physical body. Whites may suppress black history and define Africans as savages, but the words of slavemasters do not have to be taken seriously when the oppressed know that they have a *somebodiness* that is guaranteed by the heavenly Father who alone is the ultimate sovereign of the universe. This is what heaven meant for black slaves.

The idea of heaven provided ways for black people to affirm their humanity when other people were attempting to define them as nonpersons. It enabled blacks to say yes to their right to be free by affirming God's eschatological freedom to be for the oppressed. That was what they meant when they sang about a "city called heaven."

> *I am a poor pilgrim of sorrow.*
> *I'm in this world alone.*
> *No hope in this world for tomorrow.*
> *I'm trying to make heaven my home.*

Sometimes I am tossed and driven.
Sometimes I don't know where to roam.
I've heard of a city called heaven.
I've started to make it my home.

In the midst of economic and political disfranchisement, black slaves held themselves together and did not lose their spiritual composure because they believed that their worth transcended governmental decisions. That was why they looked forward to "walking in Jerusalem just like John" and longed for the "camp meeting in the Promised Land."

IX

Despite the ways that black eschatology might have been misused or the crude forms in which it was sometimes expressed, it nevertheless provides us today with the best theological foundation for enabling American theologians to develop a concept of the future that is related to black oppression. Black theologians have little patience with so-called political theologians of America who say that they are concerned about humanizing the world according to God's promised future but do not relate that future to the history and culture of that people who have been and are being dehumanized and dehistoricized by white overlords. With all the talk among American theologians about "hope theology," "humanistic messianism," "Marxist-Christian dialogue," and revolutionary theology, one would expect that such language could easily be related to black people and their thoughts on eschatology and divine liberation. But white American theologians have been virtually silent on black liberation, preferring instead to do theology in the light of a modern liberalism that assumes that black people want to integrate into the white way of life. Such silence is inexcusable, and it is hard not to conclude that they are enslaved by their own identity with the culture and history of white slavemasters. What they need is liberation, and this can only happen when they face the reality of Black Power and what that means for the oppressed of the land.

One of the effective starting points for that encounter with reality is the body of black spirituals that came to maturity in the antebellum years. Far from being poignant expressions of shattered humanity, they were affirmations of hope—hope that enabled black slaves to risk their lives for earthly freedom because they knew they had a home "over yonder."

Black Theology on Revolution, Violence, and Reconciliation

How is Christianity related to the black revolution in America? The answer to this question is not easy since we live in a white society that emphasizes the seeming discontinuity between "blackness-revolution" and the gospel of Jesus. Black consciousness as expressed in Black Power is by definition revolutionary in white America, if by revolution we mean a sudden, radical, and complete change; or as Jürgen Moltmann puts it: "a transformation in the foundations of a system—whether of economics, of politics, or morality, or of religion."[1] In America "law and order" means obedience to the law of white people, and "stability" means the continuation of the present in the light of the past—defined and limited by George Washington, Abraham Lincoln, and Richard Nixon. Revolution then means anything that challenges the "sacredness" of the past which is tantamount to usurping the rule of white oppressors. That is why J. Edgar Hoover described the Black Panthers as the most serious internal threat to the American way of life.

But for black people, revolution means that blacks no longer accept the history of white people as the key to their existence in the future. It also means they are prepared to do what is necessary in order to assure that their present and future existence will be defined by black visions of reality. We believe, as Ernst Bloch puts it: "Things can be otherwise. That means: things can also *become* otherwise: in the direction of evil, which must be avoided, or in the direction of good, which would have to be promoted."[2] The black revolution involves tension between the actual and the possible, the "white-past" and the "black-future," and the black community accepting the responsibility of defining the world according to its "open possibilities."

Moltmann is right: "Truth is revolutionary," that is, truth involves "discovering that the world can be changed and that nothing has to remain as it has been."[3] White oppressors cannot share in this future reality as defined by the black revolution. Indeed, we blacks assume that the white position of unauthorized power as expressed in the racist character of every American institution—churches and seminaries not excluded!—renders white oppressors incapable of understanding what black humanity is, and it is thus incumbent upon us as black people to become "revolutionaries for blackness," rebelling against all who enslave us. With Marcus Garvey, we say: "Any sane man, race or nation that desires freedom must first of all think in terms of blood."

In contrast to the revolutionary thrust of Black Power, Christianity usually is not thought of as being involved in radical change. It has been identified with the status quo, a condition that encourages oppression and not human liberation. Some black religionists, like Howard Thurman and Albert Cleage, say that the Apostle Paul must bear a heavy responsibility for the theological justification of human oppression. It was Paul who admonished slaves to be obedient to their masters; in Romans 13, he urged all men to be subject to the state. While it is possible to question the use of Paul in this context, especially in view of the radical eschatological vision of first-century Christians and the contrasting differences between the social and political situation of Paul's time and ours, we cannot deny that later theologies used Paul as a theological justification of economic and political oppression. Indeed, it can be said that when Constantine made Christianity the official religion of the Roman State (replacing the public state sacrifices), the gospel of Jesus became a religious justification of the interests of the state. Theologians began to equate the immoral with the unlawful and slavery with the sins of the slaves. As Augustine put it: Slavery was due to the sinfulness of the slaves. Therefore, like Paul, he admonished "slaves to be subject to their masters . . ." serving them "with a good-heart and a good-will."[4]

During the Middle Ages, Thomas Aquinas took his cue from Augustine. "Slavery among men is natural," wrote Aquinas. "The slave, in regard to his master, is an instrument. . . . Between a master and his slave there is a special right of domination."[5]

The idea that the slave should be obedient to his master and should not seek to change his civil status through revolutionary violence is found throughout the Christian tradition. In Protestant Christianity, this emphasis is found in Martin Luther and his definition of the state as the servant of God. That was why he condemned the Peasants' revolt, saying that "nothing can be more poisonous, hurtful, or devilish than a rebel." He equated killing a rebel peasant with the killing of a mad dog.[6]

It is unfortunate that Protestant Christianity did not offer a serious challenge to modern slavery in Europe and America. Calvinism seemed especially suited for America with its easy affinity for capitalism and slavery. While John Wesley, the founder of Methodism, did not endorse slavery, he appeared to be more concerned about a warm heart than an enslaved body. And his evangelist friend George Whitefield publicly defended the slave institution in Georgia. It is a sad fact that Protestants not only tolerated slavery but frequently encouraged it.

The same emphasis is found in modern Catholicism. It rarely defended the interests of the oppressed. In 1903 Pope Pius X clarified the Catholic position:

> Human society as established by God is made up of unequal elements. . . . Accordingly, it is in conformity with the order of human society as established by God that there be rulers and ruled, employers and employees, learned and ignorant, nobles and plebeians.[7]

In 1943, in a similar vein, Pope Pius XII advised the Italian workers that

> [s]alvation and justice are not to be found in revolution but in evolution through concord. Violence has always achieved only destruction not construction; the kindling of passions, not their pacification; the accumulation of hate and ruin, not the reconciliation of the contending parties. And it has reduced men and parties to the difficult task of rebuilding, after sad experience, on the ruins of discord.[8]

We may conclude, then, that the essential differences between Protestants and Catholics do not lie in their stand on revolution. Both agree that the state has divine sanction and thus violent revolution must be condemned. And if there are rare exceptions in which violence can be justified, these exceptions do not apply to black people and their liberation struggle in America. In regard to the black revolution, Protestants and Catholics alike stand solidly on their tradition. It seems that the most "radical" comment coming from the white churches is: "We deplore the violence but sympathize with the reasons for the violence"—which is equivalent to saying "Of course we raped your women, dehumanized your men, and ghettoized the minds of your children, and you have a right to be upset, but that is no reason for you to burn our buildings. If you people keep acting like that, we will never give you your freedom."

Toward Liberation

Christians, unfortunately, are not known for their revolutionary actions. For the most part, the chief exponents of the Christian tradition have been identified primarily with the structures of power and only secondarily with the victims of power. This perhaps explains why white Christians in America tend to think of "love" as an absence of power and "reconciliation" as being indifferent to justice. It certainly accounts for the inauspicious distinction made between violence and force: "The state is invested with force; it is an organism instituted and ordained by God, and remains such even when it is unjust; even its harshest acts are not the same thing as the angry or brutal deed of the individual. The individual surrenders his passions, he commits violence."[9]

True, not all Christians have defended this perspective. The Left Wing tradition of the Protestant Reformation and the Quakers' stand on American slavery are possible exceptions. Prominent examples in our century are Reinhold Niebuhr's *Moral Man and Immoral Society*, the Confessing Church in Hitler's Germany, and particularly the noble example of Dietrich Bonhoeffer. We have already mentioned Jürgen Moltmann, and we could name other European theologians who are participating in the Marxist-Christian dialogue,[10] relating theology to revolutionary change. In America, Richard Shaull and Paul Lehmann have been defining the theological task according to the "politics of God," emphasizing the divine participation in the "messianic movements dedicated to the liberation of man from all that enslaves and dehumanizes him."[11]

But these examples are exceptions and not the rule. In America, at least, the Christian tradition is identified with the structures of racism in their oppression of black people. This was the reason for the white church's compliance with black slavery, its subsequent indifference toward oppression generally, and its failure to respond to the authentic demands of black reparations. No white theologian has taken the oppression of black people as a point of departure for analyzing the meaning of the gospel today. Apparently white theologians see no connection between blackness and the gospel of Jesus Christ. Even the so-called white American "theologians of revolution" did not receive their motivation from an identification with Black Americans but from Latin America, Vietnam, and other foreign lands. I do not want to minimize their theological endeavors or question the authenticity of their verbalized identification with the poor, "undeveloped" nations, but I believe, as Sartre puts it: "The only way of helping the enslaved out there is to take sides with those who are here."

What then is the answer to the question, "What relevance has Christian theology to the oppressed blacks of America?" Since whites have ignored this question, it is necessary to look beyond the white Christian tradition to the biblical tradition, investigating the latter in the light of the past and present manifestations of the black struggle for liberation.

Taking seriously the tradition of the Old and New Testaments and the past and present black revolution in America, *black* theology contends that the content of Christian theology is *liberation*. This means that theology is a rational and passionate study of the revolutionary activity of God in the world in the light of the historical situation of an oppressed community, relating the forces of liberation to the essence of the gospel, which is Jesus Christ. Theology so defined moves us in the direction of the biblical tradition which focuses on the activity of God in history, liberating people from human bondage. God, according to the Bible, is known by what he does, and what he does is always related to the liberation of the oppressed. This is the meaning of the saying:

> You have seen what I did to the Egyptians, and how I bore you on eagles' wings and brought you to myself. Now therefore, if you will obey my voice and keep my covenant, you shall be my own possession among all peoples. . . .
>
> *(Exod. 19:4 5a RSV)*

Here the Exodus is connected with the covenant, revealing that Israel's consciousness as the people of God is bound up with her escape from Egyptian slavery. Yahweh is the God of the oppressed and downtrodden and his revelation is made known *only* through the liberation of the oppressed. The covenant at Sinai, then, is not just a pious experience of God; it is a celebration of the God of liberation whose will is revealed in the freedom of slaves.

The equation of God's salvation with human liberation is found throughout biblical history, and particularly in God's incarnate appearance in Jesus Christ. By becoming the Oppressed One, God "made plain by this action that poverty, hunger, and sickness rob people of all dignity and that the Kingdom of God will fill them bodily with riches. The kingdom which Jesus preached and represented through his life is not only the soul's bliss but *shalom* for the body as well, peace on earth and liberation of the creature from the past."[12] This is the meaning of his birth in the stable at Bethlehem, his baptism with sinners, and his definition of his ministry for the poor, not the rich. God came to those who had no rights and "he celebrated the eschatological banquet."

> His resurrection from the humiliation of the cross can be understood as the revelation of the new creation of God's righteousness. In view of this, Christians are commissioned to bring . . . the justice of God and freedom into the world of oppression.[13]

With liberation as the essence of the Christian gospel, it becomes impossible to speak of the God of Hebrew history, the God who revealed himself in Jesus Christ, without recognizing that he is the God *of* and *for* those who labor and are heavy laden.

The emphasis on liberation not only leads us to the heart of the biblical message, it also enables theology to say something relevant to the black revolution in America. The liberation theme relates Black Power to the Christian gospel, and renders as an untruth the unverbalized white assumption that Christ is white, or that being Christian means that black people ought to turn the other cheek—as if we blacks have no moral right to defend ourselves from the encroachments of white people. To explicate the meaning of God's activity as revealed in the liberation of the oppressed blacks of America means that the theologian must lose his identity with the white structure and become unqualifiedly identified with the wretched of this land. It means that there can be no authentic Christian talk unless it focuses on the empowerment of the poor—defined and limited by their past, present, and future history. If God is truly the God of the weak and helpless, then we must critically reevaluate the history of theology in America, a theology that owes more to white oppressors than oppressed blacks or Indians. What about Gabriel Prosser, Denmark Vesey, and Nat Turner as theological sources for assessing the contemporary presence of Christ? Could it be that American theologians can best understand their task by studying LeRoi Jones, Malcolm X, or the Black Panthers rather than merely mouthing the recent rhetoric of German theologians? Hopefully, the rise of black theology will force American religionists to realize that no theology of the Christian gospel is possible that ignores the reality of the divine among black people in this country.

Violence as Curse and as Right

The black revolution involves a total break with the white past, "the overturning of relationships, the transformation of life, and then a reconstruction."[14] Theologically, this means that black people are prepared to live according to God's eschatological future as defined by the present reality of the black kingdom in the lives of oppressed people struggling for historical liberation. It is this perspective that informs black theology's reflections on the religious significance of the black revolution in America.

Because the black revolution means a radical break with the existing political and social structure and a redefinition of black life along the lines of black liberation, it is to be expected that white Christians and assorted moralists will ask questions about methods and means. Theologically and philosophically, they want to know whether revolutionary violence can be justified as an appropriate means for the attainment of black liberation. If black theology is Christian theology, how does it reconcile violence with Jesus' emphasis on love and reconciliation? Is it not true that violence is a negation of the gospel of Jesus Christ?

These are favorite *white* questions, and it is significant that they are almost always addressed to the oppressed and almost never to the oppressors. This fact alone provides the clue to the motive behind the questions. White people are not really concerned about violence per se but only when they are the victims. As long as blacks are beaten and shot, they are strangely silent, as if they are unaware of the inhumanity committed against the black community. Why did we not hear from the "nonviolent Christians" when black people were *violently* enslaved, *violently* lynched, and *violently* ghettoized in the name of freedom and democracy? When I hear questions about violence and love coming from the children of slavemasters whose identity with Jesus extends no further than that weekly Sunday service, then I can understand why many black brothers and sisters say that Christianity is the white man's religion, and that it must be destroyed along with white oppressors. What white people fail to realize is that their questions about violence and reconciliation not only are very naive, but are hypocritical and insulting. When whites ask me, "Are you for violence?" my rejoinder is: "Whose violence? Richard Nixon's or his victims'? The Mississippi State Police or the students at Jackson State? The Chicago Police or Fred Hampton?[15] What the hell are you talking about?" If we are going to raise the question of violence, it ought to be placed in its proper perspective.

(1) Violence is not only what black people do to white people as victims seek to change the structure of their existence; violence is what white people *did* when they created a society for white people only, and what they *do* in order to maintain it. Violence in America did not begin with the Black Power movement or with the Black Panther Party. Contrary to popular opinion, violence has a long history in America. This country was born in violent revolution (remember 1776?), and it has been sustained by the violent extermination of red people and the violent enslavement of black people. This is what Rap Brown had in mind when he said that "violence is American as cherry pie."

White people have a distorted conception of the meaning of violence. They like to think of violence as breaking the laws of their society, but that is a narrow and racist understanding of reality. There is a more deadly form of violence, and it is camouflaged in such slogans as "law and order," "freedom and democracy," and "the American way of life." I am speaking of white collar violence, the violence of Christian murderers and patriot citizens who define right in terms of whiteness and wrong as blackness. These are the people who hire assassins to do their dirty work while they piously congratulate themselves for being "good" and "nonviolent."

I contend, therefore, that the problem of violence is not the problem of a few black revolutionaries but the problem of a whole social structure which outwardly appears to be ordered and respectable but inwardly is "ridden by psychopathic obsessions and delusions"[16]—racism and hate. Violence is embedded in American law, and it is blessed by the keepers of moral sanctity. This is the core of the problem of violence, and it will not be solved by romanticizing American history, pretending that Hiroshima, Nagasaki, and Vietnam are the first American crimes against humanity. If we take seriously the idea of human dignity, then we know that the annihilation of Indians, the enslavement of blacks, and the making of heroes out of slaveholders, like George Washington and Thomas Jefferson, were America's first crimes against humankind. And it does not help the matter at all to attribute black slavery to economic necessity or an accident of history. America is an unjust society and black people have known that for a long time.

(2) If violence is not just a question for the oppressed but *primarily* for the oppressors, then it is obvious that the distinction between violence and nonviolence is false and misleading. "The problem of violence and nonviolence is an illusory problem. There is only the question of the justified and unjustified use of force and the question of whether the means are proportionate to the ends";[17] and the only people who can answer that problem are the victims of injustice.

Concretely, ours is a situation in which the only option we have is that of deciding whose violence we will support—the oppressors or the oppressed, whites or blacks. Either we side with oppressed blacks and other unwanted minorities as they try to redefine the meaning of their existence in a dehumanized society, or we take a stand with the American government whose interests have been expressed in police clubs and night sticks, tear gas and machine guns. There is no possibility of neutrality—the moral luxury of being on neither side. Neither the government nor black people will allow that! The government demands support through taxes, the draft, and public allegiance to the American flag. Black people demand that you deny whiteness as an appropriate form of human existence, and that you be willing to take the risk to create a new humanity. With Franz Fanon, we do not believe it wise to leave our destiny to Europeans. "We must invent and we must make discoveries. . . . For Europe, for ourselves, and for humanity . . . we must turn over a new leaf, we must work out new concepts, and try to set afoot a new man."[18]

(3) If violence versus nonviolence is not the issue but rather the creation of a new humanity, then the critical question for Christians is not whether Jesus committed violence or whether violence is theoretically consistent with love and reconciliation. The question is not what Jesus *did*, as if his behavior in the first century is the infallible ethical guide for our actions today. We must ask not what he did but what he is *doing*, and what he did becomes important only insofar as it points to his activity today. To use the Jesus of history as an absolute ethical guide for people today is to become enslaved to the past, foreclosing God's eschatological future and its judgment on the present. It removes the element of risk in ethical decisions and makes people slaves to principles. But the gospel of "Jesus means freedom"[19] (as Ernst Käsemann has put it), and one essential element of that freedom is the existential burden of making decisions about human

liberation without being completely sure what Jesus did or would do. *This is the risk of faith.*

My difficulty with white theologians is their use of Jesus' so-called non-violent attitude in the Gospels as the primary evidence that black people ought to be nonviolent today. Not only have Rudolf Bultmann and other form critics demonstrated that there are historical difficulties in the attempt to move behind the kerygmatic preaching of the early church to the real Jesus of Nazareth, but, moreover, the resurrected Christ is not bound by first-century possibilities. Therefore it is possible to conclude that the man from Nazareth was not a revolutionary zealot, and still contend that the risen Christ is involved in the black revolution today. Though the Jesus of yesterday is important for our ethical decisions today, we must be careful where we locate that importance. It is not to be found in following in his steps, slavishly imitating his behavior in Palestine. Rather we must regard his past activity as a *pointer* to what he is doing now. It is not so much what he did; but his actions were signs of God's eschatological future and his will to liberate all people from slavery and oppression. To be for Jesus means being for the oppressed and unwanted in human society.

As Christians, we are commanded not to follow principles but to discover the will of God in a troubled and dehumanized world. Concretely, we must decide not between good and evil or right and wrong, but between the oppressors and the oppressed, whites and blacks. We must ask and answer the question, "Whose actions are consistent with God's work in history?" Either we believe that God's will is revealed in the status quo of America or in the actions of those who seek to change it.

Accepting the risk of faith and the ethical burden of making decisions about life and death without an infallible guide, black theology contends that God is found among the poor, the wretched, and the sick. "God chose what is foolish in the world to shame the wise [wrote Paul], God chose what is weak in the world to shame the strong, God chose what is low and despised in the world, even the things that are not, to bring to nothing things that are . . ." (1 Cor. 1:26f.). That was why God elected Israelite slaves and not Egyptian slavemasters—the weak and the poor in Israel, not the oppressors. As Jesus' earthly life demonstrated, the God of Israel is a God whose will is made known through his identification with the oppressed and whose activity is always identical with those who strive for a liberated freedom.

If this message means anything for our times, it means that God's revelation is found in black liberation. God has chosen what is black in America to shame the whites. In a society where white is equated with good and black is defined as bad, humanity and divinity mean an unqualified identification with blackness. The divine election of the oppressed means that black people are given the power of judgment over the high and mighty whites.

Two Kinds of Reconciliation?

When black theology emphasizes the right of black people to defend themselves against those who seek to destroy them, it never fails that white people then ask, "What about the biblical doctrine of reconciliation?" Whites who ask that question should not be surprised if blacks respond, "Yeah man, what about it?" The difficulty is not with the reconciliation question per se but with the people asking it. Like the question of violence, this question is almost always addressed *to* blacks *by* whites, as if we blacks are responsible for the demarcation of community on the basis of color. They who are responsible for the dividing walls of hostility, racism, and hate want to know whether the victims are ready to forgive and forget—without changing the balance of power. They want to know whether we have any hard feelings toward them, whether we still love them, even though we are oppressed and brutalized by them. What can we say to people who insist on oppressing black people but get upset when black people reject them?

Because black liberation is the point of departure of black theology's analysis of the gospel of Jesus, it cannot accept a view of reconciliation based on white values. The Christian view of reconciliation has nothing to do with black people being nice to white people as if the gospel demands that we ignore their insults and their humiliating presence. It does not mean discussing with whites what it means to be black or going to white gatherings and displaying what whites call an understanding attitude—remaining cool and calm amid racists and bigots.

To understand the Christian view of reconciliation and its relation to black liberation, it is necessary to focus on the Bible. Here reconciliation is connected with divine liberation. According to the Bible, reconciliation is what God does for enslaved people who are unable to break the chains of slavery. To be reconciled is to be set free; it is to have the chains struck off the body and mind so that the creatures of God can be what they are. Reconciliation means that people cannot be human and God cannot be God unless the creatures of God are liberated from that which enslaves and is dehumanizing.

When Paul says, "God was in Christ reconciling the world unto himself," this is not a sentimental comment on race relations. The reconciling act of God in Christ is centered on the cross, and it reveals the extent that God is willing to go in order to set people free from slavery and oppression. The cross means that the Creator has taken upon himself all human pain and suffering, revealing that God cannot be unless oppression ceases to be. Through the death and resurrection of Christ, God places the oppressed in a new state of humanity, now free to live according to God's intentions for humanity.

Because God has set us free, we are now commanded to go and be reconciled with our neighbors, and particularly our white neighbors. But this does not mean letting whites define the terms of reconciliation. It means participating in God's revolutionizing activity in the world, changing the political, economic, and social structures so that distinctions between rich and poor, oppressed and oppressors, are no longer a reality. To be reconciled with white people means destroying their oppressive power, reducing them to the human level and thereby putting them on equal footing with other humans. There can be no reconciliation with masters as long as they are masters, as long as men are in prison. There can be no communication between masters and slaves until masters no longer exist, are no longer present as masters. The Christian task is to rebel against all masters, destroying their pretensions to authority and ridiculing the symbols of power.

However, it must be remembered that oppressors never take kindly to those who question their authority. They do not like "thugs and bums," people who disregard their power, and they will try to silence them any way they can. But if we believe that our humanity transcends them and is not dependent on their goodwill, then we can fight against them even though it may mean death.

Black Theology and the Black Church:
Where Do We Go from Here?

Since the appearance of black theology in the late 1960s, much has been written and said about the political involvement of the Black Church in black people's historical struggle for justice in North America. Black theologians and preachers have rejected the white church's attempt to separate love from justice and religion from politics because we are proud descendents of a black religious tradition that has always interpreted its confession of faith according to the people's commitment to the struggle for earthly freedom. Instead of turning to Reinhold Niebuhr and John Bennett for ethical guidance in those troubled times, we searched our past for insight, strength, and the courage to speak and do the truth in an extreme situation of oppression. Richard Allen, James Varick, Harriet Tubman, Sojourner Truth, Henry McNeal Turner, and Martin Luther King, Jr., became household names as we attempted to create new theological categories that would express our historical fight for justice.

It was in this context that the "Black Power" statement was written in July 1966 by an ad hoc National Committee of Negro Churchmen.[1] The cry of Black Power by Willie Ricks and its political and intellectual development by Stokely Carmichael and others challenged the Black Church to move beyond the models of love defined in the context of white religion and theology. The Black Church was thus faced with a theological dilemma: Either reject Black Power as a contradiction of Christian love (and thereby join the white church in its condemnation of Black Power advocates as un-American and unchristian), or accept Black Power as a sociopolitical expression of the truth of the gospel. These two possibilities were the only genuine alternatives before us, and we had to decide on whose side we would take our stand.

We knew that to define Black Power as the opposite of the Christian faith was to reject the central role that the Black Church has played in black people's historical struggle for freedom. Rejecting Black Power also meant that the Black Church would ignore its political responsibility to empower black people in their present struggle to make our children's future more humane than intended by the rulers in this society. Faced with these unavoidable consequences, it was not possible for any self-respecting churchperson to desecrate the memories of our mothers and fathers in the faith by siding with white people who murdered and imprisoned black people simply because of our persistent audacity to assert our freedom. To side with white theologians and preachers who questioned the theological legitimacy of Black Power would have been similar to siding with St. George Methodist Church against Richard Allen and the Bethelites in their struggle for independence during the late eighteenth and early nineteenth centuries. We knew that we could not do that, and no amount of white theological reasoning would be allowed to blur our vision of the truth.

But to accept the second alternative and thereby locate Black Power in the Christian context was not easy. First, the acceptance of Black Power would appear to separate us from Martin Luther King, Jr., and we did not want to do that. King was our model, having creatively combined religion and politics, and black preachers and theologians respected his courage to concretize the political consequences of his confession of faith. Thus we hesitated to endorse the "Black Power" movement, since it was created in the context of the James Meredith March by Carmichael and others in order to express their dissatisfaction with King's continued emphasis on nonviolence and Christian love.[2] As a result of this sharp confrontation between Carmichael and King, black theologians and preachers felt themselves caught in a terrible predicament of wanting to express their continued respect for and solidarity with King, but disagreeing with this rejection of Black Power.

Secondly, the concept of Black Power presented a problem for black theologians and preachers not only because of our loyalty to Martin Luther King, but also because many of us had been trained in white seminaries and had internalized much of white people's definition of Christianity. While the rise and growth of independent black churches suggested that black people had a different perception of the gospel than whites, there was no formal theological tradition to which we could turn in order to justify our definition of Black Power as an expression of the Christian gospel. But if we intended to fight on a theological and intellectual level as a way of empowering our historical and political struggle for justice, we had to create a new theological movement, one that was derived from and thus accountable to our people's fight for justice. To accept Black Power as Christian required that we thrust ourselves into our history in order to search for new ways to think and be black in this world. We felt the need to explain ourselves and to be understood from our own vantage point and not from the perspective and experiences of whites. When white liberals questioned this approach to theology, our response was very similar to the bluesman in Mississippi when told he was not singing his song correctly: "Look-a-heah, man, dis yere *mah song*, en I'll sing it howsoevah I pleases."[3]

Thus we sang our Black Power songs, knowing that the white church establishment would not smile upon our endeavors to define Christianity independently of their own definitions of the gospel. For the power of definition is a prerogative that oppressors never want to give up. Furthermore, to *say* that love is compatible with Black Power is one thing, but to demonstrate this compatibility in theology and the praxis of life is another. If the reality of a thing was no more than its verbalization in a written document, the Black Church since 1966 would be a model of the creative integration of theology and life, faith and the struggle for justice. But we know that the meaning of reality is found *only* in its historical embodiment in people as structured in societal arrangements. Love's meaning is not found in sermons or theological textbooks but rather in the creation of social structures that are not dehumanizing and oppressive. This insight impressed itself on our religious consciousness, and we were deeply troubled by the inadequacy of our historical obedience when measured by our faith claims. From 1966 to the present, black theologians and preachers, both in the church and on the streets, have been searching for new ways to confess and to live our faith in God so that the Black Church would not make religion the opiate of our people.

The term *black theology* was created in this social and religious context. It was initially understood as the theological arm of Black Power, and it enabled us to express our theological imagination in the struggle of freedom independently of white theologians. It was the one term that white ministers and theologians did not like, because, like Black Power in politics, black theology located the theological starting point in the black experience and not the particularity of the Western theological tradition. We did not feel ourselves accountable to Aquinas, Luther, or Calvin but to David Walker, Daniel Payne, and W. E. B. Du Bois. The depth and passion in which we expressed our solidarity with the black experience over against the Western tradition led some black scholars in religion to reject theology itself as alien to the black culture.[4] Others, while not rejecting theology entirely, contended that black theologians should turn primarily to African religion and philosophy in order to develop a black theology consistent with and accountable to our historical roots.[5] But all of us agreed that we were living at the beginning of a new historical moment, and this required the development of a *black* frame of reference that many called "black theology."

The consequence of our affirmation of a black theology led to the creation of black caucuses in white churches, a permanent ecumenical church body under the title of the National Conference of Black Churchmen (NCBC), and the endorsement of James Forman's "Black Manifesto." In June 1969 at the Interdenominational Theological Center in Atlanta and under the aegis of NCBC's Theological Commission, a group of black theologians met to write a policy statement on black theology. This statement, influenced by my book *Black Theology and Black Power,* which had appeared two months earlier, defined black theology as a "theology of black liberation."[6]

Black theology, then, was not created in a vacuum and neither was it simply the intellectual enterprise of black professional theologians. Like our sermons and songs, black theology was born in the context of the black community as black people were attempting to make sense out of their struggle for freedom. In one sense, black theology is as old as when the first African refused to accept slavery as consistent with religion and as recent as when a black person intuitively recognizes that the confession of the Christian faith receives its meaning only in relation to political justice. Although black theology may be considered to have formally appeared only when the first book was published on it in 1969, informally, the reality that made the book possible was already present in the black experience and was found in our songs, prayers, and sermons. In these outpourings are expressed the black visions of truth, preeminently the certainty that we were created not for slavery but for freedom. Without this dream of freedom, so vividly expressed in the life, teachings, and death of Jesus, Malcolm, and Martin, there would be no black theology, and we would have no reason to be assembled in this place. We have come here today to plan our future and to map out our strategy because we have a dream that has not been realized.

To be sure, we have talked and written about this dream. Indeed, every Sunday morning black people gather in our churches to find out where we are in relation to the actualization of our dream. The Black Church community really believes that where there is no vision the people perish. If people have no dreams they will accept the world as it is and will not seek to change it. To dream is to know what is ain't supposed to be.

What visions do we have for the people today? Do we still believe with Martin King that "we as a people will get to the promised land"? If so, how will we get there? Will we get there simply by preaching sermons and singing songs about it? What is the Black Church doing to actualize the dreams it talks about? These are hard questions, and they are not intended as a put-down of the Black Church. I was born in the Black Church in Bearden, Arkansas, and began my ministry in that church at the early age of sixteen. Everything I am as well as what I know that I ought to be was shaped in the context of the Black Church. Indeed, it is because I love the church that I am required, as one of its theologians and preachers, to ask, "When does the Black Church's actions deny its faith? What are the activities in our churches that should be not only rejected as unchristian but also exposed as demonic? What are the evils in our church and community that we should commit ourselves to destroy?" Bishops, pastors, and church executives do not like to disclose the wrongdoings of their respective denominations. They are like doctors, lawyers, and other professionals who seem bound to keep silent, because to speak the truth is to guarantee one's exclusion from the inner dynamics of power in the profession. But I contend that the *faith* of the Black Church lays a claim upon all churchpeople that transcends the social mores of a given profession. Therefore, to cover up and to minimize the sins of the church is to guarantee its destruction as a community of faith, committed to the liberation of the oppressed. If we want the Black Church to live beyond our brief histories and thus to serve as the "Old Ship of Zion" that will carry the people home to freedom, then we had better examine the direction in which the ship is going. Who is the Captain of the Ship, and what are his economic and political interests? This question should not only be applied to bishops, but to pastors and theologians, deacons and stewards. Unless we are willing to apply the most severe scientific analysis to our church communities in terms of economics and politics and are willing to confess and repent of our sins in the struggle for liberation, then the Black Church, as we talk about it, will remain a relic of history and nothing more. God will have to raise up new instruments of freedom so that his faithfulness to liberate the poor and weak can be realized in history. We must not forget that God's Spirit will use us as her instrument only insofar as we remain agents of liberation by using our resources for the empowerment of the poor and weak. But if we, like Israel in the Old Testament, forget about our Exodus experience and the political responsibility it lays upon us to be the historical embodiment of freedom, then, again like Israel, we will become objects of God's judgment. It is very easy for us to expose the demonic and oppressive character of the white church, and I have done my share of that. But such exposures of the sins of the white church, without applying the same criticism to ourselves, is hypocritical and serves as a camouflage of our own shortcomings and sins. Either we mean what we say about liberation or we do not. If we mean it, the time has come for an inventory in terms of the authenticity of our faith as defined by the historical commitment of the black denominational churches to liberation.

I have lectured and preached about the Black Church's involvement in our liberation struggle all over North America. I have told the stories of Richard Allen and James Varick, Adam Clayton Powell and Martin Luther King. I have talked about the double-meaning in the Spirituals, the passion of the sermon and prayer, the ecstasy of the shout and conversion experience in terms of an eschatological happening in the lives of people, empowering them to fight for earthly freedom. Black theology, I have contended, is a theology of liberation, because it has emerged out of and is accountable to a Black Church that has always been involved in our historical fight for justice. When black preachers and laypeople hear this message, they respond enthusiastically and with a sense of pride that they belong to a radical and creative tradition. But when I speak to young blacks in colleges and universities, most are surprised that such a radical Black Church tradition really exists. After hearing about David Walker's "Appeal" in 1829, Henry H. Garnet's "Address to the Slaves" in 1843, and Henry M. Turner's affirmation that "God is a Negro" in 1898, these young blacks are shocked. Invariably they ask, "Whatever happened to the black churches of today? Why don't we have the same radical spirit in our preachers and churches?" Young blacks contend that the black churches of today, with very few exceptions, are not involved in liberation but primarily concerned with how much money they raise for a new church building or the preacher's anniversary.

This critique of the Black Church is not limited to young college students. Many black people view the church as a hindrance to black liberation, because black preachers and church members appear to be more concerned about their own institutional survival than the freedom of the poor people in their communities. "Historically," many radical blacks say, "the Black Church was involved in the struggle but today it is not." They often turn the question back upon me: "All right, granted what you say about the historical Black Church, but *where* is an institutional Black Church denomination that still embodies the vision that brought it into existence? Are you saying that the present-day A.M.E. Church or A.M.E. Zion Church has the same historical commitment for justice that it had under the leadership of Allen and Payne or Rush and Varick?" Sensing they have a point difficult to refute, these radicals then say it is not only impossible to find a Black Church denomination committed to black liberation but also difficult to find a local congregation that defines its ministry in terms of the needs of the oppressed and their liberation.

Whatever we might think about the unfairness of this severe indictment, we would be foolish to ignore it. For connected with this black critique is our international image. In the African context, not to mention Asia and Latin America, the Black Church experiences a similar credibility problem. There is little in our theological expressions and church practice that rejects American capitalism or recognizes its oppressive character in Third World countries. The time has come for us to move beyond institutional survival in a capitalistic and racist society and begin to take more seriously our dreams about a new heaven and a new earth. Does this dream include capitalism or is it a radically new way of life more consistent with African socialism as expressed in the *Arusha Declaration* in Tanzania?[7]

Black theologians and churchpeople must now move beyond a mere reaction to white racism in America and begin to extend our vision of a new socially constructed humanity for the whole inhabited world. We must be concerned with the quality of human life not only in the ghettos of American cities but also in Africa, Asia, and Latin America. Since humanity is one, and cannot be isolated into racial and national groups, there will be no freedom for anyone until there is freedom for all. This means that we must enlarge our vision by connecting it with that of other oppressed peoples so that together all the victims of the world might take charge of their history for the creation of a new humanity. As Franz Fanon taught us, if we wish to live up to our people's expectations, we must look beyond European and American capitalism.

New times require new concepts and methods. To dream is not enough. We must come down from the mountaintop and experience the hurts and pain of the people in the valley. Our dreams need to be socially analyzed, for without scientific analysis they will vanish into the night. Furthermore, social analysis will test the nature of our commitment to the dreams we preach and sing about. This is one of the important principles we learned from Martin King and many black preachers who worked with him. Real substantial change in societal structures requires scientific analysis. King's commitment to social analysis not only characterized his involvement in the Civil Rights movement but also led him to take a radical stand against the war in Vietnam. Through scientific analysis, King saw the connection between the oppression of blacks in the U.S. and America's involvement in Vietnam. It is to his credit that he never allowed a pietistic faith in the other world to become a substitute for good judgment in this world. He not only preached sermons about the promised land but concretized his vision with a political attempt to actualize his hope.

I realize, with Merleau-Ponty, that "one does not become a revolutionary through science but through indignation."[8] Every revolution needs its Rosa Parks. This point has often been overlooked by Marxists and other sociologists who seem to think that all answers are found in scientific analysis. Mao Tse-tung responded to such an attitude with this comment: "There are people who think that Marxism is a kind of magic truth with which one can cure any disease. We should tell them that dogmas are more useless than cow dung. Dung can be used as fertilizer."[9]

But these comments do not disprove the truth of the Marxists' social analysis which focuses on economics and class and is intended as empowerment for the oppressed to radically change human social arrangements. Such an analysis will help us to understand the relation between economics and oppression not only in North America but throughout the world. Liberation is not a process limited to black-white relations in the United States; it is also something to be applied to the relations between rich and poor nations. If we are an African people, as some of the names of our churches suggest, in what way are we to understand the political meaning of that identity? In what way does the economic investment of our church

resources reflect our commitment to Africa and other oppressed people in
the world? For if an economic analysis of our material resources does not
reveal our commitment to the process of liberation, how can we claim that
the Black Church and its theology are concerned about the freedom of oppressed peoples? As an Argentine peasant poet said:

> *They say that God cares for the poor*
> *Well this may be true or not,*
> *But I know for a fact*
> *That he dines with the mine-owner.*[10]

Because the Christian Church has supported the capitalists, many
Marxists contend that "all revolutions have clashed with Christianity because *historically* Christianity has been structurally counter-revolution-
ary."[11] We may rightly question this assertion and appeal to the revolutionary expressions of Christianity in the black religious tradition, from
Nat Turner to Martin Luther King. My concern, however, is not to debate
the fine points of what constitutes revolution, but to open up the reality
of the Black Church experience and its revolutionary potential to a world
context. This means that we can learn from people in Africa, Asia, and
Latin America, and they can learn from us. Learning from others involves
listening to creative criticism; to exclude such criticism is to isolate ourselves from world politics, and this exclusion makes our faith nothing but
a reflection of our economic interests. If Jesus Christ is more than a religious expression of our economic and sexist interests, then there is no reason to resist the truth of the Marxist and feminist analyses.

I contend that black theology is not afraid of truth from any quarter. We
simply reject the attempt of others to tell us what truth is without our participation in its definition. That is why dogmatic Marxists seldom succeed
in the black community, especially when the dogma is filtered through a
brand of white racism not unlike that of the capitalists. If our long history
of struggle has taught us anything, it is that if we are to be free, we black
people will have to do it. *Freedom is not a gift but is a risk that must be taken.*
No one can tell us what liberation is and how we ought to struggle for it,
as if liberation can be found in words. Liberation is a process to be located
and understood only in an oppressed community struggling for freedom.
If there are people in and outside our community who want to talk to us
about this liberation process in global terms and from Marxist and other
perspectives, we should be ready to talk. But *only* if they are prepared to

listen to us and we to them will genuine dialogue take place. For I will not listen to anybody who refuses to take racism seriously, especially when they themselves have not been victims of it. And they should listen to us *only* if we are prepared to listen to them in terms of the particularity of oppression in their historical context.

Therefore, I reject dogmatic Marxism that reduces every contradiction to class analysis and thus ignores racism as a legitimate point of departure in the process of liberation. There are racist Marxists as there are racist capitalists, and we must struggle against both. But we must be careful not to reject the Marxist's social analysis simply because we do not like the vessels that the message comes in. If we do that, then it is hard to explain how we can remain Christians in view of the white vessels in which the gospel was first introduced to black people.

The world is small. Both politically and economically, our freedom is connected with the struggles of oppressed peoples throughout the world. This is the truth of Pan-Africanism as represented in the life and thought of W. E. B. Du Bois, George Padmore, and C. L. R. James. Liberation knows no color bar; the very nature of the gospel is universalism, that is, a liberation that embraces the whole of humanity.

The need for a global perspective, which takes seriously the struggles of oppressed peoples in other parts of the world, has already been recognized in black theology, and small beginnings have been made with conferences on African and black theologies in Tanzania, New York, and Ghana. Anther example of the recognition of this need is reflected in the dialogue on black theology between South Africa and North America. From the very beginning black theology has been influenced by a world perspective as defined by Henry M. Turner, Marcus Garvey, and the Pan-Africanism inaugurated in the life and work of W. E. B. Du Bois. The importance of this Pan-African perspective in black religion and theology has been cogently defended in Gayraud Wilmore's *Black Religion and Black Radicalism.* Our active involvement in the "Theology in the Americas," under whose aegis this conference is held, is an attempt to enlarge our perspective in relation to Africa, Asia, and Latin America as well as to express our solidarity with other oppressed minorities in the U.S.

This global perspective in black theology enlarges our vision regarding the process of liberation. What does black theology have to say about the fact that two-thirds of humanity is poor and that this poverty arises from the exploitation of the poor nations by rich nations? The people of the U.S.

compose 6 percent of the world's population, but we consume 40 percent of the world's resources. What, then, is the implication of the black demand for justice in the U.S. when related to justice for all the world's victims? Of the dependent status we experience in relation to white people, and the experience of Third World countries in relation to the U.S.? Thus, in our attempt to liberate ourselves from white America in the U.S., it is important to be sensitive to the complexity of the world situation and the oppressive role of the U.S. in it. African, Latin American, and Asian theologians, sociologists, and political scientists can aid us in the analysis of this complexity. In this analysis, our starting point in terms of racism is not negated but enhanced when connected with imperialism and sexism.

We must create a global vision of human liberation and include in it the distinctive contribution of the black experience. We have been struggling for nearly 400 years! What has that experience taught us that would be useful in the creation of a new historical future for all oppressed peoples? And what can others teach us from their historical experience in the struggle for justice? This is the issue that black theology needs to address. "Theology in the Americas" provides a framework in which to address it. I hope that we will not back off from this important task but face it with courage, knowing that the future of humanity is in the hands of oppressed peoples, because God has said, "Those who hope in me shall not be put to shame" (Isa. 49:23).

Martin and Malcolm

Although Martin King was a Christian preacher of the black Baptist tradition and Malcolm X was a minister in the religion of Islam, the distinguishing mark of their thought and practice was their commitment to justice for the poor and their willingness to die for it.

—*For My People: Black Theology and the Black Church*, 1984

Martin King belongs to *all* Americans (blacks, whites, Asians, Hispanics, and Native peoples) who are struggling for justice and peace in this society. He represents what this land should mean for all its inhabitants, namely, a place in which the dignity of everyone is recognized and respected.

—*Union Seminary Quarterly Review*, 1986

The Theology of
Martin Luther King, Jr.

Centuries ago Jeremiah raised a question, "Is there no balm in Gilead? Is there no physician?" He raised it because he saw the good people suffering so often and the evil people prospering. Centuries later our slave foreparents came along and they too saw the injustices of life and had nothing to look forward to morning after morning but the rawhide whip of the overseer, long rows of cotton and the sizzling heat, but they did an amazing thing. They looked back across the centuries and they took Jeremiah's question mark and straightened it into an exclamation point. And they could sing, "There is a balm in Gilead to make the wounded whole. There is a balm in Gilead to heal the sin-sick soul."[1]

It seems clear that the major obstacle in viewing Martin Luther King, Jr., as a creative theologian (and one of the most important in American history) is the narrow, elitist, and racist definition of theology that limits its methods and subject matter to problems that whites identify. If by contrast one insists that the struggle for freedom is the only appropriate context for doing theology, then King's importance as a theologian can be appreciated.

King was no armchair theologian. He was a theologian of action, an engaged theologian, actively seeking to transform the structures of oppression. His thinking emerged from his efforts to establish a just society. Therefore, it is possible to analyze his thought only in connection with such events as the successful Montgomery bus boycott (1955–56), his defeat in Albany (1961), the Birmingham demonstrations (1963), the Selma March for voting rights (1965), his encounter with racism in Chicago (1966), his dialogue with Black Power advocates during and after the Meredith, Mississippi, March (1966), his preparation for the Poor People's

March on Washington (1967), his stand against the Vietnam War (1967–68), and his last march with garbage workers in Memphis (1968). In each of these crises, King refined his theology according to the needs of the people with whom and for whom he was struggling. His theology was not permanent or static but was dynamic, constantly emerging from the historical circumstances in which he was engaged.

King's theology focused on the themes of justice, love, and hope, all grounded in the Black Church's faith in Jesus Christ. In addition to the Black Church tradition, King drew from other intellectual sources, namely, black "secular" integrationism, Protestant liberalism, and the nonviolent protest tradition of Gandhi and Thoreau. From these four sources, King created a coherent theology in the midst of the freedom struggle. The first part of this essay consists of an examination of the four sources and their contributions, including the themes of justice, love, and hope. The second part examines the function and interrelationship of the sources. The third part shows the development of King's thought from 1955 to 1968. I will conclude with a brief assessment of King's importance as an American theologian.

The Sources of King's Theology

The Black Integrationist Tradition

It is important to recognize that there has been a black integrationist tradition in this country for a century and a half, related to the Black Church but often at odds with it. It was founded in the black abolitionism of Frederick Douglass and redefined for this century in the protest of W. E. B. Du Bois and his allies against Booker T. Washington's accommodationism. It was institutionalized in the NAACP and the National Urban League. This line of black thought precedes by decades the Social Gospel movement within liberal Protestantism, which in any case seldom included the liberation of blacks in its agenda.

No one embodied in his life and thought the central ideas of the integrationist tradition more clearly than did Martin Luther King, Jr. No one proclaimed the vision of an integrated society with the oratorical power comparable to his sermons and speeches. In this regard, his greatest moment was his "I Have a Dream" address in Washington in 1963. King gave many versions of this speech before and after the Washington address, because his idea of the "American Dream" was the political symbol for his theological claims about the "beloved community." While Walter Rauschenbusch and other liberal theologians influenced his views regarding the American dream and the beloved community, the integration tradition of Douglass, NAACP, and the Urban League was more decisive in determining King's ideas.

The integrationist tradition shared the political optimism of Protestant liberalism and, even more than the latter, embraced the values of the American democratic tradition as embodied in the Declaration of Independence and the Constitution, providing a bridge for King's approach to white America. Furthermore, integrationist thought resonated with the Black Church tradition, particularly in its sense of hope and the worth of the human personality, leading many blacks to see King as the prophet of a new day.

Protestant Liberalism

This tradition made far less impact on King's thought than most of his interpreters have claimed and than King himself suggested.[2] Nevertheless, it contributed significantly to the process of his intellectual development.

First, liberalism showed King how to deal with elements of naive conservatism in the Black Church that had repelled him even as a child. Liberal theology rejected both rigid orthodoxy and modern humanism, each of which emerged in response to the secular spirit of the eighteenth century Enlightenment, largely defined by the rise of scientific thinking. Liberal theologians who influenced King included Walter Rauschenbusch, George Davis, and L. Harold DeWolf. They applied the critical spirit of rational reflection to theology and the Bible and insisted upon the reasonableness of the Christian faith. They rejected almost everything that the fundamentalist and orthodox theologians were affirming as essentials of the faith: the inerrancy of the Bible, virgin birth of Jesus, substitutionary theory of atonement, bodily resurrection of Jesus, miracles, and similar creedal formulations.

Secondly, liberal thinkers introduced King to Hegel's dialectical method of analyzing history. King went to Boston University to study with Edgar S. Brightman, who guided him in a serious study of Hegel. After Brightman's untimely death during King's first year of graduate study, King continued his study of Hegel under the direction of Peter A. Bertocci and L. Harold

DeWolf. King said of Hegel: "His contention that 'truth is the whole' led me to a philosophical method of rational coherence. His analysis of the dialectical process . . . helped me to see that growth comes through struggle."[3] It also gave his own theology a dialectical quality. King's thought, like Hegel's, emerged out of his encounter with two opposites and his endeavor to achieve a synthesis of the truth found in each. For example, King's philosophy of integration and his strategy of nonviolent direct action were developed out of his rejection of both the accommodationism of black conservatives and the separatism of black nationalists. Black conservatives failed to realize that passivity in response to injustice merely contributes to its continued existence. Black nationalists failed to realize that a just community cannot be created in an atmosphere of hate and violence. A just community is an integrated community, black and white together, and it can be created only through nonviolence (love) and not violence (hate). Jesus and Gandhi provided a synthesis that moved beyond two opposites—powerless love and loveless power. Robert Penn Warren correctly said of King that "his philosophy is a way of living with intense polarity."[4]

Thirdly, liberalism showed him, as the classical integrationists could not, a rationale for relating religion to social change. King found his own concern for ethics and justice present in liberal theology, especially that of Walter Rauschenbusch. There is no doubt that Rauschenbusch's *Christianity and the Social Crisis* (1907) made a profound impact on Martin King's theology, particularly Rauschenbusch's interpretation of the message of the Hebrew prophets and the "social aims of Jesus."[5] King's admiration of Brightman grew from an appreciation of the ethical implications of Brightman's philosophy of personalism. "It [personalism]," said King, "gave me metaphysical and philosophical grounding for the idea of a personal God, and it gave me a metaphysical basis for the dignity and worth of all human personality."[6]

King shared the liberals' rejection of the neo-orthodox theology of the middle decades of this century. Though he probably did not study Barth seriously, he regarded Barth as anti-rational and semi-fundamentalist.[7] To be sure, King read Reinhold Niebuhr and was deeply influenced by his *Moral Man and Immoral Society* (1932), especially Niebuhr's analysis of the self-interested orientation of groups when compared to individuals. He was also deeply moved by Niebuhr's critique of pacifism. Nevertheless, King felt that Niebuhr's estimate of human nature was too low and his view of love was restricted to relations between individuals and not applicable to society.[8]

In his essay entitled "Pilgrimage to Nonviolence," King analyzes the impact of liberal theology upon his thinking. The influence of liberal theology can be seen clearly in many of the major emphases of his theology: optimism regarding human nature, accent on the beloved community, love as the central meaning of the gospel, the "unique God-consciousness of Jesus," the value of human personality, ethical activity as a necessary corollary of the Christian faith, God's imminent presence in the world —all of these ideas are prominently present in liberal Protestant thought.

Mohandas K. Gandhi and Henry David Thoreau

Though liberal theology influenced King's philosophical understanding of love, it was the philosophy of Mahatma Gandhi, the "little brown man" from India, as King called him, who provided the intellectual justification and the methodological implementation of his perspective on nonviolent direct action. Thoreau provided the philosophical justification for civil disobedience in the context of the North American democratic tradition. Martin King was introduced to Thoreau's *Civil Disobedience* during his student days at Morehouse and to the importance of Gandhi as a student at Crozer Seminary and, in a special way, at a lecture by Mordecai Johnson during the same period. Under the influence of Bayard Rustin and Glen Smiley, King became a firm devotee of Gandhi's theory of nonviolence. He connected Gandhi with Jesus and began to see his philosophy of nonviolence as similar to Jesus' suffering love on the cross. The idea that "unmerited suffering is redemptive" emerged as a dominant theme in King's theology as he constantly reminded blacks that they would experience a "season of suffering" before justice is achieved.[9]

The centrality of Gandhi and Jesus, nonviolence and the cross in his speeches and publications undergirded King's messages to blacks that there will be no freedom apart from suffering. The idea that the unearned suffering of blacks was redemptive appeared early in his theology and remained dominant throughout his life. When the bombing of his house aroused blacks to the potential for violence, King gave the anxious crowd in Montgomery a message that he would emphasize many times during his ministry:

We must not return violence under any condition. I know this is difficult advice to follow, especially since we have been the victims of no less than ten bombings. But this is the way of Christ; it is the way of the cross. We must somehow believe that unearned suffering is redemptive.[10]

A similar emphasis on the necessity for suffering is found in Gandhi. Explicating *satyagraha* (soul force), Gandhi wrote: "[It] is the vindication of truth not by infliction of suffering on the opponent but on one's self. . . . Rivers of blood may have to flow before we gain our freedom, but it must be our blood."

After much reflection on Gandhi's philosophy, and following a journey to India during which he discussed his views with many scholars there, King began to speak more forthrightly regarding the inevitability of black suffering through nonviolence before the goal of an integrated, beloved community can be achieved. No statement expressed this idea more forcefully than his often repeated statement:

> We will match your capacity to inflict suffering with our capacity to endure suffering. We will meet your physical force with soul force. We will not hate you, but we cannot in all good conscience obey your unjust laws. Do to us what you will and we will still love you. Bomb our homes and threaten our children; send your hooded perpetrators of violence into our communities and drag us out on some wayside road, beating us and leaving us half dead, and we will still love you. But we will soon wear you down by our capacity to suffer. And in winning our freedom we will so appeal to your heart and conscience that we will win you in the process.[11]

There is no doubt that King was deeply influenced by Gandhi's philosophy of nonviolence as a potent weapon for the practical implementation of Jesus' idea of love in the context of the black struggle for justice. But it is obvious that his unshakeable commitment to nonviolence and the inevitability of black suffering was much more appealing to liberal whites than to oppressed blacks. Many black scholars, like Kenneth Clark, warned King of the psychological damage to black personality when black people are urged to assume the heavy burden that his theology required.[12]

King's use of Thoreau's concept of civil disobedience was to come later in the course of his political development. Open disobedience to the law happened first during the sit-ins (1960), freedom rides (1961), and the Birmingham demonstrations (1963). Civil disobedience was initially limited to regional laws of discrimination against blacks in the South. Thoreau said that "it is not desirable to cultivate a respect for the law, so much as for the right. The only obligation which I have the right to assume is to do at anytime what I think right."[13] A firm opponent of slavery, Thoreau was also jailed for his refusal to pay taxes to support the war with Mexico. When his friend Ralph Waldo Emerson reportedly asked, "Thoreau, why are you in jail?" Thoreau replied, "Emerson, why are you out of jail?"

Although Martin King could apply Thoreau's logic of civil disobedience in his protest against regional segregation laws of the South, he had more difficulty applying it to federal laws, because he used the federal laws as the basis for his disobedience of discriminatory laws of the South. He expected and received the legal support of the federal courts, the President, and the Congress in the achievement of black people's civil rights. His concern about federal support probably accounted for his retreat in the second attempt to cross the Pettus Bridge during the Selma to Montgomery march. In Memphis, however, he resolved to disobey a federal injunction against the march but was assassinated before it actually happened.

The Faith of the Black Church

Without seeking to minimize the importance of the other three sources, they should be interpreted in the light of the faith of the Black Church which decisively influenced the development and final shape of King's theology. King's theology was defined by the themes of justice, love, and hope. The meaning of each, while influenced by the other sources, achieved their distinctiveness as King attempted to fulfill his vocation as a black preacher. He believed that the gospel demanded that he speak the truth and that he work toward its establishment in human relations.

Justice, love, and hope are central themes in the history of the black religious tradition. It was black people's concern for justice in the church and society that led them to organize independent churches during the late eighteenth and early nineteenth centuries. It was their concern for love in human relations that prevented their fight for justice from degenerating into an attitude of vengeance and violence. It was black people's focus on God's eschatological hope that enabled them to "keep on keeping on," fighting for the right with love in their hearts, even though the achievement of justice seemed bleak and doubtful.

Martin King deeply internalized the values of the black religious tradition in which he was born.

> I am many things to many people; Civil Rights leader, agitator, trouble-maker and orator, but in the quiet resources of my heart, I am fundamentally a clergyman, a Baptist preacher. This is my being and my heritage for I am also the son of a Baptist preacher, the grandson of a Baptist preacher, and the great-grandson of a Baptist preacher. The Church is my life and I have given my life to the Church.[14]

The distinctiveness of King's ideas of justice, love, and hope were developed in the context of his vocation as pastor of Dexter and Ebenezer Baptist Churches and as president of SCLC, an organization composed mainly of preachers. His theology, therefore, can be properly understood only from the vantage point of his belief that he had been set aside by God to be the leader of blacks, the people whom he believed God had chosen to "save the soul of America." His belief that black people were called by God to redeem America through their suffering love was derived from the black religious tradition.

The most appropriate way to decide what was primary for King's theology is to identify the source to which he turned in moments of crisis during his fight for justice. Where he turned when his back was up against the wall and when everything seemed hopeless will tell us far more about his theology than the papers he wrote in graduate school. Engulfed by the "midnight of despair," where did he receive the hope that "morning will come?"[15]

The evidence is clear: Whether we speak of the Montgomery bus boycott, the Birmingham demonstrations, the Selma March, Black Power, or Vietnam, King turned to the faith of the Black Church in moments of frustration and despair. His existential appropriation of black faith occurred a few weeks after the inauguration of the Montgomery bus boycott. He not only referred to this event in his writings but especially in many of his sermons in black churches.[16] One night, January 27, 1956, King received a nasty telephone call: "Nigger, we are tired of you and your mess now and if you aren't out of this town in three days, we're going blow your brains out and blow up your house." Though he had received many similar threats (about forty daily), for some reason that one stunned him, preventing him from going to sleep. He began to realize that his wife and newly born baby daughter could be taken from him or he from them at any moment. He got up out of bed and went to the kitchen to heat some coffee, "thinking," he said, "that coffee would give me a little relief."

In the midst of one of the most agonizing experiences of his life, he searched for a place that he could stand. "I started thinking about many things; I pulled back on the theology and philosophy that I had just studied in the universities trying to give philosophical and theological reasons for the existence and the reality of sin and evil, but the answer didn't quite come there." Unable to cope with his frustration and despair, King turned to the God of the black faith that he had been taught as a child:

> Something said to me, you can't call on daddy now; he's in Atlanta, a hundred-seventy-five miles away. . . . You've got to call on that something, on that person that your daddy used to tell you about, that power that can make a way out of no way. And I discovered then that religion had to become real to me and I had to know God for myself. And I bowed down over that cup of coffee. I never will forget it. Oh yes, I prayed a prayer. And I prayed out loud that night. I said, "Lord, I'm down here trying to do what's right. I think I'm right. I think the cause that we represent is right. But Lord, I must confess that I'm weak now, I'm faltering, I'm losing my courage, and I can't let the people see me like this because if they see me weak and losing my courage they will begin to get weak."

It was in the midst of this crisis of faith that King experienced the liberating presence of God as never before. He heard an inner voice saying: "Martin Luther, stand up for righteousness. Stand up for justice. Stand up for truth. And lo, I will be with you, even until the end of the world." After that liberating experience he said: "I was ready to face anything."[17] From that point onward, King never doubted God's presence in the struggle for justice, reassuring him that love and nonviolence, despite the odds, will triumph over hate and violence.

King's theology was defined by an eschatological hope, God's promise not to leave the little ones alone in struggle. In his sermons, he spoke often of "midnight," "darkness," and the "cross," usually referring to racism, poverty, and war. But in spite of the great difficulties he encountered in fighting these evils, King was certain that "we shall overcome," because "truth crushed to the earth will rise again."

> Sometimes I feel discouraged. And I don't mind telling you this morning that sometimes I feel discouraged. I felt discouraged in Chicago. As I moved through Mississippi and Georgia and Alabama I feel discouraged. Living everyday under the threat of death I feel discouraged sometimes. Living everyday under extensive criticism, even from Negroes, I feel discouraged sometimes. Yes, sometimes I feel discouraged and feel my work's in vain, but then the Holy Spirit revives my soul again. There is a balm in Gilead to make the wounded whole.

The Function and Interrelationship of the Sources

The black religious tradition always remained at the heart of King's thought and practice, even though he rarely articulated its importance in most of his writings and speeches. He seldom referred to the theological significance of the Black Church, because almost everything he published was intended primarily for a white audience who had doubts about the legality and morality of nonviolent direct action and civil disobedience. Many whites complained about the violence which civil rights demonstrations evoked, and they strongly urged King to "wait," "cool off," and "not to move too fast." Martin King's frequent appeals to Gandhi and a variety of Euro-American theologians and philosophers were intended to persuade the white public that he had sound philosophical and Christian reasons for his nonviolent demonstrations. He wanted to demonstrate that his claim that "segregation is a cancer in the body politic" as well as a "tragic evil which is utterly unchristian" was not simply the rhetoric of a black preacher but was derived from the most influential thinkers in the West.

On the other hand, when Martin King spoke to an audience in a black church, he may have referred to white theologians and philosophers, but they were secondary to his overall purpose. Blacks did not need to be persuaded that segregation was morally evil and contrary to democratic values and thus should be eliminated. They needed inspiration and courage to struggle against tremendous odds. It was black people's faith that "God can make a way out of no way" that King knew in his heart and articulated so well in his sermons.

Focusing primarily on the themes of justice, love, and hope as they are grounded in faith, King integrated the four sources into a coherent whole, with each theme emerging as dominant at different periods of his life as he sought to communicate his ideas to black and white audiences. Protestant liberalism and the philosophies of Gandhi and Thoreau were the sources that provided the intellectual structure that King used to interpret his ideas and actions regarding nonviolence and civil disobedience to the white community. They gave him a method of fighting for justice that was consistent with American democratic values and the theological and philosophical tradition of the West.

When King spoke to a black audience, his chief source was the Bible, as mediated through the Black Church tradition. It can be said that as long as King was confident that justice would be achieved in a reasonable amount of time and with the support of the federal government, white moderates of the South and North, labor, and the churches, he relied primarily on liberal Protestantism, Gandhi, and Thoreau to express his theology. The dominant theme was always love with justice and hope interpreted in its light. But when the problem of injustice seemed insurmountable and the white support for justice was not visibly present, King turned to the faith of the Black Church, with an emphasis on God's eschatological promise to "transform dark yesterdays into bright tomorrows," "the fatigue of despair into the buoyancy of hope."

The faith of the Black Church and the integrationist tradition in black history provided the political and religious sources for expressing King's views to the black community. Because white racists controlled the centers of sociopolitical power, many blacks were paralyzed by the fear of loss of property and life. They were uncertain of their courage to challenge the white power structure and of their spiritual strength to sustain themselves in that challenge.

Furthermore, some blacks were not sure that integration into white society was the most appropriate goal of the Civil Rights movement or whether nonviolence was the right method for achieving that goal. The black political tradition of Frederick Douglass and the NAACP provided the rationale that integration was the correct political goal and that nonviolent direct action was the only way to achieve it. But it was the faith of the Black Church that provided black people with the courage to fight against great odds, giving them the hope that the goal of justice would eventually be achieved.

Change and Continuity in King's Theology

The function and interrelationship of the sources are illuminated when seen in the context of an analysis of the continuity and change in King's theology. The character of King's theological development was shaped by two overall concerns: what he was fighting *against* and what he was fighting *for*. He began his public ministry by fighting against racism, and the events of the 1960s forced him to connect it with poverty and militarism. Though King's theology went through several developmental changes between 1955 and 1968, this aspect of his thought should be analyzed in relation to the continuity in his thinking. As the changes can best be illuminated in relation to what he was fighting against and the strategies he developed to overcome evil, so the continuity in King's theology can best be demonstrated when it is analyzed in relation to what he was fighting for. King's goal was not simply the elimination of racism, poverty, and war, but rather the establishment of an integrated community of persons of all races, working together toward the building of the kingdom that he called the "beloved community." Everything King did and said regarding the church and society was intended to create a new community in which love and justice defined the relationship between all people.

Martin King began his public career with an emphasis on the justice of God. He derived its meaning from the Hebrew prophets, as interpreted in the faith and history of the Black Church and liberal Protestant theology. He also used the American democratic tradition, especially as found in the Constitution and the Declaration of Independence. As blacks in Montgomery began the bus boycott, King based their actions on the theme of justice in the Christian faith, and love and hope were interpreted in its light. But shortly after the boycott began, white and black advisors, concerned about the development of a method of social change that would avoid violence, urged King to adopt Gandhi's method of nonviolent direct action and thereby place love at the center of his thought. During this period, love replaced justice as the dominant theme, and King derived its meaning from the life and teachings of Jesus and Gandhi. Also useful were the theologians and philosophers he studied in graduate school. With an emphasis on love strongly influenced by liberal Protestantism, justice was defined as the absence of segregation and the establishment of an integrated community, and hope became similar to the liberal optimism that King had studied in graduate school.

When King realized that the life-chances of the poor had not been affected by the gains of the Civil Rights movement, that the federal government was not nearly as committed to fighting the war on poverty as it was to fighting the war in Vietnam and that white moderates were not as concerned with the establishment of justice in the North as they had been in fighting legal segregation in the South, the idea of hope became the dominant theme in his theology. His reflections on hope were derived almost exclusively from biblical religion as mediated through the faith and history of the Black Church. Hope was carved out of the suffering and disappointments he experienced in fighting injustice in urban ghettos (especially Chicago), in dialoguing with Black Power advocates, and in taking his stand against the war in Vietnam. He placed love and justice in an eschatological context, with an emphasis on bearing witness to God's coming freedom by taking a stand for justice *now*, even though the odds against its establishment are great.

Between 1955 and 1968, Martin King moved from an optimistic integrationist to a temporary separatist;[18] from a social reformer to a militant nonviolent revolutionary;[19] from an intellectual dependence on classical Western philosophy to a call for the study of black philosophers;[20] from a naive belief that southern white moderates (especially ministers) would join him in the struggle for an integrated society to a deepening skepticism regarding whether even white northern liberal Christians, labor, and government officials had the moral sensitivity to understand the depth of the disadvantages that African-Americans must overcome in order to survive in a society that does not recognize their humanity;[21] from his inspiring "I Have a Dream" oration to his despairing assertion that "the dream I had in Washington back in 1963 has often turned into a nightmare";[22] from his silence about the Vietnam war to his well-known "Beyond Vietnam" speech at New York's Riverside Church (April 4, 1967), proclaiming that "America is the greatest purveyor of violence in the world today."[23]

To understand the character of King's theological development, it is important to note its three phases, with each being defined by an emphasis on justice, love, and hope. When he reluctantly became the leader of the

Montgomery bus boycott, he was not an advocate of nonviolent direct action or a follower of Mahatma Gandhi. Indeed, as white violence increasingly emerged as a threat to his life, King applied for a license to carry a gun in his car but was refused by the Montgomery police department. The guiding principle for his initial involvement in the bus boycott was the justice of God as defined by the prophets and Jesus Christ. Reflecting back on the preparation for his first major speech at Holt Street Baptist Church (December 5, 1955), King said that his chief question was: "How could I make a speech that would be militant enough to keep my people aroused to positive action and yet moderate enough to keep this fever within controllable and Christian bounds?"[24]

After referring to the "right to protest" as an inherent part of American democracy, and then connecting what happened to Rosa Parks with the "long history of abuses and insults that Negro citizens had experienced on the city buses," King creatively articulated the balance between active protest and appropriate moderation with the passion and rhythm so typical of the best in the Black Church tradition. As he increased the volume of his voice, seeking to allow himself to be used by God's Spirit to empower poor blacks to "walk the streets in dignity rather than ride the bus in humiliation," King said:

> There comes a time when people get tired of being trampled over by the iron feet of oppression. There comes a time . . . when people get tired of being flung across the abyss of humiliation where they experience the bleakness of nagging despair. There comes a time when people get tired of being pushed out of the glittering sunlight of life's July and left standing amidst the piercing chill of an Alpine November. We are here this evening because we're tired now.[25]

Martin King justified the boycott on both legal and moral grounds, emphasizing that the "great glory of American democracy is the right to protest for right" and that the Christian faith demanded that black people "stand up for their rights." In sharp contrast to King's later description of this speech in *Stride Toward Freedom* in which he said "love your enemies" was his chief emphasis,[26] my examination of the tape and printed text revealed that *justice*, and not love was his major theme.

> We only assemble here because of our desire to see right exist. . . .
> We're going to work with grim and firm determination to gain justice

on the buses of this city. And we are not wrong . . . in what we are doing. If we are wrong, then the Supreme Court of this nation is wrong.
If we are wrong, the Constitution of the United States is wrong. If we
are wrong, God Almighty is wrong. If we are wrong, Jesus of Nazareth
was merely a utopian dreamer and never came down to earth. If we
are wrong, justice is a lie. . . . We are determined . . . to work and fight
until "justice runs down like waters and righteousness like a mighty
stream."[27]

There is a great difference between King's report of this speech in *Stride
Toward Freedom* and the tape of what he actually said on that occasion.
Even as King urged blacks to keep "God in the forefront," his emphasis re-
mained on justice and not love, *coercion* and not persuasion.

I want to tell you this evening that it is not enough for us to talk about
love. Love is one of the pinnacle parts of the Christian faith. There is
another side called justice. And justice is really love in calculation.
Justice is love correcting that which would work against love. The Almighty God . . . is not . . . just standing out saying, "Behold Thee, I
love you Negro." He's also the God that standeth before the nations
and says: "Be still and know that I am God, and if you don't obey me
I'm gonna break the backbone of your power, and cast you out of the
arms of your international and national relationships." Standing beside love is always justice. And we are only using the tools of justice.
Not only are we using the tools of persuasion but we've got to use the
tools of coercion.[28]

On the tape of King's Holt Street Address, there is no mention of Gandhi's method of nonviolent direct action and no reference to Jesus' command to "love your enemies." His stress was almost exclusively on justice
as defined by the American democratic tradition of equality and the biblical theme of the righteousness of God.

As King's involvement in the Montgomery bus boycott deepened and
the appeal for white support was accentuated, the Christian idea of love
emerged as the central theme of his theology. Love became the modifier of
justice as he sought to eradicate the fears of both blacks and whites regarding violence. By the time King wrote *Stride Toward Freedom* (1958), he had
become an international figure, with white and black advisors assisting
him in his work, including the editing of his book manuscript and ad-

dresses. I am convinced that the change in emphasis from justice to love was partly due to the editorial hand of his advisors.[29]

As the boycott proceeded, King's practical concern about the dangers of violence, along with his acceptance of the naive optimism of liberal theology, caused him to change his primary emphasis from justice to love. While acknowledging the important role of the Black Church and the absence of any reference to Gandhi, King seemed to have forgotten about his original accent on justice. For example, in *Stride Toward Freedom*, he recalls:

> The first days of the protest . . . the phrase most often heard was "Christian love." It was the Sermon on the Mount, rather than a doctrine of passive resistance, that initially inspired the Negroes of Montgomery to dignified social action. It was Jesus of Nazareth that stirred the Negroes to protest with the creative weapon of love.[30]

Likewise, King's focus on Gandhi and nonviolent resistance was a later development, emerging simultaneously with his new emphasis on love. The connection between Gandhi and the Montgomery bus boycott was suggested initially by Juliette Morgan's letter to the editor of the *Montgomery Advertiser*. Later on, nonviolent direct action was intellectually defined and practically implemented when Bayard Rustin and Glen E. Smiley of the Fellowship of Reconciliation (FOR) joined Martin King as advisors about two months after the boycott began.[31]

During the phase in which love was dominant in King's theology, he defined racism as segregation and designated it as America's "chief moral dilemma." But the more he fought racism the more he came to realize that it was much more complex than the discrimination laws in the South. To King's surprise, he not only found racism in the North, but discovered also that northern racism, though less visible, was more destructive to human personality and also more deeply embedded in the sociopolitical structures than what he had seen in the South.

After the Selma March and the passage of the Voting Rights Act (1965), several events caused King to undertake a deeper analysis of racism, which in turn disclosed the severe limitations of what had been achieved in the southern-based Civil Rights movement. Five days following the signing of the Voting Rights Bill by President Johnson (August 6), the Watts riot erupted (August 11), initiating a radical change in King's per-

spective regarding the nature of racism and what would be needed to eliminate it. His struggle and frustrations in Chicago, the rise of Black Power,
drastic cuts in the domestic budget, and a rapid escalation of expenditures
for the war in Vietnam—all these events contributed to King's movement
toward the left. His analysis of racism disclosed its global manifestations,
especially its connection with two other evils: poverty and war. King began to acknowledge publicly the limitations of his earlier views and started
to connect racism with "class issues . . . the privileged as over against the
underprivileged," and even openly advocating democratic socialism.[32]

When King saw the depth of the problem of racism as reflected by exten-
sive poverty in the northern ghettos and its devastating effects on the self-
worth of black people, he became so incensed that he could no longer keep
silent regarding the moral contradictions involved. It was during the period between the end of 1965 and his assassination in 1968 that Martin
King entered a revolutionary path that led him to declare "God's judgment
. . . on America" because of its failure to use its vast economic resources
for life rather than death.

> There is something wrong with our nation. Something desperately
> wrong. . . . There is confusion in the land. . . . This is why we've made
> a decision to come to the seat of government [and] will seek to say to
> the nation that if you don't straighten up, and that if you do not begin
> to use your vast resources of wealth to lift God's children from the
> dungeons of despair and poverty, then you are writing your own obit-
> uary. We are coming to Washington to say to America, "straighten
> up, and fly right."[33]

The primary source for King's prophetic critique of President Johnson's
war policies was the black church tradition. There is nothing in liberal
Protestant theology, Gandhi or Thoreau, or even the integrationist tradition of Douglass and the civil rights organizations that can explain the
content and the style of King's devastating critique of America's involvement in Vietnam. He was unrelenting in his criticisms, and he refused the
advice of any of his black and white friends who warned him about his lack
of competence in foreign policy and the danger of mixing peace and civil
rights. Some even questioned his patriotism. But King was quick to respond that he was speaking out against the war not because he was a civil
rights activist or an expert in foreign policy. He spoke solely in the name of

God's righteousness and human decency. As a minister of the God of Jesus, he could not keep silent, for the truth of the gospel was at stake.

Although his "Beyond Vietnam" address was perhaps his greatest hour and best known indictment of U.S. policies in Vietnam, it is in his unpublished sermons that one can clearly observe the depth of the agony of King's concerns and the source of his theological criticism. Most of these sermons were delivered at Ebenezer Baptist Church in Atlanta. Hardly anyone can read them or listen to the tapes and fail to acknowledge the decisive impact of the black and biblical traditions upon the content of his sermons and the forcefulness in which he delivered them. They include: "Why I Am Opposed to the War in Vietnam," "Mastering Our Fears," "The Drum Major Instinct," "A Knock at Midnight," "Standing by the Best in an Evil Time," "Who Is My Neighbor?," "Unfulfilled Dreams," and "But If Not. . . ."

In these sermons, King takes his stand with the prophets of the biblical tradition and rejects the advice of many of his friends and followers in SCLC, NAACP, labor, government, and even black and white churches, all of whom told him to keep silent about the war in Vietnam, because he was alienating President Johnson and the financial supporters of SCLC. With prophetic passion, so typical of the best in the Black Church tradition, King told them:

> I'm sorry, you don't know me. I'm not a consensus leader. I don't determine what is right and wrong by looking at the budget of the Southern Christian Leadership Conference, or by taking a Gallup Poll of the majority opinion. Ultimately a genuine leader is not a searcher for consensus but a molder of consensus.[34]

King deeply believed that just as Shadrach, Meshach, and Abednego had to take their stand against King Nebuchadnezzar and refuse to worship the King's golden image, even though they faced the flames of the fiery furnace, so he, Martin King, had to take his stand against Lyndon Johnson's war policies and refuse to bow down to the economic and political pressures of the State Department and its supporters. As the intensity of the pressures increased, even to the extent that the FBI was trying to force him to commit suicide, King turned to the God of black faith, because he believed that, as was true of the "three Hebrew children," God could deliver him "if it be so" (Dan. 3:17).

Using the response of the three Hebrews to Nebuchadnezzar as a sermon title, "But If Not . . . ,"[35] King made it clear that he was prepared to
give his life for the truth of God. Nothing, absolutely nothing, was more
important to Martin King than speaking and doing the truth. The more
he was pressured to keep silent, the more forcefully he spoke out against
the evils of racism, poverty, and war. In fact King became so disturbed
about injustice that many of his biographers and some close friends have
suggested that he was on the verge of a mental breakdown. I am sure that
many contemporaries of the Hebrew prophets had similar feelings about
them. The nature of the prophets' vocation almost always threw them into
conflict with the values of their time. Prophets of every age are truth-
tellers, and the "powers that be" never want to hear the truth in a world
based on their lies. When Whitney Young of the Urban League, a colleague and friend, cornered King in public and reprimanded him about his
views on Vietnam, King responded sharply: "Whitney, what you are saying may get you a foundation grant but it will not get you into the kingdom
of truth."

One cannot understand correctly Martin King's convictions about Vietnam, Black Power, racism, and poverty without a keen knowledge of the
role of the "preacher as prophet" in the black community. When the black
preacher is true to his/her vocational calling, he/she must speak the truth
of God regardless of who is affected by its judgment. That was why King's
most severe indictments against the evils of racism, poverty, and war were
delivered as sermons. As a prophet of God, he had no choice but to speak
the Word of God. In the sermon entitled "Standing by the Best in an Evil
Time," King made a forceful and prophetic statement on why he could not
keep silent on the evil of America's involvement in Vietnam.

> I've decided what I'm going to do. I ain't going to kill nobody in Missis-
> sippi [and] in Vietnam. I ain't going to study war no more. And you
> know what? I don't care who doesn't like what I say about it. I don't
> care who criticizes me in an editorial. I don't care what white person
> or Negro criticizes me. I'm going to stick with the best. On some posi-
> tions, cowardice asks the question "is it safe?" Expediency asks the
> question, "is it politic?" Vanity asks the question, "is it popular?" But
> conscience asks the question, "is it right?" And there comes a time
> when a true follower of Jesus Christ must take a stand that's neither

safe nor politic nor popular but he must take that stand because it is right. Every now and then we sing about it, "if you are right, God will fight your battle." I'm going to stick by the best during these evil times.[36]

Conclusion

When Americans celebrate Martin Luther King, Jr.'s birthday as a national holiday, seminary students and faculty, church leaders and Christians throughout the world should not forget his importance *as theologian*, perhaps the most important in American history. In saying this, I do not wish to minimize the significant contribution of other theologians —whether Jonathan Edwards, Walter Rauschenbusch, or the Niebuhr brothers. There are three reasons that make Martin King a candidate for the status of America's most outstanding theologian:

1. If theology is a disciplined endeavor to interpret the meaning of the gospel for the present time, and if the gospel is God's liberation of the poor from bondage, then I would claim that no one has articulated the Christian message of freedom more effectively, prophetically, and creatively in America than Martin Luther King, Jr.

2. Unlike many American theologians who often look toward Europe to identify theological problems that require disciplined reflection, Martin King's theological perspective achieved its creativity by engaging uniquely American issues. He was truly an *American* theologian and not simply a theologian who happened to live in the United States. No theologian has made a greater impact on American culture than Martin Luther King, Jr. Making his birthday a national holiday merely symbolized that fact.

3. Unlike most white theologians who do theology as if their definitions of it are the only ones and as if their problems are the only ones that deserve the attention of disciplined theological reflection, Martin King did not limit his theological reflections to the problems of one group. While he began with a focus on the racial oppression of blacks, his theological vision was universal. He was as concerned about the liberation of whites from their *oppression as oppressors* as he was in eliminating the racial oppression of blacks. He was as concerned about the life-chances of brown children in Vietnam as he was about black children in America's cities. King's vision was truly international, embracing all humanity. That is why his

name is invoked by the oppressed around the world who are fighting for freedom. Teachers of theology do themselves, their students, and their discipline a great disservice when they ignore the outstanding contribution that King has made to American theology and to all who are seeking to understand the gospel today. For if one wishes to know what it means to be a theologian, there is no better example than Martin Luther King, Jr.

Martin Luther King, Jr., Black Theology—Black Church

During a decade of writing and teaching Black Theology, the most frequent question that has been addressed to me, publicly and privately, by blacks and especially by whites, has been: "How do you reconcile the separatist and violent orientation of black theology with Martin Luther King's emphasis on integration, love, and nonviolence?" I have always found it difficult to respond to this question because those who ask it seem unaware of the interrelations between King, black theology, and the Black Church.

While it is not my primary intention to compare King and black theology, I do hope that an explication of his theology in the context of the Black Church will show, for those interested in a comparison, that black theology and King are not nearly as far apart as some persons might be inclined to think.

I

The white public and also many white scholars have misunderstood King, because they know so little about the Black Church community, ignoring its effect upon his life and thought. An example of this misguided interpretation are the books by Kenneth Smith and Ira Zepp, Jr., *Search for the Beloved Community: The Thinking of Martin Luther King, Jr.* (Judson, 1974), and John Ansbro, *The Mind of Martin Luther King, Jr.* (Orbis, 1982). These authors analyze the thought of Martin King as if the Black Church community had no decisive impact on him, indeed as if thought itself is limited to the white intellectual community. While these books are useful in telling us what King learned in graduate school and what intellectual resources he used in communicating his ideas to the white community, they are not helpful in identifying the heart of King's theology and faith that sustained him in his fight for justice.

When one uses exclusively the perspectives of white theologians to interpret Martin King, it is difficult to explain the consistency of his thinking and actions. How is it possible for King to reconcile his use of the neo-orthodox theology of Reinhold Niebuhr and the Boston Personalism of Edgar S. Brightman? King appeals to so many resources for his ideas that it is conceptually impossible to reconcile them into one coherent whole when these white philosophers and theologians are used as the primary source of their origin and analysis. That is why many of King's interpreters find it nearly impossible to explain the entirety of his theological perspective in a consistent and wholistic manner.

What is true for the interpreters of Martin King is also true for many interpreters of my own perspective on black theology. As King used evangelical liberalism and Boston Personalism in defining his theology, many of my interpreters claim that I use the so-called neo-orthodox theology of Karl Barth. When I also begin to use Tillich, Marx, Bonhoeffer, and other white interpreters for the presentation of my ideas, my interpreters get a little confused in explicating the consistency of my perspective, because the different ideas I use for interpreting black theology do not belong in the same theological school of thought.

What is most interesting is that even I myself used to think that the sources for explaining my theology were Barth, Bonhoeffer, and Tillich, because these were the theologians who made the most conscious intellectual impact on me during my seminary days. After writing a Ph.D. dissertation on Karl Barth's anthropology, I naturally turned to him for communicating my deepest feelings about the theological implications of the black struggle for freedom. At that time, Barth and others like him were the only intellectual resources at my command for explicating the theological meaning of the black struggle, even though the truth of it did not arise from the experience of white neo-orthodox theologians.

Since the publication of *Black Theology and Black Power* (1969), I have come to realize the limitation of this procedure and have attempted to correct it as much as possible, while not denying the usefulness of ideas from all cultures. I now know that even though I may not have recognized it, the Black Church was and still is the most dominant element for a proper understanding of my own theological perspective. While I do not rule out other influences, they are not in any way decisive. I can discard Barth and Tillich as easily as I can choose to use them. They, as well as others, are merely instrumental in giving conceptual structure to a primary commitment determined by the Black Church community.

II

With that community in mind, one can then understand both the similarities and differences between King's theology and my own perspective on black theology. Although our differences on violence versus nonviolence, love and reconciliation, and the possibility of change in the white community are real, they are differences between two persons who are deeply committed to the same faith of the Black Church. Our differences are not so great as is usually believed. They are more semantic than substantive, and can best be understood by investigating our different circumstances in the black community and the audiences to which we address our viewpoints.

King was not nearly as nonviolent as many claimed, and his faith in whites and the accomplishment of his movement was not uncritical. For example, when he spoke about black progress in the area of civil rights, he knew that all was not as well as whites liked to think and that for the masses of blacks the movement had left their situation of oppression untouched. In a 1965 interview with Alex Haley, King said:

> Though many would prefer not to, we must face the fact that progress for the Negro—to which white moderators like to point in justifying gradualism—has been relatively insignificant, particularly in terms of the Negro masses. What little progress has been made—and that includes the Civil Rights Act—has applied primarily to the middle class Negro. Among the masses, especially in the Northern ghettoes, the situation remains the same, and for some it is worse.[1]

Speaking about his disappointment regarding southern white ministers, King said:

> The most pervasive mistake I have made was in believing that because our cause was just, we could be sure that the white ministers of the South, once their Christian consciences were challenged, would rise to our aid. . . . I ended up, of course, chastened and disillusioned.[2]

Both of these quotations show that Martin King did face the failure of the Civil Rights movement to reach the masses of black people. He also realized that whites, even liberal clergy, could not always be counted on to act out in life what they claim in their confessions of faith or in their theological textbooks.

My own perspective on black theology, unlike Martin King, begins with the assumption that the people who benefit from the unjust social, political, and economic order are not likely to be the ones who will change it radically. I do not make this claim because I think that whites are by nature more evil than any other group of people. I make this claim because of the Christian doctrine of sin which says that individuals or groups will claim more than what they ought to, if they can get away with it. I think that the reality of sin has already been validated by history. I do not believe that any group of people will do right, because of the demands of faith alone.

As Reinhold Niebuhr forcefully demonstrated in his *Moral Man and Immoral Society,* individuals may stand outside of themselves and therefore act against their interests as defined by the existing social arrangements. But groups seldom, if ever, can transcend their interests for the sake of another. Martin King was certainly aware of Niebuhr's analysis, but it apparently made little impact on his theological consciousness, since his optimism regarding whites could not be shaken radically. King's optimism, however, is not derived primarily from the theological liberalism of Boston Personalism or of the Social Gospel movement.

I think King received this faith in whites from the Black Church tradition which has always extended its openness to reconciliation to the white community. What is most amazing about the black community as a whole and the Black Church in particular is their willingness to forgive whites their brutality during slavery, lynching, and even oppression today in the ghettos of the urban cities. But despite our willingness to extend the right hand of fellowship, whites continue their massive assault upon the humanity of our people and get angry with us if we say we don't like it. It seems that whites have been allowed to do what they wish to us so long that they regard such inhumane invasion of black humanity as synonymous with their freedom.

With regard to what black people can expect from white people in our struggle for freedom, there are some genuine differences between King and me. I do not believe that whites or any other group holding power will voluntarily empower those who are powerless. Freedom is not a gift but must be taken. While the Gospel of God can and does empower people to change sides in the struggle for freedom, we must realize that many people publicly testify that they are for the poor but are in fact against them.

Even though there are important differences between King and me, I think they can best be understood from within the context of the Black Church rather than in the context of white liberal and neo-orthodox theologies of North America and Europe. Such views as represented by King and me, as well as many others, can be found throughout the black religious tradition. There is no need to turn to white Western theology for an explanation. King's perspective has its antecedents in Frederick Douglass, while my view is partly found in the life and writings of Henry Highland Garnet, both of whom were contemporaries in the nineteenth century and stressed somewhat different views regarding the place of whites in the black struggle for freedom.[3]

III

What was the main content of King's thought which he derived from the Black Church tradition? This question is not easy to answer because the Black Church has not done much systematic reflection in the area of theology. Our theologies have been presented in the forms of sermons, songs, prayers, testimonies, and stories of slavery and oppression. In these sources we have given our views of God and the world, and how each may be understood in relation to our struggle for freedom. We did not write essays on Christian doctrine because our descendents came as slaves from Africa and not as free people from Europe. Many blacks were prevented from learning to read and write either by the circumstances of our birth or by the legal restrictions defined by the government. Therefore, we had to do theology in forms other than rational reflections. We sang and preached our theology in worship and other sacred contexts. The central meaning disclosed in these nonrational sources is found in both their *form* and *content* and is identical with *freedom* and *hope*.

The influence of the Black Church and its central theme of freedom and hope can be seen in the language of King's speaking and writing. Everything he said and wrote sounds like a black sermon and not rational reflection. To be sure, King finished first in his class at Crozer and also wrote a Ph.D. dissertation at Boston on Henry Nelson Wieman's and Paul Tillich's conceptions of God. But it is significant to note that he did not adopt the style of theological presentation from any of his white theological mentors. He may have referred to white theologians and philosophers when he needed to explain his views to a white public, but the style of his presentation was unmistakably from the tradition of black preaching.

Like his predecessors and contemporaries in the Black Church, King preached his theology, because the theme of freedom and hope had to be reflected in the movement and rhythm of his voice, if he expected a black congregation to take his message seriously. The eschatological hope of freedom is not only an idea to be analyzed in the conceptual language of white theologians and philosophers. It is primarily an event to be experienced when God's word of freedom breaks into the lives of the gathered community through the vehicle of the sermon's oration. No one understood the relationship between style and meaning in the context of the Black Church any better than Martin King.

In the Black Church, the meaning is found not primarily in the intellectual content of the spoken word but in the *way* the word is spoken and its effect upon those who hear it. That was why King could speak on Plato, Augustine, or even Boston Personalism, about which most blacks know nothing and care even less, and still move the congregation to tears and shouts of praise, even though they did not understand the content of his discourse. What they understood was the appropriate tone and movement of his speech which the people believe is the instrument for the coming presence of God's Spirit, thereby empowering them with the hope for freedom. The people believe that freedom is coming because a foretaste of it is given in the sermon event itself. When King spoke of his dream at the 1963 March on Washington, and when he spoke the night before his assassination in Memphis of his hope that we will reach the Promised Land, black people did not believe him because of the cogency of his logic but rather because of the spirit of empowerment generated by the style of his sermon oration. The people believed him because they contended that they experienced in their hearts the Spirit of God's liberating presence.

I think style is important in doing theology, and I try to reflect it in my own theology. How can black theology claim to be derived from the black community if it does not reflect in its style the language of the people? If black people do not recognize themselves in the language of theology, how can theology really claim blackness as its identity? For any theology to be truly black, its blackness must be expressed in the form in which it is written. This point was impressed on my own theological consciousness by the black critics of my early books *Black Theology and Black Power* (1969) and *A Black Theology of Liberation* (1970). With the publication of *The Spirituals and the Blues* (1972), *God of the Oppressed* (1975), *My Soul Looks Back* (1982), and other subsequent writings, I have tried to incorporate the *content* of liberation not only in theology but also in the very form of the language itself. Martin King has been helpful in the accomplishment of this task.

IV

In addition to the style of King's theology pointing toward freedom and hope, the same theme is also found in the *content* of his message. The influence of the Black Church on the content of King's theology is not easy to demonstrate. Anyone can easily notice the influence of the Black Church on his sermonic delivery and in the form of his writings. But that is not the case with the content of his message, since he does not explicitly refer to the Black Church. What is clear, however, is that the central theme of freedom and hope do define the content of King's life and message. It is summarized in his March on Washington speech:

> I have a dream that my four little children will one day live in a nation where they will not be judged by the color of their skin but by the content of their character. . . . With this faith we will be able to transform the jangling discords of our nation into a beautiful symphony of brotherhood. With this faith we will be able to work together, to pray together, to struggle together, to go to jail together, to stand up for freedom together, knowing that we will be free one day.

The words were spoken in 1963, but few of us today can speak with the confidence of Martin King, because events since that time are difficult to reconcile with his optimism. Between 1965 and 1968, even King had to move away from the optimism defined in the 1963 Washington speech, because his sermons and speeches did not dislodge the entrenchment of white power as he appeared to think. But despite the failure of his sermons and speeches to move whites to change the social, political, and economic situation, the content of his message of freedom and hope did move blacks to action. Without the response of the Black Church people, King would have had his hope for freedom destroyed, because even liberal whites seemed incapable of embodying the hope and freedom about which he preached.

In the Black Church, King knew that the people had a hope that stretched back to the beginnings of the black Christian community in the eighteenth and nineteenth centuries. All he had to do was restate that hope for freedom in the songs and language of the people and they would respond to the content of the message. That was why King used the language of the so-called Negro Spirituals in his sermons in black churches. His sermons always contained the hope for freedom, and he always related it to his current struggles to attain freedom in this world. But when it seemed as if freedom was difficult to realize in this world, Martin King did not despair but moved its meaning to an eschatological realm as defined by the Black Church's claim that "the Lord will make a way somehow." The night before he was assassinated, King, in a Black Church worship service, restated that hope with the passion and certainty so typical of the black preacher: "I may not get there with you, but I want you to know tonight that we as a people will get to the Promised Land. . . . Mine eyes have seen the glory of the coming of the Lord."

King's emphasis on the eschatological hope of freedom as defined by "the coming of the Lord" was not derived from white theologians and philosophers, but from his own religious tradition. These words of faith and hope were derived from the black tradition as defined by our pain and suffering. People who have not lived in the context of hundreds of years of slavery and suffering are not likely to express an eschatological hope of freedom. Hope in God's coming eschatological freedom is always derived from the suffering of people who are seeking to establish freedom on earth but have failed to achieve it. In their failure to establish freedom in their existing present, black people prevented despair from becoming the defining characteristic of their lives by looking forward to God's coming, eschatological freedom.

As with King, black theology, and the Black Church generally, we blacks do not deny that trouble is present in black life. What we deny is that it has the last word, for we believe, in the words of Charles Tindley, that "we will understand it better by and by."

Trials dark on every hand, and we cannot understand.
All the ways that God would lead us to the Blessed
    Promised Land
But he guides us with his eye and we'll follow till
    we die.
For we'll understand it better by and by.

By and by, when the morning comes,
All the saints of God are gathered home
We'll tell the story how we've overcome
For we'll understand it better by and by.

Martin Luther King, Jr., and the Third World

When Martin Luther King, Jr., achieved international fame as the leader of the Montgomery bus boycott in 1955–56, no African country below the Sahara had achieved political independence from the colonial regimes of Europe. When he was assassinated in Memphis, Tennessee, twelve years later, in 1968, the great majority of African countries had gained their independence. Since 1968 black Africans have continued their "stride toward freedom," overcoming the political domination of Europeans in every country except South Africa.[1]

As in Africa, similar struggles for freedom occurred in Asia and Latin America. The struggles of the poor in all societies remind us that the fires of freedom are burning and that nothing short of justice for all will establish peace and tranquility in the world.

As we reflect on the significance of the life and thought of Martin Luther King, Jr., for the people of America, it is important to remember that the meaning of his life is not bound by race, nationality, or creed. Speaking of the international significance of his son, Daddy King was correct when he said: "He did not belong to us, he belonged to the world."[2] I would add that Martin Luther King, Jr., belonged particularly to the Third World, the world of the poor and the disinherited. It is therefore important to ask about his significance for peoples of Africa, Asia, and Latin America and about their significance for him. In this essay I will limit my analysis to the impact of Third World liberation movements on the development of King's theology.

Martin King's thinking falls into two periods.[3] The first began with the Montgomery bus boycott in December 1955 and ended with the enactment of the Voting Rights Act in August 1965. The second period commenced in the fall of 1965 as King began to analyze more deeply the interrelationship of racism, poverty, and militarism in the policies of the United States government. In both periods his ideas were defined by his faith in the God of justice, love, and hope. The difference between the two periods is the shifting emphases he gave to each of those theological attributes as he sought to develop a nonviolent philosophy of social change that would eliminate racial and economic exploitation and establish peace in America and the world.

During the first period, King's thinking was defined by an optimistic belief that justice could be achieved through love, which he identified with nonviolence. The place of the Third World liberation movements in his thinking was to reinforce his liberal optimism regarding the certainty of the rise of a new world order of freedom and equality. In the early months of the Montgomery bus boycott, Martin King began to interpret the black struggle for justice in America as "a part of [an] overall movement in the world in which oppressed people are revolting against . . . imperialism and colonialism." He believed that black people's fight against segregation in America expressed the same spirit that led Africans, Asians, and Latin Americans to revolt against their European colonizers. Both revolts (that of blacks in America and that of the poor in the Third World), according to King, signified "the birth of a new age." Using that phrase for the title of an address in 1956, he said that Third World people had "lived for years and centuries under the yoke of foreign power, and [that] they were dominated politically, exploited economically, segregated and humiliated."[4] Because King saw little difference between colonialism in Africa and segregation in America, he employed the same language to describe both experiences. Speaking about the impatience of black and Third World peoples with oppression, King repeated the words he had first used at the Holt Street Baptist Church in 1955:

> There comes a time when people grow tired, when the throbbing desires of freedom begin to break forth. There comes a time when people get tired of being trampled over by the iron feet of the tramper. There comes a time when people get tired of being plunged across the abyss of exploitation, where they have experienced the bleakness and madness of despair. There comes a time when people get tired of being pushed out of the glittering sunlight of life's July and left standing in the pitying state of an Alpine November.[5]

In this and many similar statements, King's point was to emphasize that black and Third World people were fed up with segregation and colonialism. "In the midst of their tiredness," something happened to them. They began to reevaluate themselves, and as a result, they "decided to rise up in protest against injustice." The protests of the oppressed throughout the world, King believed, were nothing but a signal that "the time for freedom has come." No resistance from the oppressors could abort freedom's birth because, as King often said (quoting Victor Hugo), "there is no greater power on earth than an idea whose time has come."[6] Martin King's travel to the independence celebration of Ghana (1957), the rapid achievement of independence by other Third World nations, and his study tour of India (1959) deepened his optimism that freedom would soon be achieved.[7]

King's optimism regarding the prospect of freedom's achievement was derived partly from the success of the Civil Rights movement in America and liberation movements in the Third World. The Montgomery bus boycott, sit-ins and freedom rides, the demonstrations in Birmingham, the March on Washington, the Selma March, and other less publicized civil rights victories throughout the South—all were linked with the success of anticolonialist movements in the Third World. King believed that freedom's time had come, because oppressed peoples all over the world were demonstrating that they would no longer accept passively their exclusion from the material riches of God's creation.

In Martin King's view, segregation in America and colonialism in the Third World were nothing but the denial of the dignity and worth of human beings. Both the segregationist and the colonialist said by their actions that blacks and other coloreds are inferior beings, incapable of governing themselves or living in a relationship of equality with white Americans and Europeans. As long as there was insufficient resistance from black and Third World peoples, the old order of segregation and colonialism remained unchanged. The new age of freedom began to break forth when a "New Negro" was born in America and a "New Human Being" began to rise up from among the ragged and hungry masses of the world. Armed with a new sense of dignity and self-respect, both started to march together toward the promised land of freedom.

Of course, Martin King was aware that oppressors do not voluntarily grant freedom to the oppressed. He was also aware that white segregationists and European colonists had much more military power than their victims. Yet he contended that the coming of a new world order of freedom was inevitable. How could he be so sure? The answer is found in his faith in the biblical God of justice, love, and hope. No idea or strategy that King advocated can be understood correctly apart from his deep faith in the Christian God as defined by the black Baptist and liberal Protestant traditions. The new age is coming and cannot be stopped, because God, who is just and loving, wills that the oppressed be liberated. That is why King could say:

> Oppressed people cannot remained oppressed forever. The urge for freedom will eventually come. This is what happened to the American Negro. Something within has reminded him of his birthright of freedom; something without has reminded him that he can gain it. Consciously and unconsciously, he has been swept in by what the Germans call the *Zeitgeist*, and with his black brothers of Africa, and his brown and yellow brothers of Asia, South America, and the Caribbean, he is moving with a sense of cosmic urgency toward the promised land of racial justice.[8]

King often employed the German word *Zeitgeist* to refer to his belief that "the universe is under the control of a loving purpose, and that in the struggle for righteousness [we have] cosmic companionship." That is what he had in mind when he said that Rosa Parks "had been tracked down by the *Zeitgeist*—the spirit of the times."[9]

The role of God in King's idea of the coming new age is reflected also in his use of the striking image of the "dream." He spoke often of the "American Dream," referring to the idea of equality in the Declaration of Independence, the Constitution, and the Jewish-Christian Scriptures. King's dream, however, was not limited to racial equality in the United States but was defined by its universality and eternality. To say that the dream is universal means that it is for all—blacks and whites, men and women, the peoples of Africa, Asia, and Latin America, and those of the United States and Europe. To say that it is eternal means that equality is not a right conferred by the state; it is derived from God, the creator of all life.[10]

When Martin King urged people to "make the dream a reality" or to "face the challenge of a new age," he almost always told them to "develop a world perspective." "All life is inter-related," because God is the creator of all. "No individual . . . [or] nation can live alone," because we are made for each other. No people can be who they ought to be until others are who they ought to be. "This is the way the world is made."[11]

When Martin King received the Nobel Peace Prize in 1964, it deepened his commitment to global justice and peace and reinforced his belief that God willed it. "I have the audacity to believe," he said in his acceptance speech, "that people everywhere can have three meals a day for their bodies, education and culture for their minds, and dignity, equality and freedom for their spirits." For King, the Nobel Prize was an "unutterable fulfillment," given in recognition of those fighting for freedom all over the world. His dream of a coming new age of freedom is eloquently expressed in his Nobel Lecture.

> What we are seeing now is a freedom explosion. . . . The deep rumbling of discontent that we hear today is the thunder of disinherited masses, rising from dungeons of oppression to the bright hills of freedom. . . . All over the world, like a fever, the freedom movement is spreading in the widest liberation in history. The great masses of people are determined to end the exploitation of their races and land. They are awake and moving toward their goal like a tidal wave. You can hear them rumbling in every village, street, on the docks, in the houses, among the students, in the churches and at political meetings.[12]

Because God is involved in the freedom struggles, King believed, they cannot be halted. Victory is inevitable. Success in the Civil Rights and Third World liberation movements combined with his deep faith in God's loving justice gave King an optimistic hope that freedom was not too far away.

Turning to the second period of King's thought, 1965–68, I want to emphasize that certain bedrock ideas did *not* change. He did not change his mind about the basic principles of his faith or about the Civil Rights movement's goal of freedom. In fact, his convictions regarding God's will to inaugurate a new age of freedom deepened in the last years as he gave himself totally to the struggles for justice and peace in America and the world. His faith in nonviolence remained completely unshakable. What then was new or newly emphasized in the later period?

One new thing was his great disappointment with the failure of the majority of white moderates in the North and South (in government, labor, church, business, and even the Civil Rights movement) to support the goal of genuine equality for blacks and poor people. For several years he thought that he could win the support of the decent "white majority" in America through a moral appeal to religion and the democratic traditions that they claimed to live by. But as early as his *Playboy* interview (January 1965), he acknowledged his great letdown regarding government officials and white moderates:

> [A]bysmal ignorance seems to prevail among many state, city, and even Federal officials on the whole question of racial justice and injustice. . . . But this white failure to comprehend the depth and dimension of the Negro problem is far from being peculiar to government officials. . . . It seems to be a malady even among those whites who like to regard themselves as "enlightened." . . . I wonder at [persons] who dare to feel that they have some paternalistic right to set the timetable for another [person's] liberation. Over the past several years, I must say, I have been gravely disappointed with such white "moderates." I am often inclined to think that they are more of a stumbling block to the Negro's progress than the White Citizen's Counciler or the Ku Klux Klanner.[13]

When summer riots became a regular occurrence during the second half of the 1960s, King grew impatient with whites who withdrew their support from the Civil Rights movement and began to say that "law and order" ought to be the highest priority of government. "I say to you," proclaimed King, "the riots are caused by nice gentle, timid white moderates who are more concerned about order than justice."[14]

Another new disappointment for Martin King was his failure to win the support of the majority of blacks to nonviolent direct action as the primary method for gaining their freedom. The Watts riot (August 1965) and others that followed in the urban centers (along with the Black Power movement) revealed the great gap between King's optimism about nonviolence and the despair expressed in the random violence of American ghettos.

During the first ten years, King and others in the southern-based Civil Rights movement had assumed that blacks in the North would benefit in a derivative fashion from the victories gained in the South. The Watts riot and the subsequent rise of Black Power during the Meredith March (June 1966) showed that King had badly miscalculated the self-esteem that northern blacks would receive from the "straightened up backs" of southern blacks. When he went to Watts, he was surprised that many blacks there had never heard of him and even more astonished when he heard a group of young blacks boasting, "We won." "How can you say you won," King asked, "when thirty-four Negroes are dead, your community is destroyed, and whites are using the riots as an excuse for inaction?" "We won because we made them pay attention to us," they responded to him.[15] When King reflected on that response and the hostile reactions his message of nonviolence received from Chicago street gangs and young Black Power advocates during the Meredith March, he began to realize that the Civil Rights Act (1964) and the Voting Rights Act (1965) did not significantly affect the problems of racism and poverty, especially among northern blacks.

Martin King experienced a third disappointment. He expected American blacks' success with nonviolence to help persuade the majority of the oppressed of Africa, Asia, and Latin America to adopt a similar method in their struggles for freedom. But instead of adopting the creative method of nonviolence, many Third World people were openly advocating armed revolution. King was aware that even some theologians in Latin America were joining revolutionary groups in their efforts to overthrow oppressive governments.

All of this caused him to reevaluate *not* the efficacy of nonviolence, but the depth of the problem of injustice in a global context. When King began seriously to analyze global injustice, he concluded that the three evils of racism, poverty, and militarism were interrelated and deeply rooted in both the sociopolitical life of America and the international economic order. King's focus on the global implications of racism in relation to poverty and war led him to conclude that the slums in American cities were a "system of internal colonialism" not unlike the exploitation of the Third World by European nations.[16]

King's global vision helped him to see that the sociopolitical freedom of blacks was closely tied to the liberation of their sisters and brothers in Africa, Asia, and Latin America. Token integration (that is, a few professionals moving into the existing mainstream of American society) was not true freedom. "Let us," wrote King in 1967, "not think of our movement as one that seeks to integrate the Negro into all the existing values of American society."[17]

The economic exploitation of Third World nations and the deepening poverty of the poor in the United States led King to the conclusion that there was something desperately wrong with America.

> Why are there forty million poor people in a nation overflowing with such unbelievable affluence? Why has our nation placed itself in the position of being God's military agent on earth, and intervened reck-lessly in Vietnam and the Dominican Republic? Why have we substi-tuted the arrogant undertaking of policing the whole world for the high task of putting our own house in order?

These questions suggested to King the "need for a radical restructuring of the architecture of American society," so that it can serve the needs of hu-manity throughout the world.[18]

The later years of Martin King's theology are also defined by a shift in the emphasis and meaning given the themes of love, justice, and hope. Ex-cept for his great Holt Street Address, with its powerful focus on justice, the first period of King's spiritual and intellectual development centered on love, with justice and hope being interpreted in its light. But as a result of the experiences and bleak reflections just described, hope becomes the center of Martin King's thinking, with love and justice being interpreted in *its* light. The main difference between his early and later years in regard to hope was this: In the early period, King's hope was similar to a naive op-timism, because it was partly based on the progress of the freedom move-ment in America and the Third World and the support it received both from the oppressed (by their active commitment to nonviolence) and from the majority in the dominant classes (by their apparent commitment to formal equality). In contrast, King's hope, in the later years, was not based on the backing he received from blacks and whites in the United States or from the international community. Rather, his hope was grounded almost exclusively on his faith in the God of the biblical and black traditions who told him, during the early months of the Montgomery bus boycott: "Stand up for righteousness. Stand up for justice. Stand up for truth. And lo I will be with you, even until the end of the world."[19]

Instead of trusting human allies to produce a victory over the forces of organized evil, King's hope was now a transcendent one, focusing on the biblical God of the oppressed who "put down the mighty from their thrones, and exalted those of low degree."[20] The shift came out in his critique of United States policy in Vietnam, which he knew would alienate his former allies.

Among the many disappointments that shaped the second period of his thinking, none pained King more than America's military involvement in Vietnam and the criticisms he received from his white and black friends (in government, the media, and the Civil Rights movement) for opposing it. The escalation of the war in Vietnam by the United States, along with a deescalation of the War on Poverty, and American indifference toward massive poverty in the Third World motivated King to become one of the severest critics of the domestic and foreign policies of his government during the second half of the 1960s. He began to speak like a prophet, warning of the Day of Judgment, proclaiming God's wrath and indignation on a rich and powerful nation that was blind to justice at home and indifferent to world peace. Instead of speaking of the American dream as he had done so eloquently in the first half of the 1960s, he began to speak, over and over again, of an American nightmare, especially in Vietnam.[21]

Martin King did not enjoy criticizing his government. He loved America deeply, particularly its democratic and religious traditions of equality and justice. But he could not overlook the great contradictions of racism, poverty, and militarism. For King there was no greater inconsistency between creed and deed than America's military adventures in Vietnam. He frequently referred to Vietnam as a small nation whose own document of freedom, declaring independence from France in 1945, had quoted our Declaration of Independence. "Yet," King said, "our government refused to recognize them. President Truman said they were not ready for independence. So we fell victim as a nation at that time of the same deadly arrogance that has poisoned the international situation for all these years."[22]

The arrogance King referred to was racism. He believed "our disastrous experiments in Vietnam and the Dominican Republic have been . . . a result of racist decision making. Men of the white West . . . have grown up in a racist culture, and their thinking is colored by that fact. . . . They don't really respect anyone who is not white." King also felt that the vehement criticisms of his opposition to the Vietnam War emanating from the white community were motivated by racism. He spoke against his white allies in government and the media who had supported his stand on nonviolence during the sit-ins and freedom rides and in Birmingham and Selma and then rejected his position on Vietnam.

> They applauded us in the sit-in movement when we nonviolently decided to sit in at lunch counters. They applauded us on the freedom rides when we accepted blows without retaliation. They praised us in . . . Birmingham and Selma, Alabama. Oh, the press was so noble in its applause and . . . praise when I would say "Be nonviolent toward Bull Connor. . . . Be nonviolent toward Jim Clark." There is something strangely inconsistent about a nation and a press that would praise you when you say, "Be nonviolent toward Jim Clark," but will curse and damn you when you say, "Be nonviolent toward little brown Vietnamese children!"[23]

Martin King refused to accept the idea that being an American citizen obligated him to support his country in an unjust war. He refused to equate "dissent with disloyalty," as many of his critics did. On the contrary, he contended that he was the true patriot, because in his opposition to the war, he was in reality defending America's tradition of freedom and democracy, which was being violated in Vietnam. Furthermore, King believed that as a Nobel Laureate he was obligated to transcend nationalism, and thereby to take a stand for world peace. But much more important than his obligation as a citizen of the United States or of the world was his vocation as a minister of God. When people queried him about the wisdom of mixing peace and civil rights, King responded:

> Before I was a civil rights leader, I answered a call, and when God speaks, who can but prophesy? I answered a call which left the spirit of the Lord upon me and anointed me to preach the gospel. . . . I decided then that I was going to tell the truth as God revealed it to me. No matter how many people disagreed with me, I decided that I was going to tell the truth.[24]

For Martin King, telling the truth meant proclaiming God's judgment on America for its failure to use its technological resources for the good of humanity. "Here we spend thirty-five billion dollars a year to fight this terrible war in Vietnam and just the other day the Congress refused to vote forty-four million to get rid of rats in the slums and the ghettoes of our country." "The judgment of God is on America now," he said. He compared America to the rich man, Dives, who passed by the poor man, Lazarus, and never saw him. And like Dives, who went to hell because he refused to use his wealth to bridge the gulf that separated him from Lazarus, "America," King said, "is going to hell too, if she fails to bridge the gulf" that separates blacks from whites, the United States and Europe from the Third World.[25]

Because Martin King believed that America's war in Vietnam violated its own democratic values and the moral principles of the universe, he could not keep silent. There comes a time "when silence is betrayal." A nation that spends five hundred thousand dollars to kill an enemy soldier in Vietnam and only fifty dollars to get one of its citizens out of poverty is a nation that will be destroyed by its own moral contradictions. "If something doesn't happen soon," King said, "I'm convinced that the curtain of doom is coming down on the U.S."[26]

Although King was often depressed about his government's refusal to stop the war in Vietnam and to eliminate poverty at home and in the Third World, he did not lose hope. In December 1967, in "A Christmas Sermon on Peace," he proclaimed that despite the nightmare of racism, poverty, and war, "I still have a dream, because . . . you can't give up on life. If you lose hope . . . you lose that courage to be, that quality that helps you to go on in spite of all."[27]

It was Martin King's hope that sustained him in the midst of controversy, enabling him to make solidarity with the victims of the world, even though he failed to achieve the justice for which he gave his life. King's hope was grounded in the saving power of the cross of Jesus Christ, and it enabled him to see the certainty of victory in the context of an apparent defeat.

> When you stand up for justice, you never fail. The forces that have the power to make concession to the forces of justice and truth . . . but refuse to do it . . . are the forces that fail. . . . If there is no response from the federal government, from the Congress, that's the failure, not those who are struggling for justice.[28]

It is difficult for people who do not share Martin King's faith or his solidarity with the Third World to understand his meaning for poor people today. King's name is well known and greatly admired in the Third World because his life and thought disclose profound insights about humanity that are relevant to all who struggle for freedom.

"There is nothing in all the world greater than freedom."[29] Martin King gave his life for it. South African blacks, endowed with the same liberating spirit, are facing death daily, because they do not believe that whites have the right to determine the nature and the date of their freedom. Poor people throughout the world are demonstrating with their bodies that one cannot begin to live until one is ready to die for freedom.[30] Freedom is that quality of existence in which a people recognize their dignity and worth by fighting against the sociopolitical conditions that limit their recognition in society.

Martin King's foremost contribution as a moral thinker was his penetrating insight into the meaning of justice during his time. No one understood justice with more depth or communicated it with greater clarity in the area of race relations in the United States and the world than Martin Luther King, Jr. Because of King, the world is not only more aware of the problem of racial injustice but equally aware of its interrelatedness with poverty and war. "Injustice anywhere is a threat to justice everywhere."[31]

The "anemic democracy" to which King pointed is still present in America and around the world. The dream is still unfulfilled. Whether we speak of the relations between nations or of the relations between persons within nations, the rich few are still getting richer and the poor many are getting poorer. To incorporate the true meaning of Martin Luther King, Jr., into America's national consciousness would mean using our technological resources to bridge the huge economic gap that separates the rich and poor nations.

Martin King's greatest contribution was his ability to communicate a vision of hope in extreme situations of oppression. No matter how difficult the struggle for justice became, no matter how powerful were the opponents of justice, no matter how many people turned against him, King refused absolutely to lose hope, because he believed that ultimately right will triumph over wrong. He communicated that hope to the masses throughout the world, enabling them to keep on struggling for freedom and justice even though the odds were against them.

> I am not going to stop singing "We shall overcome" [he often said], because I know that "truth crushed to the earth shall rise again." I am not going to stop singing "We shall overcome," because I know the Bible is right, "you shall reap what you sow." I am not going to stop singing, "We shall overcome," because I know that one day the God of the

universe will say to those who won't listen to him, "I'm not a playboy. Don't play with me. For I will rise up and break the backbone of your power." I'm not going to stop singing, "We shall overcome," because "mine eyes have seen the glory of the coming of the Lord. He's trampling out the vintage where the grapes of wrath are stored. Glory hallelujah, his truth is marching on."[32]

Demystifying Martin and Malcolm

Martin Luther King, Jr., and Malcolm X evoke contrasting images among most Americans. When people think of Martin King, they usually think of his philosophy of love, nonviolence, and integration—a dream of blacks, whites, and other Americans living and working together in the beloved community. When people think of Malcolm X, they often think of hate, separation, and violence—a nightmare of blacks, whites, and other Americans fighting one another in riot-torn cities. These two contrasting images were created by the mainstream media in the 1960s, and they are still influential today.

When Martin King was assassinated on April 4, 1968, America mourned his tragic death. Prominent government officials acknowledged his great contribution to the nation. President Lyndon Johnson called King an "American martyr," and the U.S. Senate passed a resolution expressing its "appreciation for the immense service and sacrifice of this dedicated American." More than thirty-thousand people attended King's funeral, including eighty members of the U.S. Senate and House of Representatives.

When Malcolm X was assassinated on February 21, 1965, few tears were shed outside of Harlem and America's poorest black neighborhoods. No mainstream media had a kind word to say about him. The *New York Times* called him an "irresponsible demagogue," and *Time* magazine said he was "a disaster to the Civil Rights movement." The black press was not any kinder. They called Malcolm a "professional race baiter" who, as the *Michigan Chronicle* of Detroit put it, "reaped the harvest of his own philosophy." Even black churches did not want to be associated with him. Several churches, including Adam Clayton Powell, Jr.'s Abyssinian Baptist, declined the request to open their doors for Malcolm X's funeral.

Martin King was soon elevated to the status of a national hero. On November 2, 1983, the Congress and President Ronald Reagan established King's birthday as a national public holiday, first observed on January 20, 1986. He is the only American with a holiday in his name alone. By contrast, after Malcolm's death, little attention was paid to him, except among a small group of black nationalists and even smaller number of white and black leftists, who remembered his birthday and assassination.

Recently, however, a strong wind of change began to blow in the African-American community. Many blacks began to question whether the nonviolent, integrationist philosophy of Martin King was adequate for dealing with the economic deprivation of the inner cities and the lack of cultural self-esteem and political power of their inhabitants. Of course, few people deny that the Civil Rights movement enabled blacks to make significant strides toward social and political freedom and equality in America, especially those among the college-educated. There are forty blacks in the U.S. Congress and more than 800 elected public officials throughout the nation. There are more black students and professors in predominantly white colleges and universities, more black lawyers in the big law firms, more black doctors at the major hospitals, and more black professionals in every segment of American society than ever before. Blacks have been "moving on up," to use the theme song of the once popular television sitcom called "The Jeffersons."

But despite the progress in middle-class black America, the black underclass are poorer today than they were in the 1960s. One-half of black babies are born in poverty, and nearly 25 percent of black men between the ages of nineteen and twenty-eight are in jails, prisons, or awaiting their day in court. With no respect for themselves or for anybody else, black youth are dropping out of school, having babies, joining gangs, selling drugs, and killing one another with a frequency that boggles the imagination.

A New Look at Malcolm

Eight years of Ronald Reagan's savage attack upon the black poor shocked the African-American community into taking another look at Malcolm X. Rap musicians and other hip-hop artists, along with Spike Lee's epic movie and the controversy that preceded it, created a resurgence of interest in Malcolm X. "Who is this Malcolm the Tenth?" a black college student asked me, inquiring about my announced lecture and wondering why he had never been told about him. On urban street corners, in college and university classrooms, at conferences and other large community events, on television and radio talk shows, people—particularly younger people—of all races and ethnic groups began talking about Malcolm. A new generation learned of the one-time Harlem hustler and pimp who became the national spokesperson for Elijah Muhammad's Nation of Islam and later an international African-American leader who linked the black freedom struggle in the U.S. with liberation movements in the Third World. Tapes of Malcolm X's speeches are selling well on the streets of inner cities and in music stores. Literature by and about him abounds in bookstores and libraries and is regularly assigned in college and university classes in black studies and other subjects. *The Autobiography of Malcolm X* was on the *New York Times* paperback best-sellers list for nineteen weeks and has appeared on the *Chronicle of Higher Education*'s best-selling list called "What They're Reading on College Campuses."

Malcolm X evokes much more respect today among blacks than he did during his lifetime. In a 1964 *New York Times* poll, only 6 percent named Malcolm as "doing the best work for Negroes." Yesterday's "Negroes" are *black* today. This transformation is reflected in their enhanced appreciation of Malcolm. According to a November, 1992 *Newsweek* poll, 57 percent of all blacks regard Malcolm as a "hero." The younger the respondents, the greater the agreement: a respectable 33 percent among blacks over fifty, but an amazing 84 percent among blacks between fifteen and twenty-four. Young grassroots blacks, alienated from the civil rights organizations and the churches, respect Malcolm like no other person in African-American history. He is an inner city cultural icon who often receives as much devotion from the hip-hop generation as Christians give to Jesus. "Saint Malcolm" is what they sometimes call him. Walking through any big city, one can feel and see the reverence that Malcolm's image evokes. He is a symbol of young blacks' rage against white America's racism and also against middle-class blacks who have forgotten the plight of their poor brothers and sisters left behind in the ghetto.

Malcolm represents an abrasive, "in-your-face" assertion of blackness, a "don't mess with me" attitude. Young blacks love Malcolm's courage to speak the truth that whites did not want to hear. They love his righteous and fearless anger, his eloquence, wit, and self-confidence. Malcolm said in public what most blacks felt but were afraid to say except in private among themselves. He was able to talk defiantly to white people because he did not want anything from them. Here was a black man with only an eighth grade education who, through self-discipline, acquired the intellectual ability to hold his own in debates with black and white scholars. On tee-shirts, sweaters, jackets, and caps, young blacks wear Malcolm's name and face with pride. It is their way of saying, "We are proud to be black like Malcolm, and we don't care who is offended by it." This may sound like a trivial statement to whites, who have never had their identity as human beings seriously questioned. But for young blacks who did not make it in the white man's society and who are told daily by its institutional structures that they are worthless, Malcolm X is a source of inspiration and hope that they can be somebody even in an environment of despair and death.

A Reversal of Places

In contrast to the contemporary "Malcolmania," as one scholar called it, interest in Martin King is declining, especially among young blacks. Martin's vision of the beloved community is sometimes openly denounced as ineffectual, or worse, as complicit with white racism. One does not see caps with K's and not many tee-shirts, sweaters, and jackets with Martin's face and name. He is rarely quoted by rap musicians, and other hip-hop artists seem to pay no attention to him. No epic movie is being planned on Martin's life, and there is little debate about him in the African-American community. Even black college students, who benefit the most from Martin's civil rights work, are more enamored of Malcolm X and black nationalism. From the middle of the 1950s to the middle of the 1980s, Martin King occupied the dominant place in the pantheon of African-American leaders. Among blacks over fifty he still holds that place, but among the young grassroots and college blacks today, the dominant place belongs to Malcolm, with King hardly ever being mentioned.

What are we to make of this reversal of places between Malcolm and Martin? Is it a good or a bad thing for the pendulum to swing toward Malcolm and away from Martin? Anyone who has read my book *Martin & Malcolm & America: A Dream or A Nightmare* or has heard me talk about Martin and Malcolm knows that nothing could please me more than the resurgence of interest in Malcolm X. Uncritical adoration of Martin by both blacks and whites and knee-jerk disparagement of Malcolm have created the false impression that Martin had all the answers and Malcolm had nothing to contribute, or worse, was a hindrance in the black free-dom struggle.

Both Martin and Malcolm are needed for a critical understanding of the meaning of America from the vantage point of its inhabitants of African descent. Martin and Malcolm symbolize the two great resistance tradi-tions in black history—integrationism and black nationalism. Who are we? Are we African or American or both? In 1903, the great black scholar W. E. B. Du Bois, in *The Souls of Black Folk*, called the struggle for black iden-tity in America a "peculiar sensation," a "double-consciousness," "two warring ideals in one dark body, whose dogged strength alone keeps it from being torn asunder." Martin and Malcolm together embodied both aspects of the African-American struggle for identity. If we choose one and reject the other, it is like splitting ourselves in half, leading to our certain death. We cannot choose between them and still survive as a healthy people.

What concerns me the most about the resurgence of interest in Mal-colm X is that many young blacks are acting as if they do not need Martin King. They are committing the same mistake that their elders made when they ignored Malcolm and exclusively embraced Martin. Civil rights lead-ers of the 1970s and 1980s gave uncritical praise to Martin's achieve-ments without even acknowledging the contribution of Malcolm. Young blacks are making a similar error today. They rap about Malcolm's pro-found analysis of America's racism without even mentioning how Martin organized a movement to fight against the racism that Malcolm analyzed. Spike Lee's movie, although a good introduction to the life of Malcolm, makes this same mistake. He portrays Malcolm's life and message without paying sufficient attention to Martin's challenging critique, thereby creat-ing a Malcolm devoid of his complexity. Erring on either side of the mis-take, taking Malcolm without Martin or vice versa, is detrimental to black self-understanding. Both mistakes distort the meaning of America for blacks and whites and hide the nature of their struggle to create in Amer-ica a meaningful life together.

The Radical Martin

Looking at Martin King without sufficient attention to the provocative presence of Malcolm X created an image of King that was primarily defined by and for white America. He is portrayed as the acceptable Negro leader, standing in front of the Lincoln Memorial in 1963, frozen there, looking into the heavens, proclaiming his dream of an America without racial animosity. White people adore the nonviolent "I Have a Dream" Martin, as if he said nothing else about America on that day or afterwards. Without Malcolm's challenging presence, we cannot see clearly the radical Martin, the one who in 1966 to 1968 moved toward Malcolm.

The radical Martin acknowledged that racism was much more deeply embedded in American life than he had initially realized. Many northern whites who supported Martin's campaign against racism in the distant South opposed him when he took the movement to the North and challenged de facto segregation in housing, education, and government. He quit talking about his dream. "I saw that dream turned into a nightmare," he said. Martin declared that there was more racism in Chicago and other northern cities than in Mississippi and the rest of the South. He even acknowledged that "temporary segregation" may be the only way to achieve a genuinely integrated society. He realized, as Malcolm did before him, that tokenism seemed to be the only kind of integration that white people would accept.

The radical Martin was also an anti-war activist and a challenger of the economic order. He called racism, war, and poverty the three great evils of his time. Opposition to the war in Vietnam and to poverty and racism at home and abroad became Martin's major obsession as he proclaimed God's judgment upon America. His opposition was more than just a political protest. It was a theological and prophetic condemnation of America. He had a deep spiritual conviction that the God of the universe is going to establish justice in the world whether America likes it or not. "God is not a playboy," Martin shouted in a sermon, as if he were a biblical prophet, proclaiming God's wrath upon nations that "trample on the needy" and "bring ruin to the poor." "If something doesn't happen soon," Martin said, "I'm convinced that the curtain of doom is coming down on the U.S."

The radical Martin King sounds like Malcolm X. That is why we seldom hear about him during the King holiday celebrations in January. When President Reagan and the Congress established the King holiday, "They voted for Martin's 'I Have a Dream' speech," Andrew Young correctly said. "They didn't vote for his anti-Vietnam speech or his challenge to Lyndon Johnson about ending poverty." Unfortunately, civil rights leaders have done too little to correct the distorted image that whites created for Martin. Putting him in conversation with Malcolm would go a long way toward correcting the distortion.

Malcolm Distorted

Just as Martin King's followers separated him from Malcolm X, thereby allowing his image to be co-opted by white America, Malcolm X's devotees are separating him from Martin, thereby allowing his image to be co-opted by black conservatives and vulgar, dogmatic black nationalists. Malcolm is often portrayed as a black Republican or as a gun-toting black revolutionary. In reality, he was neither. But without an informed, critical portrayal of Malcolm's life and message in dialogue with Martin King and in the historical context of the black freedom struggle of the 1950s and 1960s, Malcolm's image can be manipulated into a point of view he would have despised.

"Was Malcolm X a Republican?" asked Juan Williams, a national correspondent for *The Washington Post.* In an article by that title in the *Gentlemen's Quarterly,* Williams cites several black conservatives who give an affirmative answer. "If Malcolm X were alive today, he would be a black conservative," says Robert L. Woodson, President of National Center for Neighborhood Enterprises. "Everything I do comes right out of Malcolm's playbook." Tony Brown, the TV talk show host, agrees. "I think Malcolm X was essentially a black Republican by today's standards," Brown says. "I use two basic criteria to come to that conclusion. Number one, Malcolm was for individual opportunity. Number two, he was for self-help. This is Republican philosophy. It is right in line with Garvey, Elijah Muhammad, Booker T. Washington, and, most of all, Malcolm X." Even Clarence Thomas, the Supreme Court Justice, claims Malcolm's legacy and can quote him from memory and at length.

What black conservatives are doing in claiming Malcolm X is "proof-texting." Like some people reading the Bible, they select only the passages that support what they already believe. They do not present the complete Malcolm, the one who was critical of white society and of black intellectuals who use their minds to make whites feel better about the crimes they committed against blacks. Black conservatives say what their white counterparts, like Pat Buchanan and Senator Jesse Helms, want to hear, something Malcolm, after his break with the Black Muslims, could never have done. It is true that, as a spokesperson for Elijah Muhammad, Malcolm found himself in conversation with the Ku Klux Klan. That was Elijah Muhammad's Malcolm and not Malcolm thinking for himself. Black conservatives are closer to the philosophy of Elijah Muhammad (who today is represented by Louis Farrakhan) than they are to Malcolm X. Malcolm was a sophisticated international thinker whose philosophy was too political to be contained by the religio-economic philosophy of Elijah Muhammad.

Black conservatives want African-Americans to choose between affirmative action programs (which they reject) and self-help programs (which they embrace), as if the two are contradictory. This is a false choice, and no groups in America are expected to make that choice except blacks and other people of color. Whites do not have to make that choice, especially the men of their group. No group has had more affirmative action programs than they—more than 200 years of them. While blacks were reduced to slavery and Indians were being massacred by the U.S. Army, white men established themselves as the sole rulers of the country and owners of the land. They have doled out privileges to one another as if people of color were not human beings. Only in the last two decades have people been talking about affirmative action programs for blacks, women, and other people of color, and white men have been the first to protest about their rights being denied. The people who took everyone else's rights and never treated any other group as their equal are now claiming that affirmative action programs and entitlements for blacks, women, and other people of color deny them equal justice. Statements like that would not deserve a serious reply but for the fact that they are uttered by the mighty. Such people would not know what true justice means if they saw the Statue of Liberty walking down the street. We need Malcolm X to give us the words to reply to their twisted logic. Malcolm warned blacks about tricky whites who can make the criminal look like the victim and the victim like the criminal. He also warned us about the black intellectuals, who are so interested in being accepted by their white peers that they cannot think in the interest of their community.

Turning to the other distortion of Malcolm, young blacks who separate Malcolm from Martin emphasize his rejection of nonviolence and, by implication, suggest that he advocated violence. But they must be reminded that Malcolm did not carry a gun and never committed an act of violence.

It is interesting to note that Martin, the apostle of nonviolence, did more to create situations of violence between blacks and whites than Malcolm, the so-called prophet of violence. Of course, Malcolm exposed the hypocrisy of whites, who advocated nonviolence for blacks but were not themselves nonviolent. But he did not advocate violence. Malcolm advocated self-defense, the right of blacks to defend themselves when violently attacked by their enemies.

However, even Malcolm's self-defense philosophy was misunderstood. He did not fight whites with guns. He fought them with his intelligence. He contended that the pen was more powerful than the sword. He studied hard so that he could effectively argue the case of blacks in the world court of reason. Malcolm spoke of his debates with white intellectuals as verbal battles, in which the most effective weapons were words, which he called philosophical and theological bullets. He loved to fight with his mind because he believed that he had the truth on his side. He could not wait to do battle with the professors and students at Harvard, Yale, Oxford, and other white institutions of learning. It did not matter what discipline persons represented or who was in the audience, Malcolm was always ready to shape his presentation to what he needed to defeat the opponents of freedom.

Young blacks often fail to grasp the intellectual Malcolm. They are often more interested in "X" clothes and caps than in Malcolm's ideas. Many have not even read his *Autobiography* or any serious commentary on his life and message. They merely cite slogans, like "by any means necessary" as if it were equated with picking up the gun. "Any means," as Malcolm's daughter Attallah Shabazz rightly said, "can involve reading books and studying hard." "Without education," Malcolm warned, "you are not going anywhere in this world."

Young blacks need to get in touch with the intellectual Malcolm and to be transformed by the encounter. To know Malcolm is also to know him in relation to Martin because they were fighting in the same struggle for the same cause. "Dr. King," Malcolm said, "wants the same thing I want—freedom." For both, freedom meant black people affirming their dignity as human beings and demanding that white people treat them accordingly. "If you are not ready to die for it, put the word 'freedom' out of your vocabulary," Malcolm told blacks. Martin told them the same thing: "A [person] who won't die for something is not fit to live." Both Martin and Malcolm did more than just talk about freedom. And they both paid the ultimate price.

Most people who talk about Martin and Malcolm have not studied them, do not know them in the context of their time, and thus cannot assess their meaning for us today. When Supreme Court Justice Clarence Thomas and other black conservatives can claim allegiance to Malcolm and President Ronald Reagan and other white conservatives can claim Martin, then we know that a lot of intellectual work needs to be done so that the true meanings of Martin and Malcolm are not co-opted by their enemies.

Martin was a *political revolutionary*. He transformed the political and social life of black and white Americans. The impact of Martin King's life and message is so profound and widely acknowledged that one hardly needs to make a case for it.

But what about Malcolm X? "What did Malcolm X ever do for the black people," asks Carl T. Rowan, the well-known syndicated black columnist. Both Rowan and Virginia Governor L. Douglas Wilder (now former) agreed with the late Supreme Court Justice Thurgood Marshall, who said that Malcolm never did "one concrete thing" to lift the level of black people's lives and thus "would not miss him if Malcolm had never lived."

It is unfortunate that prominent black professionals are often so blinded by their own success in this society that they cannot see the obvious. Malcolm was a *cultural revolutionary*. He changed the way black people think about themselves. He revolutionized the black mind, transforming docile Negroes and self-effacing colored people into proud blacks and self-confident African-Americans. Both Carl Rowan and Douglas Wilder should acknowledge that Malcolm's legacy created the cultural space for them to be *black* people. They were once Negroes, as most of us were. Even Justice Marshall, the great defender of the political rights of blacks, was transformed from a Negro to an Afro-American. It is unfortunate that he did not acknowledge Malcolm's contribution to his changed identity.

More than anyone else, Malcolm taught blacks that they should be proud of their African origin. "You can't hate the roots of the tree," he said, "and not hate the tree. You can't hate your origin and not end up hating yourself." Malcolm emphasized that the self-confidence to live as free human beings could be achieved only through a people's knowledge of their past. "Just as a tree without roots is dead," he said, "a people without history or cultural roots become a dead people." Malcolm ridiculed blacks who said, "I ain't left nothing in Africa." "Why, you left your mind in Africa," he retorted.

Embracing Martin and Malcolm

Martin and Malcolm embodied in their lives and work the African American struggle for identity in a society that is not sure what to do with us. There is a little bit of Martin and Malcolm in all African-Americans. But many, especially those among the middle class, are reluctant to reveal the Malcolm part of themselves, especially in the presence of whites. They push Malcolm down below their consciousness, sometimes even forgetting that he was ever a part of them.

Most whites are not prepared to listen to the harsh truths of Malcolm X. They like Martin King because, as one white university student said, he "went about everything in the right way," which really means white people's way. Malcolm chose "a more destructive way," which really means a way contrary to the desires of whites. Since Martin spoke a message that appealed to whites, they saw their own image in him and embraced what they saw. That is why they joined with blacks to make King's birthday a national public holiday. There is no possibility that America will bestow the same honor on Malcolm X.

Most whites want blacks to choose Martin over Malcolm, but blacks and other Americans interested in justice should never celebrate Martin without giving equal place to Malcolm. We should not listen to Martin's "I Have a Dream" speech without also listening to Malcolm's answer in his "Message to the Grass Roots." "While King was having a dream," Malcolm said, "the rest of us Negroes are having a nightmare." Without confronting the American nightmare that Malcolm bore witness to, we will never be able to create the beloved community articulated so well by Martin King. How can we overcome racism if we do not admit how deeply this cancer is embedded in American history and culture? Malcolm, not Martin, is the best source for understanding racism and its consequences in America.

But the Afrocentric lovers of Malcolm must be reminded that destroying racism is not the only goal of the struggle for freedom. We blacks must be free not only for ourselves but also for others. On this point, Martin was right, and we must listen to his counsel. "All life is interrelated," he said. "All . . . are caught in an inescapable network of mutuality. Whatever affects one directly affects all indirectly." Neither blacks nor whites or others can be what they ought to be until all realize their full potential.

Blacks must begin with Malcolm, that is, with a healthy regard for themselves—their history and culture as it stretches back to the continent of Africa. But we must not stop with Malcolm. To do so would stunt our growth and thus hinder the realization of our human potential. We must embrace Martin too, as passionately and lovingly as we embrace Malcolm. I know that such a demand will be difficult for many lovers of blackness. But Martin's vision of black people living together with all human beings as brothers and sisters is as important as Malcolm's vision of blacks living together as one. The human family is as important as the black family, because we either learn to live together with others, or we will perish together. We must choose life and not death.

To choose life means to see that racism is not the only contradiction affecting the quality of human life. There are other social evils just as harmful as racism. They include sexism, classism, heterosexism, and the wanton disregard of the earth. Accenting Malcolm's and Martin's critique of racism is not enough. We also must criticize Malcolm and Martin for their failures, especially their blatant sexism, and their silence on homophobia in the black community and the larger society. If we are going to make a new future for ourselves with others, we will need to develop creative and self-critical leadership. We must not deify Martin and Malcolm. They were only human beings with assets and liabilities like all of us. If we do not identify their weaknesses and seek to overcome them, then we will perpetuate them.

Let us, therefore, create an America—not just for Martin and Malcolm, or for whites and blacks but for Latinos, Indians, and Asians and for women in all groups, for gay men and lesbians—for every people, every culture and every faith in this land. When we can do that, we will have achieved the goal for which Martin, Malcolm, and all freedom fighters have struggled.

Going Forward

The church must always be that community of people that is looking for and identifying with those who are voiceless.

—*Enquiry*, March–May, 1971

New Roles in the Ministry:
A Theological Appraisal

Many problems arise concerning the church and its ministry, because we forget what these terms mean in the context of the gospel of Jesus. Aside from the customary verbal confessions of belief in Jesus Christ that we have been conditioned to say in prayers, sermons, and other religious situations, a large number of churchpeople seldom reflect in their everyday lifestyle a faith commitment to the One who was crucified on Golgotha's hill. Our church is an impostor, because we no longer believe the gospel we proclaim. There is a credibility gap between what we say and what we do. While we may preach sermons that affirm the church's interests in the poor and the downtrodden, what we actually do shows that we are committed to the "American way of life," in which the rich are given privileged positions of power in shaping the life and activity of the church, and the poor are virtually ignored. As a rule, the church's behavior toward the poor is very similar to the society at large: The poor are charity cases. Our negligence of them is symbolized in the small offering taken in their name every Sunday morning in most black churches. It is appalling to see some black churches adopting this condescending attitude toward the victims, because these churches were created in order to fight against slavery and injustice. For many slaves, the Black Church was God's visible instrument for freedom and justice. Therefore, to have contemporary middle-class black Christians treating the poor as second-class members of the church is a disgrace not only to the Scripture but also to our black religious heritage.

Because our churches adopt their value system from the American capitalistic society and not from Jesus Christ, church offices are more often than not valued as indications that one has achieved a certain status in life. This partly accounts for the fact that women are not permitted in any denomination to exercise power commensurate with their numbers, and in some denominations are even denied ordination. Although there is room for legitimate debate in these matters, it seems clear that no appeal to Scripture or church tradition can remove the suspicion that all who stand against the equality of women in every dimension of the Church's life do so in the light of the political and social interests of men. Whatever the exegesis of Scripture and tradition one may advocate, one fact is certain: When a particular interpretation of Scripture benefits people who hold positions of power, it can never be the gospel of Jesus.

No amount of clever reasoning can camouflage the obvious social, economic, and political interests involved in the subordination of women in the church. Black women know that their ministry has been severely limited, and they also know why. That is, they know *who* benefits from their oppression. That is the reason they now openly speak of "new roles in the ministry." Such a theme is not only appropriate, but necessary, so that attention can be called to certain apostasies and heresies in the Black Church.

The need for a definition of new roles for women and men in the Black Church arises not from the fact that the gospel is new or is changing. The opposite is the case: There is a *constancy* about the gospel that is derived from the One who is the content of its message. Anyone who encounters the biblical God experiences the divine constancy. In the Scriptures, God's constancy is spoken of as divine faithfulness, that is, God's promise to be with and for the people in time of trouble. Theologians of the early church, paying more attention to Greek philosophy than to the Bible, spoke of the divine constancy in terms of the absence of suffering in the Being of God. But more than one thousand years later, black slaves took the tradition *back* to the Scriptures by expressing their confidence in a divine constancy that was clearly derived from biblical roots.

> *God is a God!*
> *God don't never change!*
> *God is a God*
> *An' He always will be God.*

This constancy was the foundation of their faith and the source of black slaves' confidence that God had not left them alone in servitude. In this essay I want to examine the idea of new roles in the ministry for black men and women in the light of the constancy of the gospel of Jesus.

The Holy Spirit and Social Reality

One of the most important and perplexing questions in systematic theology is the relation between the gospel and culture. What is this gospel that does not change? What is it that we preach and sing about that is the same today as yesterday and will be the same tomorrow and forevermore? Unless we answer this question, then there is no way to identify the new roles that our ministry is required to take in our faithfulness to the gospel of Jesus. By failing to identify the universal dimension of the gospel and to subject it to the judgment of Scripture and the traditions of the church, we leave ourselves vulnerable to the charge of ideology, that is, allowing the gospel to be defined by our cultural and political interests. While I do not agree with Karl Barth's assertion that there is an "infinite qualitative distinction" between God and humanity, it is still true that we seek a Christian lifestyle and proclamation that are not simply the values of our society or community. This means that we must ask the critical question, "What is the gospel, and how is it different from my own social conditioning?"

However, before we can define the gospel and then develop new roles in the ministry on the basis of its proclamation, it is necessary to describe the theological and social context in which my perspective on the gospel has been shaped. I do not believe that it is possible to understand what the gospel is all about in terms of its demands on people in our world unless one encounters the Spirit, that is, God's presence with the people. The Spirit refers to God's gift of the power of insight so that one can hear and do the truth as revealed in the biblical witness. Without an openness to the power and guidance of the divine Spirit and her presence in the world, we will not understand what the gospel is. One should not belittle the value of disciplined intellectual effort in the life of the church, but the gospel is more than intellectual study. Sometimes intellectual formulations give us a false confidence about our understanding of the truth. This has often been the case with the literary and historical criticism of the Bible. The truth of the Bible is simply not accessible apart from the Spirit.

To claim that the Spirit is needed to understand what the gospel is, is to say that our resources alone are not enough to know who Jesus is. To speak of Jesus and his gospel is to speak of his Spirit who opens up dimensions of reality that are not reducible to our intellectual capacity. The Spirit is the power to hear and do the truth as lived by the people. Without an openness to walk and talk with Jesus and to be led by a Spirit not of our own creation, there is no way to hear the gospel and to live out its meaning in our ministry.

But lest we think that God's Spirit is merely a pious feeling in our hearts, it is necessary to point out the relations between social reality and God's presence in the world. The only way to encounter God's Spirit is to have one's religious consciousness formed in a political context. The social and political context of the victims is indispensable for hearing our true calling, a vocation that is always bound up with the liberation of victims from servitude. It is not possible for anyone to hear the divine Spirit's call into the Christian ministry, and at the same time derive his or her perception of that ministry from an ecclesiastical structure that oppresses women.

One does not need a seminary education to know that oppression in any form is a contradiction of God's Spirit. Indeed, I firmly believe that the insight into the radical contradiction between the divine Spirit and human oppression is disclosed to people only when they find their consciousness being formed in a community of victims. There will be no new roles in the ministry for women and men unless they are created in the struggle of freedom for the victims of the land. We do not learn this insight in seminaries, because they are largely defined by the existing structures of power. We may hear about Marx, Fanon, and Gutiérrez in white seminaries, but we must not mistake revolutionary rhetoric for actual praxis in the community of victims. Rhetoric is learned in the classrooms by reading Marx's *Das Kapital* and Fanon's *Wretched of the Earth*. But if we are to take Marx seriously when he says, "It is not consciousness that determines life but life that determines consciousness," then we must conclude that a true revolutionary consciousness is formed only in the social context of victims. Only as we join the poor in their struggle can we encounter the divine Spirit of liberation disclosed in their fight for justice.

The Gospel Defined

What is this gospel that can only be understood in the social and political context of victims and from which new styles of ministry must be shaped in the Black Church? I do not want to spend too much time repeating what I have written and said elsewhere. Yet I will say something about defining the gospel, partly to avoid being misunderstood, but more because I come from that tradition of black preachers who contended that one should never pass up an opportunity to say a word about Jesus. Therefore I am compelled by the nature of my vocation to say a word about what we call the "gospel of Jesus."

To put it as clearly as I know how: *The Christian gospel is God's good news to the victims that their humanity is not determined by their victimization.* This means that the poor do not have to adjust to poverty; the oppressed do not have to reconcile themselves to humiliation and suffering. They can do something to change not only their perception of themselves, but also the existing structures of oppression. Indeed, this is what the Exodus, the prophets, and the Incarnation are all about. These events and people are God's way of saying that injustice is a contradiction of the divine intention of humanity. Persons, therefore, who embark on a vocation in the Christian ministry and do not view their calling as a commitment to the victims of the land are not really servants of the gospel of Jesus. We may be servants of the United Methodist or A.M.E. denominations, but not of the One whom the Lucan Evangelist reported as saying:

> The Spirit of the Lord is upon me
> because he has anointed me to preach good news to the poor.
> He has sent me to proclaim release to the captives
> and recovering of sight to the blind,
> to set at liberty those who are oppressed,
> to proclaim the acceptable year of the Lord.
>
> *(Luke 4:18–19)*

Jesus' consciousness was defined by his identity with the liberation of the weak and helpless. That is why the Lucan account tells us that he was born in a stable at Bethlehem. We are also told that Jesus defined his ministry for the poor and not the rich. Jesus' identity with the victims led to his condemnation as a criminal of the Roman State. If Jesus had been born in the emperor's court and had spent most of his life defending the interests of the rulers of that court, then what I am saying would have no validity at all. It is because the Scripture is so decisively clear on this matter that I insist on the liberation of the victim from social and economic oppression as the heart of the gospel. Anything less than this message is an ideological distortion of the biblical message.

Therefore, whatever new styles we create, they must never be allowed to camouflage the true meaning of the gospel. Our endeavor to "get with it," to be "up-to-date" or avant-garde must never deter us from our calling.

I like being fashionable as much as anybody else. There is nothing wrong with that, if it does not become a substitute for the substance of our faith. This faith is universal and is identical with God's will to liberate the victims of the land.

To go further, not only must the new styles not obscure the gospel, they must actually be derived from the gospel. Otherwise we run the risk of having our ministry controlled by another Lord. This is the danger of every theological movement. Whether one speaks of the old or new quest of the historical Jesus, liberalism or neo-orthodoxy, secular theology or liberation theologies among Latin Americans, white women, or black people, we must never forget the basic proclamation and praxis that make the gospel *the* gospel in our cultural and political settings.

Whatever we do at Garrett-Evangelical, or Union and Yale, we must not forget about the faith of our mothers and fathers. For it was this faith that enabled our grandparents to survive the slave ships and a lifetime of servitude in North America. Not much has been written about their faith, since they were not white and thus not privileged to learn to read and write theological discourses. Instead, we read about their enslavers and the theological justifications they made in defense of white supremacy and American domination. Of course, the validity of the faith of our mothers and fathers must not be determined by theological criteria devised by the descendents of slave masters. Rather, the authenticity of our parents' faith should be decided by whether or not that faith empowered them to live as they sang. They sang that Jesus is a "bridge over troubled water," that he is the "lily of the valley and the bright and morning star." To test the validity of these faith claims is to ask whether our parents gave up in despair in slavery and oppression or whether they continued to fight in the knowledge and hope that oppressors did not have the last word about their humanity. I think the historical record speaks for itself. We have been bequeathed a faith that brought our grandparents through hard trials and great tribulations. Therefore we should not abandon it in our search of new lifestyles in the ministry. Since this faith has survived the tests of slavery, lynchings, and ghettos and has sustained our parents in their struggle to be something other than what white people said they were, we black heirs of this faith should not be too quick to discard the religion of our ancestors. I believe that we ought to follow unashamedly in their footsteps and sing as they once sang:

Give me that old-time religion,
Give me that old-time religion,
Give me that old-time religion,
It's good enough for me.

The epistemological reason for our confidence in that "old-time religion" is grounded in our claim that "it was good enough for our mothers,"
and "it was tried in the fiery furnace." Therefore, "it's good enough for you
and me." Our parents also claimed that "it will make you love everybody,"
and "will do when you are dying." This religion must be the source for our
definition of new roles in the ministry.

New Roles in the Ministry: Black Women and Men

What are these new roles that are required for the Church to remain faithful to the gospel of Jesus expressed in black people's old-time religion? To
answer the question, I would like to say a word about new roles in the
Black Church for women and men. For obvious reasons, this is not an easy
subject for me to talk about in that I, like most, have been socially conditioned to accept what white culture has defined as the woman's place in
the church and society. And even though I may assert the liberation of
black women, that public assertion alone is no guarantee that I truly
share the commitment that black women should not be oppressed by
anybody, including black male clergy. But regardless of the question that
may remain about the validity of my conversion, the gospel is quite clear
on this matter. The gospel bears witness to the God who is against oppression in any form, whether inflicted on an oppressed group from the outside
or arising from within an oppressed community. The Exodus is the prime
example of the first instance, and the rise of prophecy is a prominent example of the second. But in both cases, Yahweh leaves no doubt that oppression is not to be tolerated. Therefore, people who claim to believe in the
biblical God and also claim that this God supports the subordination of
women to men have not really understood the Bible. They have distorted
it and thus confused cultural limitations and errors with the message
itself.

If the biblical message is one of liberation, then a ministry based on that
message must be creative and liberating. There is no place for differences

in the roles of men and women in the ministry. God has created man and woman as equals, that is, as co-partners in service of freedom. Therefore, whatever differences are found in present-day churches arise from human sin, that is, the will of men to dominate and control women. If we are to be true ministers of the gospel, then we must create new roles for everyone so that the distinctions between man and woman for the purpose of domination are no longer a reality for our churches. We must liberate our own community from its own internal destructiveness, so that we will be free to fight against oppression in the larger society.

It is a contradiction for black men to protest against racism in the white church and society at large and then fail to apply the same critique to themselves in their relation to black women. This contradiction led Sister Frances Beale to comment that the black man "sees the system for what it is for the most part, but where he rejects its values on many issues, when it comes to women, he seems to take his guidelines from the pages of the *Ladies Home Journal.*"[1]

If black people are going to create new roles in the ministry, black men will have to recognize that the present status of black women in the ministry is not acceptable. Since the gospel is about liberation, it demands that we create structures of human relations that enhance freedom and not oppression.

I know that such affirmations are more easily said than done. Where then do we begin? Liberation is not an individual's agenda but, rather, the commitment of the black community. If we black men and women shall achieve freedom, we must do it together. Accordingly, the test of the authenticity of our commitment to freedom is found not only in what we say about freedom generally, but in what we do about the liberation of victims within our community. We cannot support a subordinate ministry for women and also claim to be for the liberation of the oppressed. How is black men's insistence on the subordination of black women in the church and society any different from white people's enforcement of black subordination? No matter how much we wish the similarity to be nonexistent, it is unmistakably present. This point has been clearly stated by Anna Hedgman:

> We have had the extra burden of being women. But if you just review
> the problems that women face, you need only substitute the word

Afro-American people for the word women and you have the same
problems—job discrimination, want ads that discriminate, and false
stereotypes.[2]

Moreover, when the heat has cooled and the dust has cleared in the black
man and woman debate, the black male's arguments against authentic female empowerment, as defined from the black woman's perspective, are
virtually the same as the white racist arguments against black people. The
similarity of the arguments should at least be enough to cause black men
to question heretofore accepted dogma about the secondary role that has
been created for women in the Black Church.

I think the time has come for black men and women to create new roles
in the ministry so that the church can better serve as a liberating agent in
the community. But the question is, Where do we look for role models in
the ministry? Who will provide the resources that we will use for the definition of our ministry? Where will we turn for inspiration, that is, for images that will shape our perceptions of ourselves and what our ministry
ought to be? We could say the gospel of Jesus, but that is too easy and consequently does not reflect sufficiently the ambiguity of the relation between culture and the gospel. There is no gospel that is not at the same
time related to politics and culture. Therefore whatever we may say about
the otherness in the gospel, we cannot avoid asking what cultural and historical resources we will use to organize our perceptions and images of the
Christian ministry. Will we turn to Europe or Africa, to white American
Christianity or to the black religious tradition?

This question is especially applicable to black men whose definition of
ministry in relation to women appears to be derived from white church
traditions. If our definitions of the ministry are uncritically derived from
people who have systematically tried to oppress us, is it not reasonable to
conclude that we ought to be suspicious of their models of the ministry? If
our perception of the woman's place in the ministry is derived from beliefs
and doctrines concocted by people who enslaved our grandparents, how
do we know that their doctrines about the woman's place are not inti-
mately connected with their beliefs concerning black people's place? Is it
not possible that the two doctrines are derived from the same root disease?
This does not necessarily mean that the struggles of white women are
identical with black people's liberation. It does mean that oppressions are

interconnected, and if black men are incapable of self-criticism, we will be guilty of the same crimes against our women as white men are against theirs.

I believe that the resources for our creation of new roles must come from our own tradition. Whatever we may think about the difficulties of male-female relations in the black community, we know that we have a common heritage, which reaches back to our African homeland. We are an African people; we cannot affirm that too often, because we live in a land where people try to make us believe that we have no identity except what is given by white oppressors. Both black women and men were stolen from Africa and brought on ships in chains to the shores of the Americas. Both were made to work in the fields from sun-up to nightfall. No distinctions were made between black men and women in relation to the brutality meted out in slavery. A Gullah woman's comment is graphic and to the point: "Ah done been in sorrow's kitchen and ah licked de pots clean."

But despite white brutality, we have not been destroyed or defeated. We still believe that "we shall overcome." This hope is not a "pie-in-the-sky" religion, but the religion of our grandparents who tested it in the cotton fields of Arkansas, Alabama, and Mississippi. If we create new roles in the ministry on the basis of this religion, there will be no place for those who want to oppress their sisters. We need all the strength, courage, and power that we can get in order to fight against the principalities and powers of this world.

Therefore we conclude with an appeal to black sisters and brothers in the church: The time has come for us to deal honestly with our differences, our hurts, and our pains. We cannot pretend any longer that all is well and that the problem of male-female relations is limited to the white community. It is in the black community as well; and it is time that we face up to the need to speak openly and frankly about what is right and wrong in our community in relation to black men and women. We must continue the hard task of healing the wounds that we inflict on one another. For it is only as we build strong and healing relationships with each other that we are then given the strength and courage to "keep on keeping on" until freedom comes for all humankind.

Black Theology and the Black College Student

B lack religion and theology are not popular subjects among young blacks, especially those who attend white colleges and universities. Most university blacks are alienated from the religion of their mothers and fathers, and, like their white counterparts, often identify religion as the opiate of the people. Sometimes young black students uncritically equate black religion with white Christianity and thus contend that all talk about Jesus and God, so dominant in black churches, must cease if black people are going to liberate themselves from the values that enslaved them. During the sixties and early seventies it was not uncommon to hear young black radicals proclaim that "Christianity is the white man's religion, and it must be destroyed along with white oppressors." When they did appeal to religion in their articulation of black consciousness, they embraced Islam or African Traditional Religions rather than Christianity. The assumption was that nothing white could liberate black people from a bondage created and perpetrated by whites. Black Christianity was also rejected, because it was regarded as the defender of the white values of American life and culture.

An illustration of this attitude toward black Christianity was found at the Congress of African People (CAP), held in Atlanta, Georgia, in 1970. At that time, CAP was thoroughly nationalist under the leadership of Amiri Baraka (LeRoi Jones). I was asked by Baraka to lead the religion workshop, because he had been impressed by my book *Black Theology and Black Power.* I will never forget that meeting. Many participants contended that we are an African people and that that continent will be the source of our liberation. There were about one hundred people in my workshop and nearly as many views on religion. Each person was sure that he or she had the whole truth and nothing but the truth, and any deviation from the party line was interpreted as heresy or apostasy. Needless to say, there were many heresy battles between the various viewpoints expressed. I spent most of my time trying to referee so that the discussion would stay at a level of mutual respect of opposing views. But all participants agreed that Christianity was the white man's religion, and that it deserved no status in an African Congress. I felt very uneasy with denunciations of black Christianity, because I was a *Christian* theologian and a preacher. From childhood I had come to know the Black Church as an instrument of survival and liberation in my community. Therefore, when these young blacks, who appeared to know very little about the past and present reality of the Black Church, began to denounce the God of my parents and grandparents, I wanted to challenge the authenticity of their denunciations.

I began to think about the function of religion in black life and the role it has played in the affirmation of black humanity. The same religion these young blacks were denouncing has been the source of black people's hope that "trouble won't last always." The particularity of that hope was expressed every time the people made their stand against white structures that attempted to delimit black humanity. In a personal manner, this hope was concretized when my father made his stand against the white folks of Bearden. The year was 1954. Whites had declared that they were going to lynch Charlie Cone because he refused to withdraw his name from a legal school case. I can remember my father's defiant response: "Let the sons of bitches come, they may get me, but they can be sure that I will take some of them with me." He stayed up all night waiting, but they never came. His courage to stand was derived from the very source that these young blacks in Atlanta were denying.

How was it possible for one to grow up black in America and not be aware of the spiritual sources of strength and courage in black culture and history? This was my question as I tried to reconcile the apparent contradictions between the faith of the young university student and the mature Black Church member. It appeared that the young had grown up without any knowledge of the faith of their parents and were thus cut off from the true origin of their struggle.

I can remember clearly my father's contention that he could stand against white folks and the evil they represented because God was standing with him. Other black people of Macedonia made the same faith affirmation. That was why they shouted and prayed so passionately on Sunday morning. Contrary to the popular opinion on college and university campuses, Black Church worship is not primarily compensatory or otherworldly in any negative sense. Black Church worship was born in the struggle of the people to affirm worth in their lives and not to let personhood be destroyed by white people. This is what the black folks of Macedonia meant when they sang:

> *Through the years I kept on toiling.*
> *Toiling through the storm and rain.*
> *Patiently, waiting and watching till*
> *my Savior comes again.*
> *I am comin' Lord,*
> *Trustin' in your word.*
> *Keep me from the path of sin;*
> *Hide me in thy love,*
> *Write my name above.*
> *O when the gates swings open,*
> *I'll go walkin' in.*

The very presence of the people together meant that God had given them a little more strength and courage to fight until freedom comes. The people's singing and preaching was not primarily an outward display of piety but an acknowledgment of the felt presence of God in their midst, "buildin' them up where they are torn down and proppin' them up on every leanin' side." The songs of Zion always took on an added meaning in the context of an immediate crisis as with my father. When a brother or a sister was in trouble, the people put a little extra passion and soul into their songs and prayers in order to express their solidarity with the one in trouble. Their religious expressions also confirmed their confidence that God does not leave the little ones alone in a world full of trouble. In situations of extreme suffering, as is so often the case in black life, the people turn to God as that *other* reality who places an indelible stamp of humanity on their being. That is the meaning of the song:

> *Without God I could do nothing;*
> *Without God my life would fail;*
> *Without God my life would be rugged;*
> *Just like a ship without a sail.*

It is an interesting and sad contradiction that many nationalists of the sixties and seventies had little or no place for their elders in the struggle. The struggle was almost exclusively youth-oriented, a very un-African way to run a revolution. And perhaps that is why the revolution had very little staying power. It had no roots in the culture of our ancestors. I think that the lack of staying power of most so-called radicals, of whatever revolutionary persuasion, is due to their failure to ground the struggle in the life and culture of the *people*. We may claim that we do but our actions betray what we say. Most of us are too busy being black, African, or whatever recent term we select as the "in" word than to care about our people. The absence of radical blacks in the Black Church is all the evidence needed to show that they do not mean what they say.

The rejection of Christianity by young blacks is not simply a nationalist phenomenon or simply an event of the past. It is found today in many college and university settings. Many young black college students, especially on white campuses, dismiss Christianity and the Black Church on intellectual grounds. They tend to identify both with a lack of intelligence. They view the Black Church as the place where unintelligent blacks go to sing and shout about another world, because they cannot do anything to change this world. I have lectured at more than 150 colleges and universities in the United States and have taught in the North, South, East, and West. I think it is fair to say that I have been exposed to a broad range of what black college students think about religion. One thing is sure: Black religion is not a popular course of study among blacks in academic circles.

Another way of noting the rejection of black Christianity and the Black Church is to notice their absence in most Black Studies programs. Black Studies have been known to offer courses ranging from "cornbread and black-eye peas" to the most remote kingdoms in African history, all of which have their place and validity in an appropriate context. But seldom does one find courses dealing with the historical and contemporary Black Church in a positive and creative manner. How is it possible to deal with the center of the black experience and history, however they might be defined, without coming to terms with the most visible faith of the people? How is it possible to tell our story without Richard Allen, James Varick, and Henry McNeal Turner? How can we really understand Harriet Tubman and Sojourner Truth without probing the faith that they claim held them together for struggle? How can we say we are leading a struggle of, for, and by the people when we have no knowledge of, nor respect for, the Jesus they claimed "picked them up, turned them around, and placed their feet on solid ground?" Even if we cannot hold the faith they affirm, are we not at least obliged to respect their faith if we expect to understand why the people regard it as the only source of their survival?

I am the first to admit that there is much validity for this young black critique of the Black Church. There are pimps in religion as there are on the streets in the black community. Far too many black preachers are more concerned about their personal interests than they are about the liberation of black people from white political oppression. Far too many church people are more concerned about erecting a new church building than they are about building a new black community so that all black children will have a more humane place in which to live. I do not deny that many black churches contradict what they claim to affirm. One could spend hours and days talking about the shortcomings of the Black Church. So let us admit that it is a black middle-class institution that tends to reflect the values of white America. Then why should anyone be concerned about the absence of young blacks in the church and especially a black liberation theologian?

There are several responses to this question. First of all, my difficulty with young college and university blacks who rejected black Christianity and the church was their failure to apply their logic in other contexts. If the Black Church reflects white values, then so do the universities, hospitals, legal institutions, and other aspects of black life of which these radicals avail themselves, but with no apparent contradictions in their consciousness. Practically every institution in America is white. Indeed, the institution that is perhaps least white in terms of actual control is the very one that many radical blacks rejected. Why did these ultra-black revolutionaries reject a black institution? Such a question was almost impossible to ask. Black radicals were concerned about revolution, not discussion, understandably so, because the pain of black life was and is an ever present reality. People get tired of talking about alternatives when blood is flowing in the streets. Black radicals were not about to discuss alternatives with black preachers whom they sometimes accurately identified with passivity. When David Hilliard, then chairman of the Black Panther Party, spoke at the annual convention of the National Committee of Black Churchmen in Oakland (1969), his comment to black preachers was: "You are the enemy unless you are ready to pick up the gun and shoot the pigs." There was no dialogue. Hilliard had all the answers, black preachers were at best questionable allies, and he was simply testing out that possibility.

While I can understand black radicals' impatience with the church during and after that period, we still must ask, what function does the criticism have? Does it bring us together for struggle or does it separate us into the "good" and the "bad," as if there are no contradictions among the so-called radicals and the educated. Every black person lives a life full of contradictions, but the greatest contradiction of all is to pretend that they are absent. The critique we apply to the church and its preachers ought to be applied to ourselves as well. For self-criticism is the beginning of wisdom. What we claim to be wrong with the Black Church is also wrong in other professional and institutional contexts. The task, then, is not to be destructive in our critique of the Black Church but creative so that the church can become what it was created to be: the liberating agent of the oppressed of the land.

My second response is directed toward the tendency of young university blacks to let white people define what Christianity or black religion is. The power of definition is the key to one's ability to control one's future and thus one's perception of the self. If white people are allowed to define what is going on in our community, then they can enslave us mentally. They can tell us who we are, and we will believe it.

Unfortunately, most young blacks do not recognize that what they think about the Black Church is often determined by what whites have taught them to believe. One can hardly doubt that there is a connection between the education in white institutions and alienation from one's roots in the black community. When one studies in white institutions from fourteen to twenty years, reading about white Western civilization, one cannot emerge from that brainwashing experience without being affected at the center of one's consciousness. The one institution that still shows a measure of black consciousness and control is the Black Church, and the extent of black alienation from the church in the university shows how much white people have succeeded in dividing our community. One thing is certain: If we are to be liberated, we will have to do it *together*. The oppressor knows that. Therefore, much of his strategy is designed to separate us so that we will fight among ourselves rather than against the oppressive structures that dehumanize us.

I hope the young university blacks will realize this and thus find their way back into the church. For I must admit that I cannot support any revolution that excludes my mother, and she believes in Jesus. She claims that "when you are in trouble and burdened with care and don't know what to do, take it to Jesus and he will fix it for you. He will lift your burdens and ease your pain. Jesus," she contends, "can do most anything." Now I know this testimony will not go over big with young blacks whose theoretical frame is derived from white educational institutions. But if we believe that white oppressors will not provide the means of black liberation, then we had better become suspicious of what is happening to black consciousness in white educational contexts. It could be that our freedom is not found in Karl Marx or any black facsimile thereof, but in the shouts and moans in the black experience. If freedom is found in our experience, it must have something to do with the triumph of the weak over the strong. This is the theme of black folklore with Br'er Rabbit, High John the Conquerer, and Stagolee. This same theme is found in the songs and sermons of black people. Is it possible that our freedom is found here in black life and culture and nowhere else? This is certainly the belief of the Black Church.

Most university blacks have a distorted view of the Black Church. They think of it too superficially, as if all that preaching and shouting are nothing but a reflection of black people's passive acceptance of their oppression. Sometimes this is true, of course; the exciting fact is that sometimes it is not. The black struggle for freedom was born in the church and has always had religious overtones. We must not forget that Nat Turner was a Baptist preacher. It was the Reverend Henry H. Garnett, a Presbyterian minister, who urged slaves in 1843 to demand their freedom, because liberty was a gift from God. The same biblical theme was present in David Walker's *Appeal*. It was Bishop Henry M. Turner who, in 1898, said that "God is a Negro," thereby separating black religion from white religion and connecting the AME Church with the black struggle of freedom. Whatever we might think about Adam Clayton Powell, Jr., and Martin Luther King, Jr., we must not forget their contribution to our struggle. Both connected their struggle with the Black Church and with Jesus' claim that he came to set at liberty those who were oppressed. When we look at the history of the Black Church as told in Gayraud Wilmore's *Black Religion and Black Radicalism*, there are many shortcomings and failures. But there is also the constant theme of liberation and God's will to establish justice in the land.

Let us return momentarily to the situation of slavery. We must not forget that slavery was brutal and cruel and not every black could expect to escape from its oppressive structures. Not every black could buy his freedom or run away in the night. What is a people to do when there are so few concrete possibilities for the affirmation of their humanity? When the existing societal structures define them as nobody, how are they to know that they are somebody? Must their humanity always depend upon their willingness to fight politically against impossible odds as if the affirmation of their somebodiness depends upon their willingness to commit suicide? Must every black take Nat Turner's option in order to affirm his humanity? I do not think so.

Black religion and theology provided additional options for black slaves to fight for freedom in history without being determined by their historical limitations. This is what the concept of heaven means in the slave songs and sermons. Heaven was not so much a cosmological description of the next world as it was a theological affirmation that black humanity cannot be defined by what white people do to our physical bodies. Whites may enslave us and define Africans as savages, but the words of slavemasters do not have to be taken seriously when we know that we have a heavenly Father who cares about his own.

In the midst of political economic disfranchisement, black slaves held themselves together and did not lose their spiritual composure because they believed that their worth transcended governmental decisions. That was why they looked forward to "walking in Jerusalem just like John" and longed for the "camp meeting in the Promised Land."

I know that some blacks will be suspicious of the so-called political implications of the slave songs and sermons that emphasized heaven. They have been taught so much about the opiate character of heaven that it is hard for them to see any political significance in the term. Frederick Douglass's claim about double-meaning notwithstanding, heaven-talk for many blacks is a sign of weakness and passivity. I do not want to debate this point because there is evidence on both sides, and it is not my intention to show that black Christianity is the whole truth and nothing but the truth. But we must ask about present alternatives and their *sources*. Do we have alternatives that are more meaningful than the struggles of our grandparents? If we do, then where do they come from?

My contention is simply this: black religion does not have to be, and often is not, the opiate of the people. If we believe that our struggle is dependent on the majority of black people and not on an intellectual elite, then we must go where the masses are—the church. No one speaks to as many people on a regular basis as the black preacher. Anyone who claims to be for the liberation of the people and yet remains separated from their religious hopes and dreams is a liar. To be for the people is to be united with them in their struggle to realize on earth what they have seen in heaven. We must not play intellectual games with the people's conception of their struggle. Rather, we must get down with them and feel what they feel so that we, like they, will know that "we'll soon be free." This freedom, about which the people prayed and preached, is not a pious feeling in the heart. Freedom is a struggle wrought out of the blood and tears of our mothers and fathers. It is a risk derived from the conviction that death is preferable to life in servitude.

White Theology Revisited

> Are doctors of divinity blind, or are they hypocrites? I suppose some are
> the one, and some the other, but I think if they felt the interest in the poor
> and the lowly, that they ought to feel, they would not be so *easily* blinded.
> Linda Brent [Harriet Jacobs], *Incidents in the*
> *Life of a Slave Girl*, [1861] 1973

People often ask me whether I am still angry as when I wrote *Black Theology and Black Power*. When I hear that question I smile to contain my
rage: I remain just as angry because America, when viewed from the perspective of the black poor, is no closer to Martin Luther King, Jr.'s dream of
a just society than when he was killed. While the black middle class has
made considerable economic progress, the underclass, despite America's
robust economy, is worse off in 1998 than in 1968. The statistics are well
known, yet they still fail to shock or outrage most Americans.

America is still two societies: one rich and middle-class and the other
poor and working-class. William J. Wilson called the underclass "the truly
disadvantaged,"[1] people with few skills to enable them to compete in this
technological, informational age. To recognize the plight of the poor does
not require academic dissection. It requires only a drive into the central
cities of the nation to see people living in places not fit for human habi-
tation.

What deepens my anger today is the appalling silence of white theologians on racism in the United States and the modern world. Whereas this
silence has been partly broken in several secular disciplines, theology remains virtually mute. From Jonathan Edwards to Walter Rauschenbusch
and Reinhold Niebuhr to the present, progressive white theologians, with
few exceptions, write and teach as if they do not need to address the radical
contradiction that racism creates for Christian theology. They do not write
about slavery, colonialism, segregation, and the profound cultural link
these horrible crimes created between white supremacy and Christianity.
The cultural bond between European values and Christian beliefs is so
deeply woven into the American psyche and thought process that their

identification is assumed. White images and ideas dominate the religious life of Christians and the intellectual life of theologians, reinforcing the "moral" right of white people to dominate people of color economically and politically. White supremacy is so widespread that it becomes a "natural" way of viewing the world. We must ask therefore: Is racism so deeply embedded in Euro-American history and culture that it is impossible to do theology without being antiblack?

There is historical precedent for such ideological questioning. After the Jewish Holocaust, Christian theologians were forced to ask whether anti-Judaism was so deeply woven into the core of the gospel and Western history that theology was no longer possible without being anti-Semitic? Recently feminists asked an equally radical question, whether patriarchy was so deeply rooted in biblical faith and its male theological tradition that one could not do Christian theology without justifying the oppression of women. Gay and lesbian theologians are following the feminist lead and are asking whether homophobia is an inherent part of biblical faith. And finally, Third World theologians, particularly in Latin America, forced many progressive First World theologians to revisit Marx's class critique of religion or run the risk of making Christianity a tool for exploiting the poor.

Race criticism is just as crucial for the integrity of Christian theology as any critique in the modern world. Christianity was blatantly used to justify slavery, colonialism, and segregation for nearly five hundred years. Yet this great contradiction is consistently neglected by the same white male theologians who would never ignore the problem that critical reason poses for faith in a secular world. They still do theology as if white supremacy created no serious problem for Christian belief. Their silence on race is so conspicuous that I sometimes wonder why they are not greatly embarrassed by it.

How do we account for such a long history of white theological blindness to racism and its brutal impact on the lives of African people? Is it because white theologians do not know about the tortured history of the Atlantic slave trade, which, according to British historian Basil Davidson, "cost Africa at least fifty million souls"?[2] Have they forgotten about the unspeakable crimes of colonialism? Author Eduardo Galeano claims that 150 years of Spanish and Portuguese colonization in Central and South America reduced the indigenous population from 90 million to 3.3 million.[3] During the twenty-three-year reign of terror of King Leopold II of

Belgium in the Congo (1885–1908), scholarly estimates suggest that approximately 10 million Congolese met unnatural deaths—"fully half of the territory's population."[4] The tentacles of white supremacy have stretched around the globe. No people of color have been able to escape its cultural, political, and economic domination.

Two hundred forty-four years of slavery and one hundred years of legal segregation, augmented by a reign of white terror that lynched more than five thousand blacks, defined the meaning of America as "white over black."[5] White supremacy shaped the social, political, economic, cultural, and religious ethos in the churches, the academy, and the broader society. Seminary and divinity school professors contributed to America's white nationalist perspective by openly advocating the superiority of the white race over all others. The highly regarded church historian Philip Schaff of Union Seminary in New York (1870–1893) spoke for most white theologians in the nineteenth century when he said: "The Anglo-Saxon and Anglo-American, of all modern races, possess the strongest national character and the one best fitted for universal dominion."[6]

Present-day white theologians do not express their racist views as blatantly as Philip Schaff. They do not even speak of the "Negro's cultural backwardness," as America's best known social ethicist, Reinhold Niebuhr, often did and as late as 1965.[7] To speak as Schaff and Niebuhr spoke would be politically incorrect in this era of multiculturalism and color blindness. But that does not mean that today's white theologians are less racist. It only means that their racism is concealed or unconscious. As long as religion scholars do not engage racism in their intellectual work, we can be sure that they are as racist as their grandparents, whether they know it or not. By not engaging America's unspeakable crimes against black people, white theologians are treating the nation's violent racist past as if it were dead. But, as William Faulkner said, "the past is never dead; it is not even past." Racism is so deeply embedded in American history and culture that we cannot get rid of this cancer simply by ignoring it.

There can be no justice without memory—without remembering the horrible crimes committed against humanity and the great human struggles for justice. But oppressors always try to erase the history of their crimes and often portray themselves as the innocent ones. Through their control of the media and religious, political, and academic discourse "they're able," as Malcolm put it, "to make the victim look like the criminal and the criminal to look like the victim."[8]

Even when white theologians reflect on God and suffering, the problem of theodicy, they almost never make racism a central issue in their analysis of the challenge that evil poses for the Christian faith. If they should happen to mention racism, it is usually just a footnote or only a marginal comment. They almost never make racism the subject of a sustained analysis. It is amazing that racism could be so prevalent and violent in American life and yet so absent in white theological discourse.

President Clinton's call for a national dialogue on race has created a context for public debate in the churches, the academy, and the broader society. Where are the white theologians? What guidance are they providing for this debate? Are they creating a theological understanding of racism that enables whites to have a meaningful conversation with blacks and other people of color? Unfortunately, instead of searching for an understanding of the great racial divide, white religion scholars are doing their searching in the form of a third quest for the historical Jesus. I am not opposed to this academic quest. But if we could get a significant number of white theologians to study racism as seriously as they investigate the historical Jesus and other academic topics, they might discover how deep the cancer of racism is embedded not only in the society but also in the narrow way in which the discipline of theology is understood.

Although black liberation theology emerged out of the Civil Rights and Black Power movements of the 1960s, white theologians ignored it as if it were not worthy to be regarded as an academic discipline. It was not until Orbis Books published the translated works of Latin American liberation theologians that white North American male theologians cautiously began to talk and write about liberation theology and God's solidarity with the poor. But they still ignored the black poor in the United States, Africa, and Latin America. Our struggle to make sense out of the fight for racial justice was dismissed as too narrow and divisive. White U.S. theologians used the Latin American focus on class to minimize and even dismiss the black focus on race. African-Americans wondered how U.S. whites could take sides with the poor out there in Latin America without first siding with the poor here in North America. It was as if they had forgotten about their own complicity in the suffering of the black poor, who often were only a stone's throw from the seminaries and universities where they taught theology.

White theology's amnesia about racism is due partly to the failure of black theologians to mount a persistently radical race critique of Christian theology—one so incisive and enduring that no one could do theology without engaging white supremacy in the modern world. American and European theologians became concerned about anti-Semitism only because Jews did not let them forget the Christian complicity in the Holocaust. Feminists transformed the consciousness of American theologians through persistent, hard-hitting analysis of the evils of patriarchy, refusing to let any man anywhere in the world forget the past and present male assault against women. It is always the organic, or "grassroots," intellectuals of an exploited group, rather than the elite, who must take the lead in exposing the hidden crimes of criminals.

While black theologians' initial attack on white religion shocked white theologians, we did not shake the racist foundation of modern white theology.[9] With the assistance of James Forman's "Black Manifesto"[10] and the black caucuses in Protestant denominations, black theological critiques of racism were successful in shaking up the white churches. But white theologians in the seminaries, university departments of religion and divinity schools, and professional societies refused to acknowledge white supremacy as a theological problem and continued their business as usual, as if the lived experience of blacks was theologically vacuous.

One reason black theologians have not developed an enduring radical race critique stems from our uncritical identification with the dominant Christian and integrationist tradition in African-American history. We are the children of the Black Church and the Civil Rights movement. The spirituals have informed our theology more than the blues, Howard Thurman more than W. E. B. Du Bois, Martin Luther King, Jr., more than Malcolm X, and prominent male preachers more than radical women writers. We failed to sustain the critical side of the black theological dialectic and opted for acceptance into white Christian America. When whites opened the door to receive a token number of us into the academy, church, and society, the radical edge of our race critique was quickly dropped as we enjoyed our newfound privileges.

Womanist and second generation black male theologians, biblical scholars, and historians are moving in the right directions. The strength of these new intellectual developments lies in their refusal to simply repeat the ideas of the original advocates of black theology. They are breaking new theological ground, building on, challenging, and moving beyond the founders of black liberation theology. Using the writings of Zora Neale

Hurston, Alice Walker, Toni Morrison, and a host of other women writers past and present, womanist theologians broke the monopoly of black male theological discourse. They challenged the male advocates of black theology to broaden their narrow focus on race and liberation and incorporate gender, class, and sexuality critiques and the themes of survival and quality of life in our theological discourse.[11] Some younger black male critics locate the limits of black liberation theology in its focus on blackness,[12] and others urge a deeper commitment to it, focusing especially on the slave narratives.[13] Still others suggest that the Christian identity of black theology contributes to black passivity in the face of suffering.[14] Biblical scholars and historians are laying exegetical and historical foundations for a critical rereading of the Bible in the light of the history and culture of black people.[15] All these critiques and proposals make important contributions to the future development of black theology. What troubles me about all these new theological constructs, however, is the absence of a truly radical race critique.

Malcolm X was the most formidable race critic in the United States during the twentieth century. He was the great master of suspicion in regard to American democracy and the Christian faith. His critique of racism in Christianity and American culture was so forceful that even black Christians were greatly disturbed when they heard his analysis. His contention that "Christianity was a white man's religion" was so persuasive that many black Christians left churches to join the Nation of Islam. The rapid growth of the religion of Islam in the African-American community is largely due to the effectiveness of Malcolm's portrayal of Christianity as white nationalism. It was Malcolm via the Black Power movement who forced black theologians to take a critical look at white religion and to develop a hermeneutic of suspicion regarding black Christianity. How can African-Americans merge the "double self"—the black and the Christian—"into a better and truer self,"[16] especially since Africa is the object of ridicule in the modern world and Christianity is hardly distinguishable from European culture?

While we black theologians appropriated Malcolm in our initial critique of white religion, we did not wrestle with Malcolm long enough. We quickly turn to Martin King. The mistake was not in moving toward King but rather in leaving Malcolm behind. We need them both as a double-edged sword to slay the dragon of theological racism. Martin and Malcolm represent the yin and yang in the black attack on white supremacy. One without the other misses the target—the affirmation of blackness in the beloved community of humankind.

Malcolm alone makes it too easy for blacks to go it alone and for whites to say "begone!" Martin alone makes it easy for whites to ask for reconciliation without justice and for middle-class blacks to grant it, as long as they are treated specially. Putting Martin and Malcolm together enables us to overcome the limitations of each and to build on the strengths of both and thereby move blacks, whites, and other Americans (including Indians, Asians, Hispanics, gays, lesbians, and bisexuals) toward healing and understanding.

There can be no racial healing without dialogue, without ending the white silence on racism. There can be no reconciliation without honest and frank conversation. White supremacy is still with us in the academy, in the churches, and in every segment of the society because we would rather push this problem under the rug than find a way to deal with its past and present manifestations.

Most whites do not like to talk about white supremacy because it makes them feel guilty, a truly uncomfortable feeling. They would rather forget about the past and think only about the present and future. I understand that. I only ask whites to consider how uncomfortable the victims of white supremacy must feel, as they try to cope with the attitudes of whites who act as if white supremacy ceased with the passage of the 1964 Civil Rights Bill. At least when people express their racism overtly, there is some public recognition of its existence and a possibility of racial healing. Silence is racism's best friend.

"A time comes when silence is betrayal,"[17] Martin King said. That time has come for white theologians. White supremacy is one of the great contradictions of the gospel in modern times. White theologians who do not oppose racism publicly and rigorously engage it in their writings are a part of the problem and must be exposed as the enemy of justice. No one, therefore, can be neutral or silent in the face of this great evil. We are either for it or against it.

Black theologians must end their silence too. We have opposed racism much too gently. We have permitted white theological silence in exchange for the rewards of being accepted by the white theological establishment. This is a terrible price to pay for the few crumbs that drop from the white master's table. We must replace theological deference with courage, and thereby confront openly and lovingly silent white racists or be condemned as participants in the betrayal of our own people.

In 1903 W. E. B. Du Bois prophesied, "The problem of the twentieth century is the problem of the color-line,—the relation of the darker to the lighter races of [people] in Asia and Africa, in America and the islands of the sea."[18] As we stand at the threshold of the next century, that remarkable prophesy is as relevant today as it was when Du Bois uttered it. The challenge for black theology in the twenty-first century is to develop an enduring race critique that is so comprehensively woven into Christian understanding that no one will be able to forget the horrible crimes of white supremacy in the modern world.

Whose Earth Is It, Anyway?

The earth is the Lord's and all that is in it,
The world, and those who live in it.

— *Psalm 24:1 (RSV)*

We say the earth is our mother—we cannot own her; she owns us.

— *Pacific peoples*

The logic that led to slavery and segregation in the Americas, colonization and apartheid in Africa, and the rule of white supremacy throughout the world is the same one that leads to the exploitation of animals and the ravaging of nature. It is a mechanistic and instrumental logic that defines everything and everybody in terms of their contribution to the development and defense of white world supremacy. People who fight against white racism but fail to connect it to the degradation of the earth are anti-ecological—whether they know it or not. People who struggle against environmental degradation but do not incorporate in it a disciplined and sustained fight against white supremacy are racists—whether they acknowledge it or not. The fight for justice cannot be segregated but must be integrated with the fight for life in all its forms.

Until recently, the ecological crisis had not been a major theme in the liberation movements in the African-American community. "Blacks don't care about the environment" is a typical comment by white ecologists. Racial and economic justice has been at best only a marginal concern in the mainstream environmental movement. "White people care more about the endangered whale and the spotted owl than they do about the survival of young blacks in our nation's cities" is a well-founded belief in the African-American community. Justice fighters for blacks and the defenders of the earth have tended to ignore each other in their public discourse and practice. Their separation from each other is unfortunate because they are fighting the same enemy—human beings' domination of one another and nature.

The leaders in the mainstream environmental movement are mostly middle and upper-class whites who are unprepared culturally and intellectually to dialogue with angry blacks. The leaders in the African-American community are leery of talking about anything with whites that will distract from the menacing reality of racism. What both groups fail to realize is how much they need each other in the struggle for "justice, peace, and the integrity of creation."[1]

In this essay I want to challenge the black freedom movement to take a critical look at itself through the lens of the ecological movement and to challenge the ecological movement to critique itself through a radical and ongoing engagement of racism in American history and culture. I hope we can break the silence and promote genuine solidarity between the two groups and thereby enhance the quality of life for the whole inhabited earth—humankind and otherkind.

Expanding the Race Critique

Connecting racism with the degradation of the earth is a much-needed work in the African-American community, especially in black liberation theology and the black churches. Womanist theologians have already begun this important intellectual work. Delores Williams explores a "parallel between defilement of black women's bodies" and the exploitation of nature. Emilie Townes views "toxic waste landfills in African-American communities" as "contemporary versions of lynching a whole people." Karen Baker-Fletcher, using prose and poetry, appropriates the biblical and literary metaphors of dust and spirit to speak about the embodiment of God in creation. "Our task," she writes, "is to grow large hearts, large minds, reconnecting with earth, Spirit, and one another. Black religion must grow ever deeper in the heart."[2]

The leadership of African-American churches turned its much-needed attention toward ecological issues in the early 1990s. The catalyst, as usual in the African-American community, was a group of black churchwomen in Warren County, North Carolina, who in 1982 lay their bodies down on a road before dump trucks carrying soil contaminated with highly toxic PCBs (polychlorinated biphenyl) to block their progress. In two weeks more than four hundred protesters were arrested, "the first time anyone in the United States had been jailed trying to halt a toxic waste landfill."[3] Although local residents were not successful in stopping the landfill construction, that incident sparked the attention of Civil Rights and black church leaders and initiated the national environmental justice movement. In 1987 the United Church of Christ Commission of Racial Justice issued its groundbreaking "Report on Race and Toxic Wastes in the United States." This study found that "among a variety of indicators race was the best predictor of the location of hazardous waste facilities in the U.S."[4] Forty percent of the nation's commercial hazardous waste landfill capacity was in the three predominant African-American and Hispanic communities. The largest landfill in the nation is found in Sumter County, Alabama, where nearly 70 percent of its seventeen thousand residents are black and 96 percent are poor.

In October 1991 the First National People of Color Environmental Leadership Summit was convened in Washington, D.C. More than 650 grassroots and national leaders from fifty states, the District of Columbia, Mexico, Puerto Rico, and the Marshall Islands participated. They represented more than three hundred environmental groups of color. They all agreed that "[i]f this nation is to achieve environmental justice, the environment in urban ghettoes, barrios, reservations, and rural poverty pockets must be given the same protection as that provided to the suburbs."[5]

The knowledge that people of color are disproportionately affected by environmental pollution angered the black church community and fired up its leadership to take a more active role in fighting against "environmental racism," a phrase coined by Benjamin Chavis who was then the Director of the UCC Commission on Racial Justice.[6] Bunyan Bryant, a professor in the School of Natural Resources and Environment at the University of Michigan and a participant in the environmental justice movement, defines environmental racism as "an extension of racism":

> It refers to those institutional rules, regulations, and policies or government or corporate decisions that deliberately target certain communities for least desirable land uses, resulting in the disproportionate exposure of toxic and hazardous waste on communities based upon certain prescribed biological characteristics. Environmental racism is the unequal protection against toxic and hazardous waste exposure and the systematic exclusion of people of color from environmental decisions affecting their communities.[7]

The more blacks found out about the racist policies of the government and corporations the more determined they became in their opposition to environmental injustice. In December 1993, under the sponsorship of the National Council of Churches, leaders of mainline black churches held a historic two-day summit meeting on the environment in Washington, D.C. They linked environmental issues with civil rights and economic justice. They did not talk much about the ozone layer, global warming, the endangered whale, or the spotted owl. They focused primarily on the urgent concerns of their communities: toxic and hazardous wastes, lead poisoning, landfills and incinerators. "We have been living next to the train tracks, trash dumps, coal plants and insect-infested swamps for many decades," Bishop Frederick C. James of the A.M.E. Church said. "We in the black community have been disproportionately affected by toxic dumping, disproportionately affected by lead paint at home, disproportionately affected by dangerous chemicals in the workplace." Black clergy also linked local problems with global issues. "If toxic waste is not safe enough to be dumped in the United States, it is not safe enough to be dumped in Ghana, Liberia, Somalia nor anywhere else in the world," proclaimed Charles G. Adams, pastor of Hartford Memorial Baptist Church in Detroit. "If hazardous materials are not fit to be disposed of in the suburbs, they are certainly not fit to be disposed of in the cities."[8]

Like black church leaders, African-American politicians also are connecting social justice issues with ecology. According to the League of Conservation Voters, the Congressional Black Caucus has "the best environmental record of any voting bloc in Congress."[9] "Working for clean air, clean water, and a clean planet," declared Representative John Lewis of Georgia, "is just as important, if not more important, than anything I have ever worked on, including civil rights."[10]

Black and other poor people in all racial groups receive much less than their fair share of everything good in the world and a disproportionate amount of the bad. Middle-class and elite white environmentalists have been very effective in implementing the slogan "Not in My Backyard" (NIMBY). As a result, corporations and the government merely turned to the backyards of the poor to deposit their toxic waste. The poor live in the least desirable areas of our cities and rural communities. They work in the most polluted and physically dangerous workplaces. Decent health care hardly exists. With fewer resources to cope with the dire consequences of pollution, the poor bear an unequal burden for technological development while the rich reap most of the benefits. This makes racism and poverty ecological issues. If blacks and other hard-hit communities do not raise these ethical and political problems, they will continue to die a slow and silent death on the planet.

Every sphere of human existence is determined by ecology. It is not just an elitist or a white middle-class issue. A clean, safe environment is a human and civil rights issue that impacts the lives of poor blacks and other marginal groups. We therefore must not let the fear of distracting from racism blind us to the urgency of the ecological crisis. What good is it to eliminate racism if we are not around to enjoy a racist-free environment?

The survival of the earth, therefore, is a moral issue for everybody. If we do not save the earth from destructive human behavior, no one will survive. That fact alone ought to be enough to inspire people of all colors to join hands in the fight for a just and sustainable planet.

Expanding the Ecological Critique

We are indebted to ecologists in all fields and areas of human endeavor for sounding the alarm about the earth's distress. They have been so effective in raising ecological awareness that few people deny that our planet is in deep trouble. For the first time in history, humankind has the knowledge and power to destroy all life—either with a nuclear bang or a gradual poisoning of the land, air, and sea.

Scientists have warned us of the dire consequences of what human beings are doing to the environment. Theologians and ethicists have raised the moral and religious issues. Grassroots activists in many communities are organizing to stop the killing of nature and its creatures. Politicians are paying attention to people's concern for a clean, safe environment. "It is not so much a question of whether the lion will one day lie down with the lamb," writes Alice Walker, "but whether human beings will ever be able to lie down with any creature or being at all."[11]

What is absent from much of the talk about the environment in First World countries is a truly radical critique of the culture most responsible for the ecological crisis. This is especially true among white ethicists and theologians in the United States. In most of the essays and books I have read, there is hardly a hint that perhaps whites could learn something of how we got into this ecological mess from those who have been the victims of white world supremacy. White ethicists and theologians sometimes refer to the disproportionate impact of hazardous waste on blacks and other people of color in the United States and Third World, and even cite an author or two, here and there throughout the development of their discourse on ecology. They often include a token black or Indian in anthologies on ecotheology, ecojustice, and ecofeminism. It is "politically correct" to demonstrate a knowledge of and concern for people of color in progressive theological circles. But people of color are not treated *seriously*, that is, as if they have something *essential* to contribute to the conversation. Environmental justice concerns of poor people of color hardly ever merit serious attention, not to mention organized resistance. How can we create a genuinely mutual ecological dialogue between whites and people of color if one party acts as if they have all the power and knowledge?

Since Earth Day in 1970, the environmental movement has grown into a formidable force in American society, and ecological reflections on the earth have become a dominant voice in religion, influencing all disciplines. It is important to ask, however, whose problems define the priorities of the environmental movement? Whose suffering claims its attention? "Do environmentalists care about poor people?"[12] Environmentalists usually respond something like Rafe Pomerance puts it: "A substantial element of our agenda has related to improving the environment for everybody."[13] Others tell a different story. Former Assistant Secretary of Interior James Joseph says that "environmentalists tend to focus on those issues that provide recreative outlets instead of issues that focus on equity." Black activist Cliff Boxley speaks even more bluntly, labeling the priorities of environmentalists as "green bigotry." "Conservationists are more interested in saving the habitats of birds than in the construction of low-income housing."[14]

Do we have any reason to believe that the culture most responsible for the ecological crisis will also provide the moral and intellectual resources for the earth's liberation? White ethicists and theologians apparently think so, since so much of their discourse about theology and the earth is just talk among themselves. But I have a deep suspicion about the theological and ethical values of white culture and religion. For five centuries whites have acted as if they owned the world's resources and have forced people of color to accept their scientific and ethical values. People of color have studied dominant theologies and ethics because our physical and spiritual survival partly depended on it. Now that humanity has reached the possibility of extinction, one would think that a critical assessment of how we got to where we are would be the next step for sensitive and caring theologians of the earth. While there is some radical questioning along these lines, it has not been persistent or challenging enough to compel whites to look outside of their dominating culture for ethical and cultural resources for the earth's salvation. One can still earn a doctorate degree in ethics and theology at American seminaries, even here at Union Seminary in New York, and not seriously engage racism in this society and the world. If we save the planet and have a society of inequality, we wouldn't have saved much.

According to Audre Lorde, "the master's tools will never dismantle the master's house."[15] They are too narrow and thus assume that people of color have nothing to say about race, gender, sexuality, and the earth—all of which are interconnected. We need theologians and ethicists who are interested in mutual dialogue, honest conversation about justice for the earth and all of its inhabitants. We need whites who are eager to know something about the communities of people of color—our values, hopes, and dreams. Whites know so little about our churches and communities that it is often too frustrating to even talk to them about anything that matters. Dialogue requires respect and knowledge of the other—their history, culture, and religion. No one racial or national group has all the answers, but all groups have something to contribute to the earth's healing.

Many ecologists speak often of the need for humility and mutual dialogue. They tell us that we are all interrelated and interdependent, including human- and otherkind. The earth is not a machine. It is an organism in which all things are a part of one another. "Every entity in the universe," writes Catherine Keller, "can be described as a process of interconnection with every other being."[16] If white ecologists really believe that, why do most still live in segregated communities? Why are their essays and books about the endangered earth so monological—that is, a conversation of a dominant group talking to itself? Why is there so much talk of love, humility, interrelatedness, and interdependence, and yet so little of these values reflected in white people's dealings with people of color?

Blacks and other minorities are often asked why they are not involved in the mainstream ecological movement. To white theologians and ethicists I ask, "Why are you not involved in the dialogue on race?" I am not referring primarily to President Clinton's failed initiative, but to the initiative started by the Civil Rights and Black Power movements and black liberation theology more than forty years ago. How do we account for the conspicuous white silence on racism, not only in the society and world but especially in theology, ethics, and ecology? I have yet to read a white theologian or ethicist who has incorporated a sustained, radical critique of white supremacy in his/her theological discourse similar to the engagement of anti-Semitism, class contradictions, and patriarchy.

To be sure, a few concerned white theologians have written about their opposition to white racism but not because race critique was essential to their theological identity. It is usually just a gesture of support for people of color when solidarity across differences is in vogue. As soon as it is no longer socially and intellectually acceptable to talk about race, white theologians revert back to their silence. But as Elie Wiesel said in his Nobel Peace Prize Acceptance Speech, "we must always take sides. Neutrality helps the oppressor, never the victim. Silence encourages the tormentor, never the tormented."[17] Only when white theologians realize that a fight against racism is a fight for *their* humanity will we be able to create a coalition of blacks, whites, and other people of color in the struggle to save the earth.

Today ecology is in vogue and many people are talking about our endangered planet. I want to urge us to deepen our conversation by linking the earth's crisis with the crisis in the human family. If it is important to save the habitats of birds and other species, then it is at least equally important to save black lives in the ghettos and prisons of America. As Gandhi said, "the earth is sufficient for everyone's need but not for everyone's greed."[18]

Notes

Introduction: Looking Back, Going Forward

1. James Baldwin, *The Fire Next Time* (New York: Dell, 1964), p. 61.

2. Ibid., p. 21.

3. Ibid., p. 14.

4. Cited in Manning Marable, "The Black Faith of W. E. B. Du Bois: Sociocultural and Political Dimensions of Black Religion," *The Southern Quarterly* 23 (spring 1985), p. 21.

5. Theologian Langdon Gilkey of the University of Chicago made that observation to me in a private conversation. It is unfortunate that he never made a disciplined argument about King's theological importance in his published writings. If he had done so, perhaps American white theologians would not have been as hostile as they were to the rise of black liberation theology.

6. *Malcolm X Speaks*, ed. George Breitman (New York: Grove Press, 1965), pp. 107–108.

7. See *Washington Post*, 23 January 1994, p. G6.

8. *The Fire Next Time*, p. 46.

9. Many people called Malcolm X "the angriest Negro in America." See his *Autobiography* (New York: Ballantine Books, 1986), p. 366.

10. Audrey Smedley, *Race in North America: Origin and Evolution of a Worldview* (Boulder, Colo.: Westview Press, 1993), p. 117.

11. See Reinhold Niebuhr, *Moral Man and Immoral Society* (New York: Charles Scribner's Sons, 1932).

Section I: Black Theology and Black Power

Christianity and Black Power

1. Albert Camus, *The Rebel* (New York: Random House, 1956), p. 13.

2. Stokely Carmichael and Charles Hamilton, *Black Power: The Politics of Liberation in America* (New York: Random House, 1967), p. 47.

3. Friedrich Schleiermacher, *The Christian Faith*, trans. J. Baillie, 1922, p. 9.

Black Spirituals: A Theological Interpretation

1. W. E. B. Du Bois, *The Gift of Black Folk* (1924; reprint, New York: Washington Square Press, 1970), p. 158.

2. Cited in Vincent Harding, "Religion and Resistance Among Antebellum Negroes, 1800–1860," in *The Making of Black America*, vol. 1, ed. August Meier and Elliot Rudwick (New York: Atheneum, 1969), p. 181.

3. Comment by Guy Johnson of the University of North Carolina, cited in Sterling Stuckey, "Through the Prism of Folklore," in *Black and White in American Culture*, ed. J. Chametyky and S. Kaplan (Amherst: University of Massachusetts Press, 1969), p. 172.

4. Karl Marx and Friedrich Engels, *On Religion* (New York: Schocken Books, 1964), p. 42.

5. Miles Fisher, *Negro Slaves Songs in the United States* (New York: Citadel Press, 1953), pp. 27–28, 66–67, 181–185.

6. Ibid., p. 108. It is important to note that Fisher is quoting the conservative estimate of a southern historian.

7. See ibid., chapter 4. Fisher notes that the spirituals were used to convene secret meetings among slaves, and the colony of Virginia prohibited them as early as 1676 (pp. 29, 66ff.). Most colonies joined Virginia in outlawing the secret meetings, but "neither outlawry nor soldiery prevented [them] from hemispheric significance" (p. 67).

8. B. A. Botkin, ed. *Lay My Burden Down* (Chicago: University of Chicago Press, 1945), p. 26.

9. See *Negro Slave Songs*, chapters 1–4.

10. *Life and Times of Frederick Douglass* (1892; reprint, New York: Collier Books, 1962), p. 159.

Black Theology on Revolution, Violence, and Reconciliation

1. Jürgen Moltmann, *Religion, Revolution and the Future*, trans. Douglas Meeks (New York: Charles Scribner's Sons, 1969), p. 131.

2. "Man as Possibility," in *Cross Currents* 18 (summer 1968), p. 274.

3. *Religion, Revolution and the Future*, p. 132.

4. Ernst Bloch, *The City of God*, trans. Marcus Dods (New York: Modern Library, 1950), p. 694.

5. Cited in Roger Garaudy, *From Anathema to Dialogue* (New York: Vintage Books, 1968), p. 98.

6. Cited in Roland Bainton, *Here I Stand* (New York: Abingdon Press, 1950), p. 280.

7. Cited in *From Anathema to Dialogue*, p. 98.

8. George Celestin's "A Christian Looks at Revolution," in *New Theology No. 6*, ed. Martin Marty and Dean Peerman (London: Collier Macmillan, 1969), p. 69.

9. Jacques Ellul, *Violence*, trans. C. G. King's (New York: Seabury Press, 1969), p. 3. In this quotation, Ellul is not defending this viewpoint; he is explicating it.

10. For an account of this dialogue, see Thomas Ogletree, ed., *Opening for Marxist-Christian Dialogue* (Nashville: Abingdon Press, 1968).

11. See particularly Lehmann's *Ethics in a Christian Context* (New York: Harpers, 1963) and his *Ideology and Incarnation* (Geneva: John Knox Association, 1962).

12. *Religion, Revolution and the Future*, p. 103.

13. Ibid., pp. 104–105.

14. Vitaly Baroxoj, "Why the Gospels Are Revolutionary: The Foundation of a Theology in the Service of Social Revolutions," in IDO-C, ed., *When All Else Fails* (Philadelphia: Pilgrim Press, 1970).

15. Fred Hampton was the head of the Chicago branch of the Black Panther Party. He was killed December 4, 1969, in a police raid while sleeping in bed.

16. Thomas Merton, *Faith and Violence* (Notre Dame, Ind.: Notre Dame University Press, 1968), p. 3.

17. *Religion, Revolution and the Future*, p. 143.

18. Franz Fanon, *The Wretched of the Earth* (New York: Grove Press, 1965), p. 255.

19. Ernst Käsemann, *Jesus Means Freedom*, trans. Frank Clarke (London: SCM Press, 1969).

Black Theology and the Black Church: Where Do We Go from Here?

1. This statement first appeared in the *New York Times*, July 31, 1966, and is reprinted in Warner Traynham's *Christian Faith in Black and White* (Wakefield, Mass.: Parameter, 1973).

2. For an account of the rise of the concept of Black Power in the Civil Rights movement, see Stokely Carmichael and Charles Hamilton, *Black Power: The Politics of Black Liberation* (New York: Random House). For Martin King's viewpoint, see his *Where Do We Go from Here: Chaos or Community?* (Boston: Beacon Press, 1968).

3. Cited in Lawrence W. Levine, *Black Culture and Black Consciousness* (New York: Oxford University Press, 1977), p. 207.

4. This is especially true of Charles Long, who has been a provocative discussant about black theology. Unfortunately, he has not written much about this viewpoint. The only article I know on this subject is his "Perspectives for a Study of Afro-American Religion in the United States" (*History of Religions* 11, no. 1, August 1971).

5. The representatives of this perspective include Gayraud S. Wilmore, *Black Religion and Black Radicalism* (New York: Doubleday, 1972), and my brother, Cecil W. Cone, *Identity Crisis in Black Theology* (Nashville, Tenn.: A.M.E. Church, 1976).

6. This statement, issued on June 13, 1969, is also reprinted in *Christian Faith in Black and White* by Warner Traynham.

7. See Julius Nyerere, *Ujamaa: Essays on Socialism* (Dar es salaam: Oxford University Press, 1968), especially chapter 2, entitled "The Arusha Declaration," pp. 13–37.

8. Cited in Jose Miguez Bonino, *Christians and Marxists* (Grand Rapids, Mich.: Eerdmans, 1976), p. 76.

9. Cited in George Padmore, *Pan-Africanism or Communism* (New York: Anchor Books, 1972), p. 323.

10. Cited in *Christians and Marxists*, p. 71.

11. A quotation from Giulio Girardi, cited in *Christians and Marxists*, p. 71.

Section II: Martin and Malcolm

The Theology of Martin Luther King, Jr.

1. Martin Luther King, Jr., "Thou Fool," August 27, 1967, an unpublished sermon delivered at Mount Pisgah Baptist Church, Chicago, Illinois, p. 11. Martin Luther King, Jr., Papers, Series III, Martin Luther King, Jr., Center for Nonviolent Social Change, Atlanta, Georgia (hereafter referred to as King Center Archives).

2. In King's two versions of his "Pilgrimage to Nonviolence," the black religious tradition is not mentioned as an important contribution to his theological perspective. See his *Stride Toward Freedom* (New York: Harper, 1958), pp. 90–107 and

Strength to Love (1963; reprint, Philadelphia: Fortress, 1982), pp. 147–155. On the basis of these accounts alone, one could easily conclude that King did not recognize any important contribution of black religion on his theology. Perhaps he did not during the early years of his ministry but did so in the later years, as I will seek to demonstrate in this essay.

3. *Stride Toward Freedom*, p. 101.

4. King, Jr., *Who Speaks for the Negro?* (New York: Random House, 1965), p. 213.

5. Speaking of his "intellectual quest for a method to eliminate social evil," King said, "I came early to Walter Rauschenbusch's *Christianity and the Social Crisis*, which left an indelible imprint on my thinking by giving me a theological basis for the social concern which had already grown up in me as a result of my early experiences" (*Stride Toward Freedom*, p. 91). See especially chapters 1 and 2 of Rauschenbusch's *Christianity and the Social Crisis* (New York: Macmillan, 1907). For a detailed interpretation of Rauschenbusch's impact on King, see Kenneth L. Smith and Ira G. Zepp, Jr., *Search for the Beloved Community*, chapter 2; and of Ira G. Zepp, Jr., "Intellectual Sources of the Ethical Thought of Martin Luther King, Jr.," chapter 2 (hereafter referred to as "Intellectual Sources").

King's sense of social responsibility appeared early in his thinking. Referring to his call to the ministry on his Crozer application, he wrote: "My call to the ministry was quite different from most explanations I've heard. This decision came about the summer of 1944 when I felt an inescapable urge to serve society. In short, I felt a sense of responsibility which I could not escape."

6. Ibid., p. 100. For several treatments of the impact of personalism on King, see *Search for the Beloved Community*, chapter 5; "Intellectual Sources," chapter 5; L. Harold DeWolf, "Martin Luther King, Jr., as Theologian"; John Ansbro, *Making of a Mind: Martin Luther King, Jr.*, Chapter 3.

7. See ibid., p. 99. King wrote a paper on "Karl Barth's Conception of God" during his doctoral studies at Boston. His comments are typical of many American critics who have not understood Barth or who deliberately distort his theological perspective. Barth was neither an anti-rationalist nor a semi-fundamentalist. For a perspective on Barth similar to King's, see his teacher, L. Harold DeWolf, *The Religious Revolt Against Reason* (New York: Harper, 1949).

8. See especially *Stride Toward Freedom*, pp. 97–98. During his graduate education, King wrote several papers on Niebuhr. See "Reinhold Niebuhr" (14pp.) and "Reinhold Niebuhr's Ethical Dualism" (11pp.), King Center Archives. For a discussion of Niebuhr's influence, see *Search for the Beloved Community*, chapter 4; and "Intellectual Sources," chapter 4.

9. For Gandhi's influence upon King, see his "Sermon on Gandhi," March 22, 1959, Dexter Avenue Baptist Church, Montgomery, Alabama, King Center Archives. Also "My Trip to the Land of Gandhi," *Ebony,* July 1959. See also "Intellectual Sources," chapter 3.

10. *Stride Toward Freedom*, p. 179.

11. Ibid., p. 217.

12. According to black psychologist Clark, "King's insistence that the Negro cannot afford to be corroded by hatred and must therefore discipline himself to love those who despise him is consistent with the Christian tradition and is the antithesis of the doctrine preached by the Nationalists. On the surface, King's philosophy appears to reflect health and stability, while the Black Nationalists betray pathology and instability. A deeper analysis, however, might reveal an unrealistic, if not pathological basis in King's doctrine as well. It is questionable whether masses of an oppressed group can in fact 'love' their oppressor. The natural reactions to injustice, oppression, and humiliation are bitterness and resentment. . . . It would appear, then, that any demand that a victim love his oppressor—in contrast with a mere tactical application of nonviolent, dignified resistance as a moral rebuke with concomitant power to arouse the conscience and effectiveness of others—imposes an additional and probably intolerable psychological burden" (Kenneth Clark, *Dark Ghetto: The Dilemmas of Social Power* [New York: Harper Torchbooks, 1967], p. 218).

13. Henry David Thoreau, *Civil Disobedience* (Westwood, N.J.: Fleming Revel, 1964), p. 14.

14. Martin Luther King, Jr., "The Un-Christian Christian," *Ebony,* August 1965, p. 77.

15. See his often preached sermon, "A Knock at Midnight," June 25, 1967, King Center Archives.

16. Unless indicated otherwise, my account is taken from his sermon "Thou Fool," August 27, 1967, King Center Archives. See also *Stride Toward Freedom*, pp. 134–135; *Strength to Love*, pp. 113f.

17. *Stride for Freedom*, p. 135.

18. Speaking at the sixty-eighth annual convention of the Rabbinical Assembly, King said: "What is necessary now is to see integration in political terms where there is sharing of power. When we see integration in political terms, then we recognize that there are times when we must see segregation as a temporary way-

station to a truly integrated society." "Conversation with Martin Luther King," *Conservative Judaism*, 22 (spring 1968), p. 8.

19. There is no evidence that King moved away from his deep commitment to nonviolence. But he did recognize that the riots in the cities revealed that nonviolence must be taken to a new level of militancy which involved massive disruption of the operation of government. There are many references in King's writings to this change in his thinking during 1966–68. In *The Trumpet of Conscience* (New York: Harper, 1967), he said: "Nonviolent protest must now mature to a new level to correspond to heightened black impatience and stiffened white resistance. This new level is mass civil disobedience" (p. 15). See also "Showdown for Nonviolence," *Look*, 16 April 1968. For an important interpretation of this shift in King's thinking, see David Garrow, *Martin Luther King: Challenging America at Its Core* (New York: Democratic Socialists of America, 1983); and his *The FBI and Martin Luther King, Jr.* (New York: Norton, 1981), chapter 6.

20. The best sources for King's positive affirmations of black power and pride are his unpublished speeches on the "Pre-Washington Campaign," recruiting persons for the Poor People's March on Washington. In Clarksdale, Mississippi (March 19, 1968), he said: "We're going to let our children know that the only philosophers that lived were not Plato and Aristotle, but W. E. B. Du Bois and Alain Locke came through the universe" ("Address to Mass Meeting," p. 7, King Center Archives).

21. As early as 1965, King had become greatly disappointed with many white Christians and other moderates. "The white church . . . has greatly disappointed me. . . . As the Negro struggles against grave injustice, most white churchmen offer pious irrelevancies and sanctimonious trivialities. . . . Over the past several years, I must say, I have been gravely disappointed with white 'moderates.' I am often inclined to think that they are more of a stumbling block to the Negro's progress than the White Citizen's Counciler or the Ku Klux Klanner" (*Playboy*, January 1965). King's classic critique of the white church and other moderates is found in his "Letter from Birmingham Jail" in his *Why We Can't Wait* (New York: Harper, 1963).

22. There are many references of King concerning his dream being turned into a nightmare. One of his most extended statements in this regard is found in *The Trumpet of Conscience*, pp. 75–76.

23. See "Beyond Vietnam: Dr. Martin Luther King's Prophecy for the '80s," a pamphlet of the Clergy and Laity Concerned, p. 2.

24. *Stride Toward Freedom*, pp. 59–60.

25. Martin Luther King, Jr., "Address to the Initial Mass Meeting of the Montgomery Improvement Association," Holt Street Baptist Church, December 5, 1955 (King Center Archives), hereafter referred to as "Holt Street Address."

26. See *Stride Toward Freedom*, p. 62.

27. "Holt Street Address."

28. Ibid. In *Stride Toward Freedom*, King reported: "I urged the people not to force anybody to refrain from riding the buses. 'Our method will be that of persuasion, not coercion.' Emphasizing the Christian doctrine of love, '[O]ur actions must be guided by the deepest principles of our Christian faith. Love must be our regulating ideal. Once again we must hear the words of Jesus echoing across the centuries: 'Love your enemies, bless them that curse you and pray for them that despitefully use you.' In spite of the mistreatment that we have confronted we must not become bitter, and end up by hating our white brothers. As Booker T. Washington said, 'Let no man pull you so low as to make you hate him'" (p. 62). There is nothing like this statement in the original address. There is no reference to Booker T. Washington.

29. Although much research is needed in order to determine the "essential writings" of Martin King, any student of King who has examined the materials at the King Center Archives can easily observe that many of his speeches and much of the material for his books were ghost-written. Working for the movement twenty hours a day, traveling 325 thousand miles and making 450 speeches a year, it was not possible for King to write everything that was published under his name.

30. *Stride Toward Freedom*, p. 84.

31. See Bayard Rustin, "Montgomery Diary," in his *Down the Line* (Chicago: Quadrangle Books, 1971), pp. 55–61. Originally published in *Liberation*, April 1956. See also G. Smiley, "An Interview with Martin Luther King, Jr.," February–March 1956, King Center Archives.

32. See his thirty-page speech at the staff retreat, November 14, 1966, Frogmore, S.C., p. 14. Also important is his address to the 10th Convention of SCLC, August 16, 1967, King Center Archives. Several of King's associates have confirmed his openness to socialism. See David Garrow's interpretation of his socialist leanings in "From Reformer to Revolutionary" and "The Radical Challenge of Martin King," *FBI and Martin Luther King, Jr.*, chapter 6. In a February 27, 1985, letter to David Garrow, C. L. R. James says he remembered that Martin King articulated "ideas which were fundamentally Marxist-Leninist." According to James's recollection, King said: "I don't say such things from the pulpit, James, but that is what I really believe." For a guarded assessment, see also Adam Fairclough, "Was Martin

Luther King a Marxist?" in *History Workshop,* a journal of socialist and feminist historians, spring 1983, pp. 117–125.

33. Martin Luther King, Jr., "In Search for a Sense of Direction," February 7, 1968, fourteen-page address, Vermont Avenue Baptist Church, Washington, D.C., pp. 1, 2, King Center Archives.

34. This statement appears in many of King's addresses and sermons. See especially "Address to Ministers' Leadership Training Program," "Pre-Washington Campaign—to Minister to the Valley," February 23, 1968, p. 18, King Center Archives.

35. Martin Luther King, Jr., "But If Not . . . ," November 5, 1967, Ebenezer Baptist Church, Atlanta, King Center Archives.

36. "Standing by the Best in an Evil Time," August 6, 1967, Ebenezer Baptist Church, Atlanta, King Center Archives. For two good discussions of the development of King's views on Vietnam, see Russell E. Dowdy, "Nonviolence vs. Nonexistence: The Vietnam War and Martin Luther King, Jr." M.A. thesis in the Dept. of History, North Carolina State University, 1983; Adam Fairclough, "Martin Luther King, Jr., and the War in Vietnam," *Phylon,* 45, no. 1 (1984), pp. 19–39. See also Fairclough's excellent "Study of the Southern Christian Leadership Conference and the Rise and Fall of the Nonviolent Civil Rights Movement," Ph.D. diss., University of Keele, U.K., 1977.

Martin Luther King, Jr., Black Theology—Black Church

1. Alex Haley, "Playboy Interview with Martin Luther King," *Playboy* 12 (January 1965), pp. 70–71.

2. Ibid., p. 66.

3. For an interpretation of nationalism and integration in the history of black religious thought, see Gayraud S. Wilmore, *Black Religion and Black Radicalism,* 2d ed. (Maryknoll, N.Y.: Orbis Books, 1983); see also Francis L. Broderick, "The Gnawing Dilemma: Separatism and Integration, 1865–1925," in *Key Issues in the Afro-American Experience,* vol. 2, Nathan Huggins, Martin Kilson, and Daniel Fox (New York: Harcourt Brace Jovanovich, 1971).

Martin Luther King, Jr., and the Third World

1. Today black South Africans and their supporters, under the leadership of Archbishop Desmond Tutu, Allan Boesak, Nelson Mandela, and Winnie Mandela,

and a host of others in the African National Congress and similar organizations, are currently engaged in a protracted life-and-death struggle against apartheid.

2. Cited in Coretta Scott King, *My Life with Martin Luther King, Jr.* (New York: Holt, Rinehart and Winston, 1969), p. 294.

3. In this essay I limit my analysis chiefly to two periods in Martin Luther King, Jr.'s thinking. However, I have found three periods in the development of his life and thought from the time of the Montgomery bus boycott (Dec. 5, 1955) to his assassination (April 4, 1968). The first period is quite brief (early weeks of the boycott) and is defined by his primary focus on *justice*. The second period (early 1956 to fall 1965) focuses primarily on *love*; the third period (1966 to his assassination in 1968) focuses primarily on *hope*. The distinctions are not rigid but rather a matter of emphases in his thinking. In all periods the concerns for justice, love, and hope are present and intertwined. For an interpretation of the development of King's thinking in terms of the three periods, see James H. Cone, "The Theology of Martin Luther King, Jr.," *Union Seminary Quarterly Review*, 40, no. 4 (1986), pp. 21–39.

4. See Martin Luther King, Jr., "The Legitimacy of the Struggle in Montgomery," statement, May 4, 1956, Martin Luther King, Jr., Papers (Martin Luther King, Jr., Center for Nonviolent Social Change, Atlanta), hereafter referred to as King Papers. Martin Luther King, Jr., "The Birth of a New Age," August 7–11, 1956, p. 86, ibid.

5. "Birth of a New Age." King also used this statement in his first major address, and it was repeated in several others. See "Address at Holt Street Baptist Church," December 5, 1955, King Papers.

6. Martin Luther King, Jr., "Facing the Challenge of a New Age," *Phylon* 18 (April 1957), p. 26. This is essentially the address delivered at the Alpha Phi Alpha convention in August 1956, "Birth of a New Age." See Martin Luther King, Jr., "The Time for Freedom Has Come," *New York Times Magazine*, September 10, 1961, pp. 25, 118–119, 25. The quotation from Victor Hugo was frequently used in King's addresses.

7. For King's interpretation of the impact the independence celebration of Ghana had on him, see especially Martin Luther King, Jr., "Birth of a New Nation," address, Dexter Avenue Baptist Church, April 1957, King Papers. See also Homer Jack, "Conversation in Ghana," *Christian Century*, April 10, 1957, pp. 446–448. For King's interpretation of his trip to India, see Martin Luther King, Jr., "My Trip

to the Land of Gandhi," *Ebony* 14 (July 1959), pp. 84–92; Martin Luther King, Jr., "Sermon on Gandhi," March 22, 1959, King Papers. See also Swami Vishwananda, *With the Kings in India* (New Delhi, 1959); Martin Luther King, Jr., "Farewell Statement," New Delhi, India, March 9, 1959, King Papers; and "Statement of Dr. King upon Landing at New York City," March 18, 1959, ibid.

8. "Letter from Birmingham City Jail," *New Leader*, June 24, 1963, p. 8.

9. *Strength to Love* (Philadelphia: Fortress Press, 1981), p. 154; *Stride Toward Freedom* (New York: Harper, 1958), p. 44.

10. See "The American Dream," *Negro History Bulletin* 31 (May 1968), pp. 10–15. The essay was a commencement address at Lincoln University, June 6, 1961.

11. Ibid.

12. "The Acceptance Speech of Martin Luther King, Jr. of the Nobel Peace Prize on December 10, 1964," *Negro History Bulletin* 31 (May 1968), p. 21. See "The Quest for Peace and Justice," Nobel Lecture, Oslo, Norway, December 11, 1964, pp. 1, 5, King Papers.

13. "Playboy Interview: Martin Luther King," a reprint from *Playboy* 12 (January 1965).

14. "Transforming a Neighborhood into a Brotherhood," address for the National Association of Real Estate Brokers, August 10, 1967, p. 9, King Papers.

15. See "Next Stop: The North," *Saturday Review*, 13 November 1965, pp. 33–35, 105. For his response to Watts, see *Where Do We Go from Here: Chaos or Community?* (Boston: Beacon Press, 1968), p. 112.

16. James Bevel, one of King's aides, spoke often of the Chicago slums as a "system of internal colonialism." King also adopted the same description. See his "Chicago Plan," January 7, 1966, p. 3, King Papers. "European Tour," speech, March 1966, p. 8, ibid.

17. *Where Do We Go from Here?*, p. 133.

18. Ibid.

19. See "Thou Fool," sermon, Mt. Pisgah Missionary Baptist Church, Chicago, August 27, 1967, p. 14, King Papers. This sermon includes King's account of the deep crisis of fear during the Montgomery bus boycott that led to his appropriation of the faith of his early childhood. I think this is the most critical turning point in King's life. Although I have always maintained that King's faith, as defined by the Black Church, was indispensable for understanding his life and thought, David J. Garrow was the first person to identify King's "kitchen experience" (as it might be

called) as the decisive experience in defining his faith. See David J. Garrow, "Martin Luther King, Jr., and the Spirit of Leadership," *Journal of American History* 74 (September 1987), pp. 438–438, and *Bearing the Cross: Martin Luther King, Jr., and the Southern Christian Leadership Conference, 1955–1968* (New York: W. Morrow, 1986); and Cone, "Theology of King," pp. 26–39.

20. Luke 1:52 RSV.

21. See Adam Fairclough, "Martin Luther King, Jr., and the War in Vietnam," *Phylon* 45, no. 1 (1984), pp. 19–39. See also Russell E. Dowdy, "Nonviolence vs. Nonexistence: The Vietnam War and Martin Luther King, Jr.," M.A. thesis, North Carolina State University, 1983. On King's dream being turned into a nightmare, see his *The Trumpet of Conscience* (New York: Harper and Row, 1968), pp. 75f.

22. "Why I Am Opposed to the War in Vietnam," sermon, April 30, 1967, p. 8, King Papers.

23. "A Testament of Hope," a reprint from *Playboy* 16 (January 1969), p. 4; "Why I Am Opposed," p. 6.

24. "Why I Am Opposed," pp. 3, 4.

25. "Standing by the Best in an Evil Time," sermon, August 6, 1967, pp. 7–8, King Papers.

26. *Martin Luther King, Jr.: Beyond Vietnam, April 4, 1967, Riverside Church* (New York, 1982), p. 1, pamphlet, King Papers; "Speech at Staff Retreat," May 29–31, 1967, ibid.; and address at a rally of the Pre-Washington Campaign, March 22, 1968, p. 7, ibid.

27. *Trumpet of Conscience*, p. 76.

28. "The Other America," address, March 10, 1968, p. 11, King Papers.

29. "Facing the Challenge of a New Age," p. 34.

30. Ibid.

31. Cited in Pat Watters, *Down to Now: Reflections on the Southern Civil Rights Movement* (New York: Pantheon Books, 1971), p. 366.

32. "To Minister to the Valley," address, February 23, 1968, p. 21, King Papers.

Section III: Going Forward

New Roles in the Ministry: A Theological Appraisal

1. "Double Jeopardy: To Be Black and Female," in *Black Woman*, ed. Toni Cade (New York: Signet Books, 1970), p. 92.

2. Cited by Renée Ferguson, "Women's Liberation Has a Different Meaning for Blacks," in Gerda Lerner, *Black Women in White America: A Documentary History* (New York: Random House, 1973), p. 588.

White Theology Revisited

1. See William Julius Wilson, *The Truly Disadvantaged: The Inner City, the Underclass and Public Policy* (Chicago: University of Chicago Press, 1987).

2. Basil Davidson, *The African Slave Trade: Precolonial History, 1450–1850* (Boston: Little, Brown, 1961), p. 80.

3. Eduardo Galeano, *Open Veins of Latin America: Five Centuries of the Pillage of a Continent* (London: Monthly Review Press, 1973), p. 50.

4. See Adam Hochschild, "Hearts of Darkness: Adventures in the Slave Trade," *San Francisco Examiner Magazine*, August 16, 1998, p. 13. This essay is an excerpt from his book, *King Leopold's Ghosts: A Story of Greed, Terror, and Heroism in Colonial Africa* (New York: Houghton Mifflin, 1998). Louis Turner suggests that 5 to 8 million were killed in the Congo. See his *Multinational Companies and the Third World* (New York: Hill and Wang, 1973), p. 27.

5. See especially Winthrop D. Jordan, *White over Black: American Attitudes Toward the Negro, 1550–1812* (Baltimore: Penguin Books, 1969).

6. Cited in Martin E. Marty, *Righteous Empire: The Protestant Experience in America* (New York: Dial Press, 1970), p. 17.

7. See Reinhold Niebuhr, "Man's Tribalism as One Source of His Inhumanity," in *Man's Nature and His Communities* (New York: Charles Scribner's Sons, 1965), pp. 84–105; and his "Justice to the American Negro from State, Community, and Church," in *Pious and Secular America* (New York: Charles Scribner's Sons, 1958), pp. 78–85.

8. *Malcolm X Speaks* (New York: Grove Press, 1965), p. 165.

9. In addition to *Black Theology and Black Power*, my contribution to black theology's race critique included *A Black Theology of Liberation* (1970; reprint, Maryknoll, N.Y.: Orbis Books, 1985) and *God of the Oppressed* (1975; reprint, Maryknoll, N.Y.: Orbis Books, 1998). Other critiques were Albert B. Cleage, *The Black Messiah* (New York: Sheed and Ward, 1968); J. Deotis Roberts, *Liberation and Reconciliation: A Black Theology* (1971; reprint, Maryknoll, N.Y.: Orbis Books, 1994) and *A Black Political Theology* (Philadelphia: Westminster Press/John Knox Press, 1974); and Gayraud S. Wilmore's *Black Religion and Black Radicalism* (1972; reprint, Mary-

knoll, N.Y.: Orbis Books, 1998). Significant essays included Vincent Harding, "Black Power and the American Christ," *Christian Century* (January 4, 1967), and "The Religion of Black Power," in *Religious Situation, 1968,* ed. D. R. Cutler (Boston: Beacon Press, 1968); and Herbert O. Edwards, "Racism and Christian Ethics in America," *Katallagete* (winter 1971).

10. See "The Black Manifesto," in *Black Theology: A Documentary History, vol. 1, 1966–1979,* ed. James H. Cone and Gayraud S. Wilmore (Maryknoll, N.Y.: Orbis Books, 1993), pp. 27–36.

11. See "Womanist Theology," in *Black Theology: A Documentary History, vol. 2, 1980–1992,* pp. 257–351.

12. See Victor Anderson, *Beyond Ontological Blackness: An Essay on African-American Religious and Cultural Criticism* (New York: Continuum, 1995).

13. See "The Second Generation," in *Black Theology: A Documentary History, vol. 2, 1980–1992,* pp. 15–75; see also Josiah U. Young, *A Pan-African Theology: Providence and the Legacies of the Ancestors* (Trenton, N.J.: Africa World Press, 1992); Dwight N. Hopkins and George Cummings, eds., *Cut Loose Your Stammering Tongue: Black Theology in the Slave Narratives* (Maryknoll, N.Y.: Orbis Books, 1991); Dwight N. Hopkins, *Shoes That Fit Our Feet: Sources for a Constructive Black Theology* (Maryknoll, N.Y.: Orbis Books, 1993); Garth Kasimu Baker-Fletcher, *Xodus: An African American Male Journey* (Minneapolis: Fortress Press, 1996); Riggins R. Earl, *Dark Symbols, Obscure Signs: God, Self, and Community in the Slave Mind* (Maryknoll, N.Y.: Orbis Books, 1993).

14. See Anthony B. Pinn, *Why, Lord?: Suffering and Evil in Black Theology* (New York: Continuum, 1995). Pinn is building on an earlier critique of black theology by William R. Jones, *Is God a White Racist?: A Preamble to Black Theology* (1973; reprint, Boston: Beacon Press, 1998).

15. See "New Directions in Black Biblical Interpretation," in *Black Theology: A Documentary History, vol. 2, 1980–1992,* pp. 177–254; Cain H. Felder, *Troubling Biblical Waters: Race, Class, and Family* (Maryknoll, N.Y.: Orbis Books, 1989) and his edited work *Stony the Road We Trod: African-American Biblical Interpretation* (Minneapolis: Fortress Press, 1991); Brian K. Blount, *Go Preach!: Mark's Kingdom Message and the Black Church Today* (Maryknoll, N.Y.: Orbis Books, 1998); Theophus H. Smith, *Conjuring Culture: Biblical Formations of Black America* (New York: Oxford University Press, 1994).

16. W. E. B. Du Bois, *The Souls of Black Folk* (1903; reprint, Greenwich, Conn.: Fawcett, 1961), p. 23.

17. Martin Luther King, Jr., "Beyond Vietnam," a pamphlet of the Clergy and Laymen Concerned About Vietnam, April 4, 1967.

18. *The Souls of Black Folk*, p. 23.

Whose Earth Is It, Anyway?

The second epigraph is cited in Samuel Rayan, "The Earth Is the Lord's," in *Ecotheology: Voices from South and North*, ed. David G. Hallman (Geneva: WCC, 1994), p. 142.

1. See *Justice, Peace, and the Integrity of Creation*, papers and Bible studies edited by James W. van Hoeven for the World Alliance of Reformed Churches Assembly, Seoul, Korea, August 1989; and Preman Niles, *Resisting the Threats to Life: Covenanting for Justice, Peace, and the Integrity of Creation* (Geneva: WCC, 1989).

2. See Delores Williams, "A Womanist Perspective on Sin," in *A Troubling in My Soul: Womanist Perspectives on Evil and Suffering*, ed. Emilie M. Townes (Maryknoll, N.Y.: Orbis Books, 1993), pp. 145–147; and her "Sin, Nature, and Black Women's Bodies," in *Ecofeminism and the Sacred*, ed. Carol J. Adams (New York: Continuum, 1993), pp. 24–29; Emilie Townes, *In a Blaze of Glory: Womanist Spirituality as Social Witness* (Nashville, Tenn.: Abingdon Press, 1995), p. 55; and Karen Baker-Fletcher, *Sisters of Dust, Sisters of Spirit: Womanist Wordings on God and Creation* (Minneapolis: Fortress Press, 1998), p. 93.

3. Robert Bullard, *Dumping in Dixie: Race, Class, and Environmental Quality* (Boulder, Colo.: Westview Press, 1990), p. 31.

4. Cited in Bunyan Bryant & Paul Mohai, eds., *Race and the Incidence of Environmental Hazards: A Time for Discourse* (Boulder: Westview Press, 1992), p. 2. See also "African American Denominational Leaders Pledge their Support to the Struggle Against Environmental Racism," *The A.M.E. Christian Recorder*, May 18, 1998, pp. 8, 11.

5. Cited in Robert D. Bullard, ed., *Unequal Protection: Environmental Justice and Communities of Color* (San Francisco: Sierra Club Books, 1994), p. 20.

6. Benjamin Chavis is now known as Benjamin Chavis Muhammad and is currently serving as the National Minister in Louis Farrakhan's Nation of Islam.

7. Bunyan Bryant, "Introduction" to his edited work *Environmental Justice: Issues, Policies, and Solutions* (Washington, D.C.: Island Press, 1995), p. 5. Benjamin Chavis defined environmental racism as "racial discrimination in environmental policymaking. It is racial discrimination in the enforcement of regulations and

laws. It is racial discrimination in the deliberate targeting of communities of color for toxic waste disposal and the siting of polluting industries. It is racial discrimination in the official sanctioning of the life-threatening presence of poisons and pollutants in communities of color. And, it is racial discrimination in the history of excluding people of color from the mainstream environmental groups, decisionmaking boards, commissions, and regulatory bodies" ("Foreword," in *Confronting Environmental Racism: Voices from the Grassroots*, ed. Robert Bullard [Boston: South End Press, 1993], p. 3).

8. *National Black Church Environmental and Economic Justice Summit*, Washington, D.C., December 1–2, 1993, The National Council of Churches of Christ in the USA, Prophetic Justice Unit. This is a booklet with all the speeches of the meeting, including the one by Vice President Gore.

9. See Ronald A. Taylor, "Do Environmentalists Care About Poor People?" *U.S. News and World Report*, April 2, 1984, p. 51.

10. John Lewis's quotation is cited in Deeohn and David Hahn-Baker, "Environmentalists and Environmental Justice Policy," in *Environmental Justice: Issues, Policies, and Solutions*, p. 68.

11. Alice Walker, *Living by the Word: Selected Writings, 1973–1987* (San Diego: Harcourt Brace Jovanovich, 1988), p. 173.

12. "Do Environmentalists Care About Poor People?" p. 51.

13. Ibid.

14. Ibid.

15. Audre Lorde, *Sister Outsider* (Trumansburg, N.Y.: Crossing Press, 1984), p. 110.

16. Catherine Keller, *From a Broken Web: Separation, Sexism, Self* (Boston: Beacon Press, 1986), p. 5.

17. See Elie Wiesel, "Nobel Peace Prize Acceptance Speech," <http://home.sol.no/~solhanse/wiesel.htm>, December 10, 1986.

18. Cited in Leonado Boff, *Cry of the Earth, Cry of the Poor* (Maryknoll, N.Y.: Orbis Books, 1997), p. 2.

Credits

Acknowledgments

Many people made this book, like the others, possible. A special thanks is due to Mary Graves and Louise Wareham, my assistants. Their first-rate assistance enabled me to devote my time to teaching and writing. I should also mention Adam Clark and Sylvester Johnson, my research assistants, who were adept at finding every reference I requested and called to my attention many others in my field of interest. Sylvester also read the manuscript and assisted me in the selection and the organization of the essays and the index.

A thanks is also due to Judy Diers, friend and former student. She also read most of the manuscript and made important editorial suggestions.

Thanks to the Union Seminary community for their support of my work. During my three decades at Union Seminary, I have had many provocative and challenging dialogues with my faculty colleagues. I wish I could mention all my students—past and present—during my years of teaching at Union Seminary. They heard all these essays as lectures and challenged me to think deeply about the implications of my claims. Still, every time I begin a semester of teaching, it is like the first one—tremendously exciting and deeply challenging. Union students are special. They remind me daily of the awesome responsibility and great joy of teaching and writing.

I should also express a word of gratitude to the many colleges, universities, and seminaries and to the churches and communities around the world where I presented these lectures. Their support of my work is deeply appreciated.

I also want to thank my friend Deborah Chasman, Editorial Director of Beacon Press, for passing my manuscript on to Tisha Hooks, whose encouragement and editorial expertise were much needed. An author could not ask for more.

Index

Praise for *See Through*

"She writes cunningly . . . with a commanding, spirited voice."
—*The Boston Globe*

"Reifler's oddball vignettes . . . are spring-loaded miniatures that flirt with the surreal edges of childhood and adolescence . . . you're astonished at her daring, her craft and her flair for narrative mischief."

—*Los Angeles Times*

"With unflinching precision, Reifler's debut collection of 14 short stories examines young protagonists negotiating adult-governed worlds . . . the perceptive Reifler is a writer to watch."
—*Publishers Weekly*

"With her strong New York literary scene connections and her obvious talent, Reifler is bound to receive serious attention from these chiseled tales."

—*Kirkus Reviews*

"Reifler's stories are spare with an emotional tone surprisingly subtle and restrained—a particularly admirable achievement when set against premises that are, at times, wildly absurdist. With the blackest of humor, an icy exactitude, and an ironic edge, these stories are reminiscent of Edward Gorey . . . and the diabolically psychological works of Patricia Highsmith."

—*Bookforum*

"Reifler seems to have an unflinching grasp on humanity. . . . Remarkably, considering Reifler's command of style and strength of voice, *See Through* is her first published collection."
—*Seattle Weekly*

"Nelly Reifler is one to watch. The gritty texture of her described reality and her ability to get us inside her very strange characters within a few words makes this collection one to read and enjoy."

—*The Buffalo News*

SEE THROUGH

STORIES

NELLY REIFLER

SIMON & SCHUSTER PAPERBACKS

New York London Toronto Sydney

I am deeply grateful to the friends and teachers who read these stories throughout various phases of development and helped shape them with criticism and interpretation: Elizabeth Albert, Hilary Bell, Astrid Cravens, James Gibbons, David Hollander, Siri Hustvedt, Dylan Nolfi, David Ryan, Brooke Stevens, Gina Zucker, Mary LaChapelle, Joan Silber, Linsey Abrams, and Lucy Rosenthal. More thanks go to the fine people of Darhansoff, Verrill, Feldman, especially Kristin Lang, and most of all Leigh Feldman, my frighteningly smart agent. Still more thanks go to David Rosenthal, Tara Parsons, and Victoria Meyer at Simon & Schuster—and I feel especially lucky to have worked on this book with Marysue Rucci, my wise editor. I appreciate the support given to me by the Rotunda Gallery in Brooklyn and the Henfield Foundation. And I thank my dear boss Mr. Paul.

SIMON & SCHUSTER PAPERBACKS
Rockefeller Center
1230 Avenue of the Americas
New York, NY 10020

Some of these stories were previously published as follows: "Rascal" in the *Florida Review*; "Personal Foundations of Self-forming Through Auto-identification with Otherness" in *Bomb*; "Teeny" at Failbetter.com; "Memoir" in Duckymag.com and in the *Saint Ann's Review*; "Sugar" in *Post Road*; "See Through" in *Black Book*; "Julian" in the anthology *Lost Tribe: Jewish Fiction from the Edge* (HarperCollins).

First Simon & Schuster paperback edition 2006

SIMON & SCHUSTER PAPERBACKS and colophon are registered trademarks of Simon & Schuster, Inc.

For information about special discounts for bulk purchases, please contact Simon & Schuster Special Sales: 1-800-456-6798 or business@simonandschuster.com

Manufactured in the United States of America

10 9 8 7 6 5 4 3 2 1

Library of Congress Cataloging-in-Publication Data

Reifler, Nelly.
See through : stories / Nelly Reifler.
p.   cm.
I. Title.
PS3618.E555S44 2003
813'.6—dc21
2003050379

ISBN-13: 978-0-7432-3608-9
ISBN-10:   0-7432-3608-4
ISBN-13: 978-0-7432-6150-0 (Pbk)
ISBN-10:   0-7432-6150-X (Pbk)

For my parents,
Ellen Marshall
and
Samuel Reifler

and
also
for
Josh Dorman

CONTENTS

SEE
THROUGH

TEENY

There they were.

Through the window, she could see them, one on either arm of the sofa.

They seemed to be asleep.

She had her instructions, written on a piece of lined notebook paper. She had reviewed them earlier. Now the paper was cinched in her fist, blank side out, words hidden. Her hand was sweaty.

She looked at them through the window.

She leaned forward and pressed her free hand against the glass. Her breath made a spot, which disappeared instantly from its edges inward.

What were they doing? Were they sleeping? Were they just lying there with their eyes closed? Were they dreaming? Were they thinking?

The key to the house dangled from a plastic lanyard, which she had snapped around her belt loop when she got dressed that morning.

Her fist tightened. The instructions crinkled.

It was just yesterday that she had been inside the house with her mother. Yesterday the people had shown her the plastic bowls on the kitchen floor. The litter box in the laundry room. The emergency numbers on the refrigerator. She had knelt on the kitchen floor and patted the striped one on its head, and her mother had said to the people, "See? She's a natural. She'll probably be a vet when she grows up." It was yesterday, yes, but it seemed so long ago. In her memory, yesterday's visit was a slow blur, as if her eyelashes had been glued together. Now, again, looking through the window, she felt as if she were peering through a thicket of eyelashes and glue.

She backed away from the window. Slowly, slowly, away from the house. She stumbled on a low green wire fence which guarded a flower bed. She almost fell, but she caught herself. There were no flowers there yet; it was too early. There was just dark brown earth, which had recently been turned over, and a few tiny green sprouts.

At the bottom of the driveway, she looked up and down the street. No one was around. No one saw her.

That evening, she lay on the living room carpet with a stack of chocolate chip cookies on her belly. She ate them slowly, contemplatively. She had started out with six, but somehow she had only one cookie left when she heard her mother's car in the driveway. There was the grinding noise of the garage door. Silence for a moment—then the click of the car door opening, and a thump when it closed. She shut her eyes and put a placid

expression on her face. She rested her arms by her sides and let her legs flop open.

The door between the garage and kitchen opened. She heard keys drop on the table. Water running.

"Teeny?" her mother called.

She lay still.

"I need some help here, Teeny. Where are you?"

She heard her mother's voice come closer. Her legs felt like wobbly gelatin. Her stomach turned over. Her heart started beating faster.

"What are you doing? Are you sleeping?"

She didn't answer. She felt her hands clench into fists, then let go, once again weak and droopy.

There were footsteps. She felt her mother's breath on her forehead.

"Are you okay, hon?"

She didn't answer.

"So, did you go? Did you do it? Was everything okay?"

She opened her eyes and looked at her mother. A pendant with a cameo locket hung around her mother's neck and dangled down, swinging in a small arc. There had been a baby picture inside, but her mother had taken it out. She said she was waiting for the new grown-up school photos to arrive. They were due any day.

"I was thinking today," said her mother, "you could really make this into a regular job. Everyone has pets, and there are no other children the right age on this street. Bill, Heather, Candy, Lakshmi—they're all too old, when you think about it. They have regular after-school jobs and wouldn't want to take anything else on. Brandon, Jason, those twins at the corner—they're too little to handle something like this. I'm sure that the Stines will recommend you to everyone once they see what a good job you've done."

She closed her eyes.

The next day, she dawdled on the way home from the bus stop. She walked up and down the aisles of the card shop. She opened a card that sang happy birthday in a whiny electronic voice. She tried out a highlighter pen. Then she sat on the curb outside the grocery store and watched cars come and go. By the time she got to the house, it was late afternoon, almost evening. The windows reflected the white sky, and the sun was the color of a dusty nickel.

She cupped her hands around her face and looked in at the living room.

First she saw just one, scratching at the sofa, then it darted out of sight, and then both were there, running around, chasing each other, paddling at each other's faces with their paws.

She stood there, suddenly frozen. Moving only her eyes, she looked over at the front door.

She reached for the lanyard on her belt loop. It was woven from flat vinyl string. She remembered the long crafts hall of Camp Sacajawea; she remembered the sound of rain pounding on its zinc roof the day they learned to make lanyards. She remem-

bered how some of the girls had made wallets, and burned their names into the leather with a glowing hot tool. But the counselors hadn't offered to teach her how to make a wallet. Why? Why had they only given her the vinyl string? She had lain in her bunk that night, wondering how the counselors decided who was ready to make wallets. Did they know something she didn't know for sure but suspected?—that she wasn't capable of using that burning tool? How did they know that about her? Could anyone know it just from looking at her? She had wondered if her mother would notice, at the end of the summer, that she had come back with a lanyard and not a wallet. She had wondered: What would she tell her mother if her mother asked about it? That they didn't have enough leather to go around, and she hadn't wanted a wallet anyway. Or that, instead of making a wallet, she had taught a younger camper to braid the colored vinyl.

Now she let go of the lanyard. She wiped her damp hands on her corduroys, and pulled her shirt down over her belly. Looking through the window again, she saw that they were still at it, bouncing around, hiding from each other, pouncing, rolling around under the coffee table. Sweat trickled from her temple, past her ear, down her cheek. She could feel the blood rush into her head, then flow away, then pour into her skull once again.

She turned and hurried to the end of the driveway, pausing to look up and down the street.

That night she sat on the floor, picking red gummy worms out of a waxy paper sack. Her eyes were half closed; she tried to open them all the way, but the lids just dropped back down. A couple of hours earlier, her mother had walked in, throwing her tote bag full of papers and clipboards on a chair, then rolling her knee-highs down to her ankles. "I'm sorry I'm late," her mother had said. "I was training the new agent on the com-

puter." Her mother asked if she had eaten, and she shrugged. Her mother asked if she had done her homework, and she made a gesture toward a textbook open on the table. Then her mother asked how her job went. That was when it had become necessary to walk over to the closet and get the candy bag from her jacket pocket.

Now all the red worms were gone. She sat there with her empty hand in the bag. Her mother was on the phone in the kitchen, and her mother's voice faded in and out like a faraway station on a car radio. From under her lids, she looked down at her torso, the alien bulges and folds of flesh that spilled out around her waistband, her junior bra under her T-shirt. She curled forward, folding her arms around her head, blocking out the electric light. She could smell the new smells of her armpits and crotch in the dark little room formed by her concave body. She wished she could live in a space like that; it would be quiet, and she would be the only inhabitant.

The next day, after school, she sat on one of the benches next to the gazebo in the courtyard of the shopping center. She was rereading her favorite Goosebumps book. Every few minutes, she looked around. She worried that her mother might show up. She had a story ready. She would say the science teacher was sick and she got out of school early, so she had already gone and done the feeding. She would say that she ran into Lakshmi and Mrs. Krivalli, and they had taken her to do some shopping. She would say that Mrs. Krivalli suddenly wasn't feeling well, and she had to go to the doctor. So she was sitting here, waiting to see how Mrs. Krivalli was.

But her mother did not appear. It started to get chilly. She folded down the corner of the page she was on and headed slowly back to her street. She didn't mean to, but on the way home she stopped and looked in through the windows. Inside,

they were sitting, pressed up next to each other, eyes wide
open. When she shifted forward—just the littlest bit—they
both noticed her. They stared straight at her. She watched them
open their mouths. They hopped off the sofa and ran over near
the window. Her heart flooded, then contracted. She took a
tiny step backward. They were looking at her, mouths opening
and closing. Their eyes were wild and hopeful and pleading. She
could only imagine the noises they were making. Looking at
their mouths opening and closing, she could almost hear them
saying her name. "Teeny," they were saying, "Teeny, Teeny,
Teeny. . . ."

She backed away from the window. The sky had turned gray.
She felt a raindrop. She was about to leave when she noticed
that a pile of newspapers had built up near the front door. She
opened the outer screen door, which the people kept unlocked,
and she shoved the papers inside the shallow entryway. There
was a pair of yellow plastic clogs there, and a green umbrella.
She grabbed the umbrella and pulled her jacket close to her
body. It used to zip; in fact, last spring it had been loose, but
now she had to hold it closed with her hand.

In her room, before bed that night, she unrolled the loose-leaf
paper where the couple's instructions were written in the
wife's loose, cursive hand. The wife was beautiful, and wore a
masculine haircut and glasses which made the curves under her
clothing impossible not to stare at. The day she got the job, she
had noticed how the wife's flesh had bobbed and undulated
under her big shirt. The man was friendly. He had a little beard.
They had given her the phone number of their hotel. She could
call them, she thought, she could tell them everything. She
stared at the slanting letters, the long loops and low bumps. She
saw the words "handful dry food"; she saw the word "water."
Her stomach clenched. She rolled the paper into a tight ball and
threw it under her bed. She took the green umbrella hanging

from her chair and shoved it under the bed. Finally, she grabbed the lanyard from her desk and threw it under there, too. She heard the key hit the floor.

She turned off the light. In the dark, she pinched her nipples hard, and they gathered and wrinkled. She kept going until they were sore.

She didn't stop at the house the next day. She walked the long route home from the bus stop, along the gas pipeline where the weeds were soft and pale. She stared at the tips of her tennis shoes, pushing their way through the grass like little animals. She imagined she wasn't moving her feet; they were just snuffling along on their own.

The next day was Saturday. The couple was supposed to come home on Sunday. At breakfast, her mother said, "I just want you to know how proud of you I am. You're a big girl now; you've done your first job. Have you figured out how you're going to spend your money?"

She shrugged.

"You can't spend it on candy, remember, that was a condition of taking the job. And you can't spend it on Goosebumps books, it has to be a real book. And you can't spend it on candy."

She pulled her shirt down over her belly.

Later, she stood outside the house, but she didn't look in the windows. She was tempted, but she didn't let herself. She could remember how their voices had sounded in her head, calling her name. She shoved the latest newspapers inside the vestibule. As she was leaving, she stopped at the bottom of the driveway. In

just a few days, more sprouts had come up. Some had real leaves on them. She kneeled down and put her fingers around the smallest green stem. It was silky and moist. She pulled. The one hairy white root seemed to quiver in the air. She shuddered and threw the plant down on the dirt. They were going to come home the next afternoon, around one o'clock, they had said. She counted the number of hours between now and then on her fingers. The little hairs under her arms stood up and sweat soaked her shirt.

The next morning, she said she didn't want breakfast. Then, when her mother was in the laundry room, she climbed up onto a chair and got a box of chocolate chip cookies from the cabinet. She tucked the box under her arm and went upstairs to her room to wait. She read, trembling, until twelve-fifty-five, then put her book down.

It was another wet day. She could hear the rain in the aluminum gutter outside her window. She remembered the crafts hall at Camp Sacajawea. She remembered the hair of the other girls, how it seemed to hang just right from their heads. Their limbs had seemed to belong to their bodies. She remembered watching one girl, watching the long straight hair that fanned across the girl's shoulders as she leaned forward to etch her name in brown leather. "Eleanor," the wallet said. "Eleanor"— a name like a grown-up lady's, a name like a queen from a fairy book. The girl's arms had been slender; they stretched from the short sleeves of her T-shirt, looking like the firm branches of saplings. The girl's flat, golden stomach had shown above the jeans that hung off her hips.

She finished the box of cookies. It was one-oh-five. Five minutes later, she heard car doors down the street. Soon after that, she heard voices below her window. The doorbell rang, several

urgent rings in a row. She heard her mother trotting to answer it. The doorbell rang again. And again. And then the sound of the front door opening.

She put her arms around her head and curled forward into her dark space. She inhaled and wondered how long she could hold her breath.

BABY

The baby was smart. Too smart. He was also sickly.

When he was six months old, he started to speak. By nine months he could form complete sentences. "Mom," he'd say, lying on his back in the crib, dolphin mobile dangling overhead, "I feel unwell. I'm weary. There's some kind of sticky liquid in my lungs and it hurts to breathe." Or: "Mom, my diaper's full of diarrhea again. My stomach is cramping. I'm not absorbing nutrients properly. I'm dehydrated."

His mother was at her wit's end. She tried to get him to rattle his rattle. She tried to interest him in a magnetic choo-choo train. But he'd just groan and turn over on his side.

One brilliant day in autumn, she sat on the window seat in the nursery. It was warm in the room, and she leaned against the cold window. Sunlight flickered with the movement of leaves falling off the big oak in the yard. At the baby's request, a tape of Bartók played on the yellow Fisher-Price tape player. The baby lay on his back with his arms in the air. He studied his fingers, squinting.

"Mom," he said in his reedy little voice. He paused, wheezing. He was having asthma, and she was keeping watch, ready with the inhaler.

"Yes?" she said.

"Mom, we all die, right?"

She sighed and looked out the window. A squirrel circled the base of the oak. Red and yellow leaves fluttered in the air. The squirrel picked up an acorn in its little paws.

"Mom?"

"Yes," she said, "that's right."

"Well," said the baby, still looking at his fingers, "if everyone dies, what's the point? I mean, why should I try so hard? What does it matter if I breathe or not?" He wheezed.

She watched the squirrel dash off, around the side of the house. "Because you'll grow up to be a great person," she said. "You'll do important things. You'll have friends. You'll travel."

"I know," said the baby. "But in the big picture, in the whole scheme of things, it doesn't really matter, does it? Someone else would come along and do what I would have done. The friends I might make would never know the difference if I didn't exist. The world, the universe—I'm just a speck, really," the baby said. He made fists, then rotated his arms. "The Bach cello pieces are on the other side of that tape, right, Mom?" he said. "Could you flip it over?"

His mother walked over to the tape player on its little red painted table. She remembered seeing the table in a store window one day when she was pregnant. She remembered going into the store and paying for the table. She remembered carrying it into the hush vacuum of the nursery.

Now she turned the tape over. She picked up a plush yellow duck from under the table and brought it over to the crib. She made it dance a little, then tucked it under the baby's blue flannel blanket.

"Oh," said the baby, wheezing, "this is the tape with that bad Dutch cellist. Could you find the other, please? With Yo-Yo Ma?"

The mother reached into her pocket. She produced the inhaler and leaned into the crib. She stroked the baby's fine yellow hair. She traced his white eyebrows with her finger.

She brushed away the granules of dried gunk from the corners of his eyes.

"My baby," she whispered. She brought the inhaler to his mouth. He opened wide, she squirted, he inhaled.

"Tastes like burning plastic," said the baby, wrinkling his nose.

The mother watched him breathe for a second, then went back to the window seat.

One day, early in her third trimester, she had met a friend for lunch in town after an appointment with her obstetrician. The printout from her sonogram was in a manila envelope inside her purse. As she eased herself out of her car and walked to the café, she found herself stroking and caressing the envelope. She reminded herself not to talk too much about her baby. She reminded herself that her friend, recently divorced and childless, was having a tough time and needed her attention. But after half an hour of hearing about the friend's disappointments and struggles, she couldn't help herself. She pulled the envelope out of her purse and handed the fuzzy, black and white image across the table. Her friend took a swig of wine and squinted at it. Then she laughed.

"What's so funny?" asked the pregnant woman.

"See his hands? It looks like he's saying something in sign language." Years earlier, the friend had dropped out of audiology school to get married.

"And what would that be?"

"Well . . . ," the friend giggled, raising her right thumb, and supporting her right hand with her left. "See? It looks like he's saying 'help.'"

The mother-to-be tried to laugh, but a chill began to crawl up her body, from the soles of her feet and across the hairs of her thighs to her crotch, where she felt a fluttering tremor. When she got home that day, she went straight upstairs to the nursery and lay down on the floor in the blue late afternoon light, both hands resting on the mound which housed her baby. She had sensed him moving, shifting incessantly, like an insom-

niac tossing and turning, never finding the right position.

Now she heard the baby clearing his throat. "Ahem," the baby said. "Mom?"

She opened her eyes. She hadn't realized that she had shut them.

"Mom, what about my question? What's the point?"

His mother said nothing. She looked out the window. There was the squirrel again, circling the oak again. But was it the same squirrel? She couldn't tell. All squirrels looked the same to her.

"Mom," said the baby, "Mom. My bronchi are clearing. Mom," he continued, "I said I didn't want to hear this. I said I wanted Yo-Yo Ma."

The mother groaned. She stood up, walked over to the tape player, turned it off. She unzipped the nylon case where the baby's cassettes were stored, dragged her finger along the plastic tape cases, then pulled one out, opened it, and put the tape in the player. She pressed play.

"Thanks, Mom, I really appreciate it," said the baby. The mother went back to the window seat. She looked out the window. No squirrel. A breeze passed over the lawn, and the leaves rose and swirled.

"But Mom," said the baby, "Mom, are you there? Mom, are you paying attention? What do you think? What's the answer? Why do we do it? Why do we continue, knowing all the while that life is finite? Why do people brush their teeth, go to work, eat, laugh, if they're just going to wind up things, cold flesh, food for the maggots?"

His mother watched out the window. Suddenly, two squirrels came into view, from opposite directions. So there were two of them all along, she thought. One squirrel leapt onto the tree and started to climb. The second squirrel followed. Was it chasing the first, she wondered, were they courting? Were they competing for acorns?

"Hello? Mom?" said the baby. "Hello, Mom. Are you there?"

"I'm here," said the mother. "What do you need?"

"Do you believe in God?" asked the baby. "Do you think there really is a God, or is religion just something that human beings have created to cope with the fact that their lives mean nothing?"

The mother heard the neighbor's teenage daughter pull out of the driveway in her Honda; its broken muffler coughed and rattled.

The mother stood up and walked over to the baby. She looked down at him again. His fingernails were tiny, like bits of sea glass. His skin was so thin and translucent, she could see the blue veins clearly, branching out from his arms to his hands to his fingers.

"My diaper is wet," stated the baby.

The baby had shoved his pillow to the side, and the mother picked it up, intending to put it back under his delicate skull. But then she found she had the pillow in both hands. She found herself leaning forward over the baby. She saw her hands lowering the pillow; she saw the pillow covering his face. She felt herself pressing down, hard, pressing the pillow against his nose and mouth. His arms twitched. His little fists beat against the sheet.

On tape, the bow met the cello's strings, the bow danced with the cello.

An acorn knocked against the window.

The mother jumped back from the baby. She threw the pillow on the ground.

She kicked it into the corner.

The blue paper dolphins floated over the crib.

The mother stared down at the baby. He was still. His eyes were closed.

She started to lean forward into the crib again.

Then his eyes opened. The baby opened his eyes and looked up at his mother. He looked at his mother's face. He looked into her eyes. He did not blink. Ever so slightly, he shook his head, side to side.

He said nothing. He was nine months old.

He would wait.

RASCAL

Hunter. Airborne. Wildfire. Slingshot.

Intense. Boulder. Giant. Dagger.

In the end, Robby chose a Dagger bike, because of the name. *Dagger.* He remembers that when he first saw the silver logo on the bike's shiny black frame, he imagined splitting the wind on it, stabbing up hills, ripping around curves.

Now, lying in his sleeping bag, he catalogs all the good things about getting around on his Dagger. For one thing, it's cheap. No gas. You never pay a toll, and you can usually get away with camping for free. And another thing, you never get stuck in traffic. Even if there's a traffic jam, you can just dart between the cars. Slicing like a dagger. He likes to grin into the rolled-up windows of cars that are moving about a yard an hour. *Screw you,* he thinks as he pedals past. By the time he's rolling a fresh joint in Dolores Park, they're finally leaving the city limits of San Jose.

So what if he doesn't have his own car anymore? Robby kneads his thigh muscles. They are rock-hard and knotted. These bulging forms that push against his skin are as impressive as his 'Stang ever was. He is lucky. His life has order. He's in shape, and he doesn't spend that much time with his mom and dad.

It is a bright night. The moon is big and low over Andrew Molera State Park. His nylon shorts hang on a string between two branches of a live oak. Every evening, he heats up water over a fire, washes his face with a small bar of Cashmere Bouquet, and then dips his shorts in the leftover soapy water. A rinse in the spigot, then he wrings them out and strings them up. It's part of traveling light.

Most every night, there's someone to talk to wherever he's camping. There were those bikers last summer coming back from Sturgis. They showed him their new tattoos and their customized Harleys. They offered him beer, which he declined. They were cool with that. The bikers had already laughed and patted him on the back when he told them the whole story—how he'd been arrested and had his license permanently revoked for too many DUI citations; how he had a hot girlfriend, a nineteen-year-old hippie girl with long hair and silver toe rings who lived in the Haight. He passed around a pipe, and they told a story about a guy with a Japanese bike at Sturgis. A "rice burner" they called it, an ugly thing shaped like a cockroach, with purple streaks and lots of white plastic. Fast and quiet as hell, but light, bad in the mud. The guy won a lot of races. But so what?—said the bikers—Guy wins the races and heads back to the motel the last night of the rally. He's rounding a blind spot on a little hill, and a truck pulls out of a tavern, kills the guy on the spot.

"Loud pipes save lives," said the biggest, oldest biker. Robby felt uneasy for a second. After all, Robby was the other kind of biker, a cyclist, really. But at least his bike was American.

Robby smiles when he thinks about how he impressed the bikers, even though he hadn't told them the real story. The truth was, he didn't have his license taken away for good, only for two months—he could apply for a new one any time he wanted. And there was no girlfriend, never had been. Somehow, he couldn't tell the bikers how simple his life was. Making this loop from Mom and Dad's to Dolores Park is his job, and

he's his own boss. When he first lost his license, the plan was slightly different. He thought he'd bike up to S.F., buy a big bag of weed. He thought he'd sell it to rich Bakersfield kids at a nice profit. But as it turned out, the weed was really good, and he found himself taking the long route back, camping out and getting stoned. The little monthly allowance from when his grandmother kicked it is just enough for an ounce of marijuana. He never sells it, just rides back and forth, smoking it. He rests for a couple of weeks a month, hanging out in his room with the bong, or playfully bickering at the kitchen table with his mom. After his arrest, he promised her he'd never drink beer again.

He must still look like a beer drinker, he thinks proudly. People always offer. On the way back from San Francisco last month, he met an old man at one of those fancy campgrounds where half the sites have cement rectangles for parking RV's. The old man was going to visit his grandchildren. His RV had carnival lights strung beneath the awning—not the colorful ones you usually see, but yellow with black silhouettes of naked girls, like on the mud flaps of an eighteen-wheeler. The old man assumed Robby was a serious athlete in training. Who else would refuse a Heineken? Who else would ride from Bakersfield to San Francisco on a bicycle? When Robby said he didn't drink beer, the man poured some Gatorade in a glass and pointed to the roof of his RV. There was a tiny satellite dish up there. The man told Robby he'd been following the Tour de France and Lance Armstrong on ESPN. "Even with no nuts," the old man said, "that fella's more man than all those Krauts and Dagos put together."

"What's a Dago?" Robby asked.

"You know, kiddo, an Italian."

"I thought Italian guys were Wops," said Robby.

"Either one, my friend," said the old man, grinning. "They're all mama's boys."

Robby felt nauseous for a second, and he looked down at the

ice cubes floating in his Day-Glo green drink. When he looked back up, the man was still smiling. His dentures gleamed in the lamplight. He raised his beer and said, "God bless you, kid—you've got what it takes. You're Armstrong with both balls." He clinked the can against Robby's glass, and Robby nodded, smiling back at him.

Tonight, the campground is pretty empty. It is a Tuesday night. He arrived early this afternoon. First he found a site far away from the ranger station, then he rode around and around the park, looking for someone to talk to. He avoids families, and this afternoon the only people around were families. The dads acted meek, as if they were nothing more than chauffeurs hired to drive minivans, and the moms were as stiff as sergeants in their white tennis shoes and their windbreakers. The little girls were shrill; you could hear their voices bounce off the earth. The little boys were either like sad stunted men or they were menacing, running around with sticks and rocks. He does not want to have any contact with children. He is always sure they will nail him in some way, say something true and mean that he does not want to hear.

So this evening he gave up on meeting anyone. He steamed a microwave burrito from a 7-Eleven by propping it with sticks over a pot of water. While his burrito defrosted, he went into the trees and smoked half a joint. The live oaks were so low, the top of his head poked through the upper leaves. It was the last of this ounce; he smoked with end-of-the-bag urgency. Then he lifted the hot burrito using the twigs as chopsticks. He smiled at his ingenuity. He opened the purple plastic wrapper. He wondered why plastic does not melt when it's steamed, and he thought about how his mom had soups that came in little plastic pouches. You put a pouch in hot water, then slit it open with a knife. In grade school, he recalled, there was something called Career Day, and a lady from the Sausage Makers' Union came with a filmstrip that showed a pig's bladder being slit open. Liquid flowed out like soup. Did they use the bladder for

sausage? Robby could not remember. But thinking about it made him have to pee. He ducked into the grove again, sniffing his hands before he reached into his shorts.

The Heet Mistake had happened last fall. Returning home exhausted at the end of a trip, he'd lost control as he rounded the last corner onto his mom and dad's street. He hit the Puctneys' mailbox and went flying over his handlebars. He landed on his shoulder in the gravel driveway. He lay there, just looking at all the sharp gray stones and wondering what had happened, until Mrs. Puctney came running out of the house. He sat in her kitchen, scraped up and sore, until his mother came to get him. Instead of going right home, they went to the drugstore. Robby waited in the car, and his mother came out with a bag of supplies: the largest Band-Aids he had ever seen, extra hydrogen peroxide, a quart of strawberry ice cream, and a tube of something called Heet. That evening, while he was eating ice cream and watching TV, his mother rubbed the Heet on his shoulder. It really did feel hot, and Robby inspected the aluminum tube, amazed that it was room temperature.

When his mother went out to get Robby's pizza, his shoulder started throbbing again, and he decided to rub some more Heet on it. He squeezed a blob of it out on his hands, rubbed them together, and massaged himself as best he could. Then he had to go to the bathroom. As soon as he reached into his fly, he realized he had made a mistake. He yelped from the pain once, then pulled his pants off and jumped into the bathtub. When his mother came home, he was still soaking in ice-cold water, tears drying on his face. Ever since, he always smells his hands before taking a leak.

As he watered the live oaks, he thought again about what an important lesson he had learned from the Heet Mistake, and he renewed his pledge to write a letter to the company as soon as he got home. He zipped up, grabbed his burrito, and began his stroll around the campground in his bare feet. While he walked, he planned what he would say in the letter. "Dear Heet," he

would start, "do you know how dangerous your product is?" His mother could type the letter for him.

It was growing dark. The families had built fires in their pits. Smells of hamburgers and franks came from every direction. He couldn't figure out what would come next in his letter, but smelling the cooking meat made his burrito even more enjoyable, and he chewed it slowly.

Then, as he neared his site again, he noticed that someone had come in while he was gone. A tent was pitched two sites away from his. A small Japanese car was parked between the tent and the drive. There was no evidence of children. Robby stepped into the soft dirt circle of the site. He leaned against the little red car and crumpled the purple burrito wrapper with one hand. A female voice came from inside the locust-shaped blue tent.

"Love?"

"Yeah?" A male voice came from the trees. A young guy emerged. He noticed Robby and said, "Hey."

Robby was not sure if this "hey" was an exclamation or a greeting. From the way the guy nodded and curled his lips, Robby decided it was a greeting. The guy had messy blond hair tucked behind his ears. He wore a T-shirt with a picture of a coffee mug on it. Steam rose from the mug up to the crew neck; underneath the mug, in slanted letters, was the word "Ah!"

There was movement in the tent, then the sound of a zipper. A foot in a purple sneaker poked out of the tent. It was the same purple as his burrito wrapper, Robby observed. Soon, Robby learned that the foot was attached to a red-haired girl, Sharon. The guy was Dave. They were from Maryland.

He learned these things when they were all sitting on the ground near the fire circle. Sharon had taken some blue corn chips from the trunk of the car. They ate these chips as they got to know each other. Robby was so relieved that they had shown up at Andrew Molera, and he told them so. He was imagining getting them high and making them laugh at his sto-

ries of road life. He told them how he felt about families, how all dads have fallen arches, and moms have steel-toed Reeboks for kicking the dads. Sharon nodded. Dave looked at her and squeezed her hand.

"What's your family like, then?" said Sharon.

Suddenly, Robby felt something rise from his toes to his jaw that made him stiff and hot. Did she think he was talking about his own mom and dad? He leaned forward to her, looking in her eyes, and said, "My folks are perfect. My mom . . . she bakes these snickerdoodle things"—he giggled, because the name of those cookies always makes him giggle—"and Dad . . ." He thought about how to explain Dad. "He goes back to Delaware every August to do a Revolutionary War reenactment." In his mind, Robby saw his dad—well, a photo of him—in the red jacket, holding a musket. Robby's older brother, Fred, who worked in the faucet business with Dad, had started going to Delaware each year, too. The photo in Robby's mind was actually a picture of the two of them, on a hill with an old fort in the background. They had the same broad shoulders and barrel chests, and the same serious, squinting eyes. They wore white wigs and three-cornered hats. They hadn't invited Robby yet. Everyone in the family agreed it might not be his sort of activity, just as they agreed that faucets might not hold his interest. He and his mom had fun alone, anyway, playing canasta and watching Carol Burnett. He rarely saw Fred anymore. He had bought a condo and moved in with his girlfriend.

"Dad's a redcoat," Robby said. He decided not to mention Fred.

"That's cool," Dave said. "*My* dad made a documentary film about these Elks in Arizona who reenact battles of the Civil War in their backyards." Dave laughed. Robby felt muddled. Somehow, Dave hadn't understood how much it meant for a son to have a father as brave and as strong Robby's. Dave didn't understand the difference between the Revolution and the Civil War. The Revolution was about Liberty and Justice for all. The

Civil War was about . . . something else. Robby thought of his mother's videotape of *Gone With the Wind,* that dark maid lady, with the big white eyes. Then he remembered his discomfort riding through parts of San Jose at night, the shadowy people who threaten him by lurking—it seems like they wait for him. They know things about him, the routes he takes, that he's carrying weed. He sometimes imagines how his life might be simpler if the slaves had never been freed.

There was a silence.

Sharon said, "I really wish I'd known my dad." She leaned toward Dave. Then she explained to Robby, "He died when I was two. But sometimes I dream about him. I dream he comes to my bedside and watches over me."

Dave squeezed her hand. "We're on vacation, Shar, let's not . . ." Then he kissed her near her eye. He said, "My father and my stepmother and my mom all love you, Shar."

Sharon said to Robby, "My mother is an alcoholic. I'm not talking to her until she gets help. I'm tired of being my mother's mother."

Robby looked at the two of them. He hadn't made much of an impression on either one. They were a unit, like a pair of hands stroking and holding each other. He said, "Well, I'm camping right there." He tipped his head toward his site. "If you need anything, just yell." But even as he said it, he knew he sounded dumb. What could he offer them? They seemed to have everything.

Hours later, he can't fall asleep. For all his positive thinking, he has ended up back at Sharon and Dave. What a disappointing encounter. In all his trips back and forth, he's never met people so uninterested in him. He starts to feel angry. Sharon asked him about his family, but really she just wanted to tell him about hers.

He flexes his feet and feels the tendons stretch up the backs of his legs. He remembers stepping on the back of his big brother's head once when he was a little kid. His brother screamed. His mom came out on the deck. "Oh, my little ras-

cal." He remembers her laughing. "You just don't know your own strength." But he did know his strength. He could never concentrate on math or history, but he always knew how to twist someone's arm until they begged.

Robby remembers that visit to the school counselor after something had happened in the lunchroom involving a twisted arm. Robby was in seventh grade. He and his mother and the counselor guy, Fitzman, sat in an office on the same hall as the principal. Robby remembers Fitzman, his corduroy suit and his mustache. Robby's mom said to Fitzman, "Boys are tough with each other. My boys roughhouse day in and day out."

"This is more than roughhousing," Fitzman said. Robby had a rubber band ball along that he was squeezing. He'd started it with two little rubber bands his mom gave him from around Andy Boy broccoli. Now it was as big as a softball. Fitzman was not smiling. He said, "When I was a kid, sure, we kicked, punched, all that. But it was never so . . ." He turned to Robby. "When you feel yourself getting mad, just ask yourself, Am I going over the line?"

Robby looked down at the ball.

"Can you say that?" Fitzman asked.

Robby brought the ball to his nose and sniffed. It smelled like chalk and tires.

"Robby?" Fitzman said.

"What?" Robby answered.

"'Am I going over the line?'"

Robby mumbled something, "Emuh gung ovuhlie."

"Good boy!" his mother exclaimed, patting Robby's cheek, then mussing his hair. "See?" she said.

"I don't know," said Mr. Fitzman. "Can you try again?"

Robby felt his face turning red. He shook his head.

Fitzman sighed. "Well, it's a start, I guess," he said. "Maybe this'll change when he gets interested in girls."

"Girls!" His mom laughed. "He's just a boy—all that business is a long way down the road."

On the way home, Robby's mom had taken him for a milk shake, like when he'd had his rotten baby tooth pulled out by the dentist. He sucked on the vanilla malted, and she pressed his hand with hers.

That proves it, Robby thinks. People have always been interested in him, even busy, important people like Mr. Fitzman. He decides to give Sharon and Dave another chance to be impressed. All the families have gone to bed. He hears an occasional noise from the dying fires. Snap, Crackle, Pop, he thinks—but which was which? Three little elves, and he's never thought of it before, but they look just like that cookie elf who lives in a tree, and like the Lucky Charms leprechaun without a beard. He remembers his Smurf collection, and he imagines Grandpa Smurf sitting in a blue rocker on a blue rug by a blue fireplace, with his throat slit, spurting red blood.

He yawns.

Stretching his fingers and toes, he wishes he was hanging out with the bikers tonight. They were such a great bunch of guys. The night Robby met them, the big old one was working on his saddlebags, cutting strips from a tough, strangely shaped piece of leather and tying them around the buckles. His knife caught Robby's eye. It was long for a collapsible knife, about five inches, and shiny steel. On the side was etched "Schrade." When Robby got back to his mom and dad's house, he told his mom he wanted that kind of knife. But she came back from the army-navy store with one that said "Buck" on the side. He put it back in the shopping bag and sulked for days until she asked what was wrong. "No offense, Mom, but you're not a very good listener," Robby said, and pulled the knife out of the bag, pointing at the lettering on the blade. His mother wagged her finger at him, laughing. "Picky, picky boy," she said, but then she patted Robby's cheek and apologized. She took the knife and drove away. She returned with his Schrade. Now he carries it with him all the time. Just tonight, he used it to cut the twine for hanging

up his shorts, and also for opening the burrito wrapper. He keeps it in his sleeping bag for protection at night.

This knife would impress anyone. He'll go back to Sharon and Dave. He'll say, "Psst. Hi, guys." He imagines them poking their heads out of the tent, looking sleepy. Then he'll say, "It's a beautiful night. You've got to see the moon." They'll have a better conversation. He'll show them the Schrade and tell them the big biker gave it to him. He imagines them asking to hold it.

He slips out of the sleeping bag and takes his shorts off the line. They're still damp, but that's okay. He takes a hit off the roach from earlier. He feels the weight of the Schrade in his left hand. He walks through the trees in his bare feet. He comes out right beside Sharon and Dave's tent. He's about to say, "Hi, guys, it's me." But instead, he circles the tent. Once, twice. Then he is kneeling down at the fly. He listens for noise from inside the tent. He imagines they are having sex, right now, and he almost giggles. He hears nothing, though. He waits. Are they alive? After a moment, he hears Dave cough and move. The nylon of the sleeping bag scratches along the ripstop of the tent. It sounds like insect wings.

Slowly, Robby pulls at the zipper that keeps the fly taut. In the moonlight that shines through the side of the blue tent, he can see their hair, and some of Dave's face. Dave's hair is blueblond, his skin is blue-pink. The nails of Sharon's hand that dangles off Dave's shoulder are blue-white.

Robby opens the Schrade, crouching at the maw of the tent. He's moving the knife slowly in the air, picturing the biker. Suddenly, he realizes the shape of the biker's piece of leather was the shape of an animal's back: neck, shoulders, rump. The biker's leather was the skin of an animal. He almost slaps his forehead in amazement. Of course he knew that leather came from animals, but he's never thought before of how it is skin, really skin. He doesn't slap himself, but he moves his heel and it scrapes a pebble.

In the tent, there is motion. Sharon's head turns and lifts toward him. He could still say "Hi," but nothing comes out.

Her eyes are open, looking at him. They are blue, with blue brows and lashes. She looks at him with a puzzled expression, then her eyes move down to the Schrade. They have a different look when they move back up to his face. She starts to open her mouth, but he smiles and puts his index and middle fingers to his lips. He feels cozy; he is recalling how his mom would visit his bedside while Fred slept. She would always do that, put her fingertips to her lips, before she stroked restless Robby's hair. He would fall asleep with her fingers on his scalp.

Robby moves his empty hand into the tent. It turns blue. Sharon's eyes look funny. Her eyebrows are all furrowed up, and she's not blinking as she looks into his eyes. He touches her hair with his hand. It's softer than it looks in its short, tomboy haircut. He moves the hand with the knife into the tent. The shiny steel shoots a beam of light right back out through the ripstop toward the moon. Robby smiles widely. It is a beautiful night. He lifts a small handful of Sharon's hair, some of her thick bangs. He slices through it with a swift, clean motion. She opens her mouth again; he hears a tiny squeak. He finds his hand moving the Schrade to her neck. His other hand holds her blue-red hair. He looks at her forehead, which is now exposed to the blue light. And across her forehead, he notices, is a line. Not a wrinkle but a wide, raised scar. It stretches diagonally from her part to the opposite brow. He can see that it cuts into her eyebrow; there is a hairless spot, pale and shiny. Robby has always been proud that he has not a single scar. All those cuts from roughhousing, and his skin sealed right back up every time. He moves the hand with the blade up to Sharon's forehead. Holding the handle with four fingers, Robby runs his pinkie along the waxy ridge of tissue. Then he thinks of his own body, his own skin like a rubber suit that holds his past inside.

Robby moves his hand away from her face, but his pinkie

still feels the smoothness of her scar. He eases his hand out of the tent. Then, carefully, softly, he edges backward on his haunches. He feels her watching him move away.

Back in his sleeping bag, he is still clutching Sharon's hair in his right hand. For a second, a question bobs to the surface: "Did I go over the line?" He brings the clump of hair to his nose and sniffs it—shampoo and bug spray. His stomach tightens, and he feels a little queasy. But then a TV set flashes on in his head, and he forgets everything else. He sees the Little Rascals. Alfalfa's pointy cowlick was like a horn, Robby thinks. He remembers the one when Alfalfa and Spanky went camping. Did Spanky and Alfalfa let their little brothers come on their trip? Of course not. But the kids followed the big boys all the way to the camp. Both pairs of boys pitched their tents and unrolled their sleeping bags. But when dinnertime came, Spanky and Alfalfa had forgotten their food.

The big boys sit there, looking at each other. They are close to tears. Alfalfa hits Spanky on the crown of his head. "Ow!" says Spanky, and he hits Alfalfa back. "Ow!" says Alfalfa, and he hits Spanky again. Nearby, the little ones eat bread and jam. But in the end, do they share it or keep it for themselves? Robby can't remember.

JULIAN

Julian balanced between the rungs of the cast-iron gate. He held the stationary fence and swung in a slow, small arc back and forth. The iron hinges squeaked. Rebecca rummaged in her purse for the keys. When she found them, she pushed open the front door, then turned and waited for Julian to get down from the gate.

Julian hopped down, then took a couple of uneven steps away from his mother and the front door, dragging his right foot behind him.

"Come on, time to go inside," said Rebecca.

"Today, in Yard," Julian said, "I learned to limp."

"Please, sweetie, you can play later," said Rebecca.

Julian's father, Herzl, had said he would try to make dinner. When Rebecca and Julian entered the house, there was no smell of food being cooked, no heat coming from the kitchen. Julian ran past his mother through the living room and back door, into the garden.

Herzl was in the hammock, curled up sideways, with his knees pulled up to his chest. One arm was hooked over his head, and the other covered his eyes. The ground around him

was stained black from the summer's mulberries. The hammock was big and stretchy, woven from bright green cotton string. Herzl's body weighed it down in the middle, so it supported him just above the ground and folded over him. Julian thought of a picture book they had at school about monarch butterflies, and the fields of jade-colored cocoons hanging off thousands of milkweed plants.

Julian dropped his knapsack and jacket on the ground and ran to his father. He pushed the hammock but could not move it. Julian's chest tightened. He pulled the taut ropes and looked at Herzl, then reached out a finger and poked him.

"Gentle . . ." whispered Rebecca behind him.

Herzl opened his eyes. Julian let out his breath and almost laughed. He waited for Herzl to smile or wink. He wanted his father to pull him onto the hammock, he wanted to get tangled in the stretchy webbing and fall onto his father's belly. But Herzl just looked at him; his eyes were the only part of his face that moved, and he looked Julian in the eye.

"Hi, Dad," Julian said. He made himself sound sullen and removed, like a teenager on TV.

"You didn't make dinner," said Rebecca. Then she added, "It's okay."

"I'll make dinner," said Julian. "I'm going to make dinner. I'm a good cook, Dad, right? I'll make omelets!"

"I'll make dinner," Rebecca said. Julian heard her close the door partway as she went inside the house.

Julian backed away from the hammock. His father pushed himself against the fabric and turned himself around. The hammock tipped, and he sat just inside its edge, crouching, feet on the ground. Julian could see how his father had changed: his skin did not fit his big bones, it hung slack on his chest and belly. The treatments had given him rashes and had made his hair patchy. Julian stared at his freckled scalp.

He reminded himself again of that time long ago, when he was just a little kid. Herzl had taken him upstate to the sculp-

ture park. He had been strong, and he had lifted Julian onto a couple of the giant metal monsters and taken pictures of him. Julian knew this had happened because one of these snapshots was framed on his grandmother's wall. On the way back into Brooklyn, they were stopped at a red light. Julian saw two figures in the doorway of a building. He pulled on Herzl's sleeve and pointed. A tall, thin man was bent over a tiny old lady, who was holding her pocketbook to her chest. "Wait here," Herzl said to Julian, and he pulled over and got out of the car. Julian pressed his face to the window and watched Herzl go and talk to the man; they seemed to argue. The woman backed away and opened the door with several keys. Julian was watching her when he heard shouting and saw someone run past the car. Then he didn't see his father, and then he realized Herzl was lying on the ground. Julian started screaming inside the car. He tried to open the doors, but Herzl had locked them all. Some people came over and were brushing Herzl off as he pushed himself up to sit on the sidewalk. Julian kept screaming. Herzl gave the keys to someone to let Julian out. He ran over to his father, who was talking with the people around him. Julian leapt at his father from behind and clutched onto his head. He buried his fingers in Herzl's pale, woolly hair. Julian hardly remembered the rest of the night. The important parts of that day, Julian reminded himself now, were that his dad had lifted him up and taken pictures of him; that his dad had saved a lady from being mugged; that his dad had been hurt but was okay, and had sat up all on his own.

Herzl was rubbing his hands together, and Julian could see the crisscross pattern of the strings on Herzl's arms. There was a sketch pad under the hammock. Next to it was Herzl's pen, which Julian loved to use. It was a special pen, a Rapidograph filled with India ink. Julian looked at the pad, but from where he stood, he could not make out the drawing on the page. It was small and dark and seemed to be quite detailed. He squatted to get a closer look, but Herzl reached down and closed the

pad. Julian felt himself blush. He thought he had seen wings in the picture. Was he not supposed to look? Was there another new rule?

On Friday evenings during the school year, Julian's uncle Maurice—Herzl's brother—came over with his son Peter. This visit would be their first since May. The doorbell rang at eight o'clock. Herzl was resting upstairs in the bedroom. Julian ran down the front hall in his socks, sliding the last few feet. He opened the door and let in his uncle and cousin. Uncle Maurice was divorced, and he was religious. He and Peter wore crocheted yarmulkes, which were held in place with bobby pins. Maurice bent down to hug Julian, while Peter leaned back into the shadows near the door. He was twelve, and he had recently experienced a growth spurt. He was covered in a new padding of flesh, and his black hair hung down to his chin. He wore his shirt untucked, had fancy suede sneakers, and carried a leather backpack. He said "What's up?" to Julian. His voice was husky.

Julian took Uncle Maurice's hand and pulled him into the hot, humid kitchen. The window to the garden was steamed over. Rebecca wiped her forehead on her sleeve, then turned to receive Uncle Maurice's hug. Rebecca's hands were coated in lentil loaf batter, and Julian watched them dangle in the air behind his uncle. They were caked in a drying brown crust.

There was a big rectangle cut out of the wall between the kitchen and the living room. Julian could see Peter kneeling on the rug, flipping through Herzl's record collection.

"How is he?" Maurice was asking Rebecca.

"I don't know, something happened this afternoon. He was in the backyard with Julian—" Rebecca began.

Julian walked out of the kitchen and went to kneel next to Peter, who was inspecting a Frank Zappa record he'd taken out of a faded cardboard jacket. Julian remembered Peter prying open a clamshell once on a trip to the beach, forcing it open to

see the live clam. Julian had been content to look at the pretty outsides of shells. Peter liked to open things up and touch them.

Peter handed the record to Julian and said, "Remember when we went with your dad to the radio station?" Julian nodded. Herzl's friend Al was a DJ at WROC. They went the night Al did a phone interview with Frank Zappa, and Peter had gotten to ask a question on the air. As he took the black vinyl disk from Peter, Julian saw his own slender, bony hand, with its thin skin and just a few silky blond hairs—and he saw his cousin's hand, his thick fingers, tough, chewed nails, and two skinned knuckles.

"Do you want to play?" Julian asked his cousin. His voice came out high and flutey, like a faraway child's.

"Where's your dad tonight?" asked Peter.

"Taking a nap," Julian said. "He'll wake up for dinner."

"Let's go up to your room."

The walls of Julian's room were covered in posters from *National Geographic World,* mostly fish and frogs. There was also a souvenir picture from the *Nutcracker Suite* that Julian had meant to take down before his cousin came over. He knew that Peter's walls were painted red and had pictures of Bob Dylan, Albert Einstein, and the kibbutz in Israel that he'd visited. Julian opened the door to his closet, so that it almost completely hid the Sugar Plum Fairy. He leaned against the closet door. Peter locked the door to the room.

"I'm not allowed to lock the door," said Julian.

"Don't you have any privacy around here?" asked Peter.

"Yeah . . ." Julian's voice disappeared. He sighed.

"At my mom's place," said Peter, "there are no walls, just big canvas curtains hanging from the ceiling. It doesn't have rooms, just 'spaces.' I'm having problems with my mom right now." Julian remembered Peter's mom from a long time ago, at a party, holding a cat.

"Do you still have turtles?" Julian asked.

"Yeah. But they're old. They don't move around a lot." Peter suddenly sounded weary, and he flopped down on the floor. Julian flopped down, too. Peter then half-opened his eyes and said, "I brought you something. I don't know. Maybe you wouldn't like it."

Julian tried not to sound eager. "What is it?"

"I found it in the neighbor's recycling," said Peter. "Actually, I found a lot of them."

Julian felt himself clasping his hands together like a beggar. Peter reached into his bag and pulled out a manila envelope, which he tossed to Julian. Julian caught it. He opened the envelope and pulled out a magazine. *Penthouse,* it said. Julian froze. He looked at Peter.

"It's so funny," said Peter. "Look inside. It's really, really funny."

Julian opened the magazine to the first page. On one side was an ad for menthol cigarettes, on the other a table of contents. Julian squinted so everything blurred.

Peter pulled himself across the rug to Julian's side. He giggled and opened the magazine to the middle. It rested on Julian's lap as Peter flipped through the pages.

Julian heard the door to his parents' room open. He heard his father pad into the bathroom, using the cane. Julian's stomach contracted.

"This is the one," Peter was saying.

"My dad is up," said Julian.

"It's okay. The door's locked, remember?" Peter nudged Julian.

Julian was overcome by it suddenly: the thing he'd been trying not to think about all night. It had happened earlier in the day, when he was out in the garden with his father. Right after he closed the little sketch pad, Herzl had pushed against the hammock to stand up. He was up for a second, and he reached his hand out to Julian. Then he toppled over and lay there on

the grass breathing hard. "Get your mother," he said, and as Julian dashed into the kitchen, he wondered if Herzl's hand had been about to squeeze his shoulder apologetically or hit him. Rebecca had helped Herzl up. "You have to go upstairs and lie down," she had said.

"I can't lie down forever," he had said.

Peter nudged Julian again. "Look at this."

Julian looked down at the page. His armpits tingled. He heard the toilet flush, and the door to his parents' room closed with a click. Peter nudged him again. Julian let his eyes focus. It was a picture of two women on the back of a horse, which was standing in a meadow, chewing some grass. It was a beautiful horse, sleek and brown, with a black mane. One of the women was blond and slight, and she wore a white shirt, which was unbuttoned to her waist. A globelike breast pointed toward the sky. She wore nothing on the bottom, and she leaned back against the horse's neck. She had no hair between her legs, like a little girl. The other woman straddled the horse facing her, leaning forward on the horse's back. She held a black riding crop, and her tongue pointed between the first woman's legs.

Julian looked over at his cousin. Peter now had a very serious expression on his face. Julian looked back at the picture. He heard a spatula on a pan downstairs.

Peter said quietly, "I think that one looks a little bit like you."

"Her?" Julian put his finger on the blond one's face. Peter nodded, and pushed Julian's finger away. Julian felt an ache in his thighs. He felt his testicles shift. He heard his mother's footsteps on the hardwood stairs. Rebecca called to them, "Dinner'll be ready in five minutes, kids." There was a pause, and then the footsteps descended. Julian could smell the lentil loaf. He looked at Peter, and Peter was looking at him with a strange, agonized grin. Then Peter stuck out his tongue, making it pointy like the woman in the picture. Julian stuck out his tongue, too, and leaned toward his cousin until their tongues were touching. Julian's penis pushed against his underwear. Pe-

ter put his arm around Julian's shoulder and pulled him close. Julian felt Peter's tongue, large inside his mouth. Julian thought of the Sugar Plum Fairy and moved his own tongue around. Soon they were hugging each other and lying down on the floor. They touched each other's shoulders and arms.

Then it was over. Neither pushed away, they just parted and went back to leaning against the wall. Julian inspected Peter's face. It was red and shiny. Julian still ached between his legs. He glanced down at the crotch of his cousin's pants, but they were very baggy, and Julian couldn't see anything.

"Think about something sad, and it'll go away," said Peter.

Herzl did not come down to dinner.

Rebecca asked Peter about the skateboard he was making. Peter talked about planing down the wood, picking out a finish, and why small wheels were better than the old fat kind. Then Uncle Maurice told them about two-headed tulips that had been found growing next to Three Mile Island. "How can we pray to a God who creates these things?" he said. No one answered.

"Everything in the world is somehow meant to be," Uncle Maurice continued, gesturing around the room with both his hands. "I accept that, or I try to, anyway. But think about it—normally, those bright flowers are the most prized and beautiful part of the plant. Then when you multiply them, they become bizarre—just *wrong*. Who is it that decides these things for us? Is there something we're supposed to learn? If anyone knows, please tell me."

Under the table, Julian's feet moved rhythmically. He was practicing his limp.

After dinner, Uncle Maurice and Cousin Peter went upstairs to visit Herzl. It had been months since Peter had seen his uncle. Maurice had visited after the surgery, but Peter had been in soc-

cer camp. Julian helped his mother fold the tablecloth and make tea. When Maurice came downstairs, Peter was not with him. He explained that Peter was in Julian's room, spending some "alone time."

Julian dashed upstairs. He wanted to tell Peter to take the magazine, that it was too dangerous having it in this house. The door to his room was closed. Julian knocked.

"Who is it?" Peter's voice was muffled.

"Julian."

"Come in," said Peter. Julian pushed the door open. Peter was lying on the bed, on Julian's old Star Trek quilt. When he sat up, there were glossy tear-stripes under his eyes. Julian closed the door behind himself and sat down on the edge of the bed. He was very near to Peter. Peter sniffed and wiped his nose with the back of his hand.

Peter said, "Your dad is sick."

"I know," said Julian. He looked at the Starship *Enterprise,* zooming across his bed.

"I mean, I knew he was sick, but," Peter whispered, "is he going to die?"

Julian looked back up at his cousin and he wanted to beat him. Peter was weeping, and the flesh on his body looked raw and tender. Julian's arms jerked, and for a moment, he felt he would punch Peter in the face, kick him in the belly, push him out the window to fall like a stuffed dummy into the garden.

But then Julian slid off the bed and onto the floor. He pulled his knees to his chest and wrapped his arms around them. He imagined a crisp, sunny autumn day. He imagined walking through a field of milkweed plants. As he walked, the plants started to grow. They grew taller and taller, until they were like trees around him. In his mind, he crawled up a thick stem to a fleshy leaf right below a brown pod. A thousand silk threads encircled him until he was sitting in a bright green capsule. He would hibernate in there, wait until spring. He would not come out until the time was right.

MEMOIR

My father lay in his bed, a white sheet pulled up to his chin. When I entered the attic room where he was living, he turned his head away from the round window and looked at me. His eyes were milking over. I could see his fingers, curling, twisting the bedclothes from underneath. He opened his mouth a little. His teeth were yellow, and they looked huge pushing against his peeling lips.

I sat down in the dark part of the room, holding my green satin purse. I folded my hands across my belly and looked at my father. I started to play with the clasp of my purse, listening to the noise it made opening and closing. Pop. Pop.

"I couldn't get it done," I said. He closed his mouth. "The old doctor's dead." My father turned to face the round window again. I knew he could see the old oak tree with its fresh green leaves, green hands waving in the breeze. The leaves tossed sunshine into the room through the window. The grass of the field was bright and moist, pushing up through the soft black earth. Beyond the field were the hills. Over the hills rose a snaking column of black smoke. Often, there were two columns. Sometimes, when a whole family went at once, there were as many as four or five

•

So the baby came. The trees turned scarlet and yellow, and leaves piled up like a moat around the house; apples fell to the ground and changed into wine, and drunken field mice dragged them home to their nests. And the baby came. By that time, my father couldn't move at all. He had started to flatten; his hands and feet were desiccated, papery and bloodless, curling backward. Eva from the next house over came to help me deliver. She had two of her own. She'd managed to send one away to the coast, but people there were starting to go, too. She came over to the house ready for a difficult time—she brought armfuls of towels, salves, tonics. But when she arrived, I was sitting up in the kitchen. I was feeling the pains, closer together, pushing at me. I didn't mind them. I liked the feeling. It was a feeling—so I was still alive. Instead of screaming, like Eva told me I'd do, I hummed a song. I couldn't remember where I'd heard it, and only remembered half the words.

Eva closed the screen door behind her when she entered the kitchen. She put her supplies down on the table.

"What are you doing?" she asked me.

I smiled at her. I felt sweat crawl over my cheeks to my neck. I held on to the slatted back of the chair. I never screamed. I never lay down. Eva knelt and cupped her hands, ready when the baby's head pushed through.

·

When I was small, my mother and I used to walk through the field and over the two hills, taking the shortcut to the village. One day, we went to visit Mr. Fryar, the baker. We entered at the front of the shop, as usual. The loop of bells on the door jingled. I went to stand at the picture I liked, while my mother got the bread and soup biscuits. It was a picture of a canyon, where cows waded in a stream, and sheer rock walls rose up. A path was cut in one of the dark gray sides. The valley was crisscrossed by long shadows, but up above the sun shined. A tremendous bird dove, arching away from the sun. I liked to imagine the bird swooping

down among the cows, picking one up in its great beak, and taking it back to a nest of branches for dinner.

My mother chatted with the baker longer than usual this particular day, and I noticed for the first time that there was a little cow looking out from behind one of the grown cow's bellies. Just as I discovered this new detail, I heard my mother call to me. "Come here, dear," she said. "Mr. Fryar is going to show us something very special."

Mr. Fryar, bald and round and all in white, lifted a hinged piece of the wooden counter and let us through. I'd never been in the back of the bakery before. There was a giant mixer with a spade-shaped blade, shelves of tiny bowls, and a long steel table with soft rounds of dough set on it. Mr. Fryar went over to the oven on the far wall, brick, with a chimney and decorative tiles. He opened the oven with one hand, and with the other he pushed in a flat wooden paddle. When he pulled it out, it came with a pan of loaves. He put the pan down on the metal table, and my mother curled her finger to me. "Come and look," she said.

I approached the table slowly, sniffing.

"For the festival on Saturday," said Mr. Fryar, and he held a loaf up with the paddle.

It was a bread baby, shiny with egg yolk. The dough had been shaped into a round little head, ten fingers and toes, and knobby kneecaps. Its torso was a plump braided loaf, with the bread tapering to a twisted cord at its navel.

"Here, take this," said Mr. Fryar. He unwrapped something and handed it to me. "The oven was too hot for the first batch," he said. "They fell apart."

I looked down at my hand. In it was a glossy brown baby fist. The fingers were a little burnt, but the dough on the inside was soft and melted on my tongue. I finished eating it before we got to the end of Mr. Fryar's street.

•

The first person to fall ill was the schoolteacher, Miss Trell. I saw it happen. I was in her class; my seat was in the front of the

room, right across from her desk. I remember the first day, how she licked her lips over and over. Then later that week, I noticed her eyes: that sheen they get, a white greasy layer that spreads outward from the pupil over the iris. The next week, she didn't come to school on Monday. On Tuesday, she had bandages on most of her fingertips. I didn't know her nails had shed, though soon all these signs were familiar in our town. But at the moment, I chose to pay only the slightest attention to the changes in Miss Trell. I'd discovered that every time I glanced at Chess Fulton, two seats over in the next row back, a shudder passed through me. My cheeks crawled, and between my legs there was something sticky. Once, I got excused to go to the girls' room. There I put a finger in the slickness and tasted: salt.

Two weeks after the very first signs, Miss Trell left the school. We were told it was temporary, and we had a man fill in who did tricks with apples and ball bearings. But she never came back, and eventually she was replaced by Mrs. Sargum, who rearranged the seating in the room. Now I was next to Chess. One Friday afternoon, he and I got excused at the same time, and we went to the meeting room with its soft chairs. It was next to the headmaster's office and we had to be very quiet. He unbuttoned my yellow shirt and pulled at the strap of my undershirt. He suckled and I looked at my fingers in his brown hair.

Shortly after that, Chess's mother started showing symptoms. She went into quarantine—at that point it was believed to be contagious—and Chess had to leave school to manage the thread shop.

•

When you're trapped, you want to flee. You try to flee. But a trap—by definition—is something from which you can't escape.

We soon learned that the most unbearable kind of trap is one in which no one has trapped you. In this situation, there is no one to outwit, no one to beseech, and no one to hate.

•

Neither of our village doctors—father and son—knew what to do. The younger one suddenly became religious; the older plied his patients with useless medicines.

A specialist was called in from the city, where he was head of his department at the university hospital. The specialist took a train to the next town over from ours.

He was met at the station by the knife man in his red step truck. The knife man dropped the specialist at the edge of our village, where he was greeted by the sheriff and the older doctor.

The specialist stopped at the inn just long enough to splash some cold water on his face, dot cologne on his wrists, rub some pomade in his hair, and hang up his change of clothing. Then he followed the older doctor to his office, where the specialist set up a makeshift laboratory. After that, they were off again.

They spent the rest of the afternoon visiting the homes of afflicted villagers. When they rang the first doorbell, the specialist smiled to himself—he hadn't made a house call for, he calculated, at least twenty years.

He stopped smiling when he saw the patient.

Late that evening, he looked at the samples he'd taken. The older doctor watched from a chair in the corner as the specialist bent over the microscope. The specialist almost gasped at what he saw—not from horror, exactly, but from admiration (the two aren't as far apart as you think).

This was an organism of great beauty: silky and motile, it danced on the slide, slowing down, speeding up, then whipping around to the point that it just started to break apart . . . and then stopping and resting before it began its dance again.

·

My father let go on Sally's first birthday. I'd moved him to the basement, to try and keep him damp and cool, but by then he had become so dry his arms and legs were ribbons spooled into themselves; his hips had collapsed and widened; the ribs had compressed and begun to crumble. His heart beat slowly—its bulge pushed visibly against his disintegrating ribs.

I've shown pictures of him when he was well to Sally. "That's Grandpa," I say "You look like him. He was the apple grower. Those trees down the road with the sour little fruit— they were once real apple trees, and everyone in the village ate pies from them."

And I show her pictures of her grandmother. "We used to walk over the hills together," I say. "Where the ovens are now— well, there used to be only one oven. And before the sickness came, the oven was in Mr. Fryar's bakery. We had fresh bread every day. You look like your grandmother, too."

Sometimes, Sally asks who she got her tail from. Grandma? Grandpa? She reaches behind herself and holds it; she twists around and studies it. It's a small tail, an extension of her spine. It's lively but dainty, covered in soft brown hair.

Of course people in town wonder about Sally's father. *Who is he? Where is he?* Eva asks. I never tell her.

When my father fell ill and had to stop working on the trees, I got a job at the inn, changing beds and helping serve breakfast. By that time, we rarely had visitors from out of town—just people with special permission to attend funerals. Otherwise, the guests were mostly husbands or wives kept away from their beloveds by quarantine, or spooked people who superstitiously believed that leaving their houses would keep them alive.

I was on duty when the specialist stayed over. I had noticed him come in from the train, with his dark, square-shouldered coat and his cologne and pomade. I had watched him leave again with his kit in one hand and his big book in the other.

It was very late at night, early morning really, when he came back from the old doctor's laboratory. I was at the desk near the door, half asleep, when he woke me up and asked if I had any whiskey.

"Do you want me to bring it to your room?" I asked. He shook his head. I pointed toward the end of the hall, where the lounge was, and told him to wait in there. I got the best

whiskey from the locked pantry, and put the bottle on a tray with some ice and a glass. I walked down the hall to the lounge.

Everybody in town had known that the specialist was coming; everybody hoped he'd have an answer for us; many thought he would save us. But when I saw him sitting in the dim light of the lounge, slouched in an armchair, eyes closed, rubbing his temples, I knew he was nothing, just a man from the city.

I put the tray down on the table next to him. He opened his eyes and thanked me. I sat down a few chairs away. He said I didn't need to stay. I lied and said it was against the rules to leave him alone in the lounge. He took out his deck of cards and started to play solitaire. I watched. I poured him another drink when he finished the first one, and moved to the chair across from him. When he finished that one, I poured him a third and asked him to teach me how to play cards. I already knew how to play most card games. Step by step, he showed me war, hearts, blackjack, gin rummy, and poker. I pretended to be learning them for the first time. He was arrogant in the most gentle way. I let him beat me every time. As we played, and as he drank, he told me about his day. He told me he had played cards on the train, solitaire, and that it hadn't mattered to him if he won or lost. He told me about chuckling to himself before the house call. He told me about what he had seen on the slide.

I poured him a fourth whiskey. Then I reached over, took the cards out of his hand, and pulled him toward me.

•

I've always felt Sally was charmed because of her tail.

I read in a very old book that certain charmed people can read the minds of others. Today, Sally and I sit at the kitchen table. She wears a white nightgown, and I can see her tail flicking underneath it as I bring her a cup of milk. I've told her we're going to play a game, a guessing game.

If she's charmed, then maybe she's safe forever. I want to test her. I want to see how charmed she in

I take my father's deck of cards from a drawer and shuffle them on the table. Then I pick one out and look at it. The ten of spades.

"Guess which card I have," I say to Sally.

"The six of diamonds," she says and laughs, covering her mouth with her little hand. The nightgown twitches behind her.

I tell her to pick a card and send a picture of it to me with her mind. I try to receive the message and then I say, "The queen of hearts."

"No, it's the seven of clubs," she says and laughs again.

.

THE SPLINTER

There is a beach on the eastern side of the island. It is a rocky beach, with smooth white pebbles.

It is low tide. A fine foam settles and seeps through the clustered stones. Shells and tangled weeds dry in the heat. The water beyond the beach is huge and blue, and it reflects the cloudless sky. Behind the beach is a grove of short, twisted trees. Their trunks and branches all curve in the same direction, pushed by the constant wind off the sea. Thorns grow between their leaves.

Linda runs down the slope, ducking the lowest branches. Her sandals kick dust and pebbles up in front of her. She carries an empty yellow bucket. She is six.

Last night was very windy, and the terrain has shifted. A root is exposed, the crook of it sticking up. Linda is looking ahead, at the push and pull of the water and the shiny stones. Then, like a cough or a hiccup, she finds herself pitching forward, up and over, onto her head. Her sandal stays caught in the root that tripped her. She comes to rest on her belly, breathing quickly, almost panting. Her legs and feet remain in the shade of the grove, but her torso, head, and arms have crossed into the white sunlight of the beach. She stays like this for a while, at first surprised, then almost luxuriating. Her breath slows back down to normal. She

watches a red mite make its way over the mountain of a tiny pebble. She watches a stiff gray feather shake itself free from an old brown clump of seaweed.

Then Linda starts to feel the pain in her head. She makes herself sit up, folding her sturdy legs beneath her. She lets go of the bucket and puts her fingers to her scalp, pressing on it to find the exact place that hurts. She touches a wet spot. She brings her fingers down and looks at them: there's a little blood, fresh, very thin, orange in the sunlight. She smells it, puts a finger in her mouth and tastes it—a salty, metallic taste. It makes her thirsty. She puts her fingers on the sore spot again. There's a bump there; something from the ground has dug itself into her skin, and a swelling has begun to form around it. The bleeding is stopping already.

She twists to get her sandal from the root. She tugs it free and puts it on her foot, but the tongue of the buckle has broken off. She stands slowly and walks to the wet part of the beach, dragging the foot with the broken sandal. She walks up and down along the water, squatting occasionally to dig for treasure. She finds shells and a sand dollar and the hinged claw of a crab. As she puts these in her bucket, she sometimes feels the bump on her head, presses on it. Usually she comes to the beach in the morning with the kids from next door. Today is just her second time alone. She had hesitated when her father dropped her off, hanging on to his hand, but he'd said it would be okay because it was just for a couple of hours in the afternoon, and besides, he had added, the locals would look out for her.

There is no one else on the beach.

When the sun starts to go down, she walks back through the trees, stopping for a moment at the hooked root, then carefully stepping over it. Then she comes to the other edge of the grove, where the road is, and across the road the tavern where the fishermen drink. A couple of donkeys wait patiently near the tavern, chewing on the clumps of dry grass that grow in the dirt.

Linda feels her sore spot and waits for her father. She hears mu-

sic from the tavern, the whiny instruments and tunes that get faster and faster, played on little records. Once or twice her father has taken her into the tavern for a soda, and the man behind the bar has shown Linda the records, and the plastic disks that go into the middles of them to make the holes fit the record player.

Today she is very thirsty. She would like a soda, brown and smooth, and ice knocking on her teeth. She would like to wash away the tinny taste of blood. But she can't go into the tavern without her father, so she keeps waiting, organizing her objects in the bucket.

He comes before the sun has completely set. He comes down the road with his easel strapped onto his back, and paints and paintbrushes sticking out of his pockets. He's wearing olive-colored army shorts, cut off at the knees, and a T-shirt. His legs and arms are covered with curly yellow hair.

With the bump on her head, and the blood, and the thirst, Linda has forgotten what they talked about last night, and as soon as her father reaches her, she says it without thinking: "I want my mom." He looks angry as he kneels down to her. He takes her shoulders and explains again. Mom is not here. She is in Scotland, which is part of England. Remember? he asks. He repeats what he said last night. Linda will go to Scotland to live with Mom at the end of the summer. Right now, Linda is with him, her father, here, in Greece. He takes her hand and they start up the road. "I'm thirsty," says Linda, twisting away, looking back at the tavern, thinking of a cold soda. Her father tugs on her hand, saying there's plenty to drink back at the house. It's almost dark out now, and the wind off the sea has picked up. Linda walks close to her father, careful not to drag her foot, and brushes against the fur of his arm with her face, smelling oil and turpentine.

They follow the main street, all the way to the top of the village, where their house sits at the end of a skinny cul-de-sac. It is a low white building with a wide door, made of planks and painted blue, that opens onto a small courtyard. An olive tree

grows in the courtyard, and Linda's bicycle with training wheels lies on its side here. In one corner are all the items Linda has gathered from the beach so far, washed with water from a pitcher, and sorted according to texture. Tonight, Linda puts her bucket down in this corner and touches the spot on her head, which is throbbing. When she does it again as she sips the soda he poured over ice for her, her father asks what is wrong. She shakes her foot so the broken sandal falls off. He puts down the onion he has been peeling and comes to her and picks up the sandal. He inspects the broken buckle.

"How did this happen?" he asks.

She says nothing. She touches her head again, pressing on the swollen place. She presses hard. It's an itchy kind of pain, and a little ooze comes off on her fingers. She looks at it. It's not as bloody now, more a clear, sticky substance with blood mixed in.

Her father wipes the onion juice off on his shorts. He feels around on her scalp, and when he finds the bump, Linda says, "Ow!" He tells her to sit still, and he goes to wash his hands. In the sink are the beaks and quills of squid, and on the wooden counter are the squids' flesh and tentacles, sprinkled with garlic and salt. He dries his hands on a piece of cheesecloth and brings a flashlight over to Linda. She watches her father moving around, fast and efficient. She worries about the squid, sitting out like that—she knows they're supposed to be cooked soon after they're cleaned. That way, her father always says, they're tender, more like noodles than rubber.

He shines the light on her scalp, pushes her hair away from the hurt spot. He pokes at it again. "Ow!" Linda says again.

"It's one of those damn thorns," he says. "How did you get a thorn in your head? Did you bump into a tree?"

"I fell," Linda says. "I broke my sandal."

"You fell on your head?"

She nods.

"Wasn't there anyone else at the beach?" he asks.

She shakes her head, looking at her sandal, which is balanced

sideways on the floor. He covers the squid with an upside-down
bowl, then disappears into the bathroom. He comes out with a
pair of tweezers. He takes a pack of matches out of his back
pocket and lights one, burning the angled metal pincers. He prods
the splinter a little bit. Linda's body stiffens, and she grabs on to
his shorts. He tries to get the points around the thorn, but he has
trouble finding a place to grasp. He spreads the skin around the
thorn, pressing down. Linda squeezes his leg through the soft
green cloth. He curses. "I love you, Daddy," Linda says, crying.
She feels the tears creeping from her eyes, and she tastes the salty
mucus that flows from her nostrils and rounds the curves of her
lips. She sniffles and reaches up to wipe her face.

"Just hold still," says her father. He digs with one point of the
tweezers, and her scalp starts to bleed again.

He announces that he can't get the thorn out. He pats her on
the shoulder and pries her fingers from his leg, then goes back to
the bathroom. This time he comes back with a bottle of rubbing alcohol and some cotton balls. He dabs her scalp with alcohol and tries to push her hair back into place.

He fries up the squid quickly, leaving out the onion. They sit
at the low table near the windows. The house is divided into
three rooms: there is this room, with the kitchen in one corner;
Linda's father's room, which is big and has a view of the village's roofs and the sea beyond them; and then there is Linda's
tiny room, which holds just her cot and the chair where he sits
and reads to her at night.

The throbbing calms down, and Linda does not touch the
spot on her head. It's late in the evening, the hour when he
would normally be telling her to get ready for bed, when she
would be picking out a book or asking him to tell her "Chicken
Little." But tonight, he's forgotten about her bedtime. He paces
back and forth in the main room, a glass of wine in his hand,
cursing himself and asking her questions.

"I knew I couldn't do it," he says. "I told her. I told her. This
was exactly what I was talking about. I said I wouldn't know

what to do if you got sick. Why did she have to do this to me?"

"I'm not sick, Daddy," says Linda. He does not hear her.

"She said to take you to Marisu if something happened. Marisu! Of course this would happen the one time she goes to Athens." Marisu is the next-door neighbor they get yogurt from. "I told your mother to take you with her, to take you to Edinburgh now. Right? Remember?" Linda nods. But she doesn't remember. She remembers her parents staying up and talking and talking before Mom left, and when Mom said, "I'll see you soon," Linda thought she meant tomorrow. But that was a long time ago, or at least it feels like it was.

Her father paces. "I can't do it. I can't do it," he says. He punches the kitchen counter.

"Time for bed," Linda finally says in the same tone of voice he usually uses.

He looks at the white plastic clock over the stove. He stands still for a second, then turns the flashlight on again and shines it on the swollen part of her scalp, where the blunt end of the thorn is pillowed by a blister of skin and fluid. He drips more rubbing alcohol onto it. "Okay, Linda, I don't want to try anything else—go get ready for bed. I'll be in in a minute." But then he follows her into the bathroom. Linda sees him in the mirror, watching her as she stands on the stool to brush her teeth. He looks like he's trying to smile, but his forehead is wrinkly and his eyebrows are pulled together. Linda steps off the stool, then climbs up onto the toilet to pee, then undresses herself, kicking off her shorts and underpants. She leaves her clothes in a pile on the bathroom floor and says to her father, who stands near the door, "Carry me like a baby." She's never done this with him before. It's a bedtime game she has with her mother. He picks her up, with one arm supporting her neck and the other under her bent knees, and he tilts her body toward his chest. She says, "Ga ga goo goo, me a baby." He carries her to her bed, smoothing her hair over the growing lump.

He puts her down on her cot, pulls up the sheet and cotton

blanket, and puts his hand on her forehead. He asks how she is feeling.

"I'm *not sick,* Daddy," she says. She touches her fingers to her sore spot. He reads to her, and she falls asleep quickly. He almost wakes her up to make sure she's all right, but he stops himself.

He remembers the boat ride from Athens to the island, about six weeks ago. Most of their bags were in the cargo deck below, but Nora, Linda's mother, carried the girl's plastic tote bag. It had several zippered pockets and a picture of a dancing elephant on it; inside were Linda's sneakers, a change of underpants, and a couple of her favorite books. In their hotel room in Athens, Nora had also thrown in Dr. Spock's *Baby and Child Care*—"In case she gets seasick, Tom."

"That's a good idea," he said, meaning it, but it sounded cruel and sarcastic. Nora rolled her eyes back and pushed air through her nose. It seemed too complicated to him to go back through the exchange and apologize.

They went to different decks on the boat. Nora watched Linda run up and down the upper deck, laughing at the gulls who picked at their feet with their beaks. He went to the bar. He had his easel with him, and he leaned it against a pole. He ordered a glass of ouzo and smoked a brown Turkish cigarette. There was a French businessman who was going to one of the islands to discuss building a television station. Tom practiced his French with this man. They joked about Americans. Tom was always ready to ridicule the kind of people he saw wandering supermarket aisles like zombies. Then he started to feel sick. They were further out on the water, and the boat was rocking. The easel slid down and hit the floor with a clatter.

Tom excused himself and went up to find Nora and Linda, dragging the easel behind him. Nora had wrapped her white Spanish shawl around herself. She looked up at him and laughed. He tried to grin. Linda ran over and looked up at him.

She asked her mother what was wrong with Daddy. He made his way as quickly as he could to the stern and vomited into the sea. When he came back, he sat on the chair next to Nora's, and Linda came over and patted him on the shoulder. Nora took Dr. Spock out of the bag and read aloud. "Why didn't we bring any arrowroot biscuits!" she said, laughing. He laughed too. He was feeling better. Linda climbed up the side of the chair onto his lap, and Nora got him a bottle of club soda.

They had laughed together, he remembers now. Every time they laughed together, he thought it would be okay. He thought that everything they had said and done to each other could be remedied. He believed the things they talked about in the dark, late nights meant nothing as long as they could laugh the way they did when they first met. For Tom, once the sun rose, it was almost as if those conversations hadn't actually happened: they became distant and abstract, as fleeting as dreams. But even in the daylight—over breakfast, with the *Herald Tribune* spread out in front of her, or at a museum, standing before a Miró etching—Nora acknowledged those nighttime subjects: betrayal, disappointment, regret. And she still laughed with him.

When they arrived on the island, they discovered they had left Dr. Spock under one of the canvas chairs on the boat.

Now Tom gets up and plans tomorrow. He starts pacing again. He takes a couple more glasses of wine and tries to read. Finally, though, he sits back down in his chair by Linda's bed, and falls asleep there.

When Linda wakes up the next morning, her head is throbbing again. Her skin itches around the thorn, and she runs her nails over it. She gets out of bed and walks, naked, into the kitchen. Her father is stirring a spoonful of instant coffee into some hot water. It's bright in the main room, but he still shines the flashlight on her head, parting her dark hair to look at the splinter. He says it doesn't look good. He asks her if she's been touching

it a lot. She shakes her head and takes a piece of bread off his plate. He cuts another slice of bread, spreads butter and marmalade on it, and passes it to Linda.

"We're going to see Marisu's grandmother today." This was Tom's inspiration at six this morning, when he woke up and started pacing again.

Linda remembers the old woman who lives all the way on the other side of town.

While she slept, her father made a new tongue for her buckle out of a paper clip. He helps her into her shorts and T-shirt and sandals.

They walk down the hill into the village. Linda skips ahead of her father, then runs back to meet him. "No more skipping today," he says.

"Why?" she says.

"Because of your head."

Marisu's grandmother is very happy to see them. She speaks only Greek, so everything is communicated with sign language. She pushes them down onto chairs in her sunny whitewashed parlor. She wears a long black skirt and a black shirt and shawl, and her head is wrapped in black cheesecloth. She brings in bowls of canned fruit cocktail for each of them. Linda devours hers, sticking the spoon all the way into her mouth, swinging her legs as she chews. The old woman fusses over the girl, stroking her cheeks. She takes out pictures of her great-grandchildren, not the ones from next door that Linda knows, but ones who live in Thessaly. Linda nods. She's not very interested in the pictures but knows she's expected to be polite. After a while, Tom takes the woman's wrist and pulls it toward Linda's head. He parts the hair for her and shows her the swelling. He shows the woman his worried expression and shrugs. He says, "Can you help me?" hoping she'll understand something from his voice. The old woman pushes the skin down and tries to squeeze the thorn out. Linda screams, and Marisu's grandmother keeps pushing and forcing, talking to the girl in Greek. Linda continues to wail, and finally

Tom can't take the violence of it anymore. He pulls the woman's hands off his daughter's head. He puts a sheepish, apologetic expression on his face for her. She gets a pencil and a piece of brown paper and writes something in Greek.

Tom takes Linda away as fast as he can, trying to act respectful, but angry at the old woman for hurting her. What had he expected Marisu's grandmother to do? He wanted her to be wise and sympathetic, to transcend language, and to have an ancient herbal remedy that would make the blister go down and the splinter come out. Linda is still crying and clutching his hand as they walk back up the hill. "I hate her! I hate her!" she is saying.

"It was wrong of her to squeeze so hard," her father says.

"Not her!" says Linda. "I hate Mommy."

There is a young woman at the money-changing window of the bank who speaks some English. Tom greets her and asks her to translate what's written on the slip of paper. He picks up Linda and rests her on the ledge that is meant for pocketbooks. The young woman wears a short denim skirt and panty hose, and a single comb encrusted with rhinestones holds back the hair over her right ear. Most of her hair falls in her face as she reads the note. For a second, Tom feels a familiar receding, and his eyes blur as he notices, as if looking at a landscape from a great distance, the zigzagging pattern that the young woman's hair makes against her skin, which is the same color—though a much paler tone—as the piece of paper she holds. He imagines mixing the color of the notepaper on his palette, then adding white to get the skin. And then he hates himself. He closes his eyes and presses his thumb and forefinger against his lids, then makes himself tune in to the young woman's voice. She says that the note directs him to take the little girl to Mr. Gregos. She looks at Linda and smiles. Tom becomes conscious of the shiny stripes left by his daughter's tears on her cheeks.

"Who is Mr. Gregos?" he asks.

"Oh, he is very good," says the young woman. She gives

Linda a chocolate wrapped in pink foil. She draws a map of the streets and puts a circle where Mr. Gregos is.

"Is he a doctor?"

The young woman laughs and shrugs, looking like she does not understand. She tosses her hair back and waves at Linda as they leave. A picture of the Dr. Spock book in the shade of a canvas deck chair enters Tom's mind.

He carries Linda now. She's tired from all the walking they have done. He lets her hold the map and pretends she is helping to navigate.

Mr. Gregos's place is another low, whitewashed building, but with a tiny dome on top. The door has a brass plaque bearing what Tom guesses is his name in Greek, then, written on a piece of loose-leaf paper, the name in Roman characters. It's spelled differently than by the woman at the bank. Here it's Gregous.

Her father puts Linda down and knocks on the door. Linda touches her head. It's still sore from the old lady. Forgetting everything for a moment, Linda turns, expecting to see her mother, but then reminds herself: Mom is in Scotland, which is part of England. Linda looks toward her feet and sees a shell sticking out of the ground. She squats down and tugs it out. There is a clear indentation in the dry, hard-packed earth. She shows the shell to her father. "How did it get all the way up here?" she asks. He says he doesn't know and knocks on the door again.

The door opens now. Linda stands, staring, with her mouth open. Her father steps back and puts his hands on her shoulders. In the doorway is a dwarf, only a few inches taller than the child. He has long arms, and his hands dangle past his bowed knees. He has a trim white beard and white hair. He wears a dark suit and a shirt buttoned all the way to his neck, but no tie. He does not smile but nods and says something in German.

"Not German. American. English," Linda's father says. Linda has backed up into her father completely.

"English," the dwarf echoes. He steps aside for Linda and her father. Linda's eyes are level with the dwarf's mouth, and she sees

that his front teeth, both bottom and top, are gold. She looks at his feet. He wears black shoes, one of which has a built-up sole several inches thick. Linda has a windup dump truck that is missing a wheel, and the dwarf's feet make her think of it.

Neither Linda nor her father moves. What would Nora do, Tom wonders. Nora's not timid. She would probably enter Mr. Gregos's house. If he were crazy or evil, wouldn't the woman at the bank have given him a clue? Tom gives Linda a gentle tap on her back, and tells her it's okay. She looks up at him, squinting. He understands she's probably skeptical. They enter the house, and the dwarf leads them down a short, dim hallway, and through a door into an office.

It's just an office. There is a big oak desk and a leather blotter. A green desk lamp and piles of papers and journals in Greek and German sit on the desk. On the wall is a matted reproduction of a Monet water lily painting. There are also two diplomas or certificates, very official looking, in Greek. Across from the desk are two matching chairs with chrome frames and woolly orange seats. Mr. Gregos climbs onto a raised chair behind his desk, and he motions for Linda and her father to sit down.

Linda approaches one of the chairs and touches its arm, but then turns and waits to be lifted onto her father's lap. For a second, Tom feels embarrassed, feels she's acting like a baby; then he remembers that she could be crying from fear, or she could be laughing at the dwarf, and he pulls her up onto his knee. Behind the desk, with the squat bottom half of his body hidden, Mr. Gregos looks intelligent and authoritative. Linda's father smiles, starts to relax. Mr. Gregos smiles and shows his gold teeth. Linda smiles for a second, but then turns and presses her face into her father's shirt. The three remain like this for minutes, Mr. Gregos observing the father and child, and Tom trying to smile, wanting Mr. Gregos's approval.

Finally, the dwarf gets down from his chair and comes over to Linda. He puts one of his big hands on the back of her head. Her father points to the place where the thorn is lodged. Mr.

Gregos nods. He does not touch it but points to the floor and says something in German. Suddenly uneasy again, Tom lowers Linda off his lap. Mr. Gregos puts his hand out for Linda to hold, leads her out of the office, across the hallway. Tom follows as they enter another room. This one is small, windowless, all white like a doctor's office.

The dwarf's hand is dry and warm, and squeezes Linda's hand firmly as he leads her. He smells good, clean, not perfumed. He wears a ring on his pinkie, which presses into Linda's pinkie. The metal is smooth—it does not hurt her. She looks around this room. All the shelves and cabinets are low, as if they were built for her, like ones in a playhouse or a nursery school.

Mr. Gregos gestures for Linda's father to wait behind her, near the door, and he takes a key ring out of his jacket pocket. He opens a cabinet and pulls from it a plastic tray full of small pharmaceutical bottles and tubes. He picks up a tube, uncaps it, punctures the seal with the reverse end of the cap, and squeezes some clear jelly onto his fingers. He takes Linda's hand again, then dabs the substance onto her puffy scalp. Linda's father steps forward. Mr. Gregos puts out his hand to stop him and taps Linda's scalp. She does not flinch. Tom understands: it was just an anesthetic. He smiles, nods. This is fine. He knows what he's doing, this dwarf.

Then Mr. Gregos reaches into the cabinet again. Linda's father watches him, and it seems to be all in one motion that the dwarf produces a bottle of spirits, uncaps it, tips it back over his mouth, and swigs from it. Then he pulls Linda's head toward him and puts his mouth over the bump on her scalp. Tom jumps forward, but the dwarf has already done it. Linda doesn't feel the pain, just a jagged tugging, a drawing out. The dwarf looks up at her father and smiles, showing him the intact thorn held between his gold teeth.

Tom's heart is racing. He wants to strangle the dwarf, or pound him into the floor, splitting him in two like Rumpelstiltskin. But he just kneels down and turns Linda to face him.

"Are you okay?" he asks his daughter.

"I'm fine," she says. "Is that it?" she asks, twisting away from her father to point at Mr. Gregos's mouth. Her father says yes, it is. "Thank you," she says to the dwarf. He nods and takes the thorn from between his teeth. He pulls a handkerchief from his pocket, wraps the thorn in it, and hands the bundle to Linda. Tom stares. The dwarf rummages in the tray and finds another tube. He hands it to Tom. Then he writes his price down on a notepad, elegant European numerals. Tom has just enough money along. Tom nods, says *danke,* the only German word he knows, and hurries Linda out of the house.

As soon as they round the corner, Tom stops, pulls Linda aside. He looks at her head. It's greasy with ointment, but the swelling has begun to go down. Linda gives him the handkerchief package to keep in his pocket, then holds up her hand for him to take. It's the same hand the dwarf held. Tom suddenly does not want to touch Linda. She waits, looking up at his face, her brown eyes looking into his. He makes himself wrap his hand around hers. It is soft, and a little sticky. Her bones are tiny. He could break them with one forceful squeeze.

They walk up the hill toward the house. Linda's father starts to think about his paintings. He remembers how it used to be, to spill color onto the canvas. It felt like it came from his body, some organ with no name. Ever since he arrived on the island, he's been painting perfect landscapes, blue skies, rippled water, sunsets over the whitewashed village. He hates them now, this afternoon. *What's wrong with beauty?* he has been saying to himself all summer. But they weren't beautiful, just flawless.

Linda looks down at the dust clouds that she kicks up with each step.

UPSTREAM

In early August the family went on vacation to Seattle. Late in August, back in Hadley, Massachusetts, David was dropped off after his softball team lost badly to East Hampton. When he walked into the living room, he saw that one of his father's students, Emily, seemed to have fallen down on the rug and his father seemed to have fallen on top of her. David was frozen in the doorway, wondering if Emily was laughing or crying, and if the two of them needed help, when his father noticed him and croaked, "Go away—I'm sorry," looking almost at David, but not quite.

David stared for one more second—just long enough to notice that Emily's skirt was pushed up around her hips, and that his father's belt was unbuckled. Then David turned and dashed upstairs to his room. He locked the door behind him and sat on the edge of his bed. His head pounded. Tiny gray squiggles, like the silverfish in the basement bathroom, danced in a space in front of him that he'd never noticed before; it was as if his eyes were made of glass, and he could suddenly see the surface of the glass instead of looking through it. He rubbed his eyes, but when he opened them, there were more squiggles. He was panting. He felt that he should try to scream, but when he opened his mouth, he made

a low, creaking noise, an embarrassing noise that made him blush, even all alone in his room. He flopped backward, bouncing a little on the mattress.

He lay there with his feet dangling. He stared at the ceiling, at the cracks in the plaster he'd been staring at almost his whole life. And for the first time in many years, he thought of how he'd seen the shapes of monsters in the cracks when he was little. There they were: a hulking, gorillalike shape, a fishy, fanged shape with one leg, and a four-armed phantom with a pointy hood floating into a corner of the molding.

A little while later, there was a knock at the door. David said nothing. He just lay there. He heard his father's voice. "David? David, I want to talk to you"— and David was about to get up and open the door when his father finished his sentence— "before Mom gets home." David pulled his feet up onto the bed and curled on his side. He slept until his mother knocked on the door and told him to come downstairs for dinner. At the table, David didn't look at his father.

So it was less of a surprise to David than to his older sister Michelle when, parked in the lot of the Rite Aid one evening in the first weekend of September, Labor Day weekend, their father and mother twisted around in their seats and looked back at the children and announced that they would be separating. For how long, they did not know, but they hoped it was not forever, for they both loved each other very much still. They said they didn't want to fail like so many of their friends, other couples who had met in college and married and stayed in the area, and whose marriages collapsed. David watched his father's mouth as he spoke—and he understood why his father had a reputation for being a great teacher. He was so eloquent; he spoke so easily and sincerely.

When his father started the car, David said, "I have one question."

"Yes, sweetie?" his mother said.

"We'll still have Christmas together, right?"

His father reached his hand across the bucket seats and squeezed David's mother's thigh. "Of course," his mother said, and she placed her hand on top of his father's.

The next week, school started, and David got his first sixth-grade homework assignment: "Write about something important that happened over summer vacation."

On Saturday, David's mother's friend Sally came over with her Volkswagen Vanagon, and David's father and mother and Sally moved his mother's belongings, some furniture, dishes, and silverware out of the house. David's mother looked thinner than usual to him, smaller in her sneakers and old blue jeans. His father made jokes. Sally gave David a hug. Later, right before they drove away, David was coming down the stairs when he heard Sally ask his father, "Why is he here today?"

David heard his father clear his throat. "We thought about having him spend the day with a friend, but then it seemed like that would be worse, to come back, you know, and have everything different," his father said. "Michelle decided not to stick around."

Later, David sat down to write his report. He could barely wedge his legs in under his low white desk where a year ago he'd had to sit on a cushion to work. He held a brand-new pencil with a fresh pink eraser, but for the first time in all his many years of writing reports, he couldn't think of what to say. He had writer's block. He looked at the college-ruled loose-leaf sheet in front of him with the assignment written on the top line: "Write about something important that happened over summer vacation."

He couldn't begin. It was as if he had lost the ability to think clearly. Images of the summer bombarded his brain; he tried to think, to pick one out of the mess, but they were a blurry, shifting jumble. He remembered his mother with watery eyes and a pile of tissues telling him she had allergies. He remembered

Michelle showing him a jar of nail polish that she claimed to have shoplifted. He remembered arguing with Jason about whether the Red Sox sucked; he remembered gluing glitter on a birthday card for his grandmother; he remembered his father storming out of the house and slamming the door after his mother won a game of Scrabble, and his mother laughing until she cried. But none of this was worthy of a report.

He closed his eyes. He breathed in and out, like his mother did when she needed to calm down, to "focus," as she said. He'd seen her this way in front of the potter's wheel, hands coated in slip, resting on a bowl that had started to go lopsided, breathing in slowly, then out even more slowly.

Finally, he began. "In August my family went to Seattle," he wrote. He hadn't wanted to be obvious, to write about the family trip the way everyone else would. But he had no choice. He was desperate. He described the Space Needle, an island where they visited an authentic pioneer house, and then the locks:

The locks are where the water level changes, and they move the boats up and down. In Seattle, it's where the river meets Puget Sound. Next to the locks are the Salmon Steps. They have built steps for the Salmon who are swimming upstream to go back to spawn in the place where they were born, they live in both salt and fresh water. You can go underground to a room. The room is dark, but a whole wall of it is made out of glass, the glass gives you a view of the salmon. The current is very strong, you can see it pushing, making bubbles and white foam. But the Salmon are strong too, and they are very big. You would see a salmon pushing and pushing against the current, it looked like it was going nowhere then suddenly it would jump up to the next step.

He'd stood down there for half an hour, while his parents and Michelle got fried clams and sodas up on the cement pier. The sunlight had poured through the churning water on the

other side of the glass, beams slicing into the turbulence and illuminating the spotted silver scales of the tremendous fishes. They were so sleek and muscular, the salmon, and so determined, their winglike fins and fanned, striated tails beating, gills opening and closing, revealing momentarily the slits of bloody redness underneath.

Finally, his mother came down to get him, and she stood there for a minute with him, watching, and squeezed him close to her, saying it was chilly.

When David read over his report, the only thing he didn't like was "very big." It didn't capture what he was trying to describe. He went over to his bookshelf and pulled out the thesaurus that his father had given him as a fifth-grade graduation present. *Sizable, great, large* . . . all boring words. He sighed and looked up at the cracks in the ceiling. Then he erased "very big" and wrote "monstrous."

He got a good grade, an A minus. The teacher had made check marks in the margin next to the parts she liked best. "Watch for run-on sentences and review rules about capitalization," she wrote at the bottom of the page.

Early in October, David started to think about his Halloween costume. He talked it over with his mother one night when he was staying over in her new house, an A-frame in the woods that she was renting from her pottery teacher. David told his mother he wanted to be scary, *really* scary—not some lame prefab Freddy Krueger hands, or Jason hockey mask, or Scream ghoul costume. He wanted to be a monster, ferocious and powerful.

David's mother got the supplies, and when he stayed with her again the next week, they made a papier-mâché head. They kept a book with pictures of the Creature from the Black Lagoon open in front of them on the table. They gave the head bulging eyes on either side, and a flat nose, and a gaping mouth

full of tiny, pointy teeth. The next day, when it had dried, they painted it green and black, with dark red lips.

On Halloween, Michelle went to a party dressed as a belly dancer. She wore a bikini top covered in sequins, and she had gotten her belly button pierced for the occasion. As she was leaving the house with her friend, she'd whispered to David: "I shaved down there." David's cheeks got hot. "Does Mom know?" he'd asked, but Michelle had just winked at him and put her finger to her lips.

David's father drove him around trick-or-treating.

"Arrrrrrrggggghhh," David would growl when people opened their doors. He wanted them to have heart attacks, or run out into the road waving their arms for help, or at least wet their pants. They did none of these things at the places he visited. Some people would say, "Oooh. You're scary," or "Eek."

The last stop of the night was a big stone farmhouse, a place where groups of college kids had been living since the time when David's parents were students. When the door opened, David smelled pot smoke and heard loud music with a mechanical, popping drumbeat and a moaning female voice. They pulled him into the living room, two boys and three girls, and gave him cookies and a sip of beer through a straw and then had him stand with his arms outstretched saying "Argghh" to get into character while one of them pointed the Polaroid. A boy wearing antennae on his head asked David what planet he was from, and David said, "Earth." "What did you say?" the boy shouted at him, and David shouted back, "Earth!" They took an extra picture, and one of the girls walked him out to the car.

"That took a long time," said David's father as the window slid open. He was listening to jazz on the car radio in the dark.

The girl leaned into the car to hand the snapshot to him.

"Oh! Professor Berg," the girl said. David's father looked at her. David could tell his father didn't recognize her. "I'm Julie Doyle, Emily's friend."

"Oh yes," said his father, "Julie. How are you."

"I got a letter from Emily. The fellowship is working out for her in Paris. Have you heard from her?"

"No," said his father, sighing and looking at the road. "Actually, it was a surprise that she left so abruptly."

"Well, you know. Shit happens. Everything changes," said Julie Doyle.

"Yes, I suppose so," said his father. Julie continued to stand there, leaning into the car. Then she dug in her pocket and got out a stubby pencil.

"Do you have a piece of paper?" she asked. David's father looked around in the car until he found a long Stop & Shop receipt. "Here's my number," said Julie, "in case you want Emily's address or something."

"Thank you," he said, tucking the receipt into his jacket pocket.

"Your son's so cute," said Julie. "Definitely the best costume we've seen here all night."

"I thought he was out of his monster phase two years ago," said David's father. "Time to start meeting girls."

"My mom made my costume," David said from inside the papier-mâché head. His breath made a warm, damp environment in there.

"What? Can't hear you," said Julie, pointing at her ear. "Well, nice seeing you, Professor Berg. Call me if you want."

The week after Halloween, David got assigned another report. This one could be about anything, as long as it used five words from the sixth-grade vocabulary workbook. On Friday night, he sat down on the rug in front of his mother's woodstove and wrote:

There have always been and will always be monsters. Monsters are terrifying, usually they are very big, but even the smallest ones scare people. They are *independent*, needing

nobody to take care of them. They are at their *apex* when
they are roaming around the land, causing mayhem. That
always happens at night, especially when the full moon is an
orb. They are at their *nadir* during the day, when they are
alone in their cave waiting for it to get dark. Most monsters
are very *wily,* but some are not very smart, they are just
strong and frightening.

Late in November, right after Thanksgiving (which David and
Michelle spent with their mother and Grandpa Fergusun and
Grandma Winnie in Deerfield), David walked up the driveway,
holding a note from his homeroom teacher. He didn't open the
sealed envelope, but he knew the gist of what was inside. It
would tell his father that although he'd done some promising
work early in the term, his grades had been slipping, and it would
single out the C-plus vocabulary report. It would say he seemed
to have trouble concentrating, that he was slow getting from one
class to the next. It might mention that he'd been caught cutting
class twice, reading monster comics with a seventh grader, Skylar,
in the boys' room. His father was out when he walked into the
house, so David dropped the envelope on the kitchen counter and
hurried up to his room, closing the door. He waited until he heard
his father's car on the driveway, and then he braced himself for
the questioning. But when David looked out the window, he saw
his father get out of the car with Julie Doyle, who was helping
him research an article and had been coming over now and then.

David opened his door and sat quietly on top of the steps, his
heart pounding so hard it hurt, at first willing his father not to
find the note; then, as he heard sounds of the kettle being filled,
papers being shuffled, crackers pouring out onto a plate, and
Julie laughing, David began to will his father to find the note.

David found himself moving down the steps one by one on his
rear end, a slow-motion version of how he used to slide down
them as a little kid. From the very bottom step, he could peek into
the kitchen. He saw the envelope, glowing white with the mid-

dle school's seal stamped on it, and he saw his father standing next to Julie, his right hand in her long brown hair, fingers combing through it, then grabbing and pulling. Julie slapped his hand playfully, and David's father said, "Look, we're not trying to prove he was a saint, just that he wasn't a total anti-Semite."

"But I've read his books, Berg. I'm not dumb. Remember I was in your class?" Julie said. "You don't remember."

David's father said, "Look, we're talking about a writer's *persona,* don't you know. Just because he's writing in the first person from the point of view of a character very similar to himself, it doesn't mean that person *is* him."

Julie groaned. "That's not what I'm saying."

On the steps, David coughed a quiet cough, then waited to see if either of them noticed.

"He removed all the good and reasonable parts, and created a character based on the darkest part of himself, the part he hated the most. If you read the letters he wrote to his friends and his editor, you see that he was a kind, rational guy. *And* deeply disturbed by the nationalistic turn that was happening in politics," David's father said, raising his voice slightly.

"He beat his wife!" said Julie, also raising her voice.

Then his father grabbed Julie's wrist and pulled her close. "Maybe she liked it," he said. Julie laughed, shaking her head.

David crept back upstairs and crawled into his room. He was suddenly aware of the drafts; the icy November air seeped into the room as if the wall was perforated with thousands of microscopic holes. He kicked off his shoes and got under his comforter, pulling it up over his chin. He stared at the fish beast on the ceiling; he imagined it half-hopping, half-swimming, chasing the phantom further and further into the little black space where the molding met the plaster. When he was little, he'd made up a sound for each monster. The fish beast had a gurgling, hiccupy noise. David remembered that his mother had laughed when he first demonstrated it, and he had crossed his arms and sulked, saying, "It's not funny, it's *scary.*"

•   •   •

The day before Christmas vacation started, David sat with his parents—*between* his parents—in the office of the school counselor, Mr. Daniel. It was their second meeting with him. Mr. Jolly, the school principal, had recommended that the family see Mr. Daniel once a week. In the principal's office a few weeks earlier, Mr. Jolly had said that, while the school believed in giving individual attention to students, the bottom line was that David's grades needed to improve or he would be held back. He'd also mentioned that he found it worrying that David's parents had taken ten days to respond to the note from Ms. Lanegan.

"No one sent me that note!" David's mother had said, her open, upturned hands batting the air. His father had looked down at his knees.

Now Mr. Daniel smiled at David and then at his father and his mother. The week before, he'd mentioned that he had friends who were friends of David's parents. His ex-wife had taken David's father's class at Smith, "Precursors of the Postmodern." David liked Mr. Daniel. He seemed to be able to get David's parents to sit quietly and talk gently to each other, something that hadn't happened much since his mother had moved out, despite what they'd said in the Rite Aid parking lot. Mr. Daniel had made them renew their promise to spend Christmas together. And this time, Mr. Daniel had brought something for David: a comic book that had been his own when he was a kid, a monster comic book, with pictures of bloblike beasts carrying women into a swamp.

"Thanks!" David said, thumbing through the pages.

"I don't think it's healthy, this monster obsession," said his father.

"All little boys like monsters," said his mother. She looked over at Mr. Daniel.

"I mean, at his age . . . ," said his father.

"Why do you like monsters?" Mr. Daniel addressed David.

David looked at the counselor, who, with his pale, freckled face and rumpled oxford shirt, looked like a kid himself. David shrugged. "I don't know. They're strong and powerful. People have to do what they want or the people get killed. Plus they don't have to talk all the time—monsters don't have to explain themselves."

"Do you have to explain yourself?" asked Mr. Daniel.

"Yeah, I'm doing it right now, aren't I," said David, smiling at the young man to let him know he wasn't being a brat to make Mr. Daniel's life hard.

On December twenty-fourth David's mother brought an overnight bag to the house, and after an awkward first hour, it became the kind of Christmas Eve the family always had: his parents made a big batch of eggnog, and his mother laughed when his father, pretending to slip, dumped extra whiskey into it. They had a goose stuffed with chestnuts, and beans covered in butter, and creamed spinach. They all sat in the living room after dinner, holding their stomachs and saying they were going to throw up. Then David's mother opened a bottle of red wine, and she and his father drank the whole thing. David and Michelle went to bed early, right after a second bottle had been opened. They knew their parents needed time to wrap presents.

In the middle of the night, David was pulled out of a dream as he became aware of noises coming from underneath his room. He turned over on his side and hung his head off the bed, staring at the floorboards, listening. Slowly, he recognized what he was hearing: his mother's little moans, rising in volume, his father's heavy breaths, which started to turn into grunts.

David slid out of bed and tiptoed out of his room and into the hall. Michelle was there, too. She was waiting for him. David and Michelle looked at each other in the blue near-darkness. Moonlight glinted off Michelle's new eyebrow pierc-

ing. They smiled at each other. Michelle reached out and squeezed David's shoulder.

David felt that a strange episode in his life had ended, as easily as his dream had floated away. When he got back into bed, he looked up at the ceiling, and even in the dark, he knew the cracks just looked like cracks.

But in the morning, everything was wrong. David recognized his father's strained, false smile, and his mother's shrill imitation of cheer. After waffles and presents, his mother left abruptly without saying good-bye to his father; she slammed the door of her Rabbit and backed down the driveway fast.

Starting the new term at school, David pretended to try harder. He'd put a look of concentration on his face in class. He'd write reports with long, complicated sentences using three-syllable words from books in his father's library. But he had no idea what he was doing. He felt as if he had forgotten how to read and write. When teachers talked, they sounded like they were underwater—David couldn't distinguish their voices from all the other noises, the footsteps in the hall, doors opening and slamming shut, birds outside the classroom windows, cars starting in the parking lot, lawn mowers, the gym teacher's distant whistle, and the breathing in and out of all his thirty classmates who knew something that he didn't.

In history class, they were studying ancient Greece. They looked at maps that resembled irregular quilts where places with crazy-sounding names were represented by colored patches, and the teacher talked about things that had happened thousands of years ago. David stared out the window, rubbing his eyes, or doodled with his erasable ballpoint pen. On the day they made yogurt ancient Greek style, David found himself claiming to be allergic to dairy, and he spent the class collating and stapling mimeos instead. Before they moved on to Rome, the teacher gave the class an assignment to write a report on

the voyage of Odysseus over midwinter break, which was really just a long weekend, a Friday and a Monday off.

David's father had a couple of days free from teaching, and announced to David over breakfast on Friday that he'd decided it was finally time to paint the upstairs bathroom and hallway. Wouldn't David like to help? he asked. It would be fun.

"No thank you," David said, looking into his bowl of granola.

"How about you, kid?" David's father asked Michelle, who was already zipping up her parka near the door. Michelle just rolled her eyes.

When they were done eating, David's father dragged the big ladder up from the basement. David watched him while he put a drop cloth down on the floor in David and Michelle's bathroom.

David went into his room and lay on his bed. He intended to do well on this history report. He was the smart kid—he thought—didn't anyone remember that? He'd show them all how precocious and clever he was. After hours of doing other things (he organized his comic books; he called his mother), he sat down at his desk and opened his heavy textbook to the page the teacher had marked:

"The Voyage of Odysseus."

David tried to read, but couldn't concentrate. He couldn't get involved in the story. He started flipping the pages, ignoring the words, glancing at the pictures. But then he saw something that made him stop: an illustration of a creature standing on a small island in the middle of a frothy sea. This creature was built like a man with no neck, it was wearing a tattered fur poncho, and in the middle of its forehead was a huge, raging, bloodshot eye.

David spent the long weekend reading as much as he could about Cyclops—he found his father's copy of the *Odyssey,* he scanned several encyclopedia articles, he looked at a coffee-table book of paintings by Redon. But by Monday night, the last few hours of his break, he still hadn't written anything. His floor

was covered in books and pieces of paper, but he still felt that he had nothing to say, nothing he wanted to share with his history teacher anyway.

His father had finished painting the hallway that morning but had left the ladder there. Now he was out to dinner. Michelle was in her room, listening to music. David opened his door and tugged on the ladder. It was lighter than he'd expected. He pulled some more, and it slid toward him on the drop cloth. He went to Michelle's room and knocked. When she came to the door, he asked her for help, and together they moved the ladder into his bedroom.

"Why do you want it in here?" Michelle asked. "Daddy can change the lightbulb."

"I don't know," said David. "It was in the way out there."

After Michelle left, he took one of his favorite pens, a permanent black Sharpie, from his desk drawer. He dragged the ladder across his floor and climbed to the top step. And in the middle of the forehead of the hulking neckless ceiling monster, he drew a big, black, wide-open eye.

At their meeting the next week, Mr. Daniel said he'd been thinking about monsters. "We've talked about how they're strong," he said, "and how they don't have to answer to anybody, right?"

David shrugged.

David's father said, "Let's get off the subject of monsters. *Please.*"

But Mr. Daniel continued, addressing David: "But also, they're kind of like babies, aren't they," he said. "When they're happy they laugh and pound their chests. When they're mad they roar and cry and rip things apart. They don't hold back, do they? Whatever they're feeling, they just let it rip. Right?"

David laughed. "Yeah," he said. "They're just like, *Roar!* I'm hungry. *Roar!* I have to pee."

Mr. Daniel laughed too, and said, "*Roar*! I'm mad. *Roar*! I'm sad."

David laughed again. Then Mr. Daniel said, "David, if you don't mind, I'd like to have a word alone with your folks."

Later that day, David learned that when Mr. Daniel was alone with his parents, he'd suggested that the family think about private school. Over the next few weeks, David and his mother and father visited five schools. Together, they filled out applications for four of them, sitting around the kitchen table at David's father's house one night. David noticed the formal tone in his mother's voice when she spoke to his father, as if they were now just business partners who had started out as friends long ago.

The Quaker school asked for an essay, and David submitted the report he wrote about going to Seattle. He made the grammatical corrections his teacher had suggested and reread it sitting in front of his father's computer. "All in all," the report had concluded, "the best thing about my whole trip to Seattle was the salmon." He now added, inspired for the first time in months, "I have never seen such majestic beauty in any other animal. Swimming upstream takes superhuman strength. Most people would give up before they even got anywhere. But the salmon have to go home. It's their nature."

In early May, David was accepted to the Quaker school, and spring finally came for real. The breeze was warm instead of chilly, the mud from April's rains dried up, the apple trees were budding. David was counting the days until the end of the semester. He did a minimum amount of work, ignored the other kids. He was even cool toward Jason, his oldest friend. Every day after school he would run through the front door of the house, drop his bag in the kitchen, and run back outside through the

rear door, over the long stretch of lawn and the scrubby field to
the small river that flowed along one border of the property.
There, he would sit and inhale the sweetness of the leaves overhead and the pungent, almost chocolaty smell of the mush-
rooms that had sprouted on the banks in the shade of the oaks
and maples. There wasn't much life in the river yet—a few small
fish, spiders, and one old turtle that David thought he recognized from the summer before.

One day, as David walked back to the house, damp and a little chilly from the riverbank, he saw that Julie Doyle was dragging a huge, olive-colored army duffel bag up the steps to the
door. David's father carried a smaller bag, which looked heavy.
David guessed it was full of books.

"Hey, guy," said Julie to David. She smiled at him. Her lips
were smooth and pink. Her teeth were crooked.

"Hey," said his father, breathing hard, mussing David's hair
with his free hand. "Julie's going to rent the spare room for the
summer."

David shrugged. He had the urge to ask his father why he
bothered lying, but he kept his mouth shut. As David expected,
the spare room became a storage space for Julie's things, but she
slept in his father's room every night.

On the last Friday of his career as a public school student, David
visited Mr. Daniel's office.

Mr. Daniel had a whole big stack of comic books for David.
When he handed them to David, David's stomach turned over
and his throat contracted. He started to cry. It hurt, his tear
ducts opening and his sinuses contracting, and the tears themselves were very salty, stinging his skin as they crawled down
his cheeks.

"I'm such a loser," he muttered.

"No, you're not," said Mr. Daniel, and he gave David some
tissues.

"Well, anyway, thank you for the comic books," said David, turning away.

"It's my pleasure to pass them on to you," said Mr. Daniel, opening the door for David.

David made sure to walk out of the big concrete school building slowly, so he wouldn't forget how it felt.

That summer, David spent every afternoon until dinnertime down on the riverbank, watching the water get more and more full of plant and animal life.

One day in July, he was squatting on a rock, sucking at the sweet raw center of a piece of grass, when he noticed something in the water. It was white and oblong, and though the water flowed rapidly downstream, the thing was staying in one place. David watched it, trying to make it out under the ripples. Suddenly, he noticed an eye, and something flapping behind the eye, almost a gill, David thought, but ragged and chunky. There was a mouth up front, opening and closing, slowly gulping, and where a tail would be on a fish, there was a stub, with a tiny shard of fanlike, translucent skin beating side to side. There was one scaly, silver patch near the head, but the rest of the flesh was spongy-looking and loose. As he watched, a piece of the gray flesh peeled back and broke off and was carried rapidly away from the creature. David found himself panting. This was a true, real-life monster, a terrible pathetic thing, a dying thing, a thing already dead but living at the same time.

David ran up to the house and into his father's study, where his father sat reading. He grabbed his father's arm and pulled him outside and through the grass to the water. It was still there, the thing, but it had changed even while David had been gone. More flesh had come off, and there was a bit of spine exposed.

"How bizarre," said his father.

"What is it?" asked David, his voice cracking.

"It's a salmon," said his father. "But it must be pretty old. Atlantic salmon don't usually get so banged up. You'd think it would have died a long time ago, huh?"

"That's not a salmon," said David, his throat closing.

"Sure it is," said his father. "I remember from when I was a kid. You know that river near Grandpa's in Vermont? After they've been swimming upstream for months, they don't look very pretty, they sort of fall apart like this."

"That's *not* a salmon," said David again.

"It's part of natural selection. A lot of them don't even make it home."

"They don't?" said David. He lowered himself to his knees on the brown dirt of the riverbank.

David could feel his father's eyes on him. They were silent for a while; then David felt his father's hand on his head, messing up his hair.

"David," said his father.

David said nothing. He kept watching the beast through the rush of water. He was breathing hard; he felt his inhalations, deep almost to the point of pain, and his exhalations, rapid expulsions of hot, moist vapor. David was still a boy. He only came up to his father's collar. He wanted to crush his father, to pulverize him, to make him into nothing. But he knew that if he sprang up and beat at his father with his fists, his father would be puzzled and disappointed, but unhurt. So David remained there, crouching, while his father patted him on the head. A minute later, his father turned and started walking back up the hill.

The thing had been moving backward inch by inch. It was just a matter of time, David knew, before the water overpowered it.

"Good-bye," David whispered to the fish, when he was sure his father was out of earshot. "Good-bye."

THE RIVER AND UNA

The search party called from a mechanic's shop. They were at our house ten minutes later. I ran out to the pickup as soon as it pulled into the drive. My mother stood on the edge of the porch and held on to the wooden railing with one hand; with the other, she shaded her eyes. The man in the driver's seat rolled down his window and reached his hand out for me to shake, which I did. He was the assistant baker from Minton's Bread Shop in town. I'd never seen him out of his white hat before. I didn't know the man in the passenger seat, didn't recognize his lean face and mustache. His arm was around a blanket-wrapped bundle: my sister.

I went to the other side of the truck and opened the door. The mustached man carefully slid out of his seat, then lifted my sister out after him. She was small in his arms; he was very tall. He held my sister like a bride, under her knees and head. Her bare white feet dangled from the blanket. I reached out and touched an icy pinkie toe.

"Come inside," I said, staring at my sister's feet another moment, then turning toward the house. I looked over my shoulder every couple of steps to make sure he was coming. The plains stretched out flat on either side of our house. The gravel drive divided two squares of shorn lawn, then there were

taller, paler grasses, then fields of wild wheat, then brambles.

The man followed right behind me, up the porch steps. My mother said to him: "Can you carry her into the parlor? My back is bad." She opened the screen door, and he tilted my sister a little so neither her feet nor her head banged against the door-jamb. My mother showed him the big wicker chair next to the woodstove. He bent his knees and lowered my sister into the chair, onto its flowered cushions. As he did this, the blanket fell away from her head. Her black hair was damp and clung together in bunches, and a few tiny twigs and stones were twisted in the locks. The man rested his cheek on her forehead for a moment before he let go of her.

I went over to her and looked at her face. It was covered in scratches. One cheek was swollen and bruised; there was a small bruise under her mouth. Her eyes were closed. I knelt down and listened.

She was breathing.

"Una's wild," said my mother. "If she doesn't change . . ." It was the beginning of a threat or a warning.

"It's not her fault," I said, as always—but this time I couldn't meet my mother's eyes as I said it.

The man had backed up to the front door.

"Do I owe you anything?" my mother asked. He stared at her for a moment, as if he hadn't understood. Then he shook his head slowly, and finally turned to leave. In a minute, I heard the pickup starting up, and the gravel crunching as they backed away.

My mother and I looked at each other. She stood with her arms folded low, her bony hands cradling her elbows. The blue veins stood out beneath her thin white skin—one zigzagged across her forehead, disappearing at her hairline into her brown and gray hair; another ran an uneven path from below one of her ears and across her throat.

My mother covered her face with her hands for a moment, then brought them down, sighing. She said she was going upstairs to the bathroom to get gauze and liniment.

Usually, I looked forward to being alone with my sister, to hearing about her brave or naughty adventures. But that morning, I wasn't sure I wanted to know. I put my mouth close to her ear. "Una," I whispered, "who were you with this time?"

My sister opened one eye and looked at me. A corner of her mouth curled: almost a smile. The tip of her tongue came out and licked the center point of her top lip. I looked into her open, unfocused eye. The surface looked greasy. I shuddered. Then I leaned away a bit and whispered the question again: "Come on," I said, "who were you with?"

The eye closed. When I realized that she wasn't going to answer me, I said, "You can tell me later." I went into the kitchen, put the tin kettle on the range, and rinsed out the teapot. For the thousandth time, I went over the morning of Una's disappearance in my head, but it blended into other mornings in my memory. I couldn't bring back the details. There had been so many mornings, so many quarrels, so many times Una had threatened to leave. As I spooned tea leaves into the pot, I asked myself—why had she finally gone through with it that morning, after that quarrel?

All of a sudden, there was a thump and a crash. I ran back into the parlor, then stopped short. The chair was empty and over-turned, and the blanket lay in a heap halfway between the chair and the front door. I hurried down the hall and out onto the porch. Una was running, naked, bent over at the waist, hands in two tight fists. She ran away from the house on the gravel.

I sprinted after her, down the drive. I could hear my sister panting before I got close enough to catch her. I finally got to her just before she reached the road. I grabbed her from behind, one arm around her belly, the other around her ribs. Her breasts were round and heavy and cold; my skinny forearm and my knobby, little girl wrist were buried under their weight as I pulled her back to the house. Una let me drag her, but she didn't help.

My mother was standing in the parlor when we got back in. She held the kettle up as I entered, pulling my sister with me.

My mother looked away from us as she showed me the bottom of the teapot.

"Now what are we going to do?" she said.

The bottom was charred, black, and a hole had burned all the way through.

The feeling of Una's cold body stayed with me for the rest of the day. Even after my mother had handed me a flannel robe to wrap my sister in, I couldn't forget the weight of her breasts on my arm, and the ghost of her belly's cool mass continued to envelop my fingers. Though we had always shared a room, for years I had been careful to turn away as she dressed or changed into her nightgown. And I never undressed in front of her—at night, I raced upstairs to slip into my pajamas; in the morning, I waited until she had left the bedroom before I put on my school clothes. Una always laughed at my modesty: after all, my figure was all angles and straight lines, and on my chest sat two hard little nubs, as if pieces of my ribs had sprouted and grown outward. I knew that when I was a very little girl I had run around on the hot days of summer completely bare. But I also remembered that when my mother told me I couldn't do that anymore, I had been content in the frilly sundresses she slipped over my head.

While I watched over Una in the parlor that afternoon, and tried to shake the feeling of her flesh from my skin, my mind kept wandering back to one afternoon when I was twelve and Una was fourteen. For one week each summer, we used to rent a cottage on the man-made lake near the river's head. And long after she should have, Una rejected her swimsuit because she liked the feeling of the sun-warmed water on her skin. We used to go on rowboat rides—one of us would row out, then pass the oars to the other for the ride back. This time, when I had rowed out to the middle of the lake, I fell asleep on the way back, lulled by the rhythmic sound of the squeaky oarlocks and the wooden oars scraping the wooden boat. When I opened my

eyes, we were floating near the little beach our family shared with the other renters in the cluster of cheap bungalows. Una had peeled off her shorts and bandanna-patterned top, and lay back against the bow wearing just her sandals. Her fingers, thick, with chewed-down nails, stroked the black, glossy tendrils that grew on the mound between her belly and her thighs. The faintest scent wafted over to my side of the boat, something that reminded me of the slick newborn kittens I had seen in the Loomises' barn once. I covered my nose with my hand, and breathed in the artificial coconut of suntan lotion, but still I watched her, my eyes locked to the motion of her hand.

When we finally drifted to shore, our mother was standing there with a big yellow beach towel, which she threw over Una as soon as my sister stepped out of the boat.

"Young lady," she said quietly, glancing for a second behind herself at the bungalows, "this has got to change."

Una never changed, though, she just intensified, and although she wasn't beautiful like the fashion models and movie stars we saw in magazines, every man who saw her watched her, every man who came close to her breathed harder, as if she were a vapor that he could inhale.

When our father left us suddenly, permanently, we found a note on the kitchen table telling us not to worry about him—"I'll be fine," the note said. "If there's one thing that every town needs, it's a piano teacher." He had taken all of his sheet music with him, and his metronome.

Our mother blamed his leaving on Una. "It's you," she said to Una. "What man could live under the same roof? He did it to protect all of us."

The doctor came the day after Una was found. He examined her in the parlor. He told us she was all right; she just needed a lot of bed rest.

My mother sent for Joe Loomis, the oldest boy from the

house across the road. He was strong—sometimes I'd go to a
school wrestling match and watch him compete. He helped us
move my sister to the bedroom upstairs. My mother offered
him a little money, but he said, "That's all right, ma'am." I
thought he smiled at me as he drank his tea in our kitchen.

I stayed home from school for a couple of days, but then my
mother said I had to go back.

It was late autumn. After school, I'd take the shortcut home.
I'd run upstairs to see my sister, and sit with her until dinnertime.

The cuts on her face healed, and the bruises turned green,
then yellow, and then they faded away. After a week, the doctor visited to check on her. I sat on my bed across the room, and
watched him touch her wrists and forehead, and tap her knees
and chest.

"She's a lucky girl," the doctor said, "all the damage was
superficial—look how she's improving. More rest. That's my
only prescription."

When he left, I lay down on my sister's bed next to her. Her
eyes were closed; she seemed to have fallen asleep. Her hair, famous in Lime Mills for being so long and wild and black, was
clean and brushed now, fanned out on the blue flannel pillow.
My own hair was short, like a boy's, and cowlicked in a single
brown curl over my forehead. I studied the shape of my sister's
body under the quilt. For the first time in many years, I didn't
feel shy looking at her. Her chest was broad, and those big, soft
breasts spread across it. Her hips curved above her round thighs.
I touched my own chest, felt its flatness and the two dense, tiny
bumps. I put my hand on my sister's cheek and turned her face
toward mine. Her brows were thick and velvety; they almost
met in the middle. With my thumb and forefinger, I touched her
eyelids, and slowly pushed them up to look into her eyes.

Her eyes were dull and unfocused. I shuddered, but kept
looking.

She had changed now, I knew, the river had changed her for
good.

I let go of her lids. She licked her lips, which had been dry and peeling since she'd come back from the river. I thought of all the older boys at school who'd kissed those lips in empty classrooms, in cars, in the woods. I felt my own lips with my tongue—thin and slack, they had never touched a boy.

"Una," I said, "how did it happen? You can tell me—you know I don't care. Tell me. How did you fall into the river?"

She licked her lips again.

"Did someone push you? Did you slip? Was it cold? It was very cold, wasn't it?"

She moved her mouth, stretching it around the whispered words: "I was pulled."

One day, about two months after he helped with Una, Joe Loomis was waiting outside my classroom at the end of school.

"I have to do an errand for my mother in town," he said. "Would you like to come with me?"

I nodded casually while I buckled my book bag, as if invitations like this were an everyday occurrence.

We went down to Division Street, where everyone could see us walking together, and we stopped in at the notions shop. He bought a yard of pink satin ribbon and a whole bolt of muslin.

Then Joe walked me home. He walked me right up the gravel to the front door. He said, "See you later." Then I watched him cross the road to his house, carrying the bolt of cream-colored fabric. He lived with his two brothers and two sisters, his father and mother, and Grandma Loomis. Behind the big old Loomis house were the hills that curved around and sloped into town. I imagined living there, how it would be warm and smell like food. I imagined looking out the back windows on a rich, rounded view instead of the flatness on our side of the road.

When I got inside, I ran through the house and tore upstairs to the bedroom. I pushed the door open and dropped my book bag

on the floor. "I went with Joe to buy notions!" I said to my sister.
She licked her lips.

The doctor kept visiting once a week. But he had stopped
telling us Una was well. I'd watch him shake his head as he
backed out of our bedroom. He'd go downstairs and close the
door to the parlor, where he'd confer with my mother.

One night I lay on my bed smelling my hands. Joe Loomis had
bought me a turnover at Minton's after school, and I could still
smell the butter and apples. I had been waiting all day to tell my
sister how Joe had unwrapped my turnover for me, how steam
had risen in the cold autumn air. I looked over at Una. Her hands
were moving under the quilt. I watched them for a minute. Maybe
this little action was a sign, I thought, a sign she was getting better after all. I went over to her bed, turned on her lamp, and pulled
back the covers. Her white sleeves were edged in lace. Her nightdress was pulled up around her waist, and her legs flopped open,
muscles slack from the months in bed. And her fingers worked in-
dustriously. Where the hair had been so thick and dark and glossy,
it was now dry and gray, and she pulled the shriveled strands out
one by one, leaving the flesh looking plucked and bare. I grabbed
her hands and pulled the nightdress down, but when I saw her doing it again a few minutes later, I just turned away.

That year, winter was hard and sudden. I pushed Una's bed
closer to the window so she could watch the snow fall.

It was the coldest season the valley had seen in years. For the
first time I could remember, the river froze. Joe and I walked
down there one afternoon. We took the back path through the
woods to the riverbank, and we sat down on a fallen maple. I
leaned up against the tree's base; the twisted roots were frozen
and exposed. I had on Una's old coat. It was soft white wool,
with fur as black as Una's hair circling the collar and lining the

hood. I'd outgrown my own coat and had taken this one from
the cedar closet one morning. I'd stood on the stool near the
front door and inspected myself in the mirror. If I pouted a little, I even looked a bit like Una. My mother made no comment
as I left the house in it every day, and I always took it off before
entering the room where Una lay.

Sitting close to the frosty ground, I was shivering, and Joe put
his arm around me. I moved closer to him, and we looked down at
the surface of the ice. It was thick but transparent; it had frozen
quickly. Beneath the ice, we saw brown plants and rocks that glit-
tered with mica. Down the river a little bit, a man stood on the ice.
He held a short rod and was digging in a bucket. A string hung from
the rod, and he hooked something from the bucket onto it.

"Can fish live in this cold?" I asked Joe Loomis.

"It's not the cold that kills them, it's the suffocation if the ice
gets too thick," said Joe. "But that doesn't really happen in
rivers—ponds and lakes maybe, but not rivers."

The man dropped his line into a hole we couldn't see. He
stood very still.

I pulled the hood around my head so that my face was framed
by the black fur. It was soft and it pressed against my cheek. It still
smelled like my sister's perfume: roses and spice. I watched Joe.
He was looking at me with half-closed eyes, and a smile I'd never
seen before. He slipped his hand, in its soft suede glove, inside the
hood. I felt it between the back of my neck and the fur. He pulled
me toward him and tilted his head. Then he kissed me. His lips
were cold and stiff, but inside his mouth, it was hot and slippery.

When we parted, we looked back at the man. He was pulling
something up from the water. It looked like an eel, long and silver, flopping on the ice. The man took a wide stick from his
bucket, and he slammed it down on the wriggling thing's head.
Redness spread out from the fish and disappeared on the ice.

I pressed myself into Joe's jacket.

• • •

When I got home, I planned to go straight up to the bedroom. I couldn't wait to tell my sister that I'd finally been kissed—*by Joe Loomis, on the riverbank!* But as I hurried down the hall toward the staircase, I glanced into the kitchen and saw my mother. She had been spending more and more time with her hands covering her face; that afternoon, she was sitting at the table, the points of her elbows balanced on the Formica, her palms supporting her chin, her fingertips pressing against her eyelids. There was something on the table in front of her. I walked slowly and quietly into the kitchen and stole a look at the object: it was a tarnished brass frame, with shiny glass. When I got closer, I saw that, behind the glass, there was a photograph of my father. I hadn't seen this one before, or I didn't remember it. In it, he was very young, with a mustache, and he sat in front of a piano. His long fingers rested on the keys, but he was looking straight at the camera, grinning.

I bumped the toe of my shoe against a table leg, and my mother brought her hands down and looked at me. We looked at each other.

"Someone needs to find him," she said. "Find him and tell him."

I nodded. Then I turned and left the kitchen. I didn't run up the stairs, I walked; I didn't want to go into the bedroom. I wanted to leave the house, to run across the street to Joe. I pushed open the bedroom door.

Una's head was turned toward the window. I looked at her hands resting on top of the quilt. They were as wrinkled as an old woman's.

She had been running a fever for the past three weeks, and the doctor had stopped attempting to cure her. "All I can do is try to make her more comfortable," he had said to my mother the last time he visited. Una had changed a little every day, so minutely I sometimes forgot she was changing. But then I also forgot how she used to be.

Her lips had lost their color. Her teeth pressed against them.

I heard something from my sister's bed. A scratching sound as her lips moved against each other. As I went over to her, I realized that I still had on her coat.

"What are you saying, Una? What do you need?" I put my ear close to her face.

I looked at her eyes but could hardly see into them, so buried were they in the dry, loose folds of her lids.

"I wish they had never found me," she said. "They should have let me be."

"Don't be silly," I said, stroking her forehead, even though a wave of revulsion went through me. I started to sweat, and I pulled her coat off, letting it fall to the floor.

"I was gone, already gone," she said. "I'm already gone."

"You'll get better," I said, like I had been saying all along. I was a liar. And I was thinking of Joe.

There was silence.

I turned to look out the window at the flat, snow-covered fields. I wondered what Joe and I would do next. Would he put his hand under my shirt? Would he put his lips on my neck and leave a mottled red mark for everyone to see? What would I do if he wanted to go further? Would he ask me to marry him, I thought, and then I imagined myself in a glorious white dress, holding a bouquet of primroses.

Then, all at once, I remembered every detail of the morning that Una had run away. We were having breakfast, our mother and Una and I, in the kitchen before school. It was still dark out; the faintest purple glow was starting to come through the windows. Una's messy hair was in her face, and she wore a blouse that our mother had tried time and again to hide in the pillowcase full of clothes for the charity shop, but that Una always pulled back out. It was tight, too tight: her flesh pushed at the seams, the buttons were pulled taut against their thread. Our mother pressed her thin, creased lips together and shook her head. "Una," she said, and my sister turned her head away, pretending to watch something out the window. My mother went on: "Una,

you're going to be eighteen next month. You'll be done with school in the spring. What are you going to do? This can't go on."

"What can't go on?" I said. A jay alighted on the windowsill and pecked at a wormlike streak of dirt. Una laughed at it.

My mother addressed me: "A girl can't live like this forever, like Una lives." Then she reached across the table and put her hand around Una's wrist. Una finally turned and looked at our mother, the corners of her mouth curled spitefully. "When I was eighteen," our mother said, "I got married. I married your father. I managed his schedule and kept the books. I billed his students and organized recitals. I had you, Una. What will you do?"

"I don't know," Una said, using the disdainful tone of voice that she reserved for my mother, "but hopefully not *that*. I mean, Daddy didn't exactly stick around, did he? I heard he's living in the city with a girlfriend."

"Damn you," said our mother, who never cursed. She slammed her free hand down on the table—not a punch but a slap, which made a hollow, belching sound. I giggled nervously. My mother ignored me and said to my sister: "You are never going to grow up. You are never going to grow up." She was still holding on to Una's wrist. "You are never going to grow up."

My mother kept repeating that sentence, and slowly, Una's smile changed, and her eyes opened wide. Una was staring—not at our mother anymore but at a spot in space, over the center of the table, where she seemed to be watching a terrible scene play itself out. She started to breathe harder, then to pant. She stood up and pulled her wrist out of my mother's grasp. She tore away from the table, running out the front door. I stood up to go after her, but my mother told me to stay, to let her get it out of her system. She was missing for a week.

Now I turned back to her and stroked the dry, tangled hair at her temple. "Una," I said, "did you know that fish live under the ice?"

NORTH CURVE

My mother was ironing. I was sitting at the kitchen table with a stack of index cards, studying for my vocabulary test. On the plain side of each card, I had written a word; on the lined side was the word's definition that I had copied from the blackboard. *Sycophant, lugubrious,* I read, *epigraph, epitaph.* I tried not to peek.

The radio was tuned to the classical music station. It was the one thing my mother would listen to. For over twenty minutes, the only sounds in the room had been the hiss of the iron and a single bow, moving across a cello's strings. My mother had taken violin lessons as a child. Whenever she talked about those lessons, she said that they were the happiest hours of her life. I didn't like the sound of the cello, but I didn't hate it. And it was better than silence. Or talking.

When the doorbell rang, my mother and I looked at each other. I've always thought, *That's when my heart started to hurt: when the doorbell rang.* But who knows how it really was. Anyway, I remember that I sat still. My mother sighed and shook her head as she walked past me.

It was a courier from the sugar factory. A boy, with a white cotton cap in his hand. He was panting. His eyes were wet and they jumped around the room; for a second, he looked at me. Then he hung his head.

This is what the courier had come to tell us: that my father

had been shot. He'd been shot by a thief. The thief had been waiting under a dock while my father helped load some containers onto a barge. My father had been shot in the neck. He was dead.

I ran to the bathroom and vomited. When I came back out, my mother was giving the boy a dollar. He put his cap on and disappeared from the doorway. I heard him stumble a couple of times as he ran down the stairs. Then my mother shut the door.

I squeezed her arm as she went back to the ironing board. She pulled away from me and picked up the brown shirt she'd been working on. "I guess I'm done ironing for the day," she said. Then she giggled a high, harsh giggle that I had never heard before.

The police never did anything. My father's friends from work were vague and told conflicting stories. We never saw his body. A couple of people said that the thief had pushed my father off the pier and into the water after shooting him. And even though the factory had surveillance cameras trained on both of the piers, management claimed that the videotape had been blank when they tried to play it back.

Years later, I found out that my father hadn't been shot, he'd been stabbed. And he wasn't at the factory when it happened, he'd been here in the North Curve. He'd been at the Belle Claire, in fact, just a few doors down from where I work now. The Belle Claire has been around forever. Unlike the other places around here, it's a house, not an apartment, and it has dusty red rugs and chandeliers missing half their teardrop-shaped jewels.

When I was first looking for a job, I walked into the Belle Claire. I don't know if I really wanted to work there, or if I just wanted to see where my father had died. It was morning when I pushed open the door. The beaded curtain rapped against the glass pane. Evelyn herself came down the curved staircase to greet me. Her skin was thin and creased, and she had deep triangular grooves under her cheekbones.

I told her I was in need of employment. That's how I phrased

it. I was wearing a white blouse and a pink skirt. I said I was new in town, that I was from the countryside, that I was saving up to go to stenography school. I knew better than to tell her I was a dropout, that I'd been working on my own for three years, meeting businessmen in bars and hotel lobbies. I knew better than to tell her that I had stopped only because I'd pretty much exhausted the downtown market, and I'd started to feel like I might get in trouble. I knew better than to tell Evelyn that I'd had more things—human things and thing things—inside me than I could count or remember.

She took me to a back room, which smelled like roses and mint liqueur, and had me unbutton my blouse and show her my breasts. She felt the weight of them in her white, bony hands. Then she hired me. I never showed up, though. After I left the Belle Claire, I went downtown and ran into a girl I knew, a barmaid from one of the hotels who was an escort on the side. She told me that Barry Snee was expanding his business. I lucked into this job: I was the last to be hired. The pay is better than anywhere else. The sheets are clean. There are three bathrooms. And the bedrooms here are modern, done in chrome, vinyl, and brand-new paneling.

One night, I had to stay overnight at work because I'd misplaced the keys to my apartment. So I was here when Barry arrived early in the morning. He was sitting at the front desk in his overcoat, waiting for the coffee to brew, scanning an accounting ledger, when the buzzer sounded.

Barry looked over the top of the ledger at me.

"Maybe it's just a delivery," I said.

Barry laughed. "You wish."

I unclipped my hair and stuck the *Daily Mirror* under the couch.

It wasn't a delivery. It was a man in the brown uniform of a sugar factory foreman. He stood in the doorway with an orange hard hat in his hands.

"Her," he said to Barry, pointing at me.

"Well, good," said Barry. "She's the only one here right now."

I stood up and took the man's hand. He was a large man, soft-bodied, and his hand was like a slab of steak—a fillet—cool and damp.

We went to the best room, the one in the corner. I looked out the window while he undressed. To my left, I could see the whole North Curve: three drawbridges, a tugboat, the closed-down box warehouse, and the canal itself, shimmering green like antifreeze. In the distance straight ahead, I saw the gold-leaf dome of Borough Hall, and the rooftops of a few of the taller downtown buildings, places where I had made money in hotel rooms, boardrooms, bathrooms. To my right was the slope, where the streets became wider and grander as they went uphill, finally ending at the park's edge with mansions and plane trees too far away for me to see. When I was a very little girl, I would close my eyes and listen to my mother's classical music on the radio and imagine marrying a man who lived near the park. He'd buy me a piano and a reclining arm-chair.

"It looks like it's going to be another rainy one," I said, turning around to the sugar factory man. He sat on the edge of the bed in his briefs, which almost disappeared in the meat of his thighs and his drooping belly.

"It's been a real rainy season," he said.

"It's good for the canal, though." I said it like my father used to. "Good for business, a nice high canal."

"You're right," he said, "good for business, but bad for the piers. The piers are wood. Wood rots."

"Yup," I said.

"What's that?" he asked. He raised one of those big hands and gestured at my shoulder.

"Nothing," I said, "a flower. It's been there a long time. I got it done when I was drunk."

"I can see the flower," he said, "but something's underneath."

· · ·

One month to the day after my father died, my mother had been standing at the ironing board. The iron was hot, but she didn't have anything left to press. For the first time, she wept. She wept and pressed the iron against the flesh of my shoulder. I had just taken a bath, and my skin was still damp. I heard the sizzle of steam as she leaned into me. The feeling had been chill for a second, then hot, hot.

When I walked into the tattoo parlor five years later, I wasn't drunk: I was stone sober. I pulled up my sleeve and showed the scar to the proprietress, a squat woman with long whiskers drooping from either side of her upper lip.

"Cover this," I said.

The woman looked at the scar for a full minute. "It's shaped like an arrow, pointing at your heart. It's a mark of love." She reached up from her stool and ran her finger along the ridges. "I don't want to cover it."

I rotated my arm and considered the old burn. It had been so long since I had seen my mother. I had left soon after the incident with the iron—though not because of it; I'd left because of a yellow-haired boy who had his own place near the city's one beach. Standing in the tattoo parlor, I imagined my mother the way she was when I walked out carrying my borrowed duffel bag: in my mind, she was still sitting by the window, listening to the radio. The thought of it made me dizzy. I swore to myself that I would go and visit her that very day . . . but even as I made the promise, I knew I would break it, as I had broken every promise I could remember making.

Then I pulled my money from my pocket and pointed randomly at a picture of a lily from a row of ink-on-paper samples.

In the bedroom with the man, I just repeated, "It's nothing," adding, "don't worry."

He folded his arms in front of him and slouched, looking at the floor.

I breathed in and out. I looked at the skin hanging above his elbows. I took a few steps toward the bed and sat down on the rug. Then I picked up one of his feet, with its crumpled toes and fallen arch, and started to stroke it. He didn't move. He pulled his arms closer to his body. He was shivering.

"I'm sick," he said.

"I can make you feel better," I said.

"No," he said, then. "*No,*" kicking at me with his foot. I fell backward, but I wasn't hurt. I stood up and moved away from the bed, back over to the window. Behind the curtain was a buzzer in case things ever got out of hand. I could reach it from where I stood.

"If you're sick," I said, "maybe you should—"

"I can't go home," he said.

He pulled on his socks first, then his stiff, creased pants and the shirt with epaulets and four pockets.

From an early age, I knew that my father sometimes visited the North Curve. One day, on my way back from elementary school, I saw him through the green windows of the B71 bus. He was wobbling down the sidewalk, his arm around the shoulder of another man in brown, a guy from the factory that I'd met once or twice. My father hung on his friend. His knees buckled with every step. Both men were shaking, holding their bellies from laughter, I'd thought. But now it occurred to me: he may have been weeping, my father.

I walked across the room to the man sitting on the bed. His seams strained as he bent over to tie his shoes. I put one hand on each of his shoulders and pressed my lips against his forehead. He was burning hot.

"I can't go home," he said again.

PERSONAL FOUNDATIONS OF SELF-FORMING THROUGH AUTO-IDENTIFICATION WITH OTHERNESS

Prologue.

Recently I came across a journal entry from my adolescence. I am living a lie, it said. How truly, truly sad.

Chapter One. Beginnings.

I never fit in with my family, kind as they were. As a youth, I never really found friends. Acquaintances, perhaps, but no one I could consider my soul mate. I had a dark imagination; I came to a nihilistic outlook too early to express my thoughts properly. Or perhaps I should say an existential outlook, for although I was painfully aware of mortality, I did not reject the idea of truth altogether. I felt that there was a truth for myself that I dared not examine—the stakes of self-examination felt much too high for me at that age. So I crawled about with a black haze around me, speaking as little as possible, refusing to participate in any of the social customs that seemed to me then a desperately thin patina of etiquette in the face of our inevitably animal natures. While my sister made friends and started to attract males, scampering about

coquettishly, I developed a battery of nervous tics and obsessive-compulsive rituals. These included winking constantly, picking at mites that were not there, and cocking my head side to side three times—it had to be left-right-left, not right-left-right. If I accidentally cocked my head right-left-right, I had to do penance by crawling about with my tail pressed down against the ground so that it would drag behind me instead of standing up perkily, normally, proud and fluffy.

One day, while I was degrading myself thus, wandering aimlessly with my limp tail collecting dust and mud, I happened to glance behind myself (I'd heard a nut fall somewhere in the distance), and a shock wave ran through me—a jolt of energy, a moment of what I call auto-frisson, a hint of at least the possibility of pleasure. The accidental sighting of my dirty, bedraggled tail gave me a glimmer of hope that there was a fuller life to be led.

About the same time, I began wandering away from the neighborhood. You must understand, my family occupied the most sleepy, protected area of the park, acres and acres away from dog runs, paved footpaths, broken glass. I'd heard stories about other places, but only in the form of cautionary tales: little Billy who got lost without a buddy and met some sadistic children with a Swiss Army knife—that kind of thing. But where we lived was far from the reality of the dangerous outer rim of the park. In our enclave, happy families ate together, sang happy songs, and slept long and restful sleeps, dreaming of the delicious nuts they would gather the next day, and the next, and the next. The next area over, down the hill, toward the edge of the field, was where the chipmunks made their home, and though we did not share society with them, we regarded these speedy little fellows with humor and respect. That was my sheltered world . . . until I began my explorations.

Chapter Two. Discovery.
By the summer after I first saw my bedraggled, limp tail, I was taking long perambulations, circling out in wider and wider cir-

cumferences away from home. My father fretted—he'd scratch himself nervously, blinking, and tell me to make sure to start home before the sun was even close to the western ridge. My mother would just sigh and say to him, "Pavel's a big boy now, Piotr, we can't rein him in, he must get this out of his system. He's like my brother, so restless as a youth, but now look, with Sonya and the quadruplets, who would've thought he'd become such a model father."

I let them talk. *Uncle Kristoff with his big belly and thinning whiskers—she compares me to him?* I thought. I cocked my head left-right-left and looked behind myself at my tail. Inside I knew that I was different and that I needed to explore, explore, explore.

I can remember with perfect kinesthetic awareness the feeling—oh, indescribable, flooding feeling—the first time I saw it—the *sight*—a large, steel-mesh basket, full of an array of objects from the world, broken umbrellas, newspapers, deflated rubber balls . . . and more important, also containing napkins saturated with rancid mayonnaise, apple cores, bottles with a little Yoo-Hoo still inside, folded pizza boxes. I stood staring at this monument, knowing I had discovered something important, but not knowing why. In a minute, my question was answered.

I was watching a greasy paper bag which seemed to be shaking in the wind. But there was no wind—my whiskers were perfectly still. I was watching, and wondering, when He emerged in all his glory.

He was dark gray, almost black in places, with sharp, quick eyes and alert, fanlike ears. But best of all, and last to come out of the bag, was his tail—low, sleek, serpentine. The tail I should have been born with. He was what I should have been. What was this otherworldly creature? I was without fear, so enrapt was I with this, the apparition of my true nature, the vision of what I should have seen in a puddle instead of perky brown eyes, little ears, and my obscenely fluffy, baroque tail. I

approached the creature, half disbelieving that a real animal could be so perfect, and asked Him, "What are you?"

He looked over at me, squinting shrewdly. "What do you want?"

"I only want to know what kind of creature you are."

"Rat."

I formed the syllable for the first time, spoke it as an answer to myself, "Rat."

"Yeah. And this is my bin, so you better back off."

I returned to my home in the trees that night feeling hope for the first time. I kissed my mother, scratched Father behind the ear affectionately. It wasn't their fault their son was born the wrong species, I thought. They were innocent little creatures with neither the scope nor the vision to understand the transformation that was beginning inside me.

Chapter Three. Friendship.

For the next three mornings, I woke up early, said a cheery "Bye!" to the folks, and returned as speedily as possible to the rat's garbage bin. I waited there for him, in silence, in shadows, under the cover of a juniper bush. All I wanted was to observe; I did not care, for the moment, if he accepted me or not. He'd slither up from a grate near a narrow footpath, then sidle over to his bin, each paw crossing in front of the last in a lovely demonstration of economy. Every motion fulfilled unanswered questions I'd always silently asked: Why *must* we scamper? Why *must* we eat nuts year in and year out? Why *must* we clean ourselves so often?

His single-minded scavenging was magnificent. The way he found crumbs of muffins, bits of gristle, rawhide shoelaces with a twitch of his finely tuned nose fascinated me. At home, in bed at night, I'd try to twitch my snubby nose in imitation of his sharp one.

Before I continue with my story, let me digress momentarily to share with you some ideas that started to take shape

during those days of Watching and have come to inform my later work. Much has been written about the so-called gaze; we all know that to Look At something or someone is an act of ownership and objectification. However, I put forth that another aspect inherent in all Looking At is a projection into the object, that is, we make ourselves into the Looked At thing, and that is the path of ownership—acquisition through becoming, one might call it. And this acquiring happens only through a losing of parts of the whole original self of the gazer. In some ways, therefore, the one being Looked At, the "Gazee," comes to own the Gazer, as the latter must give up some wholeness in looking (what else, if not this, is the process of seduction?). So for example when I watched the rat, I was becoming him by doing so.

Now I shall return to my story.

There I was, watching, watching, when I felt a tap on my back.

I turned around (glancing out of habit at my bedraggled tail) and found myself looking at a most unusual character: it was feathered and had two wings and two skinny little legs. But up front, where you'd expect a beak, there was a snout formed of gray felt with a little black button sewn on. And behind it, where you'd expect to see just a feathery tail, was attached a long gray piece of yarn. On its head was a sort of headdress, upon which two tiny cardboard ears were fastened.

I backed up further into the shade of the juniper bush, so that I was side to side with the creature. I was obsessed, I hated to be interrupted, but I gathered that if I didn't acknowledge it politely, it might blow my cover.

"May I help you?" I whispered.

"I think I can help you," it chirped quietly, its voice muffled by the felt snout.

I looked it up and down. "How can you help me?"

The creature chirped, "I'm a rat, I've been watching you."

"What do you mean you've been watching me?"

It cocked its head, whistled once, then chirped, "You're a rat too, you just don't know it yet."

I squinted back through the dark green foliage, trying to get a glimpse of my object of obsession. Then I turned to the creature again. "I'm *not* a rat, unfortunately," I said, "and neither are you—you're a two-bit sparrow dressed up like a rat."

"I'm used to hearing that kind of thing," it chirped. "I was accidentally born into this body, feathered and be-beaked, but my soul is a rat's soul, my mind is a rat's mind, and my heart is a rat's heart."

Now, years later, I have to laugh when I think of how I met Donna; then my heart aches from sorrow at what was to be her fate.

"How do you know so much about me?" I asked.

"I know about you because you're like me," she said, "and I remember."

Chapter Four. Coming of Age.
It was a remarkably brief time before I came to accept Donna as a rat almost completely. I rarely remembered she was physically still a bird. We spent all our time together, but I couldn't tell my father and mother about it. They were only grateful that my spirits had perked up. They asked no questions. My perfect sister, on the other hand, seemed annoyed by my cheer. She'd complain about me at the dinner table: "Pavel's not normal."

"He's perfectly fine," my mother would say.

"No he's not, 'cause if he was, he'd want to mate with me when I'm in heat," my sister would say.

"She's right," my father would say, looking worried.

"I'm fine," I'd say, "I just don't like the way she smells."

They decided I was a late bloomer and left it at that.

They were partly right; I *was* a late bloomer, though my awakenings were of an unusual nature. I was blooming into the rat I was . . . and still am in a way.

Donna helped me by shaving my tail down to the gray skin

with a sharp-edged stone from the stream, and she filed my teeth into little points. She taught me "the walk," low to the ground, paw across paw, and "the talk," direct, monosyllabic. At first I wasn't ready to try meeting any biologically born rats. I was happy in myself, and that was plenty.

One afternoon that I remember clearly (bright high sun directly overhead so the meadows were shadowless), we found an unclaimed garbage bin and plundered it. After we'd eaten a stale jelly donut and some baby formula, we lay on our backs looking across the lawn of the park.

And Donna told me the story of how she'd flown away from her mate, Mark, and their nestlings one day, and had found herself at the dump. She was looking at her reflection in an oily pit, despairing that she felt absolutely nothing anymore, when all of a sudden bubbles appeared on the surface. She grew very quiet when she told me this and I prompted her to continue.

"And then what?" I asked.

"Then She emerged," chirped Donna breathlessly, "and I realized . . ."

"Yes, yes!" I exclaimed.

"She wasn't about being sweet and little, she wasn't about dainty sand baths and pretty songs. She wasn't nurturing. She was elemental. And I saw what had always been wrong with my life. I saw what I needed to be. Rat. Raw Power. I am rat."

Chapter Five. Autumn.
Time passed. My sister mated and moved a couple of trees over. My mother was delighted with her grandchildren. To me they seemed dopey and boring, but I was glad everyone else was glad. It was autumn again, and my father was very busy with the nut gathering. My family had learned not to ask questions about the changes in my appearance.

I now knew every inch of the park. I knew every puddle and tuft of grass. Donna would get frustrated—hopping along behind me while I slithered on my belly. It was easier for me to

"be" a rat, and this was an underlying source of tension in our friendship. She'd show off, eating things I couldn't possibly stomach to prove she was truly rat, more rat even than I was.

Once or twice I asked her to show me her flying, but she refused. She said she had completely divorced herself from her bird past, and would make digs at me about how I had to leave my family if I wanted to really be a rat.

On the other hand, I was the one who craved contact with born, biological rats. I wanted to know them, not just observe them. I wanted to hear their thoughts, tell them mine. Donna and I would come across them—a single rat, like my first, guarding a stash of garbage, or a pack of rats—even the young were beautiful and fierce. But Donna was too scared of being laughed at and refused to approach them with me.

I still turn that cold afternoon over and over in my mind, wishing it could have been different, wondering what I could have done.

It was late autumn. All the leaves were off the trees; the air bit at the exposed flesh of my tail. My breath made steam puffs, and my paws were numb on the frosty earth. Donna had backed out many times before, but this time she promised to go through with it: *We would speak to a biological rat* (we never used the word *real,* for we had a tacit understanding of how it would negate our true ratness).

"Please," I had said as we parted the day before, "we'll find one alone, and be straightforward, like the rats we are. We'll ask it if we can have a word with it. Why not try?"

There had been a long pause. "Okay," said Donna, "this time I'll go through with it."

She arrived in a quiet mood; she had slept in a sewer, as usual, but it was getting cold down there. She'd had bad dreams. I remember I noticed that her felt snout needed mending.

We wandered slowly, looking for the perfect rat to meet. We saw a pack of violent-looking young ones, and a pair rutting. Then finally, after hours of searching, toward the western edge

of the park, near the big footpath, I saw the perfect candidate: a little white around the ears, blind in one eye, and the other eye twinkling with sharpness and humor.

"He'll talk to us, I bet he'll like us. Come on," I said to Donna.

We started toward him, and we got a yard away from where he was tugging at a piece of gum embedded in the bark of a tree trunk. He paused and looked at us and started to smile when Donna turned and ran, sobbing.

I stayed my ground. "I'm a rat," I said to him.

"So you are, so you are," he said in a creaky voice.

I was accepted. It was all I wanted. I smiled back at him, and cocked my head—left, right . . . when I heard *it*: a terrible roar and excited, terrified chirping underneath.

"Donna!" I yelled. I turned and ran in the direction of the noise. In a cluster of five bare maples, Donna was running in circles, her two tiny feet clawing at the dirt, while after her came a huge, black beast with bulging eyes. It barked and growled and yelped, and Donna screamed.

"Fly," I shouted. But she kept running on the hard autumn ground.

"Fly, goddamnit, Donna," I yelled. She was tiring, and the dog was gaining on her. In the background I heard someone calling, "Hector, come Hector!"

"Fly, Donna—it's your only hope!" I shouted, even as the dog reached her yarn tail.

And Donna, dear Donna, she turned and looked right at me. "You just don't understand," she said, and collapsed.

A minute or two later, there was the call again, "Hector, puppy, come along!" And from where I hid behind a dead fan-shaped fungus, I watched the dog trot away, licking its lips, feathers sticking to its nostrils and its jowls.

Epilogue.

As I have said in previous, less autobiographical works, definitions are prisons; divisions are useful only on the level of great

populations, not on a personal level if one ever hopes to align one's philosophy with the quotidian. I now say, "I am neither squirrel nor rat. Neither dog nor tree. I am nothing, and I am something called Pavel, and what that is I'll never know, and if I ever tell you I know—shake me, shake me hard, for the finality of self-naming is as dull as death.

SUMMER JOB

Between my junior and senior years of college, I had a summer job working at my uncle Marshall's retail business. It was a good deal: the store was located in a small, quaint New England town, and I was given an apartment over his partner Ellwig's garage. The pay wasn't fantastic, but with the free housing, I was saving a fair amount of cash.

The work itself was somewhat tedious. Sometimes an hour would go by with no customers. I'd go around and dust off the magazines and videos with the orange feather duster, or I'd alphabetize the files of back issues, or I'd talk on the phone with distributors, placing orders, listening to them pitch their newest products. Because Uncle Marshall's store was small, we couldn't go nuts with risky new items that might never turn over. Most of the salespeople at these companies were complete bores, with either droning, monotonous voices or wacky, over-enthusiastic ones.

There was one guy, though, at one of the smaller distributors, with whom I struck up sort of a friendship. He was also just working for the summer, also for a relative—his boss was an older cousin, a woman who was in the business for the love of it. The guy's name was Flaherty, and he was a college stu-

dent like me. We were relieved to talk to each other, because we could drop the sales jargon.

"So, um . . . you want the reprinted *Hairless Honeys,* right?" Flaherty would say.

"Yeah, send one or two," I'd say.

"How about that *Teen Twat*? That go yet?"

"No, things have been pretty slow. Marshall says it's the summer doldrums."

Business out of the way, we'd make small talk.

"How's Gert?" Flaherty would ask. He knew I was writing my senior thesis on Gertrude Stein.

"Okay," I'd sigh. I had *The Autobiography of Alice B. Toklas* and *Tender Buttons* on the counter next to the cash register. Something about the monotony of my job made me unable to concentrate on my reading.

"How are the bugs?" I'd ask. He was an entomology student.

"I'm not getting outside with the cicadas as much as I'd like," he'd say. "Eleanor keeps finding little things for me to do . . ."

I knew exactly what he meant. It was good to be able to talk to someone in the same position: the daily drudgery of a specialized business that none of my other friends really cared about or understood. At first, in the beginning of the summer, we'd both thought it might at least be a learning experience. Now, we agreed, it was just a matter of making each day go by painlessly.

It had been about a week since I'd last placed an order with Flaherty, and things had been more dead than ever. No one had come into the store for days except the regulars, Timmy and Bobo. Timmy was one of the town's pets. He was a somewhat "slow" young man, with a soft body and brush cut. His mother was a patient at the state mental health facility, and the townspeople looked out for him. The managers at JC Penney kept him in slacks and sneakers, the kindly waitress at the diner made sure he got fed, and Mr. Crobbar—the barber—trimmed his blond hair once a week. Timmy was an outgoing fellow. He'd stride into the basement shop from the alley, always with his

hand stuck out to shake. I'd have to reach over the counter and have my hand shaken vigorously by his fleshy, cool one. Timmy's thing was boys around the age of eight, maybe nine or ten. He always went straight for the same magazines he'd looked at the day before. He'd pick one out and bring it over, just to show me. He never bought anything.

On this particular day, I'd been dreading Timmy's visit because a magazine he really liked had been destroyed. He'd left it on the counter a couple days earlier. I'd put my iced tea down next to it, then answered the phone. The phone cord had knocked over my drink and soaked *Boy Games* right through. Now I watched Timmy search through his favorite section for that magazine. I didn't want to be the one to teach him a lesson about loss. After flipping through the rack again and again, he came over to me and said, "Where's *Boy Games*?"

I couldn't tell the whole truth. "Oh, Timmy, I'm sorry. Someone bought it."

"Who? Bobo?"

"No, a tourist—y'know, from out of town."

"*Boy Games* is gone?"

"*Boy Games* is gone. I'm sorry," I said.

"*Boy Games* is gone?" he said. This was one reason I tired of Timmy—things often got repeated many times.

"Yes," I said.

"*Boy Games* is gone," he said. He looked down at the carpet. I got off the stool and went over to the racks.

"Here, Timmy," I said. "Look at this—you'll like this one: *Tiny Cornholes*."

"I want *Boy Games*."

"Just take a look at *Tiny Cornholes*," I said. I handed him the magazine. He held it but didn't look at it. I opened it to the middle: a spread of readers' snapshots entitled "Stepson Heaven."

"See, Timmy!" I said. He looked away. "Come on, Timmy, I'll order the new *Boy Games*. Meanwhile, just take this one, okay?"

He glanced at the magazine. "I can have it?"

"Sure, Timmy."

"Thanks," he said. He held it tightly now. He stuck around for another ten or fifteen minutes, talking about the weather and the county fair that would be happening in the big town down the highway. Finally, I reminded him it was lunchtime, and he hurried out to the diner, waving as he left.

I had about an hour between Timmy and Bobo, in which I flipped through the Alice B. Toklas book, underlining every passage I could find that mentioned her mustache. Bobo came in at three, as he always did Tuesdays and Thursdays. Bobo was a neurologist over at the medical center. His specialty was migraine headaches that stemmed from facial tension. He'd developed an operation in which he loosened the nerves of the face and scalp. His area of connoisseurship in Uncle Marshall's shop was socks. He was a short man with salt-and-pepper hair and a beard. He liked to lean one elbow on the counter, his profile facing me, and expound upon the virtues of cotton anklets versus bobby or knee socks. I'd made the mistake early in the summer of asking him what the difference between anklets and bobby socks was. He'd been shocked. "You don't know?" he'd exclaimed. "And you're about to enter your final year of tertiary scholarship?"

I'd looked down, ashamed.

"I just don't know," he said, "what this world is coming to. They teach you all this fancy shmancy postmodern theory and leave out the basics." Then he went into a monologue about sheer woven cotton with a single cuff. That was exquisite, he said, but bobbies—thick, elasticized, opaque, and clumsy. "A different universe, my dear girl," he'd said. "Entirely different."

There were many magazines that featured socks in every issue, but Bobo was a purist. We special-ordered expensive Japanese limited edition folios that were devoted to the white cotton anklet. There was also a Swedish auteur who produced a series of black-and-white films of children with blond bowl-cut hairdos walking through empty rooms wearing nothing but the

anklets that Bobo so loved. That item was underwritten by Swedish public television, and the mail from them was erratic. We'd just gotten in three of these back-ordered videos, so I hoped he'd simply come in, get them, and leave to view them. But instead, he decided to discuss his work with me.

"Woman comes in today," he said, "in so much pain, she can't see straight—her vision goes back and forth between a double image and a tunnel effect."

I nodded.

He continued: "And I asked her when it started, and she said about a month ago. I asked her if anything had changed around the same time—you know, usual stressors: new job, relationship trouble, death in the family. And you know what her answer was?" I shook my head.

"No," he said. "No on all counts. In fact, in many ways, she said, things had been going better. 'Why's that?' I asked her. 'Let's look at that.' You see," Bobo said to me, "being a good physician has a lot to do with an ability to converse with one's patients. 'So, what's changed for the better?' I asked her. And she said, 'Well, I've been losing weight. I'd been really unhappy about my appearance, and then I started a diet in earnest. I've lost fifteen pounds, I met a man who's a cop, and I can wear my high school prom dress again.'

"Now, something was starting to go tick-tick-tick in my head. I asked her which dietary regime she'd been following. And you know what?" he said. I shook my head. "It turned out she was on that new dog biscuit diet. Nutritionally viable, perhaps, but a terror on the jaw. Crunch-crunch-crunch. The human mandible isn't made for such activity. The poor woman, doing something she thought was so beneficial, and creating a whole new problem in the meantime." He gazed off in the direction of the storage closet. I stifled a yawn. "I've seen it over and over again, my girl. So this is what I told her to do: If she's happy with the diet, happy with herself, great. I said, 'Heat up some nice skim or one percent milk to just below boiling—you know, so it doesn't get

that skin—and soak the dog biscuit in that for just a minute, long enough to soften it up. Then eat it, making sure to chew gently. The milk will add calcium,' I pointed out, and I guaranteed her that the headaches would go away. You see," said Bobo, "half these people don't need an operation. They just need a listening ear and some commonsense advice."

I smiled at him and nodded. He'd been in the store for half an hour. "The next person who entered my office—" he began, but just then the phone rang.

I answered. "Marshall and Ellwig's House of Juvenile Erotica—" It was Flaherty. I put my hand over the receiver and said to Bobo, "I'm sorry, I have to take this call."

He said, "See you Thursday," and left with his Swedish product.

"Flaherty," I said, "I'm so glad you called."

"Me too," he said. "I was on the phone with a big deal client in New York, and she kept putting me on hold with that smooth jazz."

I told him about Timmy and Bobo's latest visits. I told him how I felt guilty getting paid to sit around and do nothing. Then I contradicted myself by saying I had to be a darn baby-sitter to Timmy, and that wasn't in my job description. Neither was hearing about craniomandibular disorders.

"Well, I was just supposed to do sales," said Flaherty. "But Eleanor has me looking after Frederick and weeding the garden. I wish I at least had my own place like you. Living with the family is tough."

"Yeah," I said. "But living alone is weird, too. I mean, I've lived in dorms for the last few years. I'm used to eating in a cafeteria. It's an isolated life here. I thought it would be good for my research, but I can't do anything. I mean, what the hell are tender buttons? It's all completely stupid. I'm paralyzed, you know?" Suddenly, I felt tears squeezing their way out of my eyes. I tried to be quiet, but a sob escaped.

"Hey," said Flaherty, "are you crying?" I sobbed again. "Hey,"

he said again, softly. "I was calling because I'm coming to your area this weekend. Eleanor wants me to check out the fairgrounds and figure out where to request a booth."

My sobs stopped. There was silence on the line between us. I'd often wished to meet Flaherty in person, but the reality of it suddenly scared me. I realized I'd been able to be more myself with him, just on the phone, than with any man I'd known face-to-face. There was safety in our abstractness, and now that could change.

"Do you *want* to meet me?" I asked.

"Do you want to meet *me*?" he asked.

There was silence again. Then we both said, "Yes."

Business picked up over the next couple of days because of the various craftspeople and merchants who were in the area to prepare for the fair. One guy, a baseball hat manufacturer, bought all the back issues of *Soft Spots* and *Baby Love*. A woman from Oregon who made vegetarian sandals by hand fell in love with the amateur video selection, and returned every day for three days. "Stuey will love this," she'd say, clutching the videos to her heart. I was glad to be busy. I convinced myself that it was a bad idea to meet my special summer friend. We'd hate each other, he'd think I was ugly, or we'd be attracted and therefore lose that special connection we had just talking. But I knew we had to go through with it, and of course I had secret hopes. My boyfriend at school, Nino, had started to change. He was a philosophy major, and he'd been writing me letters about how every human relationship is based on a power dynamic. *Instinctively,* Nino wrote, *we all want to be dominant.* I'd written him back, *Don't you think it's the great challenge to the human soul to overcome those hierarchical urges?* It seemed like we couldn't agree on anything anymore.

Flaherty was supposed to arrive on Friday, but by closing time there was still no sign of him. I became angry and cynical.

Chicken, I thought. I'm glad I don't have to see him. I straightened up the books and magazines, put videos back in their slots, and went to lock the door.

And there he was: tall, with that shy expression, sandy hair, slightly crooked nose, and horn-rimmed glasses. I opened the door and let him in. He reached out his hand, and I took it, but neither of us shook. We just stood there.

Finally he spoke. "I wanted to come when you'd be alone."

"That's good," I said.

"I stopped in the woods on the way," he said, "and found a tree that was covered in cicadas. The noise was deafening—so high-pitched I could feel the sound beating against my eardrums. I thought I'd do some recordings, jot down some scientific observations. But instead, I just sat down under that tree. The ground was covered in those brown casings, empty husks of the insects. On the leaves and branches, cicada couples clung to each other, mating. In the grass were the ones that had already laid their eggs. These ones were dying, moving slowly, dragging their frayed wings. After seventeen years underground, not singing, not feeling the sun, they come out for that moment, that golden single moment. Then they die."

After that, we were silent. We stood and looked at each other, gazing into each other's eyes. For some reason, I thought of Alice B. Toklas's mustache, which Anita Loos once said was charming and alluring. Then I thought of the love that Gertrude must have felt to pen a full autobiography in the voice of her dear companion. There's that famous Picasso of Gertrude, with the big, asymmetrical almond eyes—not really how her eyes were. Yet maybe that strange skewed expression has to do with Gertrude's capacity for tenderness; perhaps the eyes of love are angled differently than the ones we use to read the paper or cross the street. *Tender Buttons,* I thought. And I finally understood how buttons can be tender.

SUGAR

W hat's in the box?" Mother asked. She was already standing by the closet, holding its door open with her hip. I looked
down at her brown shoes with their spongy soles. I had not
heard her come up the carpeted stairs. "It's her, isn't it,"
Mother said, "it's Sugar." The box was in the closet, on the bottom shelf, next to a pile of folded sweaters. She poked at it
with her foot.

"She'll wake up," I whispered. Actually, she was already
awake. I looked at my shiny black Mary Janes and white cuffed
socks against the pale pink chenille of the bedspread. My shoes
had hard soles, heels with taps on them. I could not come and
go silently.

"Stay right there," said Mother. She backed out of the room,
keeping her eyes on me. She yelled down to Daddy, "Frederick,
we need you up here."

I knew what would happen next. I dropped from the bed
and dashed for the closet. *Sugar's box!* I picked it up and
hugged it. She was starting to move in the box. She had been
asleep for days, and time had passed quietly in the house. Now
I could feel her stretching her limbs, could feel her nails
scratching against the cardboard. There was also the low noise
of bristly fur brushing against itself. I could feel where her

head pressed against the end of the box, and I heard the exhalation of a Sugar yawn.

Mother reappeared in the room. "I told you not to move," she said. I pressed my face against the side of the box and backed into the closet. I felt Sugar's alertness inside the box. She wasn't moving much, but she was listening. I sat down in the corner, between the hems of my winter coat and my long dress. The closet smelled like camphor and cedar. Daddy appeared behind Mother at the closet door. Inside the closet, it was very dark, and the rest of the room was filled with white sunlight: Daddy and Mother were just silhouettes.

Daddy leaned toward the closet. "How's my girl," he said, "my pumpkin? Kitten? Sweet Pea?" I said nothing. "How's my angel? My valentine?"

I whispered, "Fine." Sugar shifted inside the box.

"Why don't you just come out like a good girl and give Daddy the box?" he said. Sugar shifted again.

"She's not going to do it, Frederick," said Mother. "You know how it is."

Sugar knocked against the inside of the box with her head. I squeezed the box tight. A tiny fist punched the wall of the box.

Sugar was fine in my closet.

Every day, I woke up with Mother's eyes on me. She had my school clothes waiting for me. I had seven dresses, one for each day of the week. Plus my long party dress, for the one day each year that Mother and Daddy called my birthday. On this day, they told me I was a year older, and I blew out candles on a cake. The number of candles was always different. One year there might be thirteen candles, and the next, there would be seven.

After I dressed and ate my toast each morning, I would cross the cul-de-sac to go to school. I always turned my head and stared down the long road, a perfectly straight ribbon of pave-

ment with no other houses on it. A deep forest was on the other
side of this road, next to the schoolhouse. Something about the
density of the trees, whose roots pressed against the low stone
wall, always made me linger before Daddy or Mother tugged at
my hand and pulled me into the schoolhouse.

Daddy would complain about the expense of educating me,
but they agreed it was important to have me properly schooled.
Three walls of the schoolhouse were lined with bookshelves,
divided into different subjects: math, science, vocabulary, pen-
manship. On the back wall there was a blackboard. Every day,
detailed instructions were left for me in perfect script letters in
white chalk on this board. They told which books to take from
the shelves, which chapters to read, which words to study.
Daddy and Mother would take turns checking in to make sure I
was doing the lessons.

Sometimes the vocabulary or math books hinted at something. Words that I could not reconcile stayed with me: *post
office, bus, puppy, roller skate, freight train.* I would consider these
words and daydream, staring at the dust between the threads
of a binding, or looking out the window at the forest behind the
schoolhouse. But my work was checked each night, after sup-
per. I could not drift off very long.

While they discussed my notes downstairs, I would go and
visit with Sugar in the closet, waking her by whispering her
name until she came to silent attention in her box. We would
stay like this for three quarters of an hour, listening to each
other's wakefulness and breath.

They had taken her away once, but she came back. In the
short time since she had returned, she awakened more easily,
was noisier and stronger. Daddy and Mother would enter and
leave the room silently, inspecting and observing. But now,
whenever they approached me, she woke up and listened.
Whenever they spoke to me in a certain way, I could feel her
moving in the box, sharpening her nails.

I was not supposed to have her in the first place. She came

late at night after a strange evening at the house. It was after dinner, and Daddy and Mother had been checking my notes. I sat at my desk, looking out the window at the endless lawn behind the house. It was an expanse of even green, nothing to see besides grass, no buildings or trees in the distance. I heard voices rise downstairs. Mother and Daddy were arguing. I had never heard them argue. I crept out of my room and stood silently on the landing, and for once, they couldn't hear me over their own noise. They were standing at the dining table. At first, I could only see Mother, but then Daddy's hand appeared and grabbed her wrist. I ran downstairs and into the dining room. I took my mother's other wrist and pulled, trying to get her away from him. She laughed an unfamiliar laugh and shook herself free of Daddy easily. She turned toward me without really looking at me. Then she picked me up and carried me upstairs. It was impossible to move in her arms. She took me to my desk, put me down in the chair forcefully, squeezed my fingers around a pencil, and left the room.

I sat there. I felt my heart beating. I made a tight fist around the pencil, then let go. The pencil dropped, and I watched the blood rush back into my palm.

Later that night, as I lay in bed, thoughts entered my head like transmitted radio signals. I tried not to listen to them, but there they were, speaking, whispering: You are you, you are you, not them, but you. There is more, there is more, there is more than this. You are you, you are you. . . .

I woke up in the middle of the night to the sound of scratching. I had forgotten what had happened earlier and the thoughts that had repeated in my head. I opened my eyes and saw the bluish, moonlit box on my windowsill. The sound was coming from inside it.

• • •

Now Daddy stepped from behind Mother and put his head into the closet. "It's time, Pumpkin," he said. He chucked me under the chin—Sugar banged with a fist inside the box. Daddy tried to chuckle. He slowly reached over to ruffle my hair—then, Bang. Bang. Bang. He jumped back from the closet and stood behind Mother.

"Listen," Mother said. "Isn't it easier to hand the box over than to have it taken away?" Sugar paused, listening. I shook my head and clutched the box. "We don't want to have to do this," said Mother.

Daddy said, "Let's just wait for her to go to sleep again."

"No, Frederick, she's expecting us now. She'll never move from that closet."

They both backed to the corner of the room. They whispered to each other, all the while keeping their eyes on me. Sugar was scraping her nails against the cardboard. Slow, sharpening sounds. I pressed my lips against the bulge in the cardboard where her head was, and its roundness made me feel safe. Mother and Daddy approached the closet again. Their steps were measured. Sugar's scratching paused. We waited. Mother lunged for my arms and Daddy reached for the box, his cuffs rolled down to protect his hands—Bang. Bang. Bang. Bang. Sugar punched and kicked. Daddy dropped the box back into my lap. The punching and kicking got faster. Mother let go of my arms and tried to pick up the box herself, but it was vibrating too intensely. She dropped the box. They moved away from the closet once more and returned to the doorway. Sugar's banging slowed and stopped. We listened to silence.

Mother's voice was different when she spoke again. Low. Soft. Even-toned. "You're going to do a relaxation exercise," she said to me. Sugar and I listened. We had never heard Mother's voice like this before. "I want you to close your eyes," she said, "and imagine you're somewhere very safe."

I tried not to close my eyes, but I found I could not keep them open.

"Imagine you're somewhere very safe," she said again. I imagined I was inside my closet, holding Sugar's box. I imagined she was inside the box, awake but silent, protecting me. "Now," Mother said, "imagine you're in this safe place, and your limbs are getting very heavy. Say to yourself, 'I am going to relax my toes. My toes are relaxing. My toes are relaxed.'"

I imagined myself standing up and walking past Mother and Daddy, who were frozen like statues, not dead but still.

"I'm going to relax my knees. My knees are relaxing. My knees are relaxed."

I imagined myself walking down the stairs, barefoot, making no noise. I imagined myself going to the front door. It was unlocked, and I opened it easily. I stood at the door for a moment, then I stepped onto the lawn. The grass was soft under the soles of my feet.

I'm going to relax my hips. My hips are relaxing. My hips are relaxed. I imagined that I walked across the lawn and got to the edge of the paved road, where I looked down at a gutter clogged with leaves. Then I walked across the cul-de-sac. The rough pavement was hot from the sun.

I am going to relax my shoulders. My shoulders are relaxing. My shoulders are relaxed. The door to the schoolhouse was open, but I walked around the building to the forest.

I am going to relax my neck. My neck is relaxing. My neck is relaxed. There was a low stone wall at the edge of the forest. I stepped up onto it, still carrying Sugar's box. Cool air came from the trees, and there was a damp, growing mushroom smell. The other side of the stone wall dropped further, so I had to climb down backward. Then I turned and walked into the forest. The ground was covered with pine needles. There was a slope to the forest floor, and as I descended, the cul-de-sac disappeared behind me. Soon I found myself next to a brook. I sat on a rock and watched the streaming water split smoothly around twigs and stones. I thought, this would be a good place to let Sugar go, and I took her box over to a safe circle of reeds

growing near the water. I set the box down and walked away from it along the bank. All along the water, red flowers grew and clustered, four or five long stems together, with a spike of color on the end of each stem. The flowers were closed, petals pressing against each other like pods.

I'm going to relax my hands. My hands are relaxing. My hands are relaxed. For a second, I felt something slip through my fingers. I was vaguely aware of a tugging and heard familiar voices coming from a distant place. "I've got it," one of them said. The other said, "Well, take it far away."

I considered the flowers, and a word came to me. Snapdragon. *Snapdragons.* I had seen a picture of them once in a book at school. I bent down and touched a pod of petals. It was firm on the outside, and the petals were closed tight. I squeezed it between two fingers. It snapped open and showed a tender red center. I put a finger in the flower. It was soft now, slightly downy.

I was alone. It was all right. Sugar would come back to me. If she didn't I would go and find her.

AUDITOR

December 17, 1990

This person who called herself my friend said she feared that I was cold and unfeeling. Not that I was really that way, she said, but I seemed to have an iceberg inside of me. She said she was telling me for my own good.

This person who called herself my friend said I needed help with my personality. She said: Wasn't I worried people would think I was not nice? She said: Wasn't I worried I would never find a husband? She said *she* knew there was a lot of good deep down inside me, a goodness and sweetness I just never showed anyone. "I've seen glimpses, you know, moments, where I know you feel things very deeply," she said, "like maybe you feel *so* much *so* deeply you just like shut yourself down to hide from the pain."

But, she said, I *came off* as cruel, yes, she said—she knew it was a defense—but my silence *came off* as catty, dismissive. "Like that girl," she said, "that cashier, just now, you've never seen her before in your life. What has she ever done to you? Why did you have to act like that?"

I shrugged. I thought: This person who calls herself my friend, I hardly know her, either, barely better than I do the stupid, fat cashier at the ice cream shoppe. And obviously, my "friend" hardly knew me. But she followed me around. And

there was my first mistake. I let her trail after me for a while there, for a few weeks. While I was waiting.

If someone wants to be in my presence, that's their business, I told myself. I reminded myself it was better to let her do what she wanted than to do something that might raise her suspicions. But it gets to be too much when someone starts telling you how to better yourself, get help, talk to a professional, or take a class, that kind of nonsense. That night she followed me home, she said she was afraid I might do something terrible to myself someday if I continued living with the iceberg inside me.

She kept talking, all the way back to my house. She was walking a few paces behind me. I was striding ahead of her, not looking, but I could see her arms, waving in my peripheral vision. At one point, she lowered her voice and asked if someone had touched me the wrong way when I was a little girl. I almost spun around and socked her then, but I just continued moving forward, taking bites of my orange sherbet.

She followed me right up the porch steps. She'd been as far as my house before, but never inside. I had never invited her inside.

I just seem to be someone who people like to bother. Why, just recently, during my time in Poughkeepsie, there were several of them: that vitamin salesman with the button that said, "I lost thirty pounds in two months. Ask me how." He told me that he wanted to make love to me. He said I seemed like I needed it. And the woman from UPS who wanted me to come to church with her. Those two I managed to get rid of with simple rudeness. But not so with the person from the Midas franchise on Raymond Avenue.

I'd been in Poughkeepsie for two months when my muffler went. While they put my car up, this person, this receptionist behind a counter, sitting in front of a computer, she smiled and said, "Name?"

"Danita Connell," I said immediately.

"Work phone?"

And I said, "I don't have a work phone."

"Oh, a stay-at-home mom!" she said. "That's what I want to be."

"No," I said.

She was very young. She furrowed her brow, suddenly looking concerned. I found out soon enough that she was pretty new to the job at Midas. She still cared about her customers.

"What *do* you do?" she asked.

Again I answered instantly. "I'm an auditor. An independent, self-employed auditor. I'm based at home."

"Wow. You're new in town, aren't you?" she said, smiling still. She had thin, frosted pink lips; her hair was frizzy from a growing out perm.

I nodded.

"I've lived here my entire life," she said. "Well, really, I grew up in Fishkill. But the area."

I paid, and five minutes later, when I was waiting to make a left turn out of the lot, enjoying the new silence in my car, she ran out and knocked on my window. She kept knocking until I rolled it down.

"You're all alone, aren't you?" she said.

I looked at her but didn't say anything. I had on my sunglasses.

"Know what?" she said. "I want you to see how friendly Poughkeepsie is. Let me show you a nice place after work."

I still said nothing.

"We single gals have to stick together," she said, patting the roof of my car. I should have just driven away. I wish I had driven away. But I didn't.

I was already sick of her, that receptionist thing, when I walked into the bar four hours later.

She had picked the place; it was called Dickens, and it was English-themed, with a bartender in a top hat. Our table was under a plastic structure which, I believe, was supposed to be some kind of gazebo. She ordered a White Russian. I had my usual: club soda. We were there for a total of twenty minutes.

She asked me where I was from, and looking at the Miller Light clock behind the bartender, I said, "Milwaukee."

"Neat," she said. "That's so far away."

I shrugged.

"You must miss your family," she said. I noticed she had started to jiggle her leg under the table. I could hear the sole of her Reebok tapping the floor.

She volunteered, "Like I told you, I'm from Fishkill."

I said nothing.

She giggled and sipped her drink through the cocktail straw.

Later we stood in the parking lot. She cocked her head and gave me a pitying, corners-down smile. She was pink. Her cheeks were blotchy from the White Russian. She wore a flamingo-colored polo shirt with an alligator stitched over one of her wide, flaplike bosoms. She reached for my hand and squeezed it. Her hand was mushy. I pulled my hand away and turned, walking away without saying good night. But she called after me, "Good night, Danita!"

She called me from work the next day. I was lying on the couch, curtains drawn, waiting for the mail to arrive. I shouldn't have picked up the phone. But I admit that I wondered vaguely about her—what kind of person would telephone someone who walked away without saying good night? That was another mistake: answering the phone.

She was calling to say what a nice time she'd had, and let's do it again sometime. Two days later, she was patting my hand with her plump pink one across the table at the brick oven pizzeria.

"You're so mysterious," she said. She slurped from her wineglass. It was her third Chianti. "So tell me, any special guy in your life?"

I looked over her shoulder at the brick oven, that cavern with its arched doorway, logs like tidy sleeping children glowing red inside.

I told her what I told the occasional man who expressed interest in me; I told her what I'd told the vitamin salesman. I told her that my job made it impossible to have relationships. I

couldn't afford to get attached to anyone, not even friends, I said, hoping she'd get the point.

"Oh, you poor thing," she said. "You've been hurt—I can tell—that's why you're scared of intimacy. Don't you think you'd settle down if you met the right man? Someone who treated you like a lady? Wouldn't love change everything? I mean, couldn't you get a job where you didn't have to travel so much? And then," she said, her eyes shiny and wet, her finger tracing the rim of her wineglass, "then I could be your friend."

The cook pushed a pizza pie into the oven with a paddle. I was getting ready to move on anyway. I thought I'd be gone in a couple of days, that I would just disappear before she had a chance to foist herself upon me any further. I knew where my next stop would be—Campbell, Ohio—and my next name, Gloria Freeman, which I had borrowed from an octogenarian Poughkeepsie resident. I always try to find ones who have trouble with their eyes but whose hearing is sharp. I find them in supermarkets, on line at the bank, on park benches. I'm very discreet when I follow them home. Later, I try to sound as kindly and concerned as possible when, standing before a lady like Gloria Freeman, at her front door, I explain that I work for the IRS and I'll need to borrow her driver's license and social security card for an hour. Gloria had been especially friendly and forthcoming—she eagerly gave me her ID and threw in a file folder full of pharmacy receipts and Grand Union coupons.

So by the time that thing and I were having pizza, I was practicing already: Ms. Freeman, Gloria, Glory, Glo Freeman. I already knew my next zip code. But there had been a delay with the trailer I was supposed to move into in Campbell; instead of hitting the road and heading west anyway, the way I should have, I stuck around in Poughkeepsie. That was the second small mistake leading up to the big mistake: I was lazy.

That's how I found myself still in town two weeks after the pizzeria. And that's why it really went wrong with Miss Pink— I couldn't get away from her, and she insisted on fostering our

quote friendship. The colder I was, the ruder I was, the more I pushed her away, the more her desire to change me grew. When she wasn't at the Midas or bothering me, she was, as far as I could tell—not that I cared to think about it very much—watching those television shows where mothers and daughters reconcile, where long-lost twins reunite, where friends confront each other with grievances and then hug and make up. I gathered that some of the ideas she had about telling me how to improve my character came from viewing those programs, where women help each other by tearing each other apart.

It was a bother and a liability to have someone so concerned for me.

That last time after the ice cream parlor, it was just too much. Standing on the porch steps, I found myself blocking out her voice and running through everything I knew about her minuscule, pathetic life: single "gal," father dead, sickly mother in Florida. Lived with a roommate she'd found through an ad in the *Pennysaver*.

I invited her in.

She must have felt encouraged by that, because she marched right through the foyer, down the hall, into the parlor. I followed her. She stood between the painted green bookshelf and the basement door. I didn't turn on the light. She squinted up at me in the shadows.

"I haven't wanted to say this before," she said, "but now that we're here instead of out in public, I think I should. You really don't do enough to make yourself attractive. I mean, *I* think you look great. For your age. But when you don't do anything to cover those little gray hairs or smooth out your complexion, it sends a message to guys. It sends a message that you don't care about yourself. And if you don't care about yourself, who's going to care about you?"

I didn't answer. I reached for the handle on the basement door. I didn't plan this—she had positioned herself there, with

only one thin door between her and a long, steep flight of stairs and the cement floor at the bottom of them. In my head, I assessed her weight, estimated the distance to the base, and calculated the momentum of the projectile.

She stammered, her voice a little higher, "Who's going to care? Who? Who's going to care about you?"

"Let's go into the kitchen," I said, opening the basement door. "Careful, there's a little step up."

Since the day I left Poughkeepsie, I've picked up my pen a hundred times, trying to figure out how and where to begin. I've started scores of notes, then ripped them up—not out of guilt or fear of being caught, but out of a strange sense of embarrassment. Seeing my handwriting made me blush. I never blush. But now I blush again thinking about how close you and I will be when you've finished reading this letter.

I've imagined writing to you for so very long, but I have no idea who you are. I do know you're in a rented trailer at Countryside Estates, on Cooper Road near the border of Campbell, Ohio. You may find this a month after I've moved out, or five years, or ten. I know you must have noticed the place where one of the thin plastic wall panels buckled out of the aluminum runner that should have been holding it perfectly flat. I'm pretty proud of the spot I've picked out for these pieces of paper. Near the floor, behind the fold-down table, next to the kitchen nook.

Confession is supposed to be an act of purification. I have always wondered about those who confess. You see them on television now and then. They look embarrassed and tired, not pure. I'm tired. I'm tired all the time.

This note to you seemed like a practical way to get everything off my chest. As you noticed, I've changed the names of the people involved, and of the places (other than Campbell) where those events occurred. I've tried to put down the story in

a clear, linear fashion. In my professional days, I always had to report on my findings in a clear, linear fashion—so, while I know that I'm not a natural storyteller, I hope that, along the way, I developed some useful skills for expressing myself through the written word. Clear writing is like a logic problem.

I was a logical child. I remember, at eleven, solving problems with my teeth. One side of my mouth was if, the other was then.

Every time I took a math test, I scored 100. I could memorize a sequence of a thousand numbers and repeat them forwards and backwards, arrange them in size order, divide them, add and subtract them—all in my head, without making a single error.

When I grew up, I had a highly paid job as an auditor. I was the youngest female auditor in the country. There was even an article about me in a trade magazine, *Accounting World*. The thrust of the article was my incredible record—the perfection of my calculations, the cleanness of my reports, my superhuman endurance on difficult and complicated audits. The headline said, "Girl Wonder Promoted to Top Drawer." The color picture showed me with my beige sweater, my pocked skin, my hair tucked behind my ears.

I worked for an independent firm traveling from city to city, staying for a month while I made columns of red and black ink, my left hand dancing across the numbered keys of an adding machine. I'd have my own temporary desk in the corner of some office, and although I was so young, and female, I was always treated with respect. I didn't work with a partner the way many auditors did. Everybody trusted that my work would be perfect.

When I was twenty-four, my eyes started going a little. I began to misread numbers. Sometimes I would overlook a decimal point. Or I'd see a six as an eight, or an eight as a zero. I always caught myself, and I would go back and make the necessary corrections. I still had a perfect record.

Then, finally, I made the big mistake. I had known it was coming, I just didn't know when. I still don't know exactly what I did—or didn't do. I had recently been fitted for glasses

but was having a hard time adjusting to them—so maybe it was that. Or jet lag. I was in San Jose. It was a big, high-profile job for my firm, an audit for the second largest computer manufacturer in the country. Of course, it wasn't really San Jose, and it wasn't really a computer company, but let's imagine it was because I can't tell you the real details.

It hadn't been an easy job. The people who worked at the company had been young and intrusive. There was always a partylike atmosphere around the place: I'd seen people snorting cocaine in the ladies' room, and at lunchtime the male employees would put on shorts and play Frisbee. I wanted to be done with the job as quickly as possible. I wrote up my reports in record time and handed in my findings ten days ahead of schedule.

I always sat down at my desk one last time at the end of an audit, to make notes for my own records, notes I would keep with the original handwritten calculations in my ledger book. It was a standard precaution, a backup step that I made grudgingly and halfheartedly.

So there I was, at the end of this irritating job, sitting at my desk with the ledger open in front of me. It was late evening, and I was alone in the office, save the two cleaning ladies, who I heard chatting and laughing as they went up and down the halls emptying wastepaper baskets and recycling bins. I remember taking off my glasses and rubbing my blurry eyes. Then I squinted at the page again. The zeros looked funny; there were too many of them in some places, too few in others.

My stomach turned over. One of the ladies knocked on the door. "No thanks!" I croaked. I went down the lines of the ledger: decimal points wobbled, jumping back and forth instead of lining up in columns the way they should have. Just two zeros and hundreds of thousands of dollars of income had become tens of millions; millions in profit had become billions.

I threw up in a plastic bag left over from lunch.

First I imagined the phone message I would get from my boss: "It's Brian. Call me immediately." I imagined the panic I

would hear in his voice, and the anger, and the betrayal. How he would say, "It's my fault for trusting you."

Then I could see myself in meetings in windowless basement boardrooms, sweating, being forced to apologize, forced to resign.

Then I pictured hearings, with testimonies by my sixth-grade math teacher and my dyslexic older brother. I pictured myself inside a prison cell, with everybody I had ever audited filing past and shaking their heads. "Tsk, tsk, tsk," they were saying.

Yes, I could have told everybody that I had made some mistakes. But instead, I ripped up the ledger and threw the pieces into seven different dumpsters on the way back to my hotel.

When I arrived in my room, the red voice mail light on my phone was blinking. I almost turned around and ran right then. They had found out already, I thought. I could see it all—a conscientious junior accountant (or even an intern) had noticed a discrepancy and had started to dig. I felt dizzy. I threw up again in the toilet. When I came out of the bathroom, there it was still: the strobing red light. Each time it flashed, it accused me. "You. You. You. You," it was saying.

When the phone rang I almost fainted. The whole room seemed to stink from my sweat. Four rings. And then the ringing stopped.

I believed I was trapped. Trapped. I packed and slipped out of the hotel by the stairs. I was in Miami late the next day.

I know. I know. You would have stayed. You would have told yourself: It's a mistake. Everybody makes mistakes. I didn't think that. I didn't tell myself that. I try not to have regrets. I could have done things differently, but I have to live. Don't you agree? Obviously you've done something wrong, too. You must have made a terrible mistake as well. After all, you live in a trailer outside Campbell, Ohio.

•   •   •

At eight A.M. my last morning in Poughkeepsie, just as I was zipping up my duffel bag, the doorbell rang.

I froze.

I was heading to Campbell, Ohio. I could sleep in my car until the trailer was ready. Since the night before, everything had changed. I could no longer wait.

The doorbell rang again.

I crept over to the window and peeked out, hoping for a Jehovah's Witness or even the return of the UPS lady. But there was an unfamiliar Hyundai parked in front of the house. A man stepped off the porch and into my line of sight. Short, slight beer belly, khaki pants. He looked around, shielding his eyes from the sun with his hand. Baby face, blond.

I collected myself. I had to go downstairs. My car was parked in the driveway; I was obviously home. He didn't look like the law.

"Yes?" I said through the screen door.

"Um, Miss Connell? I'm Tyler? I'm looking for Corinne?" he said. (They were those kinds of names, names like Tyler and Corinne.)

"Corinne?"

"Yeah." His voice got a little stronger. "Corinne. My fiancée. Petite. Wavy hair."

Gloria Freeman, I thought. Glory, Glo. Daughter of Freeman. Good old Freeman. My daddy. I pictured Campbell, that red dot on the road atlas where I would soon be safe.

I opened the door just enough to squeeze through. It closed behind me with a snap.

"Oh, *Corinne*," I said. I squinted to see inside his car. Nobody. I looked up and down the block. Nobody.

"She didn't come home yesterday after work," he said. "She never came home."

She had told me her roommate's name was Mamie. Now I remembered her laughing nervously and volunteering that she didn't know much about Mamie's past. She lied to me, I

thought, and I found myself shaking my head. For a moment I wished I could go on one of her TV programs and confront her: *Why didn't you tell me about Tyler?* I imagined myself screaming. *What was the point?* And I imagined her sobbing, *I thought you wouldn't want to be my friend.*

I noticed that I was still shaking my head. I had to say something, so I said, "That's odd." I forced myself to put something like a smile on my face. I ached under my arms as my sweat glands puckered and wept.

"I know you're her friend," Tyler said, glancing down and to the right as if he could see through the piece of plywood I had hastily nailed across the basement window at three A.M. "She talks about you all the time . . ." Suddenly he relaxed and smiled a strained smile. "And I'm sure she talks about me all the time to you. I hope you don't think she's a pain in the ass. She means well."

"Oh, I'm sure she does," I said. I sounded terrified and sarcastic at the same time.

"Can I sit down?" he asked, nodding at the porch steps.

"Be my guest," I said. I realized that I had started to tremble, huge shivers running up and down my whole body. I pulled my cardigan tight across my chest.

"I guess she's kind of like my mom," he said, then half-winked at me. "Don't ever tell Corinne I said that. Deal?" I nodded. I wondered if he would ever leave. I pictured him moving into the house. I pictured him getting in my car and talking all the way to Campbell.

"I bet Corinne's told you all about Mom. I mean, Mom can be kind of nosy, kind of a busybody, but even though she annoys the hell out of me, I always remind myself that Mom has a heart of gold. Okay, for example, she'll come into our place and look at everything, pick up the pieces of mail, the dirty dishes, whatever, and comment on them. But what am I going to do, tell her not to come over? Tell her to call before she comes? You can't do that to your mom, right?"

I leaned against the wooden column under the sagging eave.

"Thing is," he said, making himself comfortable on the top step, "as you know, we're getting married next month, and, well, tell you the truth, I've been a little worried about how much time she's spending with you. She may have told you we've been fighting some."

I nodded. In the rear of the basement, the cement floor ended, and there was a five-foot strip of dirt floor, which became moist and spongy every time it rained.

"Nothing serious, not big fights—just—I don't know—she's always going 'My single friend this, my single friend that.' I was starting to think you were a bad influence. I thought that you were out partying together, maybe flirting with guys, that kind of thing . . . but now that I'm meeting you"—he looked at me with pity—"I can tell that wasn't the case."

I looked at my fingernails, the reddish brown dirt under them. I had done the best I could with the shovel, considering I had been in a hurry.

He cleared his throat. I tucked my hands into the pockets of my pants.

"She feels sorry for you," Tyler said.

"Uh-huh," I mumbled.

"Sometimes she says she feels sorry for me. She says I'm a big baby. Maybe all guys are, what do you think?"

"I don't know . . ." I said, thinking about his neck—it was thick, but not muscular. The flesh looked soft and pliant. What would the difference be? I thought. I pictured two mounds next to each other, mounds as plump and neat as the people inside them. Then my stomach turned over, saliva spouted into my mouth, I thought I would throw up.

He stood again, hiking up his pants. "Well, sorry to bother you. Maybe she went to TGIF with her mom and sis, and crashed on Mamie's sofa. She does that once in a while." He laughed and winked. "Especially when she's mad at me. Man, I

can't wait until this whole wedding thing is out of the way."

We stood there for a few seconds, facing each other. I realized I had to say something. "Well, good luck."

"Thanks a bunch," he said, reaching out his hand. He waited. I had no choice: from my pocket, I pulled my scared and sorrowful hand, with its stained nails and sore muscles. I offered it to him. He took it. He pumped it up and down. "I feel so much better now that we've talked," he said.

After I watched him drive away, I went back inside the house. I had rented it only semifurnished, and had never added a single chair or rug. I walked into the living room, where the shades were drawn as always, and I sat down on the tattered love seat in the corner. I knew that every moment I spent dawdling was a wasted one, a risky one, a dangerous one. Yet I couldn't move. I found myself thinking about the love seat. Closing my eyes, I could picture the people who had sat on it before I moved in— I imagined couples: entwined lovers; husbands and wives watching television; newlyweds giving each other backrubs; young parents, bickering from exhaustion after putting an infant to sleep. I thought about Corinne and Tyler, "Corinne" and "Tyler," how they must have nestled, snuggled, pressed their soft bellies together under the covers in some condo in Wappingers Falls, between the mall and the IBM compound. I could see her small, frizzy head moving over his groin. I could see him, shaving cream on half his face, catching her awkward breast in his hand as she stepped out of the shower.

He would never find her.

It was very hard at first when I got to Campbell. I didn't know how I would live, what I would do with myself. I kept my ear to the radio, my eyes on the seven-inch black-and-white TV. But I guess that the news about what happened in Poughkeepsie never made it that far. I spent a long stretch living in this trailer, longer than I'd been in one place for years. I cut my hair,

• • •

dyed it black. I started wearing dark nail polish. When my nails were bare, I could still see traces of dirt between them and the tender part of my fingertips. I was polite to all of my neighbors.

As I said, I try not to have regrets, but I do sometimes find myself looking back on my finest moment as an auditor. I wish you could have seen me at my best. I wish you had known me then. I had pride, I really did. I was on top of the world.

I was twenty-two, and coming to the end of a grueling stint at a PepsiCo satellite office in Spokane. It was a monthlong job that turned into six weeks. I was working down to the wire. It was midnight on the last night of the audit, and I had uncovered proof of what the corporate headquarters had suspected: that large sums of PepsiCo money allotted for supplies, petty cash, and promotions had been reabsorbed and recorded as earnings, and that the Spokane office was actually losing money instead of turning a healthy profit. I was making my way through the records of the last quarter when there was a knock at the door. It was the vice president who ran the satellite. He was wearing a sweat suit, and his velour jacket was zipped up tightly across his blubbery middle. He asked me how it was going, and I told him it was going well, and that I was just about done. He came closer to me and put his hairy hands on the edge of the desk. I kept working. After a little while, he said he guessed it wasn't looking too good for him, and I shook my head. The next thing I knew, he was down on his knees on the carpet, his jaw trembling.

"Please," he said, "please, this is going to kill me. Do you have to do this? Does it have to be so bad?"

I looked at him for a second—the greasy sweat on his temples, the tiny bald spot I'd never noticed when he was standing up.

"Isn't there anything we can do to make you stop?" he said.

I sharpened my red pencil.

SEE THROUGH

The first man says to me, "I missed you."

I say, "I missed you, too."

He says, "How was your weekend?"

I say, "Fine, fine. I went to a barbecue."

He says, "I'm having trouble hearing you."

I move the microphone. "Is that better?"

"Yeah. That's great. You look nice."

"Thanks," I say. I smooth my hair. "How's your girlfriend?"

"She's okay. I don't know. Let's talk about you."

"What do you want to talk about?" I ask.

"Tell me about the barbecue," he says.

"Well, it was in San Rafael. I took a bus there."

"A bus! Baby I woulda drove you."

I laugh. "I had spareribs."

"You're no vegetarian, no sir," he says. "My girlfriend makes wicked carne asada."

"So now you *want* to talk about her?" I say.

"No, no, baby. Forget about her. Tell me something . . ."

"Something what?" I watch my reflection in the glass. My eyebrows raise to look inquisitive.

"Aw, you know, baby doll . . ." He takes off his hat. It has a fire extinguisher over the visor. He is a fire extinguisher repairman.

"You know how I like it." A clunking noise, and he digs in his pocket for another quarter. The sound goes out until he drops it in the slot. "You *know*. Pretend I'm your man. Tell me what you're gonna do to me tonight when I get home from work."

"I'm going to lie you down on the blue velvet couch . . ."

"We got rid of that couch," he says.

"What kind of couch, then?" I say.

"Flowered. A sofa bed, so her mother can come and visit."

"Okay, I'm going to lie you down on the flowered sofa bed . . ."

"No—not there," he says. "That's where her mother sleeps."

"Okay, where, then?"

"The deck, out back," he says.

"The deck," I say. "I'm going to take your hand and lead you out to the deck. I'm going to be a little bit forceful."

"Not too forceful," he says.

"Of course not, honey," I say. "I'm going to lie you down on the plastic deck chair. . . ."

"Hey, you know what?" he says. "It's a full moon tonight."

The quarter drops, and there is silence again until he puts another in the slot. I stare over his head at my reflection.

"So you lie me down in the deck chair," he says, "and I'm looking up at the moon and you open my belt, and I can feel your fingernails on my legs." I drag my fingernails lightly across the glass in front of him. He is unzipping his pants. "Do it, okay?" he says.

I reach over to the hidden little shelf and take down the latex phallus. I shut my eyes. He once said to me, "You know, that's not nice, a girl keeping her eyes open when she's doing you." I put it in my mouth. I listen to his breath, trying to pay attention to his rhythm. The regular dropping of coins punctuates his quiet, polite panting. I open my eyes after I hear his customary gasp and sigh. I smile at him. He smiles at me as he zips up his pants and puts his cap back on.

"Really," he says.

"What," I say.

"If I was really me, and you was really you," he says, "would you? Like if you just met me at a party or something, would you?"

"Of course," I say. "See you soon."

The second man says to me, "I've never done this before."

My mike is still off. I sigh before I turn it on.

"Well, you're very cute," I say. And he *is* okay, a young man with long blond hair, wearing a Metallica T-shirt. He isn't used to the glass. He squints at me.

"I'll do whatever you command," I tell him.

"Is your name really Sheena?" he says.

"Absolutely," I say.

"My sister has a kitten named Sheena," he says.

"Where are you from?" I say.

"Marin. San Rafael."

"Oh, I was there last weekend for a barbecue," I say.

"Like, you go to barbecues?" He sounds disappointed.

"Well, orgy sort of barbecues," I say. "You have nice arms. You must be a drummer." I see my face in the glass, watch my lips pucker around the word 'drummer.'

He grins and nods. Then he says, "You have nice tits." He turns red, looks behind himself, and leans forward. "Is it okay to say that?"

The quarter drops, but he is prepared. He has a little sack of them from the front counter, where they charge one-twenty-five for four quarters.

"Of course it's okay to say that," I say when the sound buzzes on again. "Actually, I'm flattered, and I'm getting a little hot."

He pushes his hair behind his ear and says, "Like, you *are*?"

"Ooh, yeah," I say. "It's not every day that someone like you picks my booth."

"Well, I saw that picture of you outside, the one in the blue

bikini." He looks at me. "But you're not wearing a bikini now."

I make a show out of wiggling my slip over my head. "Better?" I say. I'm making my voice as high and breathy as I can and still remain audible. I sit in my bra and underpants.

"Like, *yuh*," he says. He stares at me leaning toward the glass. He just looks me up and down. His breath makes a spot of steam.

"You look a little like the girl in the Coors Light ads," he says. I giggle. "But she's thinner," he adds.

"Well, you know they airbrush the hell out of those pictures," I tell him.

"No, don't get me wrong," he says, "I'm, like, totally into you. You're gorgeous the way you are."

"Well," I say, "you are too."

He says, "I also like your legs, but not as much as your tits."

"Thank you." I spread my legs a little bit. It's always like this the first time: a cataloging of body parts.

"Could you, like, turn around?" he asks me.

"For you, baby, anything." I turn around and look over my shoulder at him. He is slipping another quarter into the slot.

"You also have a nice enough ass," he says. Then he whispers, "Kind of like my sister."

"The one with Sheena?" I sit back down.

"Uh-huh," he says. "She plays tennis. She's the pro at the Strawberry Point Country Club."

"Ah. Do you work out?" I ask him. "You look awfully strong."

"No. Just drums and I do landscaping. I help with the golf course at the club."

I start to feel I'm losing him. He may have satisfied his curiosity enough. He could get up and walk out. I've heard people say I don't work hard enough to keep the customers in my booth. And last week I was out with a cold. I can't afford to have him leave.

I look him in the eye and whisper into the mike, "You know, it's always been a fantasy of mine to make love on a golf course."

"Really? No *way!*"

"Yeah, I've always wanted to lie down in the grass, that really soft green grass, and have a hunky . . . dude . . . give it to me."

"Well, like, if you want to come to the club sometime, we could go there at night and stuff," he says.

"No, I can't wait, let's pretend right here, okay?" I say.

"Okay." He's nodding. He's catching on. I go slowly, take him through step by step. He asks if he can call me Tiffany. He isn't embarrassed to touch himself after I assure him he has a cute dick. I wiggle a lot. He seems to like that.

On my lunch break, I go to the dressing room in the basement to use the pay phone. A couple of the other girls are down there, but none of them talk to me anymore. A few weeks after I started this job, a nine-dollar lipstick fell out of my bag. One of the girls picked it up and raised her eyebrows. I told her I'd shoplifted it from Walgreens, but she just shook her head. For a while after that, they all seemed curious.

"Are you in college?" one girl asked me.

"No," I said. "I dropped out. For now." She looked down and sucked air in through her teeth.

A couple of them asked where my family was. "The East Coast," I'd answer. I didn't want to be specific. More stares, a shrug.

"You got any kids?" asked a small woman who had her twins' school pictures taped inside her locker. "No," I said, adding, "but maybe someday."

Then, one night in the dressing room, I was taking off my makeup when they all gathered around me. To this day, I have no idea if they planned it or if it just happened spontaneously, a natural culmination of the tension that had been building for weeks. One of them stepped forward and said, "So, what are you doing here anyway?"

I looked around at them. I tried to figure out how to answer, but wound up just standing there with my mouth half open. They turned away from me, looking sideways at each other with disgusted smiles. Since then, it's been the silent treatment. Still, I'd rather use the phone here than out on Market Street with its crackheads and Women Against Pornography. I dial Bill's number and reach his answering machine, a tape of him playing his talking drum—the rhythmic gulping sound, and his hands slapping its taut skin. I hang up without leaving a message.

A couple of years ago, soon after we met, Bill started to complain that his life lacked spirituality. I was working at a 970 number then, and sometimes he'd call and pay to talk to me. We'd chuckle as I spoke to him as Cherise or Maria. Then, out of the blue, he decided that he would start his own religion. He announced it to me one morning while we were waiting to order coffee and scones. He told the woman on line behind us, and the guy behind the counter, too, while our milk was being steamed.

Bill threw himself into his project: he wrote prayers and designated holidays and sacred symbols. He found a secluded spot in Golden Gate Park, and made a shrine there out of branches and rocks, velvet and novena candles. "I finally have something to believe in," he'd tell me, sighing, every night before he fell asleep. "I'm at peace for the first time in my life." In the near-dark, his eyes looked shiny and serious. I'd smile at him, and then he'd kiss me and pull me close.

About a year after Bill came up with his idea, someone told Channel 2 about his shrine and they did a news feature on him. As soon as he saw himself on television, he stopped believing. But the next time he visited his spot in the park, he was surprised to find some people waiting there for him. So he has to show up and worship. His fans expect him to be there at certain times, he says. He can't let people know he has lost faith.

Yesterday was the first day I was out and about after my

cold. I got up with Bill and walked with him to the park. On the path, right outside the spot where he has his shrine, I kissed him. I put my tongue as far back as I could and mashed my lips against his. But I was thinking that I needed to get nail polish on the way to work. The ridges on the roof of his mouth felt hard like fish bones. After I ended the kiss, I said, "Have a good day, baby."

"Don't talk to me like that," he said, turning and walking away.

"What do you mean?" I said, following him.

"You know, that *voice*."

We stepped into the clearing. There were a few kids with pierced lips standing around, waiting to see Bill worship. One of them held a video camera.

"But that's my voice."

"No it's not, Liz," he said. "It's dirty."

"But you like being dirty, baby," I said.

"That's exactly what I mean." He stamped his bare foot. "That *baby* shit."

I looked over at his audience. A girl clicked a steel ball rooted in her tongue against her teeth. She stared at me. I knew she wanted me to leave.

"I'm sorry." I lowered my voice. "I can change the way I talk. How do you want me to talk?"

Bill shook his head. "I just don't buy you anymore," he said to me, loud enough for everyone to hear. He turned to face the spectators, inhaled deeply, and rolled his eyes back into his head. Then he kneeled down in the grass and started lighting candles.

The third man sits down with his face in the shadows. "Bitch," he says. He has an older voice, high-pitched and restrained like Mr. Rogers. "Dirty bitch." I can see the sleeve of an egg yolk yellow cardigan when he puts the quarter in.

"What do you want, sir?" I ask. I lean forward.

"Get back, whore," he says quietly.

I try to work with it. I say, "I've been very bad. I need to be punished."

"Shut your dirty trap," he says.

I watch myself in the glass, sitting still, waiting. I hold my breath and try to be very quiet. Once, I read that the gaze holds power, that by looking at something you come to own it. I've also heard it said about names: if you call something by its true name, it belongs to you. I stare into my own unblinking eyes.

When I was a girl, I got a baby doll whose eyes closed when she lay down. I was scared for her, and pulled out her tiny plastic eyelids, so she could always see. Her eyes were blue, transparent, frozen. I would sit her on the bed across from me and we would look at each other in silence.

The quarter falls. I see the yellow sleeve moving in the dark.

ABOUT THE AUTHOR

Nelly Reifler has published stories in magazines such as *Bomb, Black Book, Post Road, Exquisite Corpse,* and *The Florida Review* as well as the anthologies *110 Stories: New York Writes After September 11* and *Lost Tribe: Jewish Fiction from the Edge.* A graduate of Hampshire College and of Sarah Lawrence College's writing program, she received the Henfield Prize for two of the stories in this collection. Her plays have been performed in the United States and Australia, and she currently teaches at Sarah Lawrence College. She lives in Brooklyn.

Printed in the United States
By Bookmasters

P A I D E I A (py-dee-a) from the Greek *pais, paidos:*
the upbringing of a child. (Related to pedagogy and
pediatrics.) In an extended sense, the equivalent of
the Latin *humanitas* (from which "the humanities"),
signifying the general learning that should be the
possession of all human beings.

Members of the Paideia Group

MORTIMER J. ADLER, *Chairman*
Director, Institute for Philosophical Research;
Chairman, Board of Editors, Encyclopaedia Britannica

JACQUES BARZUN, former Provost, Columbia University; Literary Adviser, Charles Scribner's Sons

OTTO BIRD, former head, General Program of Liberal Studies, University of Notre Dame

LEON BOTSTEIN, President, Bard College; President, Simon's Rock of Bard College

ERNEST L. BOYER, President, The Carnegie Foundation for the Advancement of Teaching, Washington, D.C.

NICHOLAS L. CAPUTI, Principal, Skyline High School, Oakland, California

DOUGLASS CATER, Senior Fellow, Aspen Institute for Humanistic Studies

DONALD COWAN, former President, University of Dallas; Fellow, Dallas Institute of Humanities and Cultures

ALONZO A. CRIM, Superintendent, Atlanta Public Schools, Atlanta, Georgia

CLIFTON FADIMAN, Author and critic

DENNIS GRAY, Deputy Director, Council for Basic Education, Washington, D.C.

RICHARD HUNT, Senior Lecturer and Director of the Andrew W. Mellon Faculty Fellowships Program, Harvard University viii

Contents

Contents

x

To Our Readers

THE PAIDEIA PROPOSAL *is addressed to those Americans most concerned with the future of our public schools:*

To Parents who believe that the decline in the quality of public schooling is damaging the futures of their children.

To Teachers troubled that the increasing time spent in keeping basic order in the classroom undermines the real business of schooling: to teach and to learn.

To School Boards frightened by the flight of middle-class children and youth to private and parochial schools.

To College Educators burdened by the increasing need to provide remedial education which detracts from their ability to offer a meaningful higher education.

To Elected Public Officials searching for ways to improve the quality of education without increasing the cost to taxpayers.

To Our Readers

To Employers concerned about the effects on productivity of a work force lacking skills in reading, writing, speaking, listening, observing, measuring, and computing.

To Minority Groups angered by widening gulfs between the better educated and the poorly educated, and between the employed and the unemployed.

To Labor Leaders attempting to deal with workers who lack the skills to find jobs in the new high-technology industries.

To Military Leaders needing brainpower among the troops capable of coping with sophisticated weaponry.

To American Citizens alarmed by the prospects of a democracy in which a declining proportion of the people vote or endeavor to understand the great issues of our time.

Such deep and legitimate concerns are addressed by our proposal for the reform of public schooling in America. The reform we seek is designed to improve the opportunities of our youth, the prospects of our economy, and the viability of our democratic institutions. It must be achieved at the community level without resorting to a monolithic, national educational system. It must be, in Lincoln's words, of the people, by the people, and for the people.

PART ONE
The Schooling of a People

1
Democracy and Education

We are on the verge of a new era in our national life. The long-needed educational reform for which this country is at last ready will be a turning point toward that new era.

Democracy has come into its own for the first time in this century. Not until this century have we undertaken to give twelve years of schooling to all our children. Not until this century have we conferred the high office of enfranchised citizenship on all our people, regardless of sex, race, or ethnic origin.

The two—universal suffrage and universal schooling—are inextricably bound together. The one without the other is a perilous delusion. Suffrage without schooling produces mobocracy, not democracy—not rule of law, not constitutional government by the people as well as for them.

The great American educator, John Dewey, recognized this early in this century. In *Democracy and Education*, written in 1916, he first tied these two words together and let each shine light upon the other.

3

A revolutionary message of that book was that a democratic society must provide equal educational opportunity not only by giving to all its children the same quantity of public education—the same number of years in school—but also by making sure to give to all of them, all with no exceptions, the same quality of education.

The ideal Dewey set before us is a challenge we have failed to meet. It is a challenge so difficult that it is understandable, perhaps excusable, that we have so far failed. But we cannot continue to fail without disastrous consequences for all of us. For the proper working of our political institutions, for the efficiency of our industries and businesses, for the salvation of our economy, for the vitality of our culture, and for the ultimate good of our citizens as individuals, and especially our future citizens—our children—we must succeed.

We are all sufferers from our continued failure to fulfill the educational obligations of a democracy. We are all the victims of a school system that has only gone halfway along the road to realize the promise of democracy.

At the beginning of this century, fewer than 10 percent of those of an age eligible for high school entered such schools. Today, almost 100 percent of our children enter, but not all complete such secondary schooling; many drop out for many reasons, some of them understandable.

It has taken us the better part of eighty years to go halfway toward the goal our society must achieve if it is to be a true democracy. The halfway mark was reached when

4

we finally managed to provide twelve years of basic public schooling for all our children. At that point, we were closer to the goal that Horace Mann set for us more than a century ago when he said: "Education is the gateway to equality."

But the democratic promise of equal educational opportunity, half fulfilled, is worse than a promise broken. It is an ideal betrayed. Equality of educational opportunity is not, in fact, provided if it means no more than taking all the children into the public schools for the same number of hours, days, and years. If once there they are divided into the sheep and the goats, into those destined solely for toil and those destined for economic and political leadership and for a quality of life to which all should have access, then the democratic purpose has been undermined by an inadequate system of public schooling.

It fails because it has achieved only the same quantity of public schooling, not the same quality. This failure is a downright violation of our democratic principles.

We are politically a classless society. Our citizenry as a whole is our ruling class. We should, therefore, be an educationally classless society.

We should have a one-track system of schooling, not a system with two or more tracks, only one of which goes straight ahead while the others shunt the young off onto sidetracks not headed toward the goals our society opens to all. The innermost meaning of social equality is: *sub-*

5

stantially the same quality of life for all. That calls for:
the same quality of schooling for all.

We may take some satisfaction, perhaps, in the fact
that we have won half the battle—the quantitative half.
But we deserve the full development of the country's human potential. We should, therefore, be vexed that we have
not yet gone further. We should be impatient to get on
with it, in and through the schools.

Progress toward the fulfillment of democracy by
means of our educational system should and can be ac-
celerated. It need not and must not take another century
to achieve uniform quality for all in our public schools.

There are signs on all sides that tell us the people
want that move forward now. The time is ripe. Parents,
teachers, leaders of government, labor unions, corporations—above all, the young themselves—have uttered passionate complaints about the declining quality of public
schooling.

There is no acceptable reason why trying to promote
equality should have led to a lessening or loss of quality.
Two decades after John Dewey, another great American
educator, Robert Maynard Hutchins, as much committed
to democracy as Dewey was before him, stated the fundamental principle we must now follow in our effort to
achieve a true equality of educational conditions. "The best
education for the best," he said, "is the best education for
all."

6

The shape of the best education for the best is not unknown to us. But we have been slow to learn how to provide it. Nor have we always been honest in our commitment to democracy and its promise of equality. A part of our population—and much too large a part—has harbored the opinion that many of the nation's children are not fully educable. Trainable for one or another job, perhaps, but not educable for the duties of self-governing citizenship and for the enjoyment of things of the mind and spirit that are essential to a good human life.

We must end that hypocrisy in our national life. We cannot say out of one side of our mouth that we are for democracy and all its free institutions including, preeminently, political and civil liberty for all; and out of the other side of our mouth, say that only some of the children—fewer than half—are educable for full citizenship and a full human life.

With the exception of a few suffering from irremediable brain damage, every child is educable up to his or her capacity. Educable—not just trainable for jobs! As John Dewey said almost a century ago, vocational training, training for particular jobs, is not the education of free men and women.

True, children are educable in varying degrees, but the variation in degree must be of the same kind and quality of education. If "the best education for the best is the best education for all," the failure to carry out that principle is the failure on the part of society—a failure of parents, of teachers, of administrators—not a failure on the part of the children.

There are no unteachable children. There are only schools and teachers and parents who fail to teach them.

2
Schooling—Only a Part of Education

IF ALL CHILDREN are educable, all are justified in aspiring to become educated persons. But no one can become fully educated in school, no matter how long the schooling or how good it is. Our concern with education must go beyond schooling.

The schooling of a people does not complete their education. Not even if the quality of schooling were improved to the utmost for all; not even if all who completed twelve years of compulsory basic schooling went on to optional advanced schooling in our colle: -s and universities and profited by it.

The simple fact is that educational institutions, even at their best, cannot turn out fully educated men and women. The age at which most human beings attend school prevents that. Youth itself is the most serious impediment—in fact, youth is an insuperable obstacle to being an educated person.

No one can be an educated person while immature. It would be a travesty to regard the degrees awarded by our colleges and universities as certifying the completion of education. It is all the more true of the high school diploma.

Only through the trials of adult life, only with the range and depth of experience that makes for maturity, can human beings become educated persons. The mature may not be as trainable as the immature, but they are more educable by virtue of their maturity.

Education is a lifelong process of which schooling is only a small but necessary part. The various stages of schooling reach terminal points. Each can be completed in a definite term of years. But learning never reaches a terminal point. As long as one remains alive and healthy, learning can go on—and should. The body does not continue to grow after the first eighteen or twenty years of life. In fact, it starts to decline after that. But mental, moral, and spiritual growth can go on and should go on for a lifetime.

The ultimate goal of the educational process is to help human beings become educated persons. Schooling is the preparatory stage; it forms the habit of learning and provides the means for continuing to learn after all schooling is completed.

For some, this preparation ends with the completion of basic schooling, amounting to about twelve years. For others, it means the completion of advanced schooling, which may take another four years or more. For all, schooling completed means that education has been begun, but not finished. Schooling, basic or advanced, that does not prepare the individual for further learning has failed, no matter what else it succeeds in doing.

Basic schooling—the schooling compulsory for all—must do something other than prepare some young people for more schooling at advanced levels. It must prepare *all* of them for the continuation of learning in adult life, during their working years and beyond.

How? By imparting to them the skills of learning and giving them the stimulation that will motivate them to keep their minds actively engaged in learning. Schooling should open the doors to the world of learning and provide the guidelines for exploring it.

Basic schooling in America does not now achieve this fundamental objective. It used to do so for those who completed high school at the beginning of this century. With the vastly increased numbers who enter high school now, our system may achieve this objective for a few, but it fails to do it for all. Yet doing it for all is precisely what we mean when we say we want the same quality of schooling for all.

The failure to serve all in this essential respect is one strike against basic schooling in its present deplorable condition. The reform we advocate seeks to remedy that condition. When that is done, the certificate which marks the completion of basic schooling at the end of twelve years will deserve once again to be called what it was called centuries ago—a baccalaureate diploma.

11

The Schooling of a People

In 1817, long before democracy came to full bloom in this country, Thomas Jefferson made a proposal that was radical for his day. He advocated three years of common schooling at the public expense for all the children of Virginia. But he then divided the children into those destined for labor and those destined for learning. Only the latter were to go on further to the local colleges of the time. The rest were to toil on the farms as hired hands or in the shops as apprentices.

In the twentieth century, we demand twelve years of common schooling at public expense for every child in the country. It is no longer a radical demand. But our present tracking system of public schooling still divides children into those destined only for labor and those destined for more schooling.

We believe, on the contrary, that all children are destined for learning, as most are destined for labor by their need to earn a livelihood. To live well in the fullest human sense involves learning as well as earning.

PART TWO
The Essentials of Basic Schooling

3
The Same Objectives for All

Aᴛ ᴛʜᴇ ᴠᴇʀʏ ʜᴇᴀʀᴛ of a multitrack system of public schooling lies an abominable discrimination. The system aims at different goals for different groups of children. One goal, higher than the others, is harder to accomplish. The other goals are lower—and perhaps easier, but, ironically, they are all too frequently not attained.

The one-track system of public schooling that *The Paideia Proposal* advocates has the same objectives for all without exception.

These objectives are not now aimed at in any degree by the lower tracks onto which a large number of our underprivileged children are shunted—an educational dead end. It is a dead end because these tracks do not lead to the result that the public schools of a democratic society should seek, first and foremost, for all its children—preparation to go on learning, either at advanced levels of schooling, or in adult life, or both.

Nor, in the present state of our schools, is that main objective aimed at or attained in any satisfactory measure

15

by the higher track along which a minority of favored children move during their years of basic schooling. That track is higher only in the sense that its aims are more difficult to accomplish. But even it is not now directed to the right objectives.

In the early years, before basic schooling branches out in different directions, it fails badly to teach proficiency in the indispensable skills of learning. Even in these years, when it is still a one-track system, it falls far short of delivering the goods.

To achieve the desired quality of democratic education, a one-track system of public schooling for twelve years must aim directly at three main objectives and make every effort to achieve them to a satisfactory degree.

These three objectives are determined by the vocations or callings common to all children when they grow up as citizens, earning their living and putting their free time to good use.

The first of these objectives has already been mentioned. It relates to that aspect of adult life which we call personal growth or self-improvement—mental, moral, and spiritual. Every child should be able to look forward not only to growing up but also to continued growth in all human dimensions throughout life. All should aspire to make as much of their powers as they can. Basic schooling should prepare them to take advantage of every opportunity for personal development that our society offers.

A second main objective has to do with another side of adult life—the individual's role as an enfranchised citizen of this republic. Citizens are the principal and permanent rulers of our society. Those elected to public office for a term of years are instrumental and transient rulers—in the service of the citizenry and responsible to the electorate.

The reason why universal suffrage in a true democracy calls for universal public schooling is that the former without the latter produces an ignorant electorate and amounts to a travesty of democratic institutions and processes. To avoid this danger, public schooling must be universal in more than its quantitative aspect. It must be universal also in its qualitative aspect. Hence, the second objective of basic schooling—an adequate preparation for discharging the duties and responsibilities of citizenship.

This requires not only the cultivation of the appropriate civic virtues, but also a sufficient understanding of the framework of our government and of its fundamental principles.

The third main objective takes account of the adult's need to earn a living in one or another occupation.

The twelve years of basic schooling must prepare them for this task, *not* by training them for one or another particular job in our industrial economy, but by giving them the basic skills that are common to all work in a society such as ours.

17

Here then are the three common callings to which all our children are destined: to earn a living in an intelligent and responsible fashion, to function as intelligent and responsible citizens, and to make both of these things serve the purpose of leading intelligent and responsible lives— to enjoy as fully as possible all the goods that make a human life as good as it can be.

To achieve these three goals, basic schooling must have for all a quality that can be best defined, *positively*, by saying that it must be general and liberal; and *negatively*, by saying that it must be nonspecialized and nonvocational.

Describing it as nonvocational may appear to be inconsistent with what has been said about its relation to earning a living. However, the schooling proposed is truly vocational in the sense that it aims to prepare children for the three vocations or callings common to all.

It is truly vocational in a further sense. It will prepare the young for earning a living by enabling them to understand the demands and workings of a technologically advanced society, and to become acquainted with its main occupations. It is nonvocational only in the sense that it does not narrowly train them for one or another particular job.

That kind of specialized or particularized job training at the level of basic schooling is in fact the reverse of something practical and effective in a society that is always changing and progressing. Anyone so trained will have to be retrained when he or she comes to his or her

18

job. The techniques and technology will have moved on since the training in school took place.

Why, then, was such false vocationalism ever introduced into our schools? As the school population rapidly increased in the early decades of this century, educators and teachers turned to something that seemed more appropriate to do with that portion of the school population which they incorrectly and unjustly appraised as being uneducable—only trainable. In doing this, they violated the fundamental democratic maxim of equal educational opportunity.

As compared with narrow, specialized training for particular jobs, general schooling is of the greatest practical value. It is good not only because it is calculated to achieve two of the three main objectives at which basic schooling should aim—preparation for citizenship and for personal development and continued growth. It is also good practically because it will provide preparation for earning a living.

Of all the creatures on earth, human beings are the least specialized in anatomical equipment and in instinctive modes of behavior. They are, in consequence, more flexible than other creatures in their ability to adjust to the widest variety of environments and to rapidly changing external circumstances. They are adjustable to every clime and condition on earth and perpetually adjustable to the shock of change.

That is why general, nonspecialized schooling has the quality that most befits human nature. That is why, in

19

terms of practicality and utility, it is better than any other kind of schooling.

But when we recognize that twelve years of general, nonspecialized schooling for all is the best policy—the most practical preparation for work—we should also realize that that is not its sole justification. It is not only the most expedient kind of schooling, but it is also best for the other reasons stated above: because it prepares our children to be good citizens and to lead good human lives.

4
The Same Course of Study for All

To GIVE THE SAME QUALITY OF SCHOOLING to all requires a program of study that is both liberal and general, and that is, in several, crucial, overarching respects, one and the same for every child. All sidetracks, specialized courses, or elective choices must be eliminated. Allowing them will always lead a certain number of students to voluntarily downgrade their own education.

Elective choices are appropriate only in a curriculum that is intended for different avenues of specialization or different forms of preparation for the professions or technical careers. Electives and specialization are entirely proper at the level of advanced schooling—in our colleges, universities, and technical schools. They are wholly inappropriate at the level of basic schooling.

The course of study to be followed in the twelve years of basic schooling should, therefore, be completely required, with only one exception. That exception is the choice of a second language. In addition to competence in the use of English as everyone's primary language, basic schooling should confer a certain degree of facility in the use of a second language. That second language should be open to elective choice.

The diagram on the opposite page depicts in three columns three distinct modes of teaching and learning, rising in successive gradations of complexity and difficulty from the first to the twelfth year. All three modes are essential to the overall course of study.

These three columns are interconnected, as the diagram indicates. The different modes of learning on the part of the students and the different modes of teaching on the part of the teaching staff correspond to three different ways in which the mind can be improved—(1) by the acquisition of organized knowledge; (2) by the development of intellectual skills; and (3) by the enlargement of understanding, insight, and aesthetic appreciation.

In addition to the three main Columns of Learning, the required course of study also includes a group of auxiliary subjects, of which one is physical education and care of the body. This runs through all twelve years. Of the other two auxiliary subjects, instruction in a variety of manual arts occupies a number of years, but not all twelve; and the third consists of an introduction to the world of work and its range of occupations and careers. It is given in the last two of the twelve years.

COLUMN ONE: ACQUISITION OF KNOWLEDGE

Here are three areas of subject matter indispensable to basic schooling—language, literature, and fine arts;

	COLUMN ONE	COLUMN TWO	COLUMN THREE
als	ACQUISITION OF ORGANIZED KNOWLEDGE	DEVELOPMENT OF INTELLECTUAL SKILLS – SKILLS OF LEARNING	ENLARGED UNDERSTANDING OF IDEAS AND VALUES
	by means of	by means of	by means of
eans	DIDACTIC INSTRUCTION LECTURES AND RESPONSES TEXTBOOKS AND OTHER AIDS	COACHING, EXERCISES, AND SUPERVISED PRACTICE	MAIEUTIC OR SOCRATIC QUESTIONING AND ACTIVE PARTICIPATION
	in three areas of subject-matter	in the operations of	in the
as erations Activities	LANGUAGE, LITERATURE, AND THE FINE ARTS MATHEMATICS AND NATURAL SCIENCE HISTORY, GEOGRAPHY, AND SOCIAL STUDIES	READING, WRITING, SPEAKING, LISTENING CALCULATING, PROBLEM-SOLVING OBSERVING, MEASURING, ESTIMATING EXERCISING CRITICAL JUDGMENT	DISCUSSION OF BOOKS (NOT TEXTBOOKS) AND OTHER WORKS OF ART AND INVOLVEMENT IN ARTISTIC ACTIVITIES e.g., MUSIC, DRAMA, VISUAL ARTS

THE THREE COLUMNS DO NOT CORRESPOND TO SEPARATE COURSES, NOR IS ONE KIND OF TEACHING AND LEARNING NECESSARILY CONFINED TO ANY ONE CLASS

23

mathematics and natural sciences; history, geography, and social studies.

Why these three? They comprise the most fundamental branches of learning. No one can claim to be educated who is not reasonably well acquainted with all three. They provide the learner with indispensable knowledge about nature and culture, the world in which we live, our social institutions,and ourselves.

The traditional name for the mode of instruction here is "didactic," or "teaching by telling." It employs textbooks and other instructional materials and is accompanied by laboratory demonstrations. The mind here is improved by the acquisition of organized knowledge.

Instruction in language comprises the learning of grammar and syntax, the forms of discourse, and to some extent the history of our own language. Comparisons between English and other languages being studied in the program should be stressed. Whether mathematics is also a language and how it compares with a natural language such as English should be considered.

Instruction in mathematics, beginning with simple arithmetic in the first grade, should rise to at least one year of calculus. It should be integrated from the very beginning with instruction in the use of calculators and lead subsequently to at least introductory instruction in the use of, and programming for, computers.

Instruction in the natural sciences includes physics, chemistry, and biology. Their interconnectedness and interdependence are stressed. Such instruction does not begin formally in the early grades but preparation for it can be made in a variety of attractive ways from the beginning.

History and geography are to be understood as including our knowledge of human and social affairs, not only within the boundaries of our own nation, but with regard to the rest of the world. Preparation for the formal study of history should begin in the early grades by story-telling and biographical narratives but, when formal study begins, it should be sequential and systematic, combining a narration of events with knowledge of social, political, and economic institutions and diverse phases of cultural development.

The innovative aspect of the first column lies not in the choice of subject matter but in the concentration and continuity of the study required. Those who know how inadequate and fragmentary is the knowledge offered to a large majority of those now graduating from high school will recognize the importance of our emphasis on these requirements.

COLUMN TWO: DEVELOPMENT OF SKILL

Here are the basic skills of learning—competence in the *use* of language, primarily English, aided by facility in a second language, as well as competence in dealing with a wide range of symbolic devices, such as calculators, computers, and scientific instruments.

25

The Essentials of Basic Schooling

The skills to be acquired are the skills of *reading, writing, speaking, listening, observing, measuring, estimating,* and *calculating.* They are linguistic, mathematical, and scientific skills. They are the skills that everyone needs in order to learn anything, in school or elsewhere. Without them, it is impossible to go on learning by one's self, whether for pleasure, or to qualify for a new job, or to be promoted in the present one.

It will be noted that language and mathematics appear in both Columns One and Two, but their significance is different in each. In Column One, *knowledge about* mathematics and language is acquired; in Column Two, the student learns *how to do* mathematical operations correctly and how to use language effectively for communication. "Know-how" consists in skilled performance. It differs from "knowledge about," which consists in knowing that something is the thus-and-so, and not otherwise.

The development of the Column Two skills clearly has close connections with the study of the three fundamental areas of subject matter in Column One. Only to the degree that pupils develop these skills, and form the habit of using them, can instruction in language and literature, mathematics and natural science, history and geography be successful.

Skills cannot be acquired in a vacuum. They must be practiced in the very study of the three basic areas of subject matter, as well as in the process of acquiring linguistic competence, competence in communication, com-

26

petence in the handling of symbolic devices, and competence in critical thinking.

Since what is learned here is skill in performance, not knowledge of facts and formulas, the mode of teaching cannot be didactic. It cannot consist in the teacher telling, demonstrating, or lecturing. Instead, it must be akin to the coaching that is done to impart athletic skills. A coach does not teach simply by telling or giving the learner a rule book to follow. A coach trains by helping the learner to *do*, to go through the right motions, and to organize a sequence of acts in a correct fashion. He corrects faulty performance again and again and insists on repetition of the performance until it achieves a measure of perfection.

Only in this way can skill in reading, writing, speaking, and listening be acquired. Only in this way can a similar measure of skill be acquired in mathematical and scientific operations. Only in this way can the ability to think critically—to judge and to discriminate—be developed. When coaching is not adequately undertaken, little can be expected in the development of the basic skills.

Coaching involves a different teacher-pupil relationship and a different pupil-teacher ratio than does instruction by telling and by the use of textbooks.

The innovative aspect of Column Two in the basic course of study lies in the fact that nowadays effective coaching and drilling is much too frequently absent from basic schooling. The lack of coaching and drilling by itself accounts for the present deficiencies of many high school

27

graduates in reading, writing, computing, and in following directions.

It is evident that Column Two is the backbone of basic schooling. Proficiency in all the skills that it lists—all of them the very means of learning itself—is indispensable to the efficient teaching and learning of the subject matters in Column One; and also indispensable to teaching and learning in Column Three.

Acquiring facility in the use of a second language is included in Column Two. Among modern languages, a choice can be made of French, German, Italian, Spanish, Russian, Chinese, and possibly others; it may even extend to Latin and Greek. A second language serves to enlarge the scope of the student's understanding of the culture in which English is the primary language by introducing him or her to the imagery and conceptual framework of the cultures that employ these other languages.

COLUMN THREE: ENLARGEMENT OF THE UNDERSTANDING

Here we have a mode of teaching and learning that has all too rarely been attempted in the public schools. Columns One and Two have important innovative aspects when compared with what now goes on and is either largely or totally left out. Column Three is virtually all innovative.

The materials of learning in Column Three can be described by calling them, on the one hand, books—books that are *not* textbooks—and, on the other hand, products

28

of human artistry. The books are of every kind—historical, scientific, philosophical, poems, stories, essays. The products of human artistry include individual pieces of music, of visual art, plays, and productions in dance, film, or television. The emphasis throughout is on the individual work.

The mode of learning in Column Three engages the mind in the study of individual works of merit, whether literary or otherwise, accompanied by a discussion of the ideas, the values, and the forms embodied in such products of human art.

The appropriate mode of instruction in Column Three is neither didactic nor coaching. It cannot be teaching by telling and by using textbooks. It cannot consist in supervising the activities involved in acquiring skills.

It must be the Socratic mode of teaching, a mode of teaching called "maieutic" because it helps the student bring ideas to birth. It is teaching by asking questions, by leading discussions, by helping students to raise their minds up from a state of understanding or appreciating less to a state of understanding or appreciating more.

The interrogative or discussion method of teaching to be employed in Column Three stimulates the imagination and intellect by awakening the creative and inquisitive powers. In no other way can children's understanding of what they know be improved, and their appreciation of cultural objects be enhanced.

The books in Column Three—fiction, poetry, essays, history, science, and philosophy—serve a twofold purpose.

29

On the one hand, discussion draws on the student's skills of reading, writing, speaking, and listening, and uses them to sharpen the ability to think clearly, critically, and reflectively. It teaches participants how to analyze their own minds as well as the thought of others, which is to say it engages students in disciplined conversation about ideas and values.

On the other hand, discussion introduces students to the fundamental ideas in the basic subject matters of Column One, and especially the ideas underlying our form of government and the institutions of our society.

To fulfill the objective of preparing all young people to become intelligent citizens requires the careful reading and discussion of at least the following documents: the Declaration of Independence, the Constitution, selections from the *Federalist Papers*, and the Gettysburg Address. Other books will fill this purpose out, but these few are basic to understanding our democracy.

For mutual understanding and responsible debate among the citizens of a democratic community, and for differences of opinion to be aired and resolved, citizens must be able to communicate with one another in a common language. "Language" in this sense involves a common vocabulary of ideas. This common intellectual resource is theirs only if they have read, discussed, and come to understand a certain number of books that deal with the ideas operative in the life of their time and place.

Music and other works of art can be dealt with in seminars in which ideas are discussed; but, like poetry and fiction, they need an additional treatment in order to be appreciated aesthetically—to be enjoyed and admired for their excellence. In this connection, exercises in the performance and composition of poetry, music, and visual works, as well as in the production of dramatic works, will help develop that appreciation in the most direct manner.

The best way to understand a play is to act in it, or at least to read it out loud. The best way to understand a piece of music is to sing or play it. The best way to understand a work oi dance is to try to dance it. Participation in the creation of works of art is as important as viewing, listening to, and discussing them. All children should have such pleasurable experiences.

THE INTEGRATION OF THE THREE COLUMNS

We have noted earlier the interplay between Columns One and Two. It can now be seen how Column Three supplements and reinforces the learning that is accomplished in the other two columns.

The reading of books throughout the twelve years of basic schooling, from easy books and mainly imaginative works in the early grades to more difficult books and expository as well as imaginative in the upper grades acquaints the growing mind with fundamental ideas in the subject matters of Column One, and at the same time employs and perfects all the linguistic skills of Column Two.

Without coaching, learners will lack the skills needed for the study of the basic subject matters. Without discussion, they may be memorizing machines, able to pass quizzes or examinations. But probe their minds and you will find that what they know by memory, they do not understand.

They have spent hours in classrooms where they were talked at, where they recited and took notes, plus hours (often too few) of homework poring over textbooks, extracting facts to commit to memory. But when have their minds been addressed, in what connection have they been called upon to think for themselves, to respond to important questions and to raise them themselves, to pursue an argument, to defend a point of view, to understand its opposite, to weigh alternatives?

There is little joy in most of the learning they are now compelled to do. Too much of it is make-believe, in which neither teacher nor pupil can take a lively interest. Without some joy in learning—a joy that arises from hard work well done and from the participation of one's mind in a common task—basic schooling cannot initiate the young into the life of learning, let alone give them the skill and the incentive to engage in it further. Only the student whose mind has been engaged in thinking for itself is an active participant in the learning process that is essential to basic schooling.

Without what is called for in Column Three, such participation cannot be accomplished to any satisfactory degree. It is not now accomplished at all for most of the students in our public schools, and it is accomplished to an insufficient degree for even the chosen few.

THE AUXILIARY STUDIES

Young people need physical exercise for their health's sake and also as an outlet for their abundant energy. Twelve years of physical education and participation in various intramural sports and athletic exercises are provided to fill this need. The program should be accompanied by instruction about health.

For a number of years, fewer than all twelve, boys and girls alike should participate in a wide variety of manual activities, including typing, cooking, sewing, wood- and metalworking, crafts using other materials, automobile driving and repair, maintenance of electrical and other household equipment, and so on.

In the later years, they should receive instruction to prepare them for choosing and finding a career. This is not to be done by requiring them to make a premature choice of a job and by giving them training for that particular job. Rather, the young person should be introduced to the wide range of human work—the kinds of occupations and careers, their significance and requirements, their rewards and opportunities.

If, over and above such general preparation, individuals need training for particular jobs that do not require the kind of advanced schooling that is appropriate to four-year colleges and universities with their technical and professional schools, this can be obtained after basic schooling is completed in two-year community colleges, in technical institutes, or on the job itself.

All activities and interests not included in the program as set forth should be regarded as extracurricular, to be engaged in voluntarily in afterschool hours.

The program recommended in the preceding pages is offered as a model. It can be adapted in a variety of ways to the diverse circumstances of different schools or school systems. *Our recommendation is not a monolithic program to be adopted uniformly everywhere.*

But the model does insist, for its validity, on the presence in all schools or school systems of the Three Columns—on the establishing of the three modes of learning and the three modes of teaching. The precise way in which that is to be accomplished will be determined by school boards and administrators in the light of the populations with which they are dealing and with reference to a variety of other relevant circumstances.

The system of public education in this country has always been pluralistic and should remain so. Preserving pluralism need not and should not prevent the adoption by *all* our schools of the central features of our model as an ideal to be realized in a variety of specifically different ways.

This cannot be conscientiously accomplished simply by introducing in some form the Three Columns of Learning. It also calls for the elimination of many things that now clutter up the school day. At the very least, their elimination is necessary to make room for what should displace them.

It eliminates all specialized training for particular jobs.

It eliminates from the curriculum and puts into the category of optional extracurricular activities a variety of pastimes that contribute little to education in comparison with the time, energy, and money spent on them.

If it did not call for all these displacements and eliminations, there would not be enough time in the school day or the school year to accomplish everything that is essential to the general, nonspecialized learning that must be the content of basic schooling.

Programs closely akin to what is here proposed have been instituted in other countries. Something like what is here proposed is carried on in our own country in a few exceptional schools, public and private.

Those who think the proposed course of study cannot be successfully followed by all children fail to realize that the children of whom they are thinking have never had their minds challenged by requirements such as these. It is natural for children to rise to meet higher expectations; but only if those expectations are set before them, and made both reasonable and attractive. They will respond when their minds are challenged by teachers able to give the different types of instruction set forth earlier, and who are themselves vitally interested in what they are teaching.

Worse evils than ignorance, lack of discipline, deficiency in rudimentary skills, and impoverished understanding result from most of the existing programs of instruction in our public schools. The absence of intellectual stimulation and the failure to challenge students by expecting the most of them leads to boredom, delinquency, lawless violence, drug dependence, alcoholism, and other forms of undesirable conduct.

Unless the overflowing energies of young people are fully and constructively employed, they will spill over into all forms of antisocial and destructive behavior. Their energies can be employed constructively only by a program of studies that engages their minds, that demands their taking an active part in learning, and that pushes and helps all to reach out and up for as much as they can get out of school.

The Paideia Proposal will be followed by a book of essays entitled *The Paideia Program: Pointers and Prospects*. This will provide guidelines for putting the program into effect.

5
Overcoming Initial Impediments

At this point the reader may be provoked to ask: "Isn't it obvious that the homes and environments from which children come to school will give some a distinct advantage in pursuing the program, while others will suffer from equally distinct disadvantages? Does not defective or even adverse nurturing in the years before schooling (and also afterwards) set up impediments that must be overcome?"

Yes, it is obvious, and we think something can be done about it.

The hopeful fact is that from the moment of birth children are capable of learning. They are born with the desire as well as the need to know. That desire—natural curiosity—can be nourished or it can be starved. The failure to nourish it as early as possible has dire consequences for the child's later schooling and adult life.

The individual's innate disposition to learn can be put to use in infancy and early childhood. It is then that neglect by parents or adverse circumstance maims or crushes this natural capacity. Preschool deprivation is the cause of backwardness or failure in school.

The Essentials of Basic Schooling

Schooling cannot do the job it should do equally well for all children if some are adequately prepared for school and some are not.

For the school to succeed in giving the same quality of basic education to all children, all must be prepared for it in roughly equal measure. Hence, at least one year—or better, two or three years—of preschool tutelage must be provided for those who do not get such preparation from favorable environments.

The idea behind the Head Start experiment was, indeed, a sound one. Preparation for schooling is not a dispensable accessory to the reform we are proposing. It is an essential ingredient, strongly recommended wherever it appears necessary and expedient.

A democratic society, defined as an ideal to be approximated, is one in which all, being equal in their humanity, enjoy equality of treatment. But in actuality a democratic society is limited in its ability to effect such equality. It can do so only through the public agencies it is able to finance and over which it can exercise some control. Preschool tutelage should, therefore, be provided at public expense for those who need but cannot afford it.

The home is a private, not a public, institution. The inequality of homes produces inequalities of nurture that lead some to draw wrong conclusions about the abilities of children. Instead of seeing them as differing only in the degree to which they have a present or future capacity for learning, they divide them into those who are truly educable and those who are not. This division is then used to

38

justify our not trying to give all the children the same quality of schooling. We keep all in school for the same number of years, but do not accord them equal treatment.

The sooner a democratic society intervenes to remedy the cultural inequality of homes and environments, the sooner it will succeed in fulfilling the democratic mandate of equal educational opportunity for all.

Without preparation for schooling, the chances of success in any attempted reform of the public school are greatly diminished. Without it, the country may even continue to believe the self-defeating doctrine that says not all children are educable and only some deserve the best quality of schooling we can afford.

6
Individual Differences

Aₙₒₜₕₑᵣ ₒbⱼₑcₜᵢₒₙ to the feasibility of our proposed reform is that we have overlooked a central fact. We have apparently dismissed as irrelevant the fact of individual differences. If it is not this oversight of a real obstacle with which we will be charged, then it will be our apparently thoughtless neglect of individual differences as if they did not matter, as if they had no significant bearing on the educability of the young.

"You propose," the objectors may say, "the same educational objectives for all the children." Yes, that is precisely what we propose.

"You propose the same course of study for all, and with no electives throughout the twelve years." Yes, again, that is right.

"You propose that they shall all complete this required course of study with a satisfactory standard of accomplishment regardless of native ability, temperamental bent, or conscious preferences." Yes, yes, yes!

How utopian! How outlandish! It will never work! At best it might suit the fortunate few, an elite who can measure up to what is required and who can acquit themselves with honors. But for the rest, it is pie in the sky, miles beyond their reach. To call it the kind of educational program that democracy demands and deserves is fine talk, but all the fine talk in the world cannot overcome the facts that stare us in the face when we pay a moment's attention to the actual population of our schools.

Why, anyhow, this unrelieved emphasis on *sameness* when the most obvious facts are the *manifold differences* among people—differences of all sorts, in native ability, in interests and inclinations, in temperament, in every taste and aptitude for learning, in home upbringing, in economic status and opportunity, in ethnic and racial heritage, and so on? Whether these differences are innate or acquired, whether they exist at birth or are produced by nurture and environment, is not the point. There they are. Any program of basic schooling that does not take them into account flies in the face of facts that will defeat it.

What the skeptics and scoffers forget are the samenesses in the context of which these differences exist. So we must, first of all, remind the objectors of those other facts—facts more significant than the differences upon which they dwell. Facts are facts, and calling attention to one set of facts does not justify forgetting, overlooking, or dismissing another set.

Despite their manifold individual differences, the children are all the same in their human nature. They are human beings and their human equality consists in the fact that no child is more or less human than another.

42

Their sameness as human beings—as members of the same species—means that every child has all the distinguishing properties common to all members of the species. They all have the same inherent tendencies, the same inherent powers, the same inherent capacities. The fact that individuals possess these common traits to different degrees is itself proof that they share a common nature at the same time that they differ in degree in the many ways that make each a unique individual. Individual differences are always and only differences in degree, never differences in kind.

In our democratic society, moreover, all children can look forward to a future that is the same in a number of essential respects. All will grow up to become full-fledged citizens with suffrage and with the political liberty it confers. All can demand to have their human and civil rights protected by the Constitution and by the laws that conform to it.

Those rights include preeminently rights to whatever conditions are needed for the pursuit of happiness—needed for their making the most of themselves and for their living as well as possible. They all have a right to participate in the general economic welfare and to expect a decent standard of living with enough free time to make a good life for themselves.

These are the facts of sameness that justify the sameness of the objectives at which our program for basic schooling aims. These are the facts of sameness that justify requiring the same course of study for all and a satisfactory standard of accomplishment for all.

To insist upon these facts—facts too often overlooked or ignored—is not to overlook or ignore individual differences.

What, then, must be done to temper the same to the different—to cope with individual differences?

The answer lies not in any retreat from the sameness of the program, any watering down of it, any deceptions that make it look as if it were the same for all while, in fact, it has become a two-track or a multitrack system.

The answer lies in adjusting that program to individual differences by administering it sensitively and flexibly in ways that accord with whatever differences must be taken into account. Children who, in one way or another, manifest deficiencies that would result in their not achieving the requisite standard of performance must be given special help to overcome those deficiencies. Such help would be truly remedial—remedying individual deficiencies that can and must be overcome.

What in recent years has been called remedial teaching is for the most part an effort to remedy defects that result from educational failures at prior levels of instruction. Because children were not taught what they should have been taught, or not taught well enough, the resultant defects must be remedied. What we here are calling for is remedial in another sense. It presupposes that in the course of study the subjects to be taught will be taught and taught well. But it recognizes that some children need more time or more help because of deficiencies that can be overcome by special efforts on the part of teachers and

44

parents—and the children themselves—to deal with their individual difficulties.

It may be that a considerable number of children will require such remedial teaching for a number of years. It may be that such remedial teaching will be most needed in the earlier rather than the later years of the program; but it should be available whenever it is needed so that no child is ever allowed to fall irremediably behind as is now the case.

We once again express our faith that there is no uneducable child—no unteachable child. There are only children that we fail to teach in a way that befits their individual condition. That faith rejects with abhorrence the notion that there are any irremediable deficiencies to block the attainment of the same educational goals for all.

Our program is not utopian. It is more realistic than the schooling that magnifies and overreacts to individual differences, that accepts deficiencies as irremediable, and that makes a mockery of equal educational opportunity by failing to recognize and make the best use of the samenesses that underlie the differences.

PART THREE
Teaching and Learning

7
The Heart of the Matter

THE PROCLAMATION OF PRINCIPLES, the setting of common objectives, the requirement of a well-devised course of study, the maintenance of reasonable standards of achievement—clearly, these are the essentials of the desired basic schooling for all.

But they are external prerequisites to be fulfilled. Fulfilling them, however necessary, is not enough. They are the outer structure, not the heart of the matter.

The heart of the matter is the quality of the learning that goes on during the hours spent in class and during the time spent doing assigned homework.

The course of study is nothing but a series of channels or conduits. The child goes in at one end and comes out at the other. The difference between what goes in and what comes out depends upon the quality of learning and of teaching that takes place throughout the journey.

The quality of learning, in turn, depends very largely on the quality of the teaching—teaching that guides and inspires learning in the classroom, and that directs and motivates learning to be done in homework. Largely but not entirely! Effective learning often occurs in spite of defective teaching. Teaching at its best is only an aid to learning, but that aid is most needed by those who are least adept at learning.

All genuine learning is active, not passive. It involves the use of the mind, not just the memory. It is a process of discovery, in which the student is the main agent, not the teacher.

How does a teacher aid discovery and elicit the activity of the student's mind? By inviting and entertaining questions, by encouraging and sustaining inquiry, by supervising helpfully a wide variety of exercises and drills, by leading discussions, by giving examinations that arouse constructive responses, not just the making of check marks on printed forms.

Learning by discovery can occur without help, but only geniuses can educate themselves without the help of teachers. For most students, learning by discovery must be aided. That is where teachers come in—as aids in the process of learning by discovery, not as knowers who attempt to put the knowledge they have in their minds into the minds of their pupils.

That never can be done, certainly not with good or permanent results. Teachers may think they are stuffing minds, but all they are ever affecting is the memory. Nothing can ever be forced into anyone's mind except by brainwashing, which is the very opposite of genuine teaching.

Teachers who do not understand these truths mis-understand the true character of learning. Worse, they do violence to the minds in their care. By assuming that they are the primary cause of learning on the part of their pupils, by filling passive receptacles, they act merely as indoctrinators—overseers of memorization—but they are not teachers

How should teachers—functioning properly as aids to learning—work to guide or assist the activity of the pupil's mind, the activity that is the principal cause of learning?

The answer differs according to the three ways in which learning improves the mind: (1) by the acquisition of information or organized knowledge; (2) by the development of intellectual skills; (3) by the enlargement of the understanding.

In each of these three modes of learning, there is a different kind of help to be given by the teacher.

Insofar as information and organized knowledge can be acquired from textbooks or manuals, teachers help such learning by monitoring its acquisition by drills, exercises, and tests. Their help also takes the form of didactic instruction, that is, lecturing: by telling, explaining, or pointing out the difficulties to be overcome, the problems to be solved, the connections and conclusions to be learned.

To keep this sort of teaching from becoming no more than a temporary stuffing of the memory, the telling should be tempered by questioning—back and forth across the teacher's desk. The more there is questioning and discussion, the more enlivened the class hour and the better the understanding of the subject being taught.

The development of the intellectual skills—the skills of learning itself—requires a different kind of help from teachers. Here (as we have said) the teacher must function the way athletic coaches do. John Dewey's oft-repeated but oft-misunderstood maxim that learning is by doing applies here most crucially and should govern the teaching effort.

What John Dewey had in mind was not exclusively physical doing or even social doing—engagement in practical projects of one kind or another. The most important kind of doing, so far as learning is concerned, is intellectual or mental doing. In other words, one can learn to read or write well only by reading and writing, one can learn to measure and calculate well only by measuring and calculating, just as one learns to swim or run well only by swimming or running.

To learn how to do any of these things well, one must not only engage in doing them, but one must be guided in doing them by someone more expert in doing them than oneself.

That more expert person is a teacher, who coaches and drills. Coaching requires, for at least part of the time, individual attention, but it can also be done with groups of learners if the groups are small enough to allow the coach to give individual attention where it is needed.

The third kind of learning which aims at raising the mind up from a lesser or weaker understanding to a stronger and fuller one cannot rely on telling or coaching. Here the teacher teaches by asking, not telling, and by using materials other than textbooks or manuals.

Discussion, in which the students both ask and answer questions, must prevail. In discussion the teacher must be keenly aware of the ways in which insights occur to enlarge the understanding—ways that differ from individual to individual. That demands close attention to what is happening in the student's mind as he or she asks or answers questions, and as one question or answer leads to another.

These three kinds of learning and teaching cannot take place effectively in the same kinds of classrooms or under exactly the same external conditions. To impose a uniform classroom setting, uniform class size, or uniform class hours on all three modes of instruction is to neglect and nullify their differences.

The ordinary classroom, with students sitting in rows and the teacher standing in front of them, dominating it, and the ordinary class period running for fifty minutes, properly serve the purposes of didactic instruction, but nothing else. Applied to the other two types of instruction, it will defeat them completely.

Consider the gymnasium, where athletic coaching is done. How does it permit the quite different relationship between the coach and those whose skill is to be trained?

By enabling the teacher to move from one trainee to another, standing or sitting beside the learner, spending more time with this one than with that one, and demanding of some or all more time for repeated exercises than an ordinary class period allows.

In other than physical education, exercising and practicing during after-school hours may well be required to meet the needs of the coaching teacher. When such homework is done, it must be carefully examined and corrected by the teacher. Without that, it comes to nothing. Moreover, parental support of homework is needed to see that it is done effectively. We are the only country in the world that is lax in this respect. No other country asks so little work of its children as we do. Some of our school "days" are over by noon and homework—not much of it at that—has become the exception.

Teaching by discussion imposes still other requirements. For older children, it calls for more than a fifty-minute class period. It also calls for a room in which the participants in the discussion sit around a table instead of in rows. The teacher is one of the participants, not the principal performer standing up in front of the group.

The teacher's role in discussion is to keep it going along fruitful lines—by moderating, guiding, correcting, leading, and arguing like one more *student!* The teacher is first among equals. All must have the sense that they are participating as equals, as is the case in a genuine conversation.

In all three ways of learning, the more active the learner the better. As far as possible, passivity must be discouraged and overcome. This does not mean more activity on the part of the teacher, but a different kind of activity from that which most teachers now display when they go on the assumption that teaching is transferring the contents of their own minds (or their notes) into the minds of their pupils.

Finally, a word must be said about deportment. Laxity in this respect can be completely destructive of learning and completely frustrating to the efforts of the best teachers. Students must be required to behave in class and in school in a manner that is conducive to learning.

Infraction of rules of conduct devised for this purpose must be effectively dealt with. Where discipline breaks down, where offenses against teachers or fellow students go unpunished, schools and classrooms are places where little or no effective learning and no teaching can take place.

Disturbing the peace is a serious matter in school as it is on the street—perhaps even more serious. Unquestionably, the well-taught class that awakens lively interest in learning and gives students a sense of accomplishment will help to promote decorum. But at all times it is of the first importance to let children know what is expected of them. The clearer and higher the expectations, the better the response.

Much has been said in recent years about the importance of the school in developing the moral character as well as the mind. One thing is certain. It is not by preaching moral homilies or by giving little lessons in ethics that moral character is formed. The moral sense develops under the discipline and examples that define desirable behavior. This must be supported by stern measures to check or prevent misconduct.

8
The Preparation of Teachers

THERE ARE AND ALWAYS WILL BE a relatively small number of highly gifted, strongly motivated teachers who manage, in spite of all adverse conditions, to perform creditably, even magnificently. But that number is far from enough to achieve the desired quality of teaching for all. At present, many factors work against having enough good teachers to staff our schools.

The surroundings in which many teachers work, especially in our large urban schools, would turn any other work place into a shambles. The productivity would drop below the lowest level for survival in business. It is not surprising that the level of achievement in many of our public schools falls below the comparable minimum.

Bad working conditions are not the only reason why we do not have enough able teachers, or why good ones are prevented from performing as they should. Recruiting for the profession is hampered by the average rate of pay, which is often less than that in other less taxing lines of work. Not only do we pay our teachers too little for work they are expected to do, we also fail in this country to give them the respect that the worth of their service to the community deserves. Teachers in the United States do not enjoy the social status that the importance of their position merits.

Add to all this the many administrative, public relations, and quasi-menial duties that teachers are asked to perform, duties that take mind and energy away from teaching, and it is easy to understand why our educational system is not able to attract many of the ablest young into the teaching profession, or to turn those who do join the ranks into adequate teachers.

Everything that has been said so far cites negative and external factors—bad working conditions, compensation that is too low, inferior social status, distracting demands. But there is more. Were all these negative factors eliminated or rectified, positive factors and conditions for training and holding a sufficiently large number of good teachers must be provided.

Nobody would expect all teachers to be truly educated persons—persons who possessed the requisite knowledge and understanding and were also skilled to a high degree in the art of teaching. That would be a utopian ideal. No amount of schooling, as was said earlier, can produce an educated person. To be truly educated is a state achieved by self-direction, usually long after schooling is completed, in the later years of life.

That being so, what is the goal to be aimed at, one that is practical rather than utopian? It is that teachers should be *on the way* to becoming educated persons. What signs indicate their tending in this direction? One is that they manifest competence as learners. Another is that they show a sufficiently strong interest in their own education and a sufficiently strong motivation to carry on learning while engaged in teaching.

To expect every teacher to learn in the course of every day's teaching is again utopian. But it is not utopian to expect intellectual growth in every term of teaching. The teacher who has stopped learning is a deadening influence rather than a help to students being initiated into the ways of learning.

If these are the touchstones of competence in teaching, what sort of schooling should be prescribed for those wishing to enter the profession of teaching and to practice it at the level of basic schooling?

They should themselves be at least as well-schooled as the graduates of the schools in which they are expecting to teach. They should have completed the required course of study we have recommended. Many teachers now employed in our public schools have not themselves had basic schooling of this quality, or even of the quality now provided in our better schools.

Even if all had the basic schooling that we are advocating, it would not be enough. Our future teachers should go on to take college work of the same kind at a higher level, that is, follow a course of study that is general, liberal, and humanistic. That course of study will add to their knowledge, develop their intellectual powers, and enlarge their understanding beyond the level of attainment set for

59

basic schooling. Nothing less than this will start them on the way to becoming educated persons—our first and indispensable requirement for competent teachers.

The course of study here proposed for the preparation of teachers does not include most or much of what is now taught to college students who plan to teach and specialize for it by taking their majors in departments of education or in teachers colleges.

The present teacher-training programs turn out persons who are not sufficiently equipped with the knowledge, the intellectual skills, or the developed understanding needed to guide and help the young in the course of study we have recommended.

If all children are expected to learn what is prescribed in our curriculum, it is reasonable to expect their teachers to be able to teach not just this or that portion, but all of it. Hence they should have a college education other than that which requires majoring or specializing in the subjects now required for teacher certification.

Do those who plan to teach in the twelve years of basic schooling need any specialized training? Yes, but it should come *after* they have completed a general college education, either in graduate courses in a university department or school of education or in what is comparable to internship in medicine—practice teaching under supervision.

Teaching is one of the three great cooperative arts. The other two are farming and healing—the arts of agriculture and of medicine. All three are "cooperative" because they must work with nature to produce the goods they aim at.

The cooperative art of the farmer consists in making the best use of seed, soil, and weather to produce the livestock, grains, or fruits that nature is able to produce alone, without the farmer's help. The cooperative art of the physician consists in employing the body's own resources for healing—for maintaining or regaining health.

The cooperative art of the teacher depends on the teacher's understanding of how the mind learns by the exercise of its own powers, and on his or her use of this understanding to help the minds of others to learn.

Obviously, the future teacher's own experience in learning is indispensable to such an understanding. It is by the skillful use of this self-understanding that the teacher can help others to learn. This skillfulness is developed best by practice under supervision; that is, by coaching. All the skills of teaching are intellectual skills that can be developed only by coaching, not by lecture courses in pedagogy and teaching methods such as are now taught in most schools or departments of education and are now required for certification.

One final condition must be mentioned. The effectiveness of even the best trained teachers will depend on the role played by the principal of the school in which they teach.

9
The Principal

THE SCHOOL IS A COMMUNITY. Not so, a school district or a school system. These are collections or aggregates of school communities in one locality. For this reason, the role of the school principal differs from that of the other administrators of a school system.

Like any community, the school community needs government. It needs leadership. Its affairs, internal and external, must be administered from day to day, from moment to moment. But the school is not an ordinary community like a city or state. It is a community devoted to learning, and its citizens are teachers and students engaged in that acitivity. It must also be conceived as including the parents whose cooperation with the school is essential to its success.

These things being so, the head of the school—its administrator—should not be solely or even primarily concerned with running the school efficiently or economically, or merely with keeping the peace of the community. Keeping the peace, doing justice, balancing budgets, enforcing laws is the main business of the political community at any level; they are not the *main business* of the school community. Its main business is teaching and learning. The head of the school—its principal—should, therefore, administer all other affairs in ways that facilitate the *main business.*

What does this mean? How does this redefine the role of the school principal?

The person chosen for that position should be a notably competent and dedicated teacher, with much classroom experience. It is not enough for the incumbent to be familiar with the administrative regulations, expert in bureaucratic procedures, and gifted with political acumen, important though such qualifications may be. The principal must be first and foremost what the title implies—the head teacher, or what in private schools is called the headmaster, leader of the other teachers who are also called masters. They are so called because they once were *masters* of the liberal arts.

The principal need not actually engage in teaching, though he or she will find it desirable from time to time. What is all important is that the principal provide the educational leadership that the school community needs. It has been shown in repeated studies that the quality of teaching and learning that goes on in a school is largely determined by the quality of such leadership.

Educational leadership by the principal is at present rare. Things being as they are, the principal has neither the time nor the inclination, even supposing the competence, to provide the leadership so sorely needed. Its character will, of course, vary with different schools in different places. But two conditions would appear to be linked with effective performance in the role of principal.

One is that he or she should have authority to hire and fire teachers (in consultation with faculty representatives and with regard for due process as set forth in administrative rules and union regulations). As a corollary, the principal should also have a voice—preferably a controlling voice—in assignments and promotions, so that these take place in a way most likely to advance the educational objectives of the school.

A second condition is that the principal should have the authority and be given the power to enforce standards of conduct—that measure of decorum and good behavior on the part of the student body that is indispensable to learning and teaching. It is not only necessary for the principal to have such disciplinary powers; it is also necessary for parents to recognize the principal's authority in enforcing rules of conduct that make the school community a safe and sane place for learning.

PART FOUR
Beyond Basic Schooling

10
Higher Learning

"THE GOAL at which any phase of education, true to itself, should aim," John Dewey declared, "is more education. Other objectives may surround that goal, but it is central."

For those whose schooling ends after twelve years, that basic phase has prepared them for adult learning beyond all schooling. For others, it has prepared them not solely for adult learning but also for more schooling of an advanced kind, in the so-called institutions of higher education: colleges, universities, and technical schools.

The education that takes place there is often called the higher learning. It would be more appropriate to refer to it as further learning, for there is still more education to be had and further learning to be done, beyond the higher learning.

Under whatever name, these higher institutions have been severely crippled by the inadequate preparation of those who successfully apply for entrance. The improvement of basic schooling, by which we seek to raise its

69

quality for all, will also do much more that is to be desired. It will prepare and motivate more young people to go on to college, and this enlarged and better-prepared student body will enable our colleges to raise their sights and to become the centers of higher education that they profess to be.

As things are now, they are hampered by the need to remedy the deficiencies of basic schooling. Instead of being able to rely on acquired knowledge, skills, and understanding and to build on our Three Columns of Learning, they are now compelled to teach all kinds of elementary work, to do what should have been done years earlier. Subjects supposedly learned in the upper years of basic schooling must be taught, or retaught, in college. Time must be spent in catching up with the deficiencies in reading, writing, speaking, computing, as well as doing something about poor or nonexistent habits of study.

Relieved of these burdens, our colleges would be in a position to reconceive their role. They would have the opportunity to recast the forms of higher education. Among these, two main purposes suggest themselves as appropriate for collegiate schooling to serve.

One is preparation for a vocation that requires specialized knowledge and technical training. With reformed lower schools, this could be accomplished in college, though for those going on to certain professions, further study in graduate, professional, or technical schools will be required.

70

The second purpose is the pursuit of general learning itself by students who are older and can build on their basic schooling to do more advanced work.

Those going to college to prepare themselves for vocations requiring specialized knowledge and technical training should be able to choose among a wide variety of programs. But, in addition to such elective majors, there should be for all a required minor course of study that will carry them to levels of general, liberal, and humanistic learning beyond what they received in their basic schooling.

Those going to college exclusively to advance their general education should seek institutions that offer college programs devised to satisfy this purpose. Too few such institutions now exist; they constitute the exception rather than the rule. We need more college programs in which the major course of study offered is common to all, with but few if any electives permitted. Such colleges would be ideal institutions for the preparation of the teachers to staff our reformed basic schools.

To overcome the specialization that now abounds on all sides, it may be necessary for our graduate and professional schools, at the university level, to leaven the intensity of the specialization they demand by carrying general learning forward at still higher levels.

That our technologically advanced industrial society needs technically trained specialists is beyond question. Intense specialization is always necessary for the advance-

71

ment of learning in all the learned professions, and in diverse fields of science and scholarship. We cannot turn our backs on these essential needs. Nor can we return to an earlier epoch when such intense specialization was not needed.

But we can and should do something to mitigate the barbarism of intense specialization, which threatens to be as destructive in its own way as the abandonment of specialization would be. We can reconceive the role and offerings of our colleges and universities, made possible by the time saved and the skills acquired that reformed basic schooling will provide.

We need specialists for our economic prosperity, for our national welfare and security, for continued progress in all the arts and sciences, and in all fields of scholarship. But for the sake of our cultural traditions, our democratic institutions, and our individual well-being, our specialists must also be generalists; that is, generally educated human beings.

11
Earning a Living and Living Well

Our main concern is basic schooling. It is the only schooling that is compulsory for all and that should be the same for all.

Our concern is double-edged. We have two fundamental goals in view. One is equipping all the children of this country to earn a good living for themselves. The other is enabling them to lead good human lives.

The enjoyment of a high standard of living, however desirable, still leaves more to be desired. The external, physical, material conditions of a good human life, necessary as they are, remain by themselves insufficient. They must be put to such use by the individual that the quality of his or her life is enriched internally as well as externally.

To raise the standard of living for all, we need—*for all*—a more effective basic schooling than now exists. To improve the quality of life for all, we need—*for all*—a better quality of schooling than now exists.

As compared with the human condition in other countries, most Americans are better off, more have ac-

73

cess to the comforts and conveniences of life, more enjoy the material advantages that are indispensable factors in the pursuit of happiness. This aim, the Declaration of Independence boldly asserted, belongs by right to all. As Abraham Lincoln pointed out, that was a pledge to the future; it still remains to be fulfilled.

When we hold before us the equally important results that our proposed reform of basic schooling aims at—earning a better living and enjoying a better quality of life—we are brought face to face with two obstacles that must be overcome. Even if all the others were surmounted, two things would still stand in the way of achieving the needed reform.

One is the uncertain economic status of a substantial part of the school population. The other is the understandable but nevertheless one-sided emphasis that too many parents place on economic and material advantages in thinking of their children's futures.

A basic human right is the right to obtain a decent livelihood by working for it under decent conditions. Those whom the economy leaves unemployed through no fault of their own are unjustly deprived of an essential human right which is indispensable to their pursuit of happiness.

As things stand now, that part of the school population which comes from severely disadvantaged minorities can look forward to unemployment after leaving school—thrown on the waste heap of a society that is squandering its human resources. Hopelessness about the future is bound to affect motivation in school. Why do the hard work that good basic schooling would demand if, after doing it, no opportunity exists to work for a decent living? This bleak prospect makes for the dropout, or, what is just as bad, turns the energetic into the delinquent. While still in school, they regard themselves as prisoners serving time.

The other face of the picture is the attitude of parents who regard all schooling as having no purpose beyond helping graduates to earn a living and get ahead materially.

The truth, hidden from too many, is that more than money and material advantages are necessary for the good life. Children should be prepared and motivated to make themselves the best human beings they are capable of becoming. If a better quality of schooling for all enables them to make a better use of their talents, their energies, their free time, it will also help to improve the quality of life for all.

Two things, then, must go hand in hand with the recommended reform of basic schooling. One is the commitment of our society to a policy of full employment, securing for everyone his or her right to earn a living. The other is the enlightenment of parents with regard to the goals of basic schooling—not just earning a living, but living well.

To put it another way, the monumental effort it will take to improve the quality of basic schooling cannot be justified solely by reference to economic and material advantages. It needs to be undertaken to improve the quality of human life for all.

12
The Future of Our Free Institutions

THE THRUST OF OUR ARGUMENT so far has been that basic schooling ought to prepare every child to earn a living and live a good life. But there is one more reason for exerting every effort to improve basic schooling. We must also do it to preserve our free institutions.

Democratic government and the institutions of a free society are of very recent advent in the world. They are as recent as the enactment of truly universal suffrage and the effort to secure the human and civil rights of the whole population. These are gains made in the twentieth century and not before, made only in a few places on this planet, not everywhere.

What occurred in a few countries for the first time in the twentieth century brought into existence only the initial conditions of a democratic society. It remains to be seen whether these conditions will be preserved and put to good use—whether their promises for the future will be fulfilled.

Both depend in large part on our being able to succeed in improving education in the broadest sense—to produce an educated electorate. As we know, achieving this result presupposes better basic schooling for all, as well as better advanced schooling for some.

You may be apathetic about improving your own life. You may be relatively hopeless about seeing the promises of democracy reach their full fruition. But you cannot love your children and at the same time be callous about the betterment of their lives, together with the betterment of the society in which they will live as adults.

You may be skeptical about the efficacy of your own involvement in political affairs. But you cannot love your country and at the same time be indifferent about the future of its free institutions.

Dismiss these concerns and you have little or no reason to feel a passionate commitment to reforms that will improve the quality of the schooling we give the children of this country.

Harbor no aspirations for the fulfillment of democracy's promises or the enhancement of the lives of its citizens, and you can shrug away the sorry state of our schools today.

But there cannot be more than a few among us who do not have to some degree these passions and these aspirations. The rest of us are deeply moved by them and thus cannot help being aroused to demand for all the children of this nation better schooling than any now available to the vast majority of them. Only a handful, a favored few, now have access to schooling of the quality that all deserve.

Our country faces many insistently urgent problems, on the solution of which its prosperity and even its survival depend—the threat of nuclear war, the shrinking of essential resources and supplies of energy, the pollution or spoliation of the environment, the spiraling of inflation accompanied by the spread of unemployment.

To solve these problems, we need resourceful and innovative leadership. For that to arise and be effective, we must have an educated people. Trained intelligence, in followers as well as in leaders, holds the key to the solution of the problems we face.

Achieving peace, prosperity, and plenty could put this country on the edge of becoming an earthly paradise, but only a much better educational system than now exists can carry us across the threshold.

Without it, a poorly schooled population will not be able to put to good use the opportunities afforded by the achievement of the general welfare. Those who are not schooled to enjoy the blessings of a good society can only despoil its institutions and corrupt themselves.

Human resources are the nation's greatest potential riches. To squander them is to impoverish our future.

To School Boards and School Administrators:

You ASK: *What should we do next Monday morning to get started on the Paideia reform of basic schooling?*

We ANSWER:

1. *Be sure that in every school—from grade one to grade twelve—there are the three kinds of learning and the three kinds of teaching represented by the Three Columns and see that they interact with one another.*

2. *In all Three Columns—the acquirement of organized knowledge, the development of intellectual skills (skills of learning), and the enlargement of the understanding of basic ideas and values—set standards of accomplishment that challenge both students and teachers to fulfill the high expectations you have for them.*

3. *Eliminate all the nonessentials from the school day, or, if retained, make them extracurricular activities.*

4. *Eliminate from the curriculum all training for specific jobs.*

5. *Introduce the study of a second language for a sufficient period of time to assure competence in its use.*

81

6. *Eliminate all electives from the course of study except the choice of the second language to be studied.*

7. *Use as much as possible of the school day's time for learning and teaching.*

8. *Restore homework, and home projects in the arts and sciences, in increasing amounts from grade one to grade twelve.*

9. *Devise, in your community, appropriate ways of ensuring adequate preschool preparation for those who need it.*

10. *Institute remedial instruction (in the Paideia sense of that term) for those who need it, either individually or in very small groups.*

Do these ten things in a manner that suits the population of your school, both teachers and students; do these things by making your own choice of the materials to be used and your own organization of the course of study from grade to grade; do them with the three fundamental objectives of basic schooling always in mind, and you will have started on its way the reform of basic schooling upon which the prosperity of this country and the happiness of its citizens depends.

Epilogue by a School Administrator

THE PAIDEIA PROPOSAL *is truly an educational mani-festo. It is both philosophical and practical, at once sound in theory and workable in fact.*

This proposal could well be entitled "The Reform of Our Public Schools," for it addresses all the critical areas of concern about our school system.

—Teaching children to think, and to use their minds in all forms of learning, is the pervasive concept.

—Underscoring the belief that all children are edu-cable, it affirms the right of all children in a de-mocracy to equal educational opportunity—the op-portunity to become educated human beings.

—Recognizing the importance of the preschool years, it stresses the necessity of early tutelage to provide the nurturing so essential as preparation for formal schooling.

—Differentiating between three basic kinds of learn-ing and of instruction, it draws our attention to the need for a clearly defined and carefully structured

83

curriculum. All educators can benefit from the reminder that the mind can be improved by

> *acquisition of information and knowledge*
> *development of intellectual skills*
> *increase of understanding and insight.*

—The role of the teacher is the key to the entire reform, and an acknowledgment of the necessary development and continuous education of the teacher reflects the prominence of the teacher in the learning process.

—Principals with power and knowledge corroborate other research that places the responsibility for good schools in the hands of good educational leaders.

Without a doubt, the recommendations presented in this book give hope and guidance for all educators interested in progress. Following this road map, so aptly designed, will help them to cure the many maladies of our beleaguered public schools.

It is often true that "there is nothing more difficult to carry out, more perilous to conduct, or more uncertain of success than to initiate a new order of things." A new order is what is called for. The Paideia Proposal *provides public education in this country with both a challenge and an opportunity!*

RUTH B. LOVE
General Superintendent of Schools
Chicago Board of Education

Printed in the United States
By Bookmasters